PRAISE FOR *PERS*

"This powerful and timely text shines a light into dark corners of the world where men and women face intimidation, persecution, and even death for their religious beliefs. Its authors have used their freedom of expression to uphold the liberties of others. Their book is both a challenge and a rebuke to those of us who fail to raise our own voices on behalf of the persecuted."

—David Alton, Professor Lord Alton of Liverpool has served for 18 years in the House of Commons, is an Independent Peer and one of the founders of Jubilee Campaign for religious freedom, www.davidalton.net.

"Christians are under attack to an unimaginable degree in the modern age, and, indeed, Christianity may become nearly extinct in some parts of the world because of religious extremism and despotism. *Persecuted* is a crucial primer on the threats and a clarion call to action. It is extraordinarily well-documented, tells a gripping story, and offers real solutions for reversing the alarming trend."

—Leonard A. Leo, Chairman, US Commission on International Religious Freedom (2009–2012)

"For over two millenia Christians have made enormous contributions to the societies in which they live. It therefore is a great irony, and a great tragedy, that Christian minorities are today under siege in so many spots around the globe, including countries with objectives that Christians can help achieve—including economic growth, social harmony, and stable democracy. Marshall, Gilbert, and Shea have written the definitive work on an issue that will come to haunt the 21st century: the central place of Christian persecution in the global crisis of religious liberty."

—Thomas F. Farr, director, The Religious Freedom Project, the Berkley Center at Georgetown University

"This authoritative, well-researched, formidable book should be required reading for all Christians who have the privilege of living in freedom and do not have to make any sacrifice for their faith. This deeply disturbing catalogue of escalating persecution must challenge us to respond with prayer, advocacy, practical help and political pressure on our governments to promote religious freedom more robustly wherever it is denied or diminished. Otherwise, 'comfortable Christianity' will be guilty not only of failing to fulfill the biblical mandate to speak for the oppressed but of betraying the spiritual, cultural, and political heritage which it is our duty to pass on undiminished to our children and grandchildren. *Reading this book may help 'comfortable Christians' to wake up, stand up, speak out and act in support of our brothers and sisters suffering persecution.* There is an urgent need to prevent further assaults on religious freedom in our world where more than 70 percent of people suffer persecution ranging from harassment and discrimination to imprisonment, torture and martyrdom."

—The Baroness (Caroline) Cox.

"When historians look back at this era, they will wonder why more wasn't done to stop the mass persecution of Christians in many parts of the world. Among those who will not be faulted are the three gifted authors of *Persecuted.* Make no mistake about it, this is most authoritative account to date on this subject."

—William A. Donohue, Ph.D., president, Catholic League for Religious and Civil Rights

"As shocking as the brutal murders of Christians is the silence of U.S. leadership and media that seems to embolden perpetrators of atrocity. Further, among many American Christians, we hear the unwise if not apathetic assumption that "the Church grows during persecution"—this is likely untrue as we think of the history of the Church in Japan and now the Middle East where Christians, present there for millennia are now often either dying or fleeing. Speak. Stand. Act on behalf of our siblings in Christ. They are bearers of blessing and peace. They are the Body of Christ, so intervene for Christ and the Kingdom. And let's spread the news of this book so necessary to bring justice, sanity and hope to the time which is ours."

—Kelly Monroe Kullberg, Author of *Finding God Beyond Harvard: the Quest for Veritas* and Founder of the Veritas Forum

PERSECUTED

THE GLOBAL ASSAULT ON CHRISTIANS

PAUL MARSHALL, LELA GILBERT,
NINA SHEA

Thomas Nelson
Since 1798

NASHVILLE DALLAS MEXICO CITY RIO DE JANEIRO

We dedicate this book to the great principle of religious freedom, known to Americans as the "first freedom," both because of its placement as the first clause of the First Amendment in the US Constitution, and because it is the core freedom, essential to the fulfillment of other rights and freedoms, as well as to the preservation of human dignity and the flourishing of the person. This freedom, in all its fullness, includes, but is not limited to, the freedom to worship. It encompasses the freedom to choose one's religion, and the freedom to manifest one's religion—either alone or in community with others, and in public or private—in teaching, practice, worship, and observation.

Published in Nashville, Tennessee, by Thomas Nelson. Thomas Nelson is a registered trademark of Thomas Nelson, Inc.

Thomas Nelson, Inc., titles may be purchased in bulk for educational, business, fund-raising, or sales promotional use. For information, please e-mail SpecialMarkets@ThomasNelson.com.

Library of Congress Cataloging-in-Publication Data

[Marshall, Paul A., 1948-
Persecuted : the global assault on Christians / Paul Marshall, Lela Gilbert, Nina Shea.
pages cm
Includes bibliographical references (pages) and index.
ISBN 978-1-4002-0441-0 (alk. paper)
1. Persecution--History--21st century. 2. Martyrdom--Christianity--History--21st century. 3. Christian martyrs--History--21st century. I. Gilbert, Lela. II. Shea, Nina, 1953- III. Title.
BR1601.3.M23 2013
272'.9--dc23

13 14 15 16 17 QG 6 5 4 3 2 1

CONTENTS

FOREWORD

WHEN IMPRISONED BY THE NAZIS AT TEGEL PRISON, DIETRICH Bonhoeffer wrote extraordinary and now famous letters. In one of them he wrote, "I'm now reading Tertullian, Cyprian, and others of the church fathers with great interest. In some ways they are more relevant to our time than the Reformers. . . ."

That's quite a statement for a German Lutheran. I can't read Bonhoeffer's mind, but I believe his connection to the church fathers wasn't so much theological as it was practical. Cyprian was beheaded by the Roman government. Bonhoeffer himself was soon to be hanged by the Nazis. To be a serious believer in the early days of Christianity was to be a marked man, and I think Bonhoeffer saw in Cyprian and the others a passion and a commitment that seems only to come from religious persecution—something that he personally knew and experienced.

Those of us who live in the modern West don't experience anything along these lines, and most of us are deeply ignorant of the sufferings of our brethren around the world. Indeed, as we read these words now, millions suffer. And we have been blessed with such a bounty of religious freedom that we can hardly imagine what such suffering must be like. We are relatively safe from government interference. We can say what we like and can worship where we want without legal repercussions. The current administration's much-contested HHS mandate, as well as other laws, are encroaching on our religious liberties in very real and disturbing ways, and these encroachments must be seen and must be strongly resisted. But we actually have religious liberties to encroach in the first place.

This is certainly not the case for millions around the world. We're often told, for example, that China is modernizing and becoming more open, but the reality is still very grim. Can we imagine a world where women in their third trimesters are "legally" forced to undergo the murder of the children in their wombs, children they very much want to raise and love? Why isn't the media telling us more about this? Chinese government policies today actually prohibit the gathering and worship of millions of Christians. One house church leader in China told Radio Free Asia that "the authorities have asked us to end our family church congregations, calling our gatherings 'illegal.'" *House church* may have a misleading ring to it. The church has fifteen hundred members.

Of course China is only one place where such repression exists. It's rampant in many places in the world—in the former Communist countries, and in Southeast Asia, Africa, and the Middle East.

But we hear so rarely about Christian persecution. Such stories are mostly glossed over in favor of the latest political news or, far worse, an inane story about some celebrity. Can we doubt that God will judge us for what we allow to occupy our attention?

I thank God for the book you are now holding. *Persecuted* by Paul Marshall, Nina Shea, and Lela Gilbert steps in where the broader media has turned away. It focuses on a scandalously underreported fact, that Christians are the single most widely persecuted religious group in the world today. And this terrible trend is on the upswing. Recent statistics from the Pew Research Center say that the world is an increasingly religious place. But it's also an increasingly intolerant place for Christian believers. In two-thirds of the world's countries, also according to Pew, persecution has worsened in recent years. The Vatican has reported the same conclusion. Why aren't the media talking about this?

Paul Marshall, Nina Shea, and Lela Gilbert are widely recognized as experts on the topic of Christian persecution and are powerfully and uniquely qualified to write this important book. Paul Marshall is Senior Fellow at the Hudson Institute's Center for Religious Freedom in Washington, D.C. Along with writing books and countless articles, he has spoken to Congress, the U.S. State Department, and to many other nations on religious freedom, international relations, and radical Islam. Nina Shea is Director of the Center for Religious Freedom and a Senior Fellow at the Hudson Institute. Also an author, she has been an international human-rights lawyer for thirty years. And Lela Gilbert is a freelance writer and editor who has authored and co-authored more than sixty books. An Adjunct Fellow at Hudson Institute, she is a contributor to the *Jerusalem Post, Weekly Standard*, and other publications. Informed by extensive international travel and on-the-ground reporting, their tremendous knowledge of this topic is evident in these pages, as they expose persecution in countries such as Egypt, Vietnam, Saudi Arabia, Pakistan, Burma, Somalia, Indonesia, and Iraq.

When Nina approached me at one of my Socrates in the City events about writing the foreword for this book, I was profoundly honored. I am privileged to contribute my voice to such an important topic as this. We in the West desperately need to know about our fellow believers who suffer for their faith. But I would even say that on another level, we should almost be jealous of them, because they have been privileged to know the true cost of discipleship, to quote the words of my hero, Dietrich Bonhoeffer. Might it be that by knowing of their sufferings, we might pray for them and fight for them where we can, so that we can repent of our own "cheap grace" and might also come to know the true cost of discipleship in Jesus? Might knowing their stories be God's way of drawing us closer to himself?

As you read the accounts in these pages, I think you'll see in them what Bonhoeffer found in Cyprian. Be prepared for the challenge. These stories will and should shake us. But let them all speak to your heart and drive you to "be anxious for nothing," but to pray in faith, knowing that God covets our prayers for those he loves. *Persecuted* is a profoundly important and inspiring book. May the Lord deeply bless you through it.

Eric Metaxas
New York City
October 2012

ONE

THE CURRENT STATE OF AFFAIRS

"A FORTY-SOMETHING WOMAN, WHO LIVED IN A CITY OF NORTH Pyongan Province [North Korea] was caught with a Bible in her home. She was taken out of her home. An army officer arrived to live there. The woman was publicly shot to death at a threshing floor of a farm." Government officials demanded that there be one witness to the execution, who later said, "I was curious why she was to be shot. Somebody told me she had kept a Bible at her home. Guards tied her head, her chest, and her legs to a post, and shot her dead. It happened in September 2005."[1]

Another firsthand account attests to the pervasive surveillance in North Korea that makes even private house church services almost impossible: "Based on a tip-off, around January 2005, agents from the Central Antisocialist Activities Inspection Unit raided my home in a county of North Hamgyong Province. As a result of their search, they found a Bible. I was taken into custody to a political prison camp alongside my wife and daughter. My son, who was staying in China, entered the North without any knowledge about his family's detention. He, too, was later taken to the camp."[2]

As in Korea, so in Iraq. Nineteen-year-old Sandy Shibib, like many other Iraqi Christians, braved hardship and terror to pursue an education. She faithfully commuted by bus to the University of Mosul where she studied biology. Three buses, operated by the Syrian Catholic bishopric, carried hundreds of students, faculty, and staff to Mosul from Sandy's home area in the predominantly

Christian district of Qaraqush. They traveled in a convoy for safety and were escorted by two Iraqi army vehicles.

On May 2, 2010, an explosion struck the buses without warning. Between two checkpoints on the daily route, where the convoy should have been the safest, it was targeted by twin roadside bombs. About 160 students were injured in the blasts.

"This is the hardest attack, because they attacked not only one car, but the whole convoy and in an area that is heavily guarded by the army," said the Syrian Catholic archbishop of Mosul, Georges Casmoussa. The students who were seriously injured received treatment in Erbil, the capital of the semi-autonomous Kurdish region.

Sandy died several days later from shrapnel wounds to her head. Maha Tuma, her schoolmate, said, "As students, we were heading to university, not to a battlefield. We carried no weapons. Nevertheless, we were targeted." The explosion caused nearly one thousand students to withdraw from Mosul University, the only university near the Nineveh Plains. Many never returned.[5]

UNDER ATTACK

Western Christians enjoy numerous blessings of religious freedom. Our rights, while sometimes challenged, are many. We speak freely about our faith, our churches, our denominational preferences, and our answered prayers. We treasure, read, and write comments in our Bibles, and share our beliefs with others without fear of danger. Our churches can have religious schools and broadcasts. We wear crosses around our necks, and our bishops, priests, ministers, monks, and nuns dress in a broad array of distinctive styles. Our Christianity doesn't require us to keep looking over our shoulders, unsure if we will be arrested for praying or attacked for having a Bible.

Our churches are well built, well equipped, and promoted by signs. Our pastors are able to concentrate on their ministerial responsibilities without having to worry about threats from hostile police and angry mobs. For our encouragement and entertainment, there are Christian television networks, music industries, websites, and publishing enterprises. Our religious freedom is largely protected by our governments as well as by the cultures in which we live.

Unfortunately, most of the world's Christians don't share these circumstances. Their experiences are not just dissimilar to ours; they are unimaginably different. Clearly we needn't feel guilty for our religious freedoms, which are God-given. But sometimes we have to be reminded about what life is like for Christians in other countries, whose everyday lives bear so little resemblance to ours. These men, women, and children of courage and faith are scattered in large numbers all across the globe. Even now, as these words are being written:

- A Christian pastor sat in a squalid prison cell in Iran for three years. Day after day he waited for the final word to come down from the authorities: "Tomorrow morning you will hang." The pastor was condemned for converting to Christianity from Islam, called apostasy in Iran, and sentenced to death. Still, he did not recant his Christian faith. Under international pressure, Iran finally acquitted him of apostasy, sentencing him to the lesser crime of "evangelizing Muslims." Released on September 8, 2012, the loving father and husband remains at mortal risk from Islamist death squads. His name is Youcef Nadarkhani.[4]
- In Pakistan, a woman awaits the day of her execution. She is ill, weak, and weary, and she misses her five children intolerably. She, too, has been sentenced to death because of her Christian faith. She has been tried and convicted of blaspheming the prophet Muhammad—a capital crime in Pakistan. Her name is Asia Bibi.
- In China, friends and loved ones await word of an elderly Roman Catholic priest who was abducted, never to be heard from again. He is frail but faithful to his beliefs and his church. But in his faithfulness, he has offended China's

Communist Party regime. No one is sure whether he is dead or alive. Nearly eighty years old, his name is Bishop James Su Zhimin, and he is known to all as Bishop Su.

- In Nigeria, surviving Christians can still smell the smoke and the burning flesh in their village. At least eleven worshippers were burned to death when terrorists firebombed a church in early 2012. More than twenty others were horribly injured. Christians in the surrounding area are running scared, even while wanting to be courageous and faithful. They are well aware that they also are targets. There are so many victims in Nigeria that only local people know the names of the dead.

THE WORLD'S MOST WIDELY PERSECUTED

Who are these people? Why are they in trouble? How have they offended state authorities or other members of their societies so greatly that their lives are at stake? In the pages that follow, we'll look more closely at these specific stories and many others. We'll examine the cases of those who are persecuted for their Christian faith in the context of their countries, their cultures, and the increasingly dangerous world through which they must navigate while both keeping sacred commitments and surviving.

Our book focuses on an underreported fact: Christians are the single most widely persecuted religious group in the world today. This is confirmed in studies by sources as diverse as the Vatican, Open Doors, the Pew Research Center, *Commentary*, *Newsweek*, and the *Economist*. According to one estimate, by the Catholic Bishops' Conferences of the European Community, 75 percent of acts of religious intolerance are directed against Christians.[5]

This persecution is targeted at all Christian faith traditions from Roman Catholic, Orthodox, and Protestant to liturgical, evangelical, and charismatic, including hundreds of small, little-known sects. Christian worship services vary, and traditions are stunningly different, but our churches are united in belief in the same Jesus Christ as Lord and Savior.

Contrary to the post-colonial construct that Christianity is a Western, white man's religion, we should pause and remember those for whom we write and pray.

Many people are unaware that three-quarters of the world's 2.2 billion nominal Christians live outside the developed West, as do perhaps four-fifths of the world's active Christians.[6] Of the world's ten largest Christian communities, only two, the United States and Germany, are in the developed West. Christianity may well be the developing world's largest religion. The church is predominantly female and non-white. While China may soon be the country with the largest Christian population, Latin America is the largest Christian region and Africa is on its way to becoming the continent with the largest Christian population. The average Christian on the planet, if there could be such a one, would likely be a Brazilian or Nigerian woman or a Chinese youth.

Why are Christians persecuted? As you'll soon see, there are a myriad of reasons. Persecution can be government sponsored as a matter of policy or practice, as in North Korea, Vietnam, China, Burma, Saudi Arabia, and Iran. It can be the result of hostility within the society and carried out by extremists and vigilantes who operate with impunity or are beyond the government's capacity to control. That is the situation today in Nigeria and Iraq. It can also be carried out by terrorist groups exerting control over territories, such as the Al-Shabab in Somalia and the Taliban in Afghanistan. Or it can come from the hands of combined and even conflicting powers, as in Egypt and Pakistan.

China, Vietnam, and Cuba show us that in some countries Christianity rebounds and rejuvenates when persecution becomes less intense. This, however, is not always so.

In most of the Middle East and North Africa, the percentage

of native Christians remains negligible. The Christian church in those places has never recovered from past persecution. Over the past one hundred years, according to a range of estimates, the Christian presence has declined in Iraq from 35 percent to 1.5 percent; in Iran from 15 percent to 2 percent; in Syria from 40 percent to 10 percent; in Turkey from 32 percent to 0.15 percent. Among the most significant factors explaining this decline is religious persecution.

WHAT IS PERSECUTION?

In the countries we've covered in this book, Christians suffer real oppression from serious violations of religious freedom. They are not simply offended in their religious feelings nor are they merely experiencing discrimination or encountering misfortune. Many terms, such as *persecution*, serious or *egregious* violations, *religious cleansing*, and *genocide* are ill-defined and controversial. As in all human rights reporting, the accuracy, precision, and meaning of the numbers of those persecuted can be equally uncertain.

The US International Religious Freedom Act (IRFA) of 1998 contains a useful description of what persecution actually means. It helps to determine which countries should be designated the worst offenders of religious freedom, or "Countries of Particular Concern." It defines violations of religious freedom to include arbitrary prohibitions on, restrictions of, or punishment for:

- assembling for peaceful religious activities such as worship, preaching, and prayer;
- speaking freely about one's religious beliefs;
- changing one's religious beliefs and affiliation;
- possession and distribution of religious literature, including Bibles;
- raising one's children in the religious teachings and practices of one's choice.

Other violations of religious freedom specified by IRFA include:

- arbitrary registration requirements;
- any of the following acts if committed on account of an individual's religious belief or practice: detention, interrogation, imposition of an onerous financial penalty, forced labor, forced mass resettlement, imprisonment, forced religious conversion, beating, torture, mutilation, rape, enslavement, murder, and execution.[7]

Not all the countries discussed in this book are among the world's worst persecutors. Nevertheless we have taken into consideration the IRFA standard. What we mean by the word *persecution* in this book is that there are Christians in the countries of focus who are tortured, raped, imprisoned, or killed for their faith. Their churches may also be attacked or destroyed. Their entire communities may be crushed by a variety of deliberately targeted measures that may or may not entail violence. And all of them most certainly experience, as the IRFA puts it, "flagrant denial of the right to life, liberty, or the security of persons."[8]

With this in mind, we should point out that persecution can morph into less bloody, more bureaucratic methods of abuse when a government becomes more self-conscious about its human rights reputation. For example, after several years of what some perceived as a thaw in relations with Christians, a crackdown in recent months has once again slammed China's iron fist against believers. As Meghan Clyne wrote in the May 19, 2011, *Weekly Standard*:

> The "thaw" in China's treatment of Christians was nothing more than a savvy and sophisticated new twist on its longstanding assault on religious freedom. While scaling back on bloody crackdowns that stir international condemnation, China has found subtle ways of undercutting independent churches and quietly preempting the spread of free religion. Indeed, the U.S. Commission on International Religious Freedom's report notes

that "Chinese officials are increasingly adept at employing the language of human rights and the rule of law to defend repression of religious communities."[9]

LEARNING ABOUT PERSECUTION

It is true that in the West the nightly news rarely reports about Christian persecution unless an unusually shocking case surfaces on a slow news day. But thanks to the success of a largely Christian grassroots movement in the late 1990s and to ever-expanding media sources, there is now a proliferation of reliable, detailed, and real-time information on persecuted religious believers, from both Christian (faith-based) and US governmental sources. Examples of these are cited throughout this book.

One of the great successes of past political mobilization against religious persecution, the IRFA, mandated that the US Department of State publish annual reports on religious persecution throughout the world. These reports include thousands of instances of anti-Christian persecution, along with other violations of religious freedom. They have official stature and are relied upon throughout the world.

It is important for us to seek out all the reliable information we can from trustworthy sources. If we depend entirely on the secular media, we will rarely hear about persecuted believers, and what we hear may not be accurate.

Of course, people of all religions—and those who have no faith at all—suffer persecution. We have protested and written of it, and will continue to do so. Many are persecuted by the same people who persecute Christians. For some, such as Mandeans and Yizidis in Iraq, Baha'is and Jews in Iran, Ahmadis and Hindus in Pakistan, Tibetan Buddhists and Falun Gong in China, Independent Buddhists in Vietnam, Rohingya Muslims in Burma, and Shiites in Saudi Arabia, the persecution is particularly intense and cruel.[10]

But Christians also are persecuted in each of these countries, and in many others. The persecution of Christians is massive, widespread, increasing, and still underreported. The Pew Forum on Religion and Public Life, a highly respected source of data on religion, reports that Christians have suffered harassment by the state and/or society in 133 countries—that's two-thirds of the world's nation states—and suffer in more places than any other religious group.[11]

As reported by Aid to the Church in Need, a Catholic charity relied on by the Vatican, the Commission of the Bishops' Conferences of the European Community estimates that in many countries, this persecution has worsened in recent years. As Pope Benedict XVI said at the beginning of 2011: "Many Christians live in fear because of their pursuit of truth, their faith in Jesus Christ and their heartfelt plea for respect for religious freedom."[12]

The very scale, scope, and variety of the persecution of Christians make it difficult to bring it into focus. This is only one reason why it is often not reported, or not reported well.[13] Still, there are patterns of persecution that can help us grasp the basic situation and begin to understand it.

CHRISTIAN PERSECUTION: THREE CAUSES

Most persecution of Christians springs from one of three causes. First is the hunger for total political control, exhibited by the Communist and post-Communist regimes. The second is the desire by some to preserve Hindu or Buddhist privilege, as is evident in South Asia. The third is radical Islam's urge for religious dominance, which at present is generating an expanding global crisis.

We turn first to the remaining Communist countries and their baleful cousins, the post-Communist countries. Communist regimes, which are usually officially atheistic, tried to eradicate religion in their glory days. They did so by physically exterminating millions of religious people. They have since retreated to an onerous policy of registration, supervision, and control. Those who will not be controlled are sent to prison or labor camps, or simply held, abused, and sometimes tortured. These regimes are still the largest source of Christian persecution, simply because they have the most Christian residents (especially in the case of China). Communism also reigns in the country that, overall, is today's most intense persecutor of Christians: North Korea.

In China, Christians are generally allowed to worship within the four walls of the church, but they do not have the right to select their church leaders, provide religious education to their young, or publish and broadcast freely. Traditional religious processions have been banned and violently dispersed. And in North Korea, Christians are executed or sent to prison camps for such crimes as the mere possession of a Bible. We describe these countries, together with Vietnam, Laos, and Cuba, in chapter 2.

Another collection of regimes sprang up after the breakup of the Soviet Union. Some of these post-Communist areas, like the Baltic republics, have become free societies, and nearly all the rest have now officially given up Communism but many still follow their predecessors' repressive tactics of registration and control. Some are still under the authority of the same old rulers or their children. Countries such as Belarus, Turkmenistan, and Uzbekistan remain among the most restrictive in the world. And, as with the Communist regimes, these rulers are usually fanatically secular (at least those who are not compromised by back-room dealings with religious factions). We describe these regimes in chapter 3.

We turn next to those lands in which some Hindus or Buddhists equate their religion with the nature and meaning of their country itself. Other faiths represent a threat to them. Consequently, they persecute minority tribes and religions, and often Christians. We have no wish to wrongly portray the peaceful followers who constitute the majority of their faithful. However, it is important to realize that Hindus and Buddhists do not always abjure violence. India has a great deal of religious violence, some of which occurs in a climate of impunity. The Hindu and Buddhist countries of concern, including Sri Lanka, Nepal, and Bhutan, are concentrated in South Asia. These we describe in chapter 4.

We turn finally to the dozens of countries in which Muslims are the majority population. Even though the remaining Communist countries persecute the most Christians, it is in the Muslim world where persecution of Christians is now most widespread, intense, and, ominously, increasing. Extremist Muslims are expanding their presence and sometimes exporting their repression of all other faiths.

Perhaps there is no more poignant and symbolic example of an Islamist assault on Christianity than the bombing of a church full of worshippers. In recent years, we've seen the rise of just such attacks on churches in Iraq, Egypt, and Nigeria. As we describe later in this book, Nigeria's Catholic bishops report that more than one hundred individuals, mostly Catholic worshippers, were killed or injured in coordinated Christmas bombings in 2011. Iraq has seen at least seventy church bombings in eight years, all committed by radical Muslims.

People are targeted in many countries for choosing to become Christians, but increasingly so in the Muslim world. Among those assaulted with violence on a horrific scale have been the young, fast-growing churches of Nigeria and South Sudan, which are seen as a threat to Muslim hegemony. Individual converts from Islam, such as Pastor Youcef Nadarkhani in Iran, are particularly at risk of being put to death or otherwise harshly punished by either the governments or extremist elements within society in significant parts of the Muslim world. They are denounced as apostates.

Even ancient churches, such as the two-thousand-year-old Chaldean and Assyrian churches of Iraq and the Coptic churches of Egypt, are under intense threat at this time. The rise of Salafi and other extremely intolerant Muslim movements, affecting both the Shia and Sunni traditions, makes this an especially dangerous time in some countries to be Christian, whether as a convert or as someone who was born into the faith. As Cardinal Christoph Schoenborn of Vienna said at our 2012 Arab Spring conference: "It would be a deep wound to lose Christianity's own homeland and land of origin."

Describing this persecution even briefly requires four chapters on the Muslim-majority world. The first, chapter 5, describes countries such as Malaysia, Turkey, Morocco, and Algeria, which certainly have state discrimination and restrictions that hinder the free practice of religion even without the level of violent state persecution seen elsewhere. Turkey, a democracy and a NATO member that was often held out as a so-called model during the "Arab Spring" revolutions of 2010, actually exemplifies the more subtle type of religious oppression. Turkey's Christians are being smothered beneath a dense tangle of bureaucratic restrictions that thwart the ability of churches to perpetuate themselves. After the United States Commission on International Religious Freedom (USCIRF) put Turkey on its "Countries of Particular Concern" list in 2012, USCIRF chair Leonard Leo explained:

> Some of the countries we recommend for CPC designation maintain intricate webs of discriminatory rules, requirements and edicts that can impose tremendous burdens for members of religious minority communities, making it difficult for them to function and grow from one generation to the next, potentially threatening their existence.[14]

Other countries such as Saudi Arabia and Afghanistan are so repressive that no churches are even permitted to exist, even though there are Christians there. The millions of Christians in these two countries, including some very beleaguered and oft-jailed converts, must hide their faith and seek the protection and secrecy of walled embassy compounds in order to pray in community. As we write, Saudi Arabia's grand mufti, an authoritative religious figure who is appointed by the king and supported by the state, has declared that it is "necessary to destroy all the churches of the region."[15] These are among the world's most intolerant states. Chapter 6 covers the two major sources of radical and repressive Islam: Saudi Arabia and Iran.

Chapter 7 covers situations usually regarded as brutal, such as those in Afghanistan, Pakistan, and Sudan, as well as one that is still often mischaracterized as "moderate," that of Egypt.

In chapter 8 we describe those Muslim-majority countries where persecution stems from war, failed states, mob violence, or terrorism. In these countries—Iraq, Nigeria, Somalia, Indonesia, and Bangladesh—the government itself is not the chief persecutor. Instead, a weak government or lack of government altogether is the problem. Christians in such places often suffer attacks from independent actors without protection, relief, or redress from the state.

Then there are national security states such as Burma and Eritrea that do not fit any of the other patterns. Ethiopia, a majority Christian state, is also not easily categorized. Burma could perhaps be treated as an example of Buddhist repression; the government has tried to cloak itself in Buddhism while simultaneously persecuting Buddhists. However, it is better understood simply as a regime where the military has sought to preserve its rule by any means necessary. These countries are covered in chapter 9.

In our conclusion, we look at ways for concerned Christians and religious freedom advocates to connect with governmental branches and agencies and to seek out non-governmental groups and faith-based organizations that are reaching out to provide hope and aid to persecuted Christians and others in similar straits. We also suggest some practical ways that those of us in the West can combine prayers, creativity, and resources to alleviate the ever-increasing abuse of Christian minorities around the world.

A QUICK LOOK AT CHRISTIAN HISTORY

Apart from the scholars and professors among us, most of us know little of church history outside the West. Why is this important? Because we need to understand how, very long ago, Christianity was introduced to many countries and regions—places that now seek to pull Christianity up by its ancient roots. It is important to understand that our history as Christian believers is complexly interwoven with world history.

The Acts of the Apostles tells of the church's early expansion into areas that are now the states of Turkey, Greece, and Italy. Not much later, the faith spread throughout Europe. At the same time, the church expanded west and south into Africa, reaching Ethiopia and Sudan, and east into Iraq, Iran, Afghanistan, and India. The most ancient churches in India and beyond have an almost two-thousand-year history, believed to have been founded by the apostle Thomas.

By the eighth century, the patriarch, or *Catholicos* of the Church of the East was based in what is now Iran and Iraq, and he was probably more influential than the Catholic pope.[16] The Church of the East, or Nestorian Church, was one of the great missionary churches of all times. Its patriarch appointed bishops for Yemen, Arabia, Iran, Turkestan, Afghanistan, Tibet, India, Sri Lanka, and China. A Christian cemetery in Kyrgyzstan, in Central Asia, contains inscriptions in Syrian and Turkish commemorating "Terim the Chinese, Sazik the Indian, Banus the Uygur, Kiamata of Kashgar, and Tatt the Mongol." At the time, the church's operating languages were Syriac, Persian, Turkish, Sogdian, and Chinese. The church, by then, may even have reached to Burma, Vietnam, Indonesia, Japan, the Philippines, and Korea.

In 1281, the patriarch was Markos, who had come from China as a monk. Mongols sent his traveling companion, Bar Sauma, on a diplomatic mission to Europe, seeking aid for a proposed joint attack on Egypt. The Europeans were amazed to discover both that the Christian church stretched to the shores of the Pacific, and that the emissary from the fearsome Mongols was a Christian bishop—one from whom the king of England, Edward I, subsequently took communion.[17]

Much of Middle Eastern and North African Christianity was crushed, not with the initial rise of Islam in the seventh century but later in the fourteenth century. One trigger was the Mongol invasions, which threatened Arab Islam as never before. (The

Crusades were a minor sideshow by then, not much commented on by Muslims of the time.) The Mongols sought alliances with Christian kingdoms, and there were Christians among their own ranks. This is one of the reasons Christian communities in the Muslim world were often treated as a potential fifth column and subjected to frequent massacres. Between 1200 and 1500, the proportion of Christians outside Europe fell from over a third to about 6 percent. In Philip Jenkins's words, by 1500 the European churches had become dominant only "by dint of being, so to speak, the last men standing" of the Christian world.[18]

Fast-forward to the early twentieth century. The Christian communities in the former Ottoman Empire were again savaged in a second great wave of persecution. This brought about the slaughter of as many as one and a half million Armenians, as well as numerous Syriacs, Assyrians, Pontic Greek Orthodox and Maronites. When the British took over Mesopotamia after the First World War, they judged the Assyrian Christians' situation so desperate that they considered moving them to Canada. In 1930 there were proposals to transfer them to South America. Following massacres by Arabs in 1933, the British flew the patriarch to Cyprus for safety, while the League of Nations debated moving the rest of the Assyrian Christians to Brazil or Niger.

We may currently be faced with a similar wave of persecution and destruction. Christians are fleeing the Palestinian areas, Lebanon, Turkey, Syria, and Egypt. In 2003 in Iraq, Christians were some 4 percent of the population, yet in more recent years they make up a much larger percentage of the refugees, supporting reports that some two-thirds of them have fled. Many Egyptian Copts fear that the Arab Spring, which began in late 2010, has become an Islamist Winter for them, and they wonder if they, too, must flee. Many have already done so. We'll look at the Arab Spring uprising in the Muslim world more closely in the book's conclusion, as it dramatically affects both today's most ancient Christian communities as well as new Christian converts from Muslim and other backgrounds.

THE CHURCH TODAY

Many of these early Christian communities have faithfully and courageously persevered through famine, war, and persecution. In some places, the church began remarkably to expand again and the final decades of the twentieth century saw the largest church growth in history, particularly in sub-Saharan Africa and China.[19]

But this new globalized spread of Christianity is, in a sense, not really that new. It is only a resumption of a venerable and long-standing reality. While there are many new things happening, the reality is that an ancient body of faith and the faithful are once again reemerging—much of it in sub-Saharan Africa, Central and South America, Asia, and most notably China.

In the late tenth century, an Assyrian monk from Arabia visited China and voiced his horror at discovering that Christianity, although it had churches, monasteries, cathedrals, bishops, and archbishops, had, after centuries, apparently become "extinct."[20] Today, however, Christianity is in its fourth great phase of expansion in China.

In the twenty-first century, more people in China attend church services than in all Western Europe. Despite the fact that most Christian gatherings are illegal and can bring about arrest and lengthy sentences in labor camps, China might have the largest church attendance of any country in the world.

GOD AND CAESAR

While there has always been confusion and conflict between what we now call "church and state," the mere existence of two authorities instead of one has had major influence. As George Sabine wrote,

> The rise of the Christian Church, as a distinct institution entitled to govern the spiritual concerns of mankind in independence of the state, may not unreasonably be described as the

> most revolutionary event in the history of Western Europe, in respect both to politics and to political thought.[21]

Under such a scheme, Jews and heretics could still be persecuted, and inquisitions and wars could still be defended. These are tragic and bloody historical facts. But people also came to believe that these authorities should be distinct. Hence, the church, despite its frequent desire for civil control, always had to acknowledge that there were forms of political power it should not exercise. And political leaders, despite their ongoing attempts to gain control of all things, had always to acknowledge that there were areas of human life necessarily and properly beyond their reach. Despite ongoing conflict and confusion, the political order had to acknowledge that the spiritual core of human life, and the authority this embodied, was a realm beyond civil control.[22]

This has meant that Christians, while usually loyal citizens, have repeatedly said with Peter that they must obey God rather than man, and are obliged to serve "another King" (Acts 17:7 NASB). This denies that the state is all encompassing or the ultimate arbiter of human life. The claim that *Caesar is not God* challenges every authoritarian regime, ancient Romans and modern totalitarians alike, and draws their angry and bloody response.[23]

This is the historical and living Christian church whose religious freedom rights we seek to defend, and whose contemporary story of persecution we will tell, at least in part, in the following pages.

SOME NECESSARY EXCEPTIONS

Perhaps we should take a moment to discuss what our chapters will *not* cover. This is not a book about the suffering of Christians per se. Christians, like all human beings, may suffer because of volcanic eruptions, earthquakes, tsunamis, or in blizzards, droughts, and famines. They may suffer because they are of the "wrong" language, race, or ethnic group. Or, they may be in the wrong place at the wrong time. We do not cover these, since they are not necessarily tied to the Christians' faith.

Instead we will focus solely on the suffering inflicted on people at least in part *because they are Christians*—suffering they would not have had to endure if they were not believers in Jesus.

Certainly, the dividing line is not clear and precise. Christians, especially pastors, are brutally attacked in Colombia, Peru, Mexico, Zimbabwe, and many other places. They are killed because they have stood against repressive regimes, against guerillas who may be even more repressive than the regimes they would replace, and against vicious drug cartels. The issues are complex, since many believe it is their Christian duty to stand against any form of oppression. For this they suffer and die. We do not pretend to say definitively that this is not religious persecution, but we do not include these courageous cases in this discussion.

Many churches consider foreign missionaries who die in the field from disease or criminal attack to be martyrs, even though they did not die a result of deliberate religious persecution. We do not include those cases. A partial exception may be places like Iraq, where we discuss criminal attacks on Christians, since they are being denied police protection because of their religion.

When we talk or write of the persecution of the church, many people ask us about persecution of Christians in the United States. Our response is that, yes, there are problems here, and they are increasing and must be challenged. But Christians in America have ample legal recourse to protect their First Amendment rights and do not face threats of the severity found in China, North Korea, Sri Lanka, Saudi Arabia, Eritrea, Somalia, or Nigeria. Because of this difference in the severity of persecution, we keep the focus of this book on the problems faced by the often forgotten Christians around the world.

It is clear that antipathy toward and legal restrictions on Christianity are increasing in the so-called post-Christian West. Critical battles for religious freedom are now being waged here in courts and legislatures, as well as in the public square. These developments deserve and are receiving attention, unlike the killing, imprisonment, and abuse that is found elsewhere. In the places we discuss in this book, the persecuted do not have the ability to debate freely and seek redress and reform through democratic means.

This is not to diminish the manifold forms of suffering experienced by Christians and others throughout the world. If an earthquake swallows your house, church, or family; if your husband was killed because he denounced a drug cartel; if your wife was raped and killed because she was Tutsi; the suffering is just as horrifying, just as torturous, just as repressing, and your loved ones are just as dead as if the attack was more specifically religious. We do not mean to slight such forms of suffering. It is only that we try to restrict ourselves to something more specific: *persecution of Christians because they are Christians.*

We have tried to be very selective in what we've addressed here. We do not cover every country or territory where Christians are persecuted; that would take many large volumes. And in the countries that we do cover, we cannot even try to come close to recounting every example of the religious persecution of Christians. That would quickly turn this book into an encyclopedia. Instead, we try to provide a clear sense of what is happening to Christians in the world right now. That includes many tales of woe, but also ones of hope and undeniable heroism.

Ours is not a matter of special pleading, but simply of fact. To note with Pope Benedict XVI, "At present, Christians are the religious group which suffers most from persecution on account of its faith." And together with Pope Benedict, we affirm, "This situation is unacceptable," because it is "an insult to God and to human dignity; furthermore, it is a threat to security and peace, and an obstacle to the achievement of authentic and integral human development."[24]

THE CALL AND HOPE OF PEACE

In 2002, one of us (Paul Marshall) traveled in southeastern Turkey with the distinguished patristics scholar Tom Oden.[25] We met with members of two-thousand-year-old Syriac churches, of whom only a few thousand are left in their homelands. Their language, Syriac-Aramaic, is as close as any living language to the one Jesus spoke, though they have been forbidden by the Turkish government to teach it in schools. We passed by deserted villages such as Kafro that were now sealed off, their inhabitants driven out by the attacks of Turkish Hezbollah. We visited the great monastery of Mor Gabriel in the Tur Abdin region, a major center of Eastern Christianity, now dwindling under court approved land confiscations and suffocating government restrictions. We met the only two monks remaining in the monastery in the village of Sare.

There is a church in the city of Nusaybin, where a famous Christian community dates back to the second century. In the fourth century, this church nurtured Ephrem, the greatest of the Syrian theologians, who is venerated as a saint in Eastern Christianity. The edifice was locked and abandoned after World War I, when the inhabitants, fleeing massacre, escaped into Syria. For sixty years there were no Christians in the city, but now the diocese has sent a Christian family from a local village to live in a small apartment in the church and keep the sacred space from falling apart.

We went into the deserted and dust-laden crypt to see the tomb of Jacob of Nisibis, for whom the Jacobite church is named. While we examined his sarcophagus, our driver, unprompted, began to sing an ancient hymn. His strong voice filled the tomb with almost unearthly resonance. We listened in silent awe. Afterward, we asked him what the words meant. He told us that the lyrics came from Ephrem himself. How poignant his words remain in today's troubled world.

Listen, my chicks have flown,
left their nest, alarmed
By the eagle. Look,
where they hide in dread!
Bring them back in peace!

TWO

CAESAR AND GOD: THE REMAINING COMMUNIST POWERS

China / Vietnam / Laos / Cuba / North Korea

IN 2001, CHINA'S MINISTRY OF JUSTICE RECOGNIZED GAO Zhisheng as one of the "Ten Best Lawyers" in the People's Republic of China. Deeply committed to truth and justice—a quality he attributed to his Christian faith—he fell afoul of the regime a short time later because of his dogged defense of groups and individuals targeted by the state, including fellow Christians and followers of the Falun Gong movement. He resigned from the Communist Party in 2005 and, in January 2006, barely avoided an attempt on his life, which the secret police staged to look like a traffic accident.

Gao disappeared from his sister's home in August 2006 and was officially arrested that September. He was tried, convicted of subversion, and sentenced to three years in prison, but released on so-called probation. In the years following, he was rearrested and tortured by methods including the favorite secret-police practice of piercing his testicles with toothpicks. Then he disappeared, rumored to be dead. In his memoir, *A China More Just*, Gao declared that the Communist Party uses "the most savage, most immoral, and most illegal means to torture our mothers, torture our wives, torture our children, and torture our brothers and sisters."[1]

David Aikman, author of *Jesus in Beijing*, reported, "In typical Orwellian fashion, in January 2010, a Chinese foreign-ministry spokesman said he didn't know where Gao was, but that he was 'where he should be.'"[2] In early 2012, the Christian human-rights organization China Aid reported that Gao had disappeared into police custody in April 2010.

On December 16, 2011, just days before his five-year probation period was to have ended, the Chinese government announced that it was sending him to Shaya (Xayar) prison for three years for violating his probation. This was the first word that he was still alive, but no information of his condition was released. Shaya prison is located in remote Aksu Prefecture, about seven hundred miles southwest of the Xinjiang capital of Urumqi. On March 24, 2012, he was allowed a visit from his brother and father-in-law.[3]

In Vietnam, persecution can be just as severe. In November 2009, Sung Cua Po, a Hmong villager from Ho Co in Dien Bien Dong district, Vietnam, converted to Christianity. Local officials arrested him and his wife on December 1, 2009, and beat him on his head and back to force him to recant his new faith. They threatened to beat him until "only his tongue was intact." His wife was also beaten. Po was forced to sign a paper recanting his religious convictions and told Christian leaders, "I folded—I signed when police threatened to beat me to death if I didn't recant, then they would seize my property, leaving my wife a widow, and my children fatherless—without a home."

But the persecution did not stop there. Po faced continuing pressure to show he was no longer a Christian and had resumed traditional ancestor worship, something he had previously refused to do. In February, Po and his wife were fined 8 million dong (US$430) and a pig. Police confiscated Po's cell phone and motorbike and incited his extended family and local villagers to harass him. The pressure ratcheted up on February 21, 2010, when villagers stole a year's worth of rice and all their cooking and eating utensils, and officials authorized the demolition of their home.

Local authorities ordered the family's house torn down on March 14, along with fourteen other Christians' homes in the area. On March 19, 2010, Po, his wife, and their three children fled into the forest, possibly to find refuge with Christian families. Following Po's persecution and that of two other converts, most Christians in the village stopped practicing their religion.[4]

Perhaps few places are so brutally anti-Christian, however, as North Korea. Lee Joo-Chan is the pseudonym of a middle-aged North Korean pastor who defected to South Korea. He recounted that his mother and brother were killed in front of him, and his son was tortured almost to death. Lee said, "My family has paid the ultimate sacrifice for God. In honor of them, I serve the Lord Jesus with my whole heart. Even if it will cost my life too."

He described a time when Christianity was vibrant in the North. "At Christmas time we used to sing familiar Christmas carols such as 'Silent Night' and 'Joy to the World.' Older North Korean Christians know these too. They sang these carols when they were young. Their parents were Christians at the time of the great revival in 1907. Now they are no longer allowed to sing them, because all Christian activity is forbidden."[5]

CHRISTIANS AND COMMUNIST REGIMES

The countries discussed in this chapter are the remnant of the world's Communist states. China, Vietnam, Laos, Cuba, and North Korea are all still controlled by party regimes that seized power around the middle of the twentieth century. Over the last two decades—with the notable exception of North Korea—the ideological rigidity of Stalin, Mao, and Ho Chi Minh has been tempered by openings to the larger world and an interest in global trade, but the regimes of these countries still remain highly repressive.

Today, China is emerging as a global economic powerhouse and a dynamic regional force poised to eclipse the Asian-Pacific democracies both militarily and economically. Vietnam, Laos, and Cuba remain impoverished and slower to enter global markets, but they, too, are reaching out for investment, trade, and tourism.

North Korea, in a class by itself, remains closed, openly hostile to the West, and devoted to Soviet-inspired totalitarianism.

These countries' ideologies initially viewed Christianity, like all religions, as an impediment to progress, its moral codes as mere superstition, and its spiritual consolation and message of hope as an opiate. They, and their ideological allies in the Soviet bloc, sought to eradicate all religions. They did so brutally. Over decades, the churches were devastated as Christians were martyred by the thousands for their faith in merciless prison and labor camps and by firing squads and assassins' bullets. North Korea has not changed.

By 1991, the Soviet Union had collapsed and splintered. Vietnam, Laos, and Cuba were left without a patron and with no choice but to court Western trade and aid. Around the same time, China began to shed its stagnating Marxist economic policies. With greater global engagement, these states needed to soften their reputations and internal policies. Simultaneously, foreign Christians worked to lend support and gain a greater presence.

With this internal loosening, even though it falls far short of real religious freedom, Christianity has begun to rise out of the ashes. Catholic and Protestant churches are rebuilding. Christian faith is spreading and, gradually, Christian public worship and practice is widening. In China in particular, the faith is seeing spectacular and unprecedented growth.

However, none of these states has made reforms in civil and political rights comparable to its economic liberalization. The Communist parties in these countries control all political and nearly all civic activity, including religious activity. More subtle forms of repression are replacing mass killings and penal camps; Christian practice is now put under surveillance, registered, regulated, and restricted, instead of being crushed outright as in the past.

Unauthorized or independent religious activity is still treated as a crime, and brutality against and imprisonment of Christians still continues. In Vietnam and Laos, authorities may force unregistered Christians in remote ethnic areas to recant their faith. North

Korea, the brutal exception, has made no substantial reforms regarding religious freedom since its founding more than half a century ago.

CHINA

In April 2011, a standoff between Chinese officials and a courageous group of Christian worshippers made international news. State authorities, using a range of tactics, were preventing Shouwang Church from holding indoor worship. Authorities pressured landlords to cancel leases so that Shouwang had no meeting place.

Frustrated but determined, they finally decided to meet outdoors, in the Zhongguancun public square in the Haidian district, Beijing. When the first gathering took place, the security forces were ready. They detained hundreds of worshippers, who were removed from the area in a phalanx of official buses. Four pastors and many other church leaders were placed under house arrest for weeks, lower-profile Christians for up to two days.

On April 24, 2011, Easter Sunday, the worshippers gathered outside in the square for the third time. Chinese writer Promise Hsu reported:

> Authorities rounded up more than 30 people and herded them into buses or police cars. Just as before, they were sent to local police stations. They were asked to leave their names and contact information and to promise not to attend outdoor worship again. Some declined to make any pledge, and others simply told the police they would continue to worship outdoors next Sunday. Some of them have been detained two or three times. More than half were released later that same day. But the rest, all in the eastern district of Chaoyang, were expected to gain freedom after having to stay at the police stations for 24 or 48 hours.[6]

More than five hundred worshippers were detained over the first few weeks of their standoff with the authorities. Individually, members have suffered ramifications from the detentions. In one case, a young man from Shouwang Church was arrested as he was having his mobile phone fixed, handed over to a regional office of Shandong Province, and expelled from Beijing to his parents' house in Shandong. His identity card was confiscated and he was warned to not attempt to return to Beijing before July 1. Village officials were ordered to keep an eye on him. Another member was similarly expelled to Hubei Province. He had already been forced to quit his job as a preschool teacher.[7]

As of December 29, 2011, two of the church's pastors, three elders, and several other leaders remained under house arrest. After beginning their outdoor worship again in 2012, the church's Facebook page reported on February 12: "As far as we know, on Sunday morning, at least fifteen believers were taken away for going to the planned location to join the outdoor service, either at the spot or on their way there. Four believers were released on the way, and the other eleven believers were sent to three local police stations. Till 18:30 pm on Sunday, ten believers were released home. And the last believer was released around 19:00 pm on Sunday . . ."[8]

TIGHT CONTROLS

China is now most known for its burgeoning economy, ubiquitous exports, growing military, talented people, and increasing global influence. These are real enough. After the suffocation of Communist policies, the country has gone through an economic transformation with perhaps no parallels in history. Many millions have risen out of crushing poverty. The growth and dynamism of surging cities such as Shanghai or Guangzhou is breathtaking.

But politically, the country remains a one-party state, with control and much wealth in the hands of the party elite. To maintain their position, they seek to regulate everything within the society, including religion. China has repressed religion for all sixty years of Communist Party rule. Since the Maoist era ended, the party's urgent goal of annihilating religion has been replaced by one of making religion serve the interests of the Communist state.

Nearly one-fifth of the world's people live in China, and its bloodstained record of control, discrimination, persecution, and death cannot be easily matched. In the 1990s, a human rights survey listing people held in China for both political and religious reasons comprised 630 pages. Today, such a document would tell a similar tale. Many of those who suffer are not named in any publication, or heard about at all.

The regime's tireless effort to silence the Christian lawyer Gao, described at the outset of this chapter, along with the dearth of information about his status, typifies a style of persecution that has a unique history of its own.

On October 1, 1949, Mao Zedong, the chairman of the Chinese Communist Party, proclaimed the founding of the People's Republic of China. Mao's government soon began its crackdown against religion, and specifically Christians, by imprisoning any religious believers who refused to accept the priority of Communism over their own faith. They were labeled as "counter-revolutionaries" and sentenced to twenty years or more in prison or labor camps. Churches and other religious institutions were closed. The death toll during the Cultural Revolution in the 1960s—when Chinese Marxists proudly declared "the death of God" and persecution reached its height—is unknown, but is estimated by researchers to have been in the millions, including many Christians.

Even now, more than sixty years later, while mass arrests and killings no longer take place, religious activities remain tightly controlled and are officially limited to government-sanctioned "Three-Self" or "patriotic" churches—that is, government-registered and monitored churches that are not under foreign influences. Christianity is treated as a foreign religion, even though the church is one of the oldest continuing institutions in China. There were Christian monasteries in China fourteen hundred years ago, and Italian John of Monte Corvino was the archbishop of Beijing some seven hundred years ago, while Communism is the recent product of nineteenth-century

European thought. The fact that the regime also persecutes other religions, including Tibetan Buddhism and the indigenous Falun Gong spiritual movement, and that it controls secular associations for labor, women, and youth suggests that the state's concern is control, not foreign influence.

Even government-approved Three-Self churches may be attacked. In Shandong Province, security agents forcibly occupied the Three-Self church in the town of Gucheng. When church officials went to Beijing to protest, they were detained and sentenced to several days' administrative detention. The Three-Self church in Dafeng county, Jiangsu Province, was forcibly demolished on March 13, 2012, and two church members were beaten, including a woman whose back was broken.[9]

Government religious policy is carried out by the State Administration for Religious Affairs (SARA), which oversees the five approved religions and monitors the "patriotic" associations with which all churches are required to register. In turn, SARA itself is supervised by the United Front Work Department of the Communist Party.

Seminary students are examined on political conformity as well as theological knowledge. The government regulates religious literature. Religious schools for children are banned. Meetings with foreign coreligionists require state authorization. Even the selection of church leaders must meet government approval. Meanwhile, the unofficial Catholic and Protestant churches, which comprise most of China's Christians, remain illegal, although their growth stands as a warning to the regime: there may be more Christians than members of the Communist Party.

HOW MANY CHRISTIANS?

Fifteen years ago, the US ambassador to China revealed in a meeting with us that he did not know what a house church was.[10] The State Department apparently had not bothered to brief him about this burgeoning and potentially transformative development within Chinese civil society. The house-church movement was the first national organization free of government control to emerge since Mao. Today house churches are the focus of international news articles that express wonder at their rapidly multiplying numbers. In September 2011, the BBC reported that the official Chinese Protestant church is growing, and its reporter attended five churches in downtown Beijing on Easter morning, each of which was packed with more than fifteen hundred worshippers. The Sunday school spilled out onto the street. It further reported that the authorities will not compromise over "the house churches' refusal to acknowledge any official authority over their organisation. The State fears the influence of zealous American evangelism and some of the House Church theology has those characteristics, but, in many other respects, it seems to be an indigenous Chinese movement—charismatic, energetic and young."[11]

How many Christians are there in China? In 2012, the society is still so restricted that it is impossible to know for certain, and there are numerous conflicting reports. According to the Lausanne Global Analysis, "Over the past few decades estimates for the number of Christians in China have ranged from 2.3 million to 200 million."[12]

The official figures are unsurprisingly paltry. In 2008 China estimated just 21 million Christians. But Zhao Xiao, a one-time Communist official and now convert to Christianity, put the number a bit higher at 130 million. And, as reported in the *Economist*, "According to China Aid Association (CAA), a Texas-based lobby group, the director of the government body which supervises all religions in China said privately that the figure was indeed as much as 130m in early 2008."[13] Meanwhile, in December 2011, the Pew Research Center, using conservative assumptions, estimated 67 million.[14]

"Although it may be impossible to arrive at a definitive figure," according to the Lausanne Global Analysis, ". . . an estimate of around 100 million Christians seems reasonable."[15] Whatever the real number may be—including Protestant and Catholic registered and unregistered churches—according to all reports, Christianity is exploding in China.

DETENTIONS, PRISONS, AND LABOR CAMPS

Apart from notoriously inhumane Chinese prisons, there exists a separate system of control consisting of the *laogai*, or "reeducation through labor," camps. These allow for detention, often in the most brutal form, without a trial or even a hearing.

According to Catholic human rights activist Harry Wu, who for nearly twenty years experienced the camps himself, "The core of the human-rights issue in China today is that there is a fundamental machinery for crushing human beings—physically, psychologically and spiritually—called the laogai camp system, of which we have identified eleven hundred separate camps." They are forced labor camps where everything from tea to steel pipe to chemicals are produced. Wu said, "Forced labor is the means, thought reform is the aim . . . it is not simply a prison system; it is a political tool for maintaining the Communist Party's totalitarian rule."[16] The government has refused to allow the International Committee of the Red Cross to examine its prisons and interview prisoners at its own choosing.

One house-church leader who has recently experienced the laogai directly is Pastor Shi Enhao. On March 4, 2011, while preaching in Nanyang, Henan Province, he was seized by officers from the Suqian Municipal Public Security Bureau, along with officials of the Religious Affairs Bureau, interrogated, beaten, and then released. On May 31, he was again arrested with some coworkers for holding unauthorized gatherings. Along with female lay-leader Chang Meiling, Shi was sentenced to twelve days of administrative detention.

The harassment continued on June 1, when more than ten investigators swept through Pastor Shi's home, confiscating books, literature, and other documents. Released on June 12, Shi was immediately put into police detention, and the following month sentenced to two years in labor camp. He was unexpectedly released in January 2012.[17]

VATICAN AUTHORITY: BANNED IN CHINA

Besides being illegal if they refuse to register with the government, churches are also forbidden to be under the authority of any overseas body. This means that Catholicism is officially outlawed because it is in communion with the Church of Rome. Those who insist on anchoring their faith in the church magisterium, the Roman Catholic creed, and papal authority pay a steep price. The government insists on controlling the Catholic Church and every religious association through strangling regulations, and it bans church teachings such as an unborn child's right to life.

The Vatican continues to patiently converse with Beijing and has worked hard to keep the Catholic community united. As the United States Commission on International Religious Freedom (USCIRF) reported, "an estimated 90 percent of CPA [Catholic Patriotic Association] bishops and priests are secretly ordained by the Vatican and, in many provinces, CPA and unregistered Catholic clergy and congregations work closely together." In 2007, there seemed to be an agreement whereby the Holy See would be allowed to approve and ordain bishops selected by the state-controlled Catholic Patriotic Association, but the apparent pact was violated by Beijing. In July 2011, Joseph Huang Bingzhang was made a bishop without a papal mandate—in a diocese that already had a bishop in communion with the Vatican. This was pronounced illicit by Pope Benedict XVI. In November 2010, the CPA ordained Guo Jincai bishop of Chengde without prior approval of the Vatican and without a papal mandate. Hong Kong's Cardinal Zen stated, "Our bishops are being humiliated."[18]

Arrests, disappearances, and imprisonment continue. The Congressional Executive Committee on China (CECC) reports that "at least 40 Roman Catholic bishops remain imprisoned, detained, or disappeared."[19] Many have not been seen or heard from since their arrests many years ago. Some have spent decades in Chinese prison camps.

One is Bishop James Su Zhimin, who is nearly eighty years old and has refused to participate in the Patriotic Catholic Church. He was the bishop of Baoding (Hebei), a traditional center of Chinese Catholicism, when the authorities arrested him in October 1997. Since then, the government has released no information about any charges or his place of detention.

Bishop Su had already served fifteen years in prison before his first release in 1993. He was tortured throughout his internment. In one beating, the board being used by the security police was reduced to splinters. Unrelenting, the police ripped apart a wooden door frame and used it to continue the beating until it, too, disintegrated into splinters. The bishop was then hung by his wrists from a ceiling while being beaten around the head.

Later on he was placed in a cell filled with water at varying levels from ankle deep to hip deep where he was left for days, unable to sit or sleep.[20]

There were reports that in late 2003 a relative recognized Bishop Su in a Baoding hospital, encircled by Public Security Bureau (PSB) officers. There has been no word since then, despite repeated requests from his family, the church, and the US government.

Another long-term prisoner is Bishop Cosma Shi Enxiang of Yixian (Hebei), ninety years old, who was arrested in April 2001. Auxiliary Bishop Yao Ling also has disappeared into the Chinese penal system. Nothing is known about either of them.[21]

The underground Catholic community of the Diocese of Suiyuan (Inner Mongolia), after years of official disinterest and church growth, is now facing a crackdown. On January 30, 2012, six priests, including the rector of the underground seminary, Father Joseph Ban Zhanxiong, were arrested at a rally. Four were later released but must report daily to police and undergo indoctrination sessions. They were dragged to concelebrate mass with the government-appointed bishop, but reportedly they refused to pray since, in the Catholic Church, only legitimate members of the clergy can administer the eucharistic celebration of the mass, and a counterfeit bishop would not qualify. "On January 31, the diocesan administrator, Father Gao Jiangping, was arrested along with another priest." Some thirty other priests there have gone into hiding.[22]

The government is desperately trying to stamp out the traditional May Twenty-Fourth pilgrimage to a Marian shrine. Whereas in the past, tens of thousands of Catholics from both official and underground churches came together in a spirit of reconciliation to pray at the shrine, now only hundreds from the local area manage to get through.

> Every year, the hill shrine of Our Lady of Sheshan, near Shanghai, is transformed into a battlefield. On the very day of its solemnity, May 24, Mary Help of Christians, hundreds of uniformed and plainclothes policemen swarm the mount like zealous ants, eyes and cameras peeled to ensure every corner of the hill on which the Church stands is under guard, to check pilgrims' documents, making them go through metal detectors, as if they were battling a new form of terrorism.[23]

The "terrorist" in question is none other than the pope and his followers, who since 2007 have asked Catholics worldwide to celebrate a day of prayer for the church in China, coinciding with the pilgrimage to Sheshan.

ONE-CHILD POLICY

China's cruel population programs, including the one-child policy, pit many people against the state, especially devout believers and Catholics in particular. Newly married couples have to be sterilized or take long-lasting contraceptives if one or both are diagnosed as having a hereditary disease, including allegedly relevant mental disorders that supposedly make them unsuitable for reproduction. It also forces women to have abortions, even in later stages of pregnancy.

The scope of China's coercive population-control policy was revealed in 2003 in Jeishi, Guangdong Province. In order to meet provincial quotas, "family-planning" officials were directed to perform 271 abortions, fit 818 women with intrauterine devices (IUDs), and have 1,369 women sterilized, all in 35 days. A blind, self-taught lawyer and activist, Chen Guancheng, who tried to organize a protest against coerced abortions, was placed under house arrest in Linyi, Shandong Province.[24] On August 24, 2006, he was sentenced to four years and three months for damaging property and disrupting traffic, as widely reported by the BBC and other international press. After his release Chen was kept under virtual house arrest, but on April 22, 2012, he managed to elude his captors and make his way to the US embassy in Beijing. After negotiations with the Chinese government, he, his wife, and their two children were allowed to leave for the United States, and he became a special student at the New York University School of Law.

Catholic priests and bishops, along with everyone else, are forbidden to oppose this ruthless policy. According to the state's own Chinese Academy of Social Services (CASS), the one-child policy will cause Chinese boys, who are socially favored, to outnumber Chinese girls by 24 million or more by 2020. Former ambassador Mark Lagon, who directed the US State Department's office on human trafficking said, "This phenomenon of 'missing girls' has turned China into 'a giant magnet' for human traffickers, who lure or kidnap women and sell them—even multiple times—into forced marriages or the commercial sex trade."[25]

At a 2011 briefing, US Representative Chris Smith, who has held numerous hearings and press conferences on the policy, described its horrors:

> A Chinese woman who becomes pregnant without a permit will be put under mind-bending pressure to abort. She knows that "out-of-plan" illegal children are denied education, health-care, and marriage, and that fines for bearing a child without a birth permit can be 10 times the average annual income of two parents, and those families that can't or won't pay are jailed, or their homes smashed in, or their young child is killed. If the brave woman still refuses to submit, she may be held in a

> punishment cell, or, if she flees, her relatives may be held and, very often, beaten. . . . If the woman is by some miracle still able to resist this pressure, she may be physically dragged to the operating table and forced to undergo an abortion.[26]

These cruel assaults are of course devastating for any woman, whatever her beliefs, but for many Christian women there is the added pain of being forced to violate their religious beliefs.

HOUSE CHURCHES

On September 26, 2010, local Public Security Bureau agents raided the church led by Liao Zhongxiu, a Sichuan Province house-church leader. They destroyed church property, confiscated books, and detained members. During interrogation, two of the congregation were severely beaten, and the police director personally choked one with a chain. Later, when some members went to the police seeking the return of church property, five were immediately arrested, charged with "disrupting public order under the guise of religion," and detained for fifteen days.[27] On March 11, 2011, Liao herself was arrested and taken into custody for "suspicion of utilizing a cult organization in undermining the implementation of the state law and regulations." As we write, she is still being held.[28]

Most of the explosive increase of Christians in China has taken place in house churches (or underground churches), which are usually evangelical in theology and practice. In the last thirty years, these church networks have experienced the largest pattern of church growth in world history. In no other country, at no other time, have tens of millions of people come into the Christian faith at such a pace.

Some of these house meetings consist of a dozen people gathering for Bible study or prayer, but many others have hundreds, even thousands of adherents who don't meet in houses but rather in warehouses, halls, hotels, or anywhere they can find space. As described above, the Shouwang Church has been meeting outdoors since the government pressured the landlord to cancel its lease.

Some house churches are individual congregations; others are tied into networks of many millions. Some have cordial relations with registered churches; others do not.

These churches' exponential growth puts the government in a quandary. There have been intense debates at the most senior levels about how to respond. But so far the state has reverted to its default position of trying to force them to be registered, regulated, and controlled. Those who refuse, especially leaders, face violence and imprisonment. Mark Shan of China Aid describes their situation:

> House Church always face persecution, especially church leaders are facing danger of even being sent to prison, though different regions in different times have different degree of persecutions. In recent years, a few house church leaders have been punished severely, e.g. Xinjiang Uyghur Christian leader Alimujiang sentenced for 15 years in 2008; Fa Yafeng the leader of church rights defending movement, has been in house arrest for over a year; and Beijing Shouwang Church who suffers non-stop persecution from April 10 of 2011 to now and all of the church leadership are under house arrest since then. [*sic*][29]

On November 8, 2011, fifty-two villagers were holding a meeting in a home in Xuyi village, Hebei Province, when they were raided by about 140 security officials, including some from the Religious Affairs Bureau (RAB). The RAB official declared the gathering illegal. Without legal procedure, officials confiscated 170,000 yuan (about US$27,000) in church funds and demolished the home. On Christmas Day, more than one hundred police officers broke up the church Christmas party held in the Zhuozhou City Bank Building. They took five believers into custody and, after twelve days of detention, Liu Cuiying and Yang Wenyan were sent for an undetermined period to the Shijiazhuang Forced Labor Camp for "organizing and participating in illegal cult meetings."[30]

Li Ying is a pastor of a South China Church in Hubei and

the niece of Pastor Gong Shengliang, founder of the South China Church, one of the fastest-growing house-church movements in China. She was editor in chief of the church newspaper, *South China Special Edition*, and had been arrested several times, spending a year in prison in 1996. She was arrested again in 2001 with five other church leaders and charged with "using a cult to undermine enforcement of the law." The leaders were actually sentenced to death, but in 2002, a higher court reduced the sentence to fifteen years in prison. In prison, Ying was not allowed to have a Bible and was forced to work fifteen hours a day making products for export. On Christmas Day 2011, she was released five years early. Even though she was not allowed to read the letters sent to her, she told China Aid president Bob Fu that more than eleven thousand letters from the international community and churches worldwide convinced authorities to release her. While free from prison, she is subject to "community correction," which means that she lives only in government-appointed neighborhoods and attends only government-appointed churches.[31]

Even foreign Protestant Christians seem unable to avoid the government's repressive measures. On January 12, 2012, "a Canadian businesswoman of Chinese descent was kidnapped and denied food and water for two days by Chinese security agents after she visited the leader of Shouwang Church and a house church in Shanxi Province."[32]

CHINA'S CONTINUING REPRESSION

China's stock answer to criticism is that people are not punished for their religious faith but for breaking the law—an answer that fails to acknowledge that their laws criminalize peaceful religious acts protected by international human rights agreements. In January 2011, SARA, a key part of the state apparatus supervising religion, outlined "measures to maintain extensive government supervision and control over religious communities, specifically calling on authorities to 'guide' unregistered Protestants to worship in state-sanctioned churches, continue policies to deny Catholics in

China the freedom to accept the authority of the Holy See to make bishop appointments."[33] Since 1999, the US State Department has designated China as a Country of Particular Concern under the International Religious Freedom Act for its persecution of religious believers. In 2011, USCIRF reported that religious freedom conditions had declined over the previous year.[34]

In its 2012 annual report, China Aid said that Chinese government's "persecution of Christians and churches has dramatically worsened in 2011. This trend of worsening persecution has persisted for the past six years, and in 2011 the number of Christians detained for their religious beliefs had soared almost 132 percent from 2010. A new government practice last year was targeting churches and individuals who were significantly impacting society, like Beijing's Shouwang Church." The report also highlighted an "increase in the use of torture against detainees," citing a 33.3 percent increase over 2010.[35]

VIETNAM

Father Thadeus Nguyen Van Ly, a Catholic priest and longtime religious freedom and democracy advocate, has been grievously persecuted for more than forty years. He has been imprisoned for more than seventeen years and placed under house arrest eight times. Ordained in 1974, Father Ly began his ministry teaching at a seminary in Hue Province and working in the office of the Bishop of Hue. He was imprisoned for a total of ten years between 1977 and 1992 after his attempt to lead thousands of pilgrims to La Vang, a site holy to Vietnamese Catholics since 1800, and due to his fearless calls for religious freedom.

In May 2001, Father Ly was arrested while preparing for mass. His offense was that he had submitted written testimony to the USCIRF on February 13, 2001, in which he reported, "The government has falsely accused clergy members and lay people as a pretext to detain and imprison those who protest its oppressive policy, or those who teach catechism, lead a church choir, or join a seminary. They are banished to concentration camps for years."

Under international pressure, Father Ly was released in February 2005, but two years later was back behind bars for again criticizing the Vietnamese government in the dissident publication he edited, *Free Speech*. During his March 2007 show trial, the authorities prohibited him from presenting a defense. At one point, police clamped their hands over his mouth when he loudly accused Vietnamese officials of human rights violations. He was sentenced to eight years' imprisonment.

Father Ly was held in harsh solitary confinement during some of this time. From prison, in a letter republished on May 24, 2007, by Reporters Without Borders, he wrote to friends, asking for warm clothes, blankets, medicines and "necessity articles (glasses, dictionary with large letters. . . .)" and confirming that authorities barred family and friends from visiting him.

While imprisoned in 2009, Father Ly suffered two strokes, and became paralyzed on his right side. He tried to send a letter to his family about his deteriorating health, but was not able to. In March 2010, four months after the second stroke, Father Ly was finally given medical parole and transferred to house arrest. During this period, the priest appealed to the UN for the Vietnamese government to "return seized Bibles, vestments, computers, nearly 200 books, and articles on justice, democracy and human rights," and asked for some $500,000 in compensation for the medical illnesses he suffered in prison.[36]

On July 25, 2011, the then sixty-five-year-old, partially paralyzed priest was returned to prison; his "medical parole" had ended.[37]

Vietnam has many faith groups, and none of them, not even its traditional Buddhist ones, are free of government restrictions. Like China, it has abandoned attempts to eradicate religion and instead tries to register, monitor, and ultimately control it. Religious oppression takes many forms. Catholics suffer particularly from restrictions on training their leaders. They and some

Protestants are also deprived of large numbers of churches, seminaries, monasteries, convents, and cemeteries that have been—and still are—confiscated by the government. Evangelical and some Catholic ethnic minorities in remoter regions, such as the Hmong and scores of smaller groups, face the harshest, most violent persecution. Christian human rights defenders are imprisoned, often serving long sentences.

Vietnam's eight million Catholics, whose church dates from the 1600s, and its more recent and rapidly growing Protestant population of up to two million, together form about 10 percent of the country's 90 million people. Protestants, who are mainly evangelical, are largely regulated through the government-recognized Evangelical Church of Vietnam, which is divided into a northern and a larger southern branch. Some churches are registered locally and nationally.

As in China, there is a flourishing movement of house churches that are not registered with the government and are therefore illegal. Expert on Vietnamese Christians Reg Reimer estimates there are at least 2,500 home-based groups belonging to house church organizations, with some claiming as many as 30,000 believers.[38] Some are connected to international denominations such as the Assemblies of God, Nazarenes, Methodists, Presbyterians, and Mennonites. Some in the south cooperate with the Vietnamese Evangelical Fellowship, and some in the north with the Hanoi Christian Fellowship, formed only in 2009.

Meeting illegally is strictly opposed. Compass Direct News reports that on July 26, 2009, security officials, on orders of the police chief, broke up the Sunday service at a Hanoi house church and announced that it was illegal for them to worship and teach religion. When Christians under the leadership of Pastor Dang Thi Dinh refused to sign a document admitting they were meeting illegally, an angry police officer shouted, "If I find you meeting here next Sunday, I will kill you all like I'd kill a dog!"[39]

A "religious police" unit (A41) monitors and sets policies toward groups the state considers extremist. These include unregistered

Protestants, especially among ethnic minorities; some Mennonite church leaders; and some Catholic priests and orders, particularly the indigenous Coredemptorists, a Marian religious order known especially for its devotion to the Blessed Mother and work with the poor. With wire taps, police surveillance, infiltrators, and a myriad of registration requirements, the state closely monitors the activities and reviews sermons of all groups, registered and unregistered.

RESTRICTING CATHOLIC LEADERSHIP AND PROPERTY

Rather than imprisoning, deporting, or executing leaders as it did in the past, the state is now trying to restrict the Catholic Church's hierarchical structure. The government had shut down all Catholic seminaries, preventing the training of new priests for more than a generation. Now, while allowing some seminaries to open, it can veto the appointment of bishops and limit the number of seminaries and seminarians. As a final precaution, it can restrict the appointment and transfers of priests. Vietnam still has not normalized relations with the Vatican, though in 2011 the president met with Pope Benedict XVI to continue negotiations.

From Ho Chi Minh's takeover of the North in 1954 up until 1988, the government repressed the church's formidable educational system. Orphanages, hospitals, and charities, and even the apostolic nunciature—the Vatican's embassy—were shut and confiscated. Even now, reports show that Vietnamese government authorities continue to take or destroy church property, and punish those who object or seek the return of previously confiscated church property. On September 19, 2008, the government tore down the apostolic nunciature building in Hanoi in order to develop the property.

In 2009, eight parishioners who took part in a prayer vigil for the return of the property of Hanoi's Thai Ha parish, confiscated in 1954, were put on trial for disturbing public order. On October 8, 2011, parish priest Reverend Joseph Nguyen Van Phuong was summoned to the Dong Da District People's Committee and informed that a hospital wastewater treatment plant would be built on the property. On November 3, hundreds of truncheon-wielding police and military accompanied by dogs and followed by a state TV crew attacked the Thai Ha monastery. They used loudspeakers to shout insults, throwing stones and smashing down the front door. Several priests and monks were assaulted as they tried to stop the wreckage. Drawn by pealing church bells, thousands of Catholics from neighboring parishes rushed to their defense and stopped the attack. After a further protest on December 2, 2011, by hundreds of parishioners and Reverend Joseph Nguyen Van Phuong, the vicar of Thai Ha, the police surrounded them and arrested or temporarily detained three clergy and about thirty parishioners. Others were beaten by uniformed and plainclothes police wielding sticks.[40]

Similarly, in October 2009, government authorities closed catechism classrooms, attacked parishioners who protested, and seized the last remaining property of Loan Ly parish in the Hue Archdiocese. The land, located along the scenic central coast, had been in church possession since 1956. It is thought the government was acting on behalf of developers.[41]

In 2010, local authorities in Da Nang Province decided to build an ecotourist resort and planned to confiscate the large and historic Catholic cemetery and seize and demolish houses in Con Dau parish. When the parish tried to bury eighty-two-year-old parishioner Mary Tan on May 4, police broke up the funeral procession and confiscated her remains in order to cremate them. When the parishioners resisted, more than one hundred were beaten, fifty-nine arrested and tortured, six eventually charged with "disturbing public order" and attacking state personnel, two sentenced to up to a year in prison, and one beaten to death.[42] Nam Nguyen, who was summoned to testify against the others, was reportedly beaten severely when he refused. He died under suspicious circumstances on July 3, 2010, several hours after being released from the police station on another, believed to be trumped-up charge.[43]

The US Department of State has reported additional government land grabs:

> In November 2009 in Da Lat, the government demolished a portion of a Catholic seminary built in 1964 and seized by authorities in 1980. The Church had repeatedly requested that the seminary be returned to church control for use as a training facility for local priests. The government instead decided to transform the property into a cultural park. Similarly, in Vinh Long Province, authorities demolished the Congregation of Saint Paul of Chartres monastery to transform the property into a public square.[44]

The government has also returned only a small number of churches and other sites confiscated from Protestants, and the Evangelical Church of Vietnam continues to seek restitution for more than 250 properties.[45]

CHRISTIAN HUMAN RIGHTS DEFENDERS

Protestants are also targeted for protesting injustice. In May 2011, Mennonite pastor Duong Kim Khai was arrested with seven members of his congregation for "abusing democratic freedoms" and "anti-government propaganda." Khai and his colleagues had organized poor farmers to fight land confiscations and had spoken to the international media about the situation. The defendants were given prison sentences—between two and eight years. Pastor Khai was also an active member of Viet Tan, a banned political organization that peacefully promotes democracy. He had been arrested previously in 2004 for using his property as a church without permission, and for hosting Viet Tan meetings.[46]

On December 30, 2011, Pastor Nguyen Trung Ton, the head of the Full Gospel Church in Thanh Hoa Province, was sentenced to two years of house arrest for "collecting documents and writing articles which tarnished the reputation of the Communist Party and the Socialist regime."[47]

Christian leaders defending the rights of ethnic minorities also suffer greatly. In April 2005 in the Hmong village of Ta-Phin, in Lao-Kai's Sapa district, officials seized land from twelve families, reportedly because they were Christians. Authorities demanded that they sign an agreement recanting their faith. After the authorities repeatedly beat one of them, Giang-A Tinh, he complained to the commune secretary. He was then arrested, bound with wire, and left in the blazing sun. Photographs taken several weeks later still showed the scars on his wrists. Government cadres also abused his seventy-year-old mother, forcing her to drink filthy water. His brother, Giang-A Pao, thirty-two, was beaten so severely that he was not able to walk for a month.[48]

According to an international human rights report in 2011:

> Since 2001, more than 350 Montagnards [mountain people] have been sentenced to long prison sentences on vaguely defined national security charges for their involvement in public protests and unregistered house churches considered subversive by the government, or for trying to flee to Cambodia to seek asylum. They include . . . pastors, house church leaders, and land rights activists. Charges brought against them include undermining national solidarity (Penal Code article 87) or disrupting security (article 89).[49]

PROTESTANT ETHNIC MINORITIES

Christian ethnic minorities in remote areas, far from the international spotlight, suffer the bloodiest repression. Constituting about 13 percent of the country's population, these ethnic groups represent more than half of the Protestants in Vietnam, while a smaller number of the Vietnamese ethnics are Catholic. The Hmong and other smaller ethnic minority Christians in the northwest provinces, along with the scores of ethnic minority Christians in the Central Highlands, are often collectively known as "Montagnards," or mountain people. They face ongoing campaigns of harassment, detention, beatings, surveillance, and property confiscations. There are also persistent reports that they are forced to renounce their faith, even though that practice was officially banned in 2005.

The ethnic minorities have a difficult time registering their churches with the government for many reasons. The Hmong in particular have been unsuccessful at legally registering more than six churches and meeting places, despite all attempts. Reg Reimer found: "The majority of remaining unregistered groups do not meet the 'twenty years of stable operation' requirement before registration can even be considered. Without denominational registration, or registration of local congregations, these groups remain vulnerable to arbitrary government harassment or worse."[50]

The state's Religious Publishing House has not acted on a longstanding request to allow printing of an edition of the Bible in the modern form of the Hmong language. (The government recognizes only an archaic form of the language that cannot be understood by the average Hmong.)[51] Those caught transporting Hmong-language materials have been beaten, fined, and detained.

The government continues to assert that Montagnards are operating a "Degar" (literally meaning "children of the mountain" in a local tribal language) church that calls for the creation of an independent Montagnard State. The Southern Evangelical Church of Vietnam congregations and the house churches in the provinces of Dak Lak, Gia Lai, Kon Tum, Binh Phuoc, Phu Yen, and Dak Nong experience tight government scrutiny because of feared association with separatist groups overseas. Human rights groups reported that "political security" (PA43) units join with local police to target leaders of unregistered house churches in the Central Highlands. In 2010, more than seventy Montagnards were reported detained or arrested, and more than 250 imprisoned on national security charges.[52]

A former US foreign service officer in Vietnam reported that, on August 21, 2009, Vietnamese Communist security police went to the homes of Protestant Christian pastors Phan Nay, Vong Kpa, and Hnoi Ksor in Ploi Ksing village, in Gia Lai Province. The police severely beat them with batons in front of their families, then prevented their relatives from taking them to the hospital, even though some were in severe pain. The police accused them of worshipping in a house church unauthorized by the government-controlled Montagnard church.[53]

USCIRF reports that an unknown number of Montagnards, including religious leaders, are still in detention since taking part in the 2001 and 2004 demonstrations for religious freedom and land rights. Many protestants in this heavily controlled area refuse to join government-approved denominations.[54]

FAITH RECANTATIONS

As the experience of the Po family at the start of this chapter illustrates, local officials try to force ethnic converts to Christianity in remote areas to recant their faith. The central government denies this is official policy, yet it goes on with impunity, even after incidents are reported to national officials.

In December 2010, in Bon Croh Ponan village, authorities summoned three Protestant Montagnard men, Beo Nay, Phor Ksor, and Rin Ksor, to the local police station. Beo Nay was accused of "persuading people to join the Degar Church and communicating with people in the US to disrupt [the Vietnamese] government." Without giving him a chance to reply, the police punched him three times, beat him with a rubber stick on his neck and back, and set fire to his beard. Under threat of imprisonment, he was forced to sign a statement giving up his rights to public worship, the celebration of Christmas, and freedom of movement. The other two were similarly beaten, and so injured they were bedridden for several weeks.[55]

Two Central Highlands Christian evangelists with the Vietnam Good News Mission, Ksor Y Du and Kpa Y Co, were sentenced to prison for six and four years respectively for "undermining national unity." They had been arrested on January 27, 2010, and were held for ten months without trial. Ksor was reportedly dragged to the police station behind a motorcycle, arriving bloodied and bruised. During Ksor's pretrial incarceration, police repeatedly visited his wife to pressure her to recant her Christian faith. They also bribed her with a monthly sack of rice, a new house, and promises of the immediate release of her husband.[56]

LAOS

On April 15, 2011, the Lao People's Army, supported by Vietnamese troops, raped and killed four women during a crackdown on a group of Hmong Christians. The women's husbands and children were beaten, tied up, and forced to watch. All their Bibles were confiscated. Two weeks later, this episode and others like it prompted thousands of Christians along the Vietnam-Laos border in Dien Bien Phu, Vietnam, and Phongsail, Laos, to join together in prayer and protest for human rights reforms, religious freedom, land reform, and an end to illegal logging and deforestation. Lao and Vietnamese troops promptly launched a joint attack on the peaceful demonstrators, reportedly killing forty-nine of them and injuring and/or arresting many hundreds of others, who were last seen being loaded onto trucks while being beaten by the soldiers.[57]

Laos has its own distinctive culture and delightful people, but with respect to religion, its government operates like a mini-Vietnam. The population of some 6.5 million is mostly Buddhist, with Christians accounting for only about 1.5 percent. Christians are generally viewed with suspicion of creating social divisions and chaos. A 2002 decree officially expanded religious freedom, allowing for evangelizing and distributing religious literature, but in practice many restrictions remain.

In recent years, Christians in the larger cities have seen the most reforms. The government has allowed Lao Protestants and Catholics to reopen, build, and expand religious venues. In 2010, a Catholic bishop was ordained with the Vatican's approval, and in 2008, priests were allowed to be ordained, the first since 1975.[58] However, provincial authorities continue to arrest and brutalize some Catholics, as well as ethnic-minority Protestants who refuse to join the government-approved Laos Evangelical Church or the Seventh-day Adventist Church. Christians in rural areas have also been pressured to recant their faith.

On January 4, 2011, for instance, a man known simply as

Pastor Wanna, eight other Lao church leaders, and two young children ate dinner at the pastor's house in Nakoon village, in the Hinboun district of Khammouan Province. During the meal, some twenty Hinboun district police came, guns at the ready, and arrested them. The next day, two were released from custody, but the other nine believers, including Pastor Wanna, were taken to Khammouan Provincial Prison, about one hundred miles away. The Christians were charged with conducting a "secret meeting" without approval.

This was not the first time Pastor Wanna has been harassed. In 2008, he began to hold worship services at his home. By 2009, twenty-five Nakoon families had become Christians and began to publicly practice their new faith. In 2008 and 2009, he was repeatedly summoned to police headquarters.

The police threatened to arrest and imprison him if he did not recant his Christian faith and stop evangelizing. He rejected both demands and, as a result, in May 2010, was arrested. Because he led other people to embrace the Christian faith, he was accused of destroying Lao customs and traditions. While Pastor Wanna was in prison, the other believers were sent to "re-education" programs for what in effect was governmental brainwashing. In October 2010, Pastor Wanna was released after being warned that he would be arrested again if he continued to spread the Christian faith. He refused to practice his faith secretly, which led to his re-arrest in January 2011.[59]

Another example comes from the district of Saybulim, in Savannakhet Province. On February 22, 2012, local officials confiscated a church in Kengweng village. The church had been built in 1972 by two Lao Christian families and had served the village's 178 Christians since then. To reopen, the Christians must submit a formal written request to the authorities of the village, district, and province, obtaining approval from each of the three levels. Agenzia Fides reports that, as of 2012, there are about thirty churches and church buildings in Savannakhet Province, but all except seven lack official recognition and are illegal.[60]

CUBA

Only ninety miles off Florida's coast, Cuba, once a satellite of the Soviet Union, continues today as a single-party Communist state. The government restricts all organized activity, including religion, which it still views as an ever-present threat that must be carefully managed and tightly controlled.

From 1959 until 1992, from the time Communist revolutionary Fidel Castro seized power, Cuba was officially an atheist state, openly and categorically hostile to religion. By 1992, the constitution merely declared Cuba to be a secular state. Between those years, the government used harsh labor camp detentions and other persecution to try to eradicate religious practice, and Catholic baptisms dropped from 85 percent to a fraction of 1 percent of the population.[61] Today Catholics are 60 percent of the population and the church's dialogue with the government, starting with Pope John Paul II's 1998 visit and reinforced by Pope Benedict XVI's 2012 visit, has led to a gradual opening for both Catholics and Protestants. The Catholic Church is now emerging as a social force brokering prisoner releases and defending dissidents.

Nevertheless, under the Communist Party's Religious Affairs Office, all religious activities—worship services, charities, media, human-rights work, processions, meetings with foreign co-religionists, and religious education—are either banned or tightly regulated. Not until 2010 did the Catholic Church finally receive permission to broadcast Easter mass in the state-monopolized media. The government-authorized Protestant Cuban Council of Churches (CCC) also received permission to host a radio series.

Protestants, about 5 percent of the population, are pressured to join the CCC. State interference in church affairs prompted Reverend Robert Rodriguez, president of the International Fellowship of Evangelical Pastors and Ministers, to withdraw his organization from the Cuban Council of Churches. Soon afterward, in March 2008, he was arrested and charged with "offensive behavior." The state's Registrar of Organizations removed him from the

Fellowship's presidency. Around the same time, his adult son Eric, also a pastor, was violently assaulted; his wife, Gilianys Rodriguez, was also attacked on the street in December 2008, which resulted in a miscarriage. Pastor Eric was sentenced to a year's probation for "disturbing the public order."[62]

Religious groups, including house churches, must register with the state. Any new group must certify that it is not duplicating the activities of an already recognized organization. Two house churches of the same denomination cannot be within two kilometers of each other, and the state determines how many people may attend. Any congregation wanting to construct a building must obtain the government's permission. Though many unregistered house churches operate, they live under threat.[63]

Pastor Omar Gude Perez was one of at least thirty Apostolic Reformation pastors arrested in 2009 on trumped-up charges. In 2008, he had been charged with "human trafficking," but ten months later, the charges were dismissed for lack of evidence. This time, the pastor was charged with "falsification of documents" and "counter-revolutionary conduct and attitudes." He was sentenced to six years in prison. Cuba's Supreme Tribunal barred him from appealing. In 2011, he was suddenly released on the condition that he could not preach or travel outside of the city of Camaguey. Though the government gave exit visas to his wife and children, it refuses to give one to Pastor Perez himself despite earlier promises that it would do so.[64]

As Perez's case attests, leaders of the Apostolic Reformation and other groups that refuse to affiliate with the CCC can face severe persecution. The construction of their church buildings has been blocked, their materials have been confiscated, and many of their members have lost their jobs, been evicted from their homes, or, again, been arrested on trumped-up charges.[65]

State restrictions for all churches are pervasive. Pastors have been called to State Security because of their sermons, and issued warnings. One pastor who said, "Don't be like Che, be like Christ" was harshly rebuked by local officials.[66] In April 2011, Pastors

Benito Rodriguez and Barbara Guzman were held at a police station for two hours while state officials interrogated them and ordered them to stop worship services in their home.[67] In October 2009, two Baptist pastors were arrested and held for two weeks without charge after providing financial assistance to churches in Guantanamo Province. In February 2010, members of the unrecognized denomination Creciendo en Gracia (Growing in Grace) were detained for several hours for attempting to distribute pamphlets without authorization; they were threatened with arrest for "disturbing the peace."[68]

Believers defending others can be targeted by sweeping criminal charges that include contempt for authority and the Orwellian crime of "dangerousness"—the claim that someone "is of the type likely to commit a crime in the future."[69] They can be persecuted harshly in Cuba's notoriously brutal prisons, and they and their family members can be effectively barred from going to mass, visiting a cemetery, leading a congregation, and having a Bible in prison. After a hunger strike protesting prison conditions, Orlando Zapata Tamayo died in February 2010. That spring, government-organized mobs blocked his mother, Reina Luisa Tamayo, from attending mass and visiting her son's grave, and afterward harassed her each time she went by the church and the cemetery.[70]

Dr. Oscar Elias Biscet, a committed Christian and human rights advocate, was arrested because he marched in support of freeing Cuba's political prisoners. Imprisoned for three years, he was released in November 2002. A few weeks later, he was rearrested for his opposition to abortion in a crackdown against seventy-five dissidents. Charged with "disrupting public order and disobedience" and sentenced to twenty-five years in prison, he spent much of nearly ten years in solitary confinement, was refused all visitors, was denied access to the Bible, and was deprived of needed medical treatment.[71] Seriously ill, he was finally released in May 2011 as part of a deal negotiated by the Catholic Church. Though other freed prisoners agreed to move to Spain, Dr. Biscet chose to stay in Cuba and continue advocating for human rights.[72]

In recent years, the Cuban government has gradually granted more permits for religious groups to build churches and has allowed the appointment of a new Catholic bishop approved by the Holy See, approved the opening of San Carlos y San Ambrosio Seminary, permitted some religious social services and processions, released many political prisoners, and allowed greater political disagreement and unregistered religious activity to take place without imposing criminal sanctions.[73] But Cuba, now under Raul Castro, who succeeded his older brother Fidel as president in 2008, has not stopped trying to control religious practice. In March 2012, it detained hundreds of dissidents, especially Catholics, and held them in prison or under house arrest to stop them from attending any of the events taking place during Pope Benedict's visit to the island.

NORTH KOREA

North Korea is the most militantly atheistic country in the world. It is an absolute dictatorship formed in the years following the 1948 division of the Korean peninsula, and initially headed, with Moscow's support, by a former Soviet army officer, Kim Il-Sung. Kim established his rule on Communist principles mixed with a pervasive personality cult and a homegrown ideology of *Juche* (self-reliance) or isolation. After "Great Leader" Kim's death in July 1994, power passed to his son "Dear Leader" Kim Jong-Il who died in December 2011 and then to his grandson Kim Jong-Un, who rules today.

Unequivocally, North Korea is one of the world's very worst religious persecutors. Nearly all outward vestiges of religion have been wiped out, and what exists is under tight government control. The Hudson Institute's Center for Religious Freedom's *World Survey on Religious Freedom* ranks North Korea at the very bottom of its religious freedom scale. The US State Department also designates North Korea as a Country of Particular Concern for egregious religious persecution, and it imposes comprehensive economic and diplomatic sanctions on it.

MORE THAN A HALF CENTURY OF PERSECUTION

When Kim Il-Sung took power half a century ago, he began a systematic campaign of indoctrination in his own Stalinist ideology, in which religion had no place. Kim considered religion to be superstition and a hindrance to the socialist evolution. By the early 1960s, his secret police had begun an intense effort to eradicate religious belief. All churches, temples, shrines, and other religious sites were closed, and all religious literature and Bibles were destroyed. Religious leaders were either executed or sent to concentration camps.

In place of Buddhism, Christianity, and other faiths, Kim imposed an alternative religion, a personality cult built around himself and his son. From early childhood, North Koreans have been taught to look on the "Great Leader" Kim Il-Sung and, later on, his son Kim Jong-Il as infallible, godlike beings and progenitors of the Korean race. The state energetically promotes this personality cult, along with lessons denigrating all religions, in weekly indoctrination at state study halls, replete with hagiographic photographs of Kim family members, shrines, and rites. The constitution refers to him as the "eternal President."

Documenting human rights abuses in North Korea is extraordinarily difficult precisely because its totalitarian dictatorship allows no freedom. Little is known about the full extent of religious persecution or the extent of underground Christian activity. However, two important studies by the USCIRF and a White Paper by the Database Center for North Korean Human Rights (NKDC), all based on the testimony of recent refugees, help piece together a grim picture.[74]

> [USCIRF] INTERVIEWEE 4: "It's the Kim Il Sung Institute of Revolutionary History or the Revolutionary History Institute. If you are absent . . . [there are] political consequences. At every district and village [we have] '*Chosanghwa Jeongseongsaeop*' (the policy to check whether Kim family portraits are well taken care of). North Koreans are evaluated by *Chosanghwa*

Jeongseongsaeop. Who takes care of the portraits hung in the office first? Who presents a flower basket in front of the statue [of Kim Il Sung] on New Year's Day? Who can show respect for *chosanghwijang* [Badge of Kim Il Sung] by wearing it on the chest all the time?"[75]

INTERVIEWEE 10: "Hanging pictures of Kim Il Sung and Kim Jong Il on the wall is an obligation. The purpose of hanging the pictures is to worship Kim Il Sung and Kim Jong Il. There is a ritual done before the pictures. [We] worship Kim Il Sung, the Great Leader who saved us from death and emancipated us from slavery. If a fire breaks out, people would show their loyalty by running into the fire to save the portraits. Anyone who gets burned doing this would win commendation."[76]

INTERVIEWEE 37: "When a person is caught carrying the Bible, he will be punished severely because he has brought an external influence to North Korea. A person caught carrying the Bible is doomed. When a person is caught [worshipping], he will be sent to *kwanliso* [prison camp] . . . and the whole family may disappear."[77]

Christians have been nearly annihilated over the past fifty years and continue to suffer horrifying persecution at the regime's hands. North Korea's famine in the 1990s killed one to two million Koreans, and Christian aid groups, among others, were allowed in to provide assistance. Due to this exposure, the numbers of North Korean Christians are slowly rising. But, to survive, Christians must still hide their faith from all but their most trusted family members and neighbors, since government spies are ubiquitous.

Dong-A Ilbo, a major South Korean newspaper, reported an estimate of thirty thousand Christians in the North, while non-governmental organizations have put the number as high as several hundred thousand. Some Christian aid groups estimate there are at least two hundred thousand underground Christians but the actual number may be nearly double that. Compass Direct News states that as many as four hundred thousand Christians may secretly worship.[78]

THE OFFICIAL CHURCH

The government has formed and strictly controls three religious organizations: the Buddhists' Federation, the Korea Christian Federation, and the Korean Roman Catholic Association. There are several hundred Buddhist temples, but most appear to be historical cultural sites rather than active religious centers.

Although fifty years ago the capital, Pyongyang, was nicknamed "Asia's Jerusalem" because of the strong influence of Christianity, the NKDC White Paper reports there are now only five churches, all state controlled—three Protestant (Bongsu Church, Chilgol Church, and Jeil Church, established in 1988, 1989, and 2005 respectively), one Catholic (Jangchung Cathedral, established in 1988), and one Russian Orthodox (Jongbaek Church, established in 2006). All are located in the capital and seem to be used solely to impress Western observers. As one refugee told USCIRF:

> One cannot even say the word "religion." North Korea does have Christians and Catholics. They have buildings but they are all fake. These groups exist to falsely show the world that North Korea has freedom of religion. But [the government] does not allow religion or [independent] religious organizations because it is worried about the possibility that Kim Jong Il's regime would be in danger [because] religion erodes society.[79]

Another interviewee explained: "There are churches and Buddhist temples in Pyongyang . . . built only for . . . foreigners to attend. When foreigners visit Pyongyang they would go to churches and temples to pray and bow. I never heard of religious books until I came to China."[80]

No Roman Catholic priests live in the country, so the sacraments cannot be administered even in the showplace church, unless a foreign priest is allowed to visit, which now occasionally occurs. There are no ties to the Vatican and no following of the magisterium of the Roman Catholic Church.[81]

PERVASIVE SURVEILLANCE

Pervasive state surveillance makes religious community a near impossibility and essentially makes the entire country one big prison. As one witness explained,

> North Korea is a prison without bars. The reason why the North Korean system still exists is because of the strict surveillance system. When we provide the information like "this family believes in a religion from their grandfather's generation," the [National Security Agency] will arrest each family member. That is why entire families are scared of one another. Everyone is supposed to be watching one another like this. All organizations, the Kim Il Sung Socialist Youth League, and the Women's League are [gathering information].[82]

The pervasive surveillance was confirmed to the NKDC by multiple refugees, one of whom gave the following account: "In 2001, a woman was taken into custody at a political prison camp for having talked with her neighbors, who had been to China, about religion. One of the neighbors was a government spy. She was forced to divorce her husband, and was detained at a political prison camp and died there."[83]

Another refugee told the USCIRF: "You cannot say a word about [religion or] three generations of your family can be killed. People who lived before the Korean War knew [about religion]. But religion was eradicated. We can only serve one person in North Korea [Kim Jong Il]."[84]

There has been little if any let-up in recent years. Twenty-three Christians were arrested in May 2010 for belonging to an underground church in Kuwol-dong, Pyongsong City, South Pyongan Province. Three of them were reportedly executed, and the others were sent to Yoduk political prison camp. In another case cited by the US State Department, "South Korean activists reported in June 2009 that Ri Hyon Ok was publicly executed for distributing Bibles in the city of Ryongchon near the Chinese border." The official charge was that she was spying and organizing dissidents.[85]

Some North Korean security agents are taught Christianity by the state in order to infiltrate and better interrogate detainees to determine whether they are Christian. The NKDC reports that Christian educational institutions in the North consist of a Pyongyang Seminary where Protestant pastors are trained and a program of Christian studies at the Department of Religious Studies of Kim Il-Sung University. According to the NKDC, the latter trains "future officials who will take charge of religious policies" for the Communist government.

Some government officials hold Christian services in order to trap secret Christians, and one case provides evidence that the state agent became Christian through such a process, though he continued to raid other house churches and arrest their congregations:

> When I visited a high-ranking official's house, there was another official there and we worshipped together in his house with the curtains drawn. They told me to read the Bible so I read a verse from Genesis 12:2 and that's when I first decided to study theology. They also prayed for Kim Jong Il. They told me that there are many underground churches in North Korea. They said that it was a heartbreaking job to catch Christians while they, too, were Christians, but they had to stay in their positions because their situation could turn even worse if an evil-minded person was in that position to ferret out believers. So they keep their positions and sometimes advise people to run away.[86]

HELP AND PERSECUTION IN CHINA

According to Voice of the Martyrs (VOM), ten college students from one of the northern provinces of North Korea were arrested in the spring of 2008 for reading the Bible and watching a DVD about the Bible. VOM's Todd Nettleton describes how the students acquired the Bibles: "In March 2006, 200 Life Bibles and several hundred CDs were purchased in China and secretly placed in flour bags before being smuggled into North Korea. This huge Bible smuggling case was headed by GumRung Company employees who were influenced by Christianity in China and underground Christians. All the leaders have been arrested and are being severely tortured."[87]

In some instances, North Korean security agents even cross the border into China to kidnap and kill or otherwise harshly punish North Korean Christians: The NKDC reports that in 2002, after learning that defectors were attending churches in China, North Korea sent agents to China to arrest devout Christians. In one case, because it was difficult to arrest them inside the church, agents reportedly seized a mother and son at another location, put them in a burlap sack, and took them to the North. They were put into a State Security Agency detention cell, where only Christians were detained, and their whereabouts are now unknown.[88]

UNDERGROUND FOREIGN WORKERS

Occasionally, foreign religious workers are allowed to enter the country in exchange for foreign aid. At great personal risk, some have managed to enter without government permission. One was US citizen Eddie Jun Yong-Su, who was arrested in North Korea in November 2010, along with two ethnic Koreans with Chinese passports. According to Lim Chang-Ho, a professor at a South Korean theological college, "The two others were badly beaten but they were allowed to return home as they were Chinese nationals." According to them, Jun was beaten so severely that he could hardly walk without help. He was freed on May 28, 2011, after visits from former president Jimmy Carter, Franklin Graham, and the US Special Envoy for North Korea human rights, Robert King.[89]

On Christmas Day 2009, Robert Park, a twenty-eight-year-old of Korean descent, crossed a poorly guarded stretch of the Tumen River that separates North Korea from China. According to a member of the Seoul-based human rights group Pax Koreana, Park shouted, "I am an American citizen. I brought God's love. God loves you and God bless you," in fluent Korean as he marched into the country. Park carried a letter to Kim Jong Il that the group posted on its website. "Please open your borders so that we may bring food, provisions, medicine, necessities, and assistance to those who are struggling to survive. Please close down all concentration camps and release all political prisoners today." Park was immediately arrested and, after forty-three days of detention, released only after he read a confession on North Korean television. Afterward, Park said the apology was a fake and that during his imprisonment he suffered beatings, torture, and sexual abuse.[90]

UNDERGROUND BELIEVERS

The government relies on relentless propaganda and a comprehensive surveillance system to control virtually every act, belief, and desire of its citizens. But there is emerging evidence that, at great risk, there are small Christian gatherings in private homes that may collectively encompass hundreds of thousands of people.

Even so, of those escaping North Korea, only a small fraction—4.5 percent of the Database interviewees—are aware of any underground Christian activities.[91] Typically, when asked about them, refugees respond: "I have not seen them with my own eyes, and it is unbelievable." Another added, "If underground churches really do exist, then it would be between individuals, like husband and wife."[92]

"'Underground believers' would be a more appropriate term than 'underground church,'" one interviewee told USCIRF. "Church would be something like a place where people can gather and listen to a sermon, but it's impossible to exist for long. Instead, underground believers can exist. There is a chance that two people pair up and hold their hands together to pray. However, a gathering of three or more is dangerous."[93]

Being caught by authorities while praying or possessing religious literature brings severe consequences. As refugees told USCIRF, many are taken to prison camps, where they are treated more harshly than other prisoners:

> INTERVIEWEE 19: "[My relative] brought a Bible from China and gave it to some close friends. But the rumor spread. . . . [T]he police heard [about it]. His entire family was taken to the prison camps (*kwanliso*). . . . I don't think they will ever be released."
>
> INTERVIEWEE 20: "There was even a case of a child (16 years old). That kid was the same age as my kid. They made that kid stand on the platform, in front of gathered parents. They declared that it is a big problem how teenagers cross the river too often and how they spread rumors about God. There, the kid's entire family was arrested in order to show an example. It happened in 2003 at Yuseon boys' middle school. According to the rumor, that kid had learnt whole Bible scriptures by heart and that was the reason he was arrested. He stayed in China for eight months and got caught. And because of religion, he and his family were all arrested."[94]

Defectors report that Christian prisoners are given the heaviest work, the least amount of food, and the worst conditions in prison. Those caught praying in prison are beaten and tortured. Singing a hymn can also be punished by death, as this case documented by the NKDC suggests:

> In 2005, I heard a man in the next-door cell singing a hymn while I was in detention at a county security office after being deported to the North. The man sang the hymn when a security agent told him to sing it, saying he recognized his Christian belief. But he disappeared that very night. At the time, rumors circulated that he was executed in secret.[95]

Refugee interviews confirm that Christians may have their entire families imprisoned. "In 2006 the government sentenced Son Jong-nam to death for espionage; however, nongovernmental organizations claimed the sentence was based on his contacts with Christian groups in China and alleged contact with his brother in

South Korea. In July 2010 his brother reported that Son was tortured and died in prison in December 2008."[96]

Those who have foreign contacts are singled out for especially harsh persecution. North Korea scholar Melanie Kirkpatrick observes that to a great extent the persecution in North Korea is due to "China's complicity." China inhumanely repatriates North Korea's refugees. This is so, even though "North Koreans who are suspected of having met Christians, South Koreans or Americans while in China are executed or shipped off to the gulag, where conditions are so severe and food so scarce that imprisonment is in effect a death sentence. The rest of the returnees are sent to other prisons, where conditions are little better. Pregnant women are forced to undergo abortions, even in their third trimester, for the crime of carrying 'Chinese seed.' "[97]

WHAT DOES THE FUTURE HOLD?

From their earliest days, Communist states have persecuted religious believers who refuse to bow the knee to temporal political forces or dictatorial leaders. China, Vietnam, Laos, and Cuba still view Christians as a threat to their political control, but their repression has eased somewhat since economic necessity has forced them to engage with the West following the Soviet collapse. Their governments control Christians through officially sanctioned churches and regulation by the Communist party. Those who refuse to submit are persecuted.

But state repression is proving to be a losing proposition—there are likely now more Christians than Communist party members in China. In Vietnam, Laos, and Cuba, despite continued oppression, the numbers of Christians and churches—including house churches— are rising and governments must adjust. In Vietnam, the state recently cooperated with the Vatican in appointing two bishops. In 2009 it allowed a new Jesuit seminary to open in Ho Chi Minh City, and has expanded the range of permitted religious activities to include charitable work and some religious instruction for minors.[98] There is a realistic hope that these freedoms will increase.

In North Korea, state brutality against Christians remains at peak levels. But, as UK Parliamentarians Lord David Alton and Baroness Caroline Cox point out in their 2010 report cited above, while North Korea encounters the outside world in its desperate quest to find food, it is no longer an "impregnable fortress."[99] With Christian and Western aid groups now involved, there may be change.

In the meantime, the country remains a bastion of repression and the persecuted faithful of North Korea continue to stand.

"In 2003, I watched three men being taken to a place of public execution in a county of North Hamgyong Province [in North Korea]. Among them was a man with whom I had studied the Bible together in China. He was gagged with rags before his execution. When told to say what he wanted to say before dying, he said, 'O Lord, forgive these miserable people.' And he was shot dead."[100]

THREE

POST-COMMUNIST COUNTRIES: REGISTER, RESTRICT, AND RUIN

Russia / Uzbekistan / Turkmenistan / Azerbaijan / Tajikistan / Belarus / Kazakhstan / Kyrgyzstan /Armenia and Georgia

IN 2002, AFTER YEARS OF MEETING OUTDOORS, THE NEW LIFE Church in Minsk, the capital of Belarus, scraped together enough money to buy an abandoned cowshed on the outskirts of the city. They bought it with a contractual agreement that it would be renovated as a house of religious worship. But even though they carefully fulfilled the myriad rules and regulations for renovation and registration, the state authorities still rejected New Life's application to use the building for religious purposes.

In 2005, frustrated but determined parishioners decided to hold a religious service in the renovated building. Since then, the church has been embroiled in a fierce legal battle with the government. The church's property has been confiscated—legally so, according to Belarus's restrictive religious regulations. But, when the authorities declared publicly that they would demolish the building outright, the congregation went on a widely publicized hunger strike.

When international bodies became involved and applied pressure, the government backed off and sent the case back to court on appeal. Two years later, however, New Life's claims were again denied, and again the congregants were ordered to evacuate the premises. They refused. Their lawyer spoke for them all: "We're here praying and believe God will protect us. . . . As a lawyer I believe the state could do anything, including the use of force. But as a believer I rely on God."[1]

Belarus has thrown every accusation imaginable at the Christians, including environmental infractions, property violations, and claims of building without a permit. The church faces fines exceeding US$89,300 but staunchly refuses to pay. Raids and legal attacks continue, but the New Life Church still meets in its remodeled cowshed every week. After a decade of turmoil, they are still standing their ground.[2]

AUTHORITARIAN STATES

When the Soviet Union collapsed, it left in its wake fifteen new countries. While some such as Lithuania, Latvia, and Estonia have become free and functional, many others are not so fortunate. They declare themselves "post-Communist," but their economies remain controlled and they apply the same repressive measures as before, often carried out by the very same people. In these countries, *post-Communist* means "still largely Communist but we don't want to admit it." The continuing authoritarianism of the governments of these states imposes restrictions upon Christian practice. And in Russia, Uzbekistan, Turkmenistan, Tajikistan, and Kyrgyzstan, Salafis and other radical Islamists are also in the mix of hostile forces against Christians.

The predominant pattern is to demand registration, which is often difficult and sometimes even impossible to achieve, and even if achieved, leads to increased surveillance and control. Those who refuse to register, or whose applications are refused, are harassed, invaded, intimidated, and potentially hounded out of existence.

In Muslim-majority countries, small Christian groups are often intensely pressured by both the state and Islamic radicals. In still others, such as Russia, religious freedom has increased but many problems remain. The level of restriction varies from Turkmenistan and Uzbekistan to Armenia and Georgia. In these countries, we usually do not witness the deaths and endemic violence that occur elsewhere, but we do see a pervasive and repetitive pattern of suffocating and contradictory restrictions designed to grind down those who seek to worship God according to their conscience, and policies meant to erode all free expressions of faith.

RUSSIA: SECTS, CULTS, AND ANTIEXTREMISM

In the Russian city of Kaluga, during St. George's Lutheran Church's Sunday morning service in February 2010, police forces suddenly appeared. Eleven officers armed with automatic weapons and police dogs stormed the building, blocking all exits to prevent anyone from leaving. They told the terrified congregation they were searching for "extremist literature."[3]

The police roughly inspected and tossed aside Bibles and hymnbooks, and the next day summoned Pastor Martyshenko to the police station to give a statement. The pastor later noted that the raid followed heightened hostility to the Lutheran congregation, in which they were called a "Catholic sect" that engaged actively in "proselytizing." The local police commander, who confirmed that police had raided the church, said, "There were indications that terrorists were gathering here, and distributing terrorist literature."[4]

In August 2009, in the Chernorechye suburb of Grozny, a Chechnyan couple was found in the trunk of a car, shot to death. The two were involved in children's aid projects and worked together at a Christian summer camp. After seeing their photographs on television, a group called Russian Ministries identified them as Alik Dzhabrailov and Zarema Sadulayeva, familiarly known by the camp directors and team as Umar and Rayana. The couple was Muslim, but Umar had been given a New Testament in Chechnya and had begun to ask questions about it: Who exactly was Jesus and did he truly claim to be God?

Umar's wife, Rayana, actively supported organizations that assisted children with disabilities. She also spent time in the summer camp's kitchen, helping with chores and talking to the Christians there. Umar had been jailed in the past and tortured, although he never explained why. The husband and wife were not politically active. Like so many other deaths in Chechnya, this one remains unsolved.[5]

Since 2001, an eerie silence has fallen across what was once a Christian community in Chechnya, part of the Russian Federation. It is difficult to find any record of believers. In the mid-to-late 1990s, Christians of all kinds—from Orthodox to Catholic to Baptist, as well as members of smaller groups—were driven out of Chechnya and particularly Grozny, where a bloodbath of epic proportions was carried out by radical Muslims, many of them Wahhabists. In the late 1990s, jihadists beheaded two Baptist pastors and kidnapped, beat, raped, and murdered innumerable men, women, and children who belonged to Christian communities. By the early 2000s, surviving Christians of every denomination had relocated outside Chechnya, leaving behind only a few elderly believers and others who lacked the means or will to flee.

In 2012, the Christian charitable group Open Doors ranked Chechnya twentieth on its World Watch List of the world's fifty worst abusers of Christians.[6]

AFTER THE COLD WAR

A quarter century has passed since Western nations were engaged in a forbidding Cold War with the USSR—the Union of Soviet Socialist Republics—an enemy that flexed its muscles across the world. Untold millions of lives were lost in the gulag labor camps and in mass murders. Countless more lived with constant hunger, deprivation, and despair. Many Western Christians still remember the persecution of fellow believers who were trapped in the Soviet Union's ruthless and officially atheistic totalitarianism. Those were days of heroic smugglers who carried contraband Bibles across closed borders, of dissidents who urgently needed rescue through international intervention, and tragic stories of persecution that found their way into churches and homes through *samizdat* documents, newsletters, magazines, and books.

The plight of the Pentecostal Vashchenko family, the "Siberian Seven" who had found sanctuary in the US embassy for five years, garnered world headlines. But, at that dark time, all Christian churches suffered deeply. Between 1922 and 1926 alone, twenty-eight Russian Orthodox bishops and more than twelve hundred priests were killed.[7] As late as September 9, 1990, independent Orthodox priest Father Alexander Vladimirovich Men was murdered with a blow from an ax on his way to celebrate the divine liturgy. Scholar Kent Hill writes that "most of the fifty-four thousand Russian Orthodox churches which existed in 1914 were destroyed, shut down or turned into warehouses, factories, or other 'socially-useful' enterprises." Legions of others from all Christian traditions were killed, imprisoned, or exiled, and their churches were infiltrated and controlled by Soviet authorities throughout the Soviet era.

From 1917 until around 1988, virtually all of the period of Soviet rule, the Russian Orthodox Church (ROC) existed in a state of siege.[8] The 1930s were a decade of brutal tyranny for the Russian people as Stalin's Great Purge killed or incarcerated millions; it was during this time that the church suffered its greatest repression. In the post-Purge decades, as regulations developed, changed, intensified, or disappeared, the Orthodox Church struggled to adapt to survive within the vehemently antireligious state.[9]

The vast Communist superpower ultimately collapsed in December 1991, and splintered into fifteen republics. A heady sense of liberation gripped much of the world. The Berlin Wall had fallen. And, for the religiously minded, the former Soviet Union's newly open borders invited a tide of devout visitors, eager to meet face-to-face the faithful for whom they had prayed and advocated.

Russian Orthodoxy had been the official state religion from the late tenth century, and although it was repressed, infiltrated, and frozen in place for seventy years, it survived the Marxist onslaught and quickly burst back into life. Russia expert John Bernbaum recounted: "In the early 1990s, Russians flocked to churches and the interest in religion was extraordinary. Religion, the 'forbidden fruit,' was now an object of great interest to many Russians. . . . [Churches were] filled to capacity with hundreds of people outside trying to push their way in. Many had never been inside a church before and now they were anxious to find out what religion was all about."[10]

Meanwhile, laws passed in the 1990s established freedom of conscience and opened the doors for new religious groups to enter Russia.

It wasn't long, however, before the ROC became alarmed at the influx of new religious organizations. It began to push back against what it saw as destructive alien elements that sought to undermine the ROC's historical status as the state religion and the embodiment and protector of Russian spirituality. By 1997—less than a decade after the fall of the Soviet Union—there were more than fifty-six hundred foreign missionaries in the region, representing more than twenty-five denominations and agencies. The church's leaders, the Moscow patriarchate, condemned these foreign missionaries as waging "a crusade against the Russian church, even as it began recovering from a prolonged disease, standing on its feet with weakened muscles."[11]

The venerable relationship between the Orthodox church and the Russian State laid the groundwork for the church's current, post-Soviet status. Although there is no official state religion, the ROC has de facto favored status among the four faiths listed by the government as "traditional" to Russia—Orthodoxy, Judaism, Buddhism, and Islam. As such, the ROC receives substantial government subsidies and has special arrangements with multiple government agencies, including the Ministries of Education, Defense, and Internal Affairs.

CONTROLLING CHRISTIAN SECTS

In 2009, the Ministry of Justice created a new official body, with the Orwellian name "Council of Experts for Conducting State

Religious Studies Expert Analysis" (alternately referred to as the "Experts' Religious Studies Council"). The council was instrumental in expanding the focus of antiextremism activities from Muslim groups to all so-called dangerous sects. While Muslims continued to face severe repression, the Council ominously declared that there were more than eighty "large" sects operating in Russia, with "thousands" of smaller sects.[12]

The term *sect* is itself problematic, since there is no legal definition of what actually constitutes a sect; generally it means a small religious group that governments or elites don't like. The authorities include as sects and cults charismatic Protestants (termed "neo-Pentecostals"), Jehovah's Witnesses, Mormons, and the New Apostolic Church. They describe neo-Pentecostalism as "a crude magical-occult system with elements of psychological manipulation . . . an anti-Biblical teaching furthering the personal enrichment of its pastors and the dissemination of false teachings originating in pagan cults."[13]

In the city of Khabarovsk, prosecutors alleged that the Grace Pentecostal Church had used mental manipulation to "[change] the psychological state" of parishioners. They cited such common Pentecostal practices as the laying-on of hands, the loud recitation of prayers, and speaking in tongues. The accusers also found fault with the church's use of such well-known Christian courses as the Alpha Course, Tres Dias, and Encounter.[14] In a court decision on April 27, 2011, a regional court agreed with the local prosecutors and banned Grace Pentecostal Church's activity. The church appealed the decision to Russia's Supreme Court, which overturned the regional ruling on July 5. The overturning did not mean that the church won; it meant that the case returned to the regional court in Khabarovsk. Authorities have since renewed their efforts to ban the church.[15]

Although in recent years the Council's powers have been restricted, groups it has categorized as sects and cults face widespread fear and harassment. Stifling laws and endless bureaucratic entanglements stand in the way of starting new churches, building or expanding church facilities, distributing literature, or openly bearing witness to the faith. And, depending on local authorities, far worse suffering can easily befall a hapless congregation. The US Department of State documents many raids across Russia, spanning a range of Christian denominations, which expose the arbitrary nature of many accusations and indictments against Christian churches and individuals.[16]

In the city of Blagoveshchensk, authorities have repeatedly targeted the New Generation Protestant Church, a Pentecostal organization, for a range of alleged offenses. The most recent case alleges that it engages in the illegal use of "medical technologies, including techniques which have a psychological and psychotherapeutic affect on the human psyche." Prosecutors claimed that the programs and practices used by the church are medical in nature and require medical licensing. On March 4, 2011, the local court banned these practices, as well as the distribution or use of audio and video materials, including television programs such as *Men Are from Mars, Women Are from Venus*, and the films *Cancer Treatment* and *Armenia's New Generation.*[17] The church appealed the court's decision and the regional court promptly overturned it in April 2011; the case has since been returned to the local court for re-examination by new judges.[18] It is all too likely that the accusations will be revived.

The United States Commission for International Religious Freedom (USCIRF) reported in 2011: "Religious freedom conditions in Russia continue to deteriorate . . . Russian officials continue to deem certain religious and other groups alien to Russian culture and society, thereby contributing to a climate of intolerance. High levels of xenophobia and intolerance, including anti-Semitism, have resulted in violent and sometimes lethal hate crimes. Despite increased prosecution for these acts, the Russian government has failed to address these issues consistently or effectively."

In 2012, USCIRF reported that "building or renting worship space is difficult for Jehovah's Witnesses, Mormons, Pentecostals, non-Moscow Patriarchate Orthodox, Molokans, and Old Believers." For these reasons and more, USCIRF places Russia on its watch list of serious religious freedom violators.

One beacon of hope for Christians in Russia has been the Office of the Federal Human Rights Ombudsman, which has religious affairs departments in both its main and eighty-nine regional offices. Although their authority is restricted, these offices can investigate reports of antireligious discrimination or violence. Thankfully, they have led efforts against attempts to label religious minority groups as sects or cults.

While religious life remains difficult for Russia's many Christian groups, there are far more dangerous places for Christians in the former Soviet Union. Open Doors' 2012 World Watch list of the fifty worst abusers of Christians lists no fewer than eight in the former Soviet Union. Listed from worse to better were: Uzbekistan (No. 7), Turkmenistan (No. 18), Azerbaijan (No. 25), Tajikistan (No. 34), Belarus (No. 42), Kazakhstan (No. 45), and Kyrgyzstan (No. 48).

UZBEKISTAN

The group of religious leaders cringed as Saidibrahim Saynazirov, deputy head of the city of Angren's administration, began to raise his voice. It was December 8, 2011, and he was ranting, in no uncertain terms, about their obligations to obey the religious laws of the state. What he said at first was typical of the government's power-hungry mechanisms: he warned them that they could under no circumstances involve themselves in "proselytism" and "missionary activity." He tossed the words out without defining what he meant, although most Christians could guess—they should not speak of their faith openly.

Saynazirov went on to proclaim that children and youth are not permitted to attend worship services or meetings. This was a new twist. More than a few eyebrows were raised.

And finally he demanded that each religious community provide him with a list of its members.

"That's not legal!" one outspoken Christian angrily objected. "We don't have to do that!"

"Maybe not," Saynazirov retorted coldly. "Maybe it's not in the law. But we recommend that you do it anyway." He did not add, ". . . if you know what's good for you," but everyone knew exactly what he meant.[19]

LEGAL BUT DISALLOWED

Uzbekistan is a landlocked nation with the largest population in Central Asia, as well as its most formidable military. The president faces no legal political opposition party, and notoriously turned his guns on the country's civilian population in 2005, killing hundreds of the country's own people. And as for the rule of law, many reports describe the use of torture in Uzbekistan as "systematic."

Given all this, and that Uzbekistan is a largely Muslim nation with a well-founded fear of homegrown extremism, it is no surprise it is a notorious abuser of religious freedom. Apart from Open Doors' 2012 World Watch List, it is also one of the US State Department's eight "Countries of Particular Concern" (CPC), shortlisted alongside such notorious violators as Iran, Saudi Arabia, and China.

Uzbekistan president Islam Karimov has been in power since before the fall of the Soviet Union and functions much like the Soviet strongman he was before the country fell apart around him. Although Uzbekistan is a Muslim-majority country, the government has imprisoned thousands of Muslims, sometimes detaining them for more than twenty years under horrific conditions and without real due process. This is also the case with Baha'is, Jehovah's Witnesses, and members of other small religious groups. Meanwhile, Protestants, less than 1 percent of the population, are routinely harassed, abused, and persecuted. They suffer these cruelties for entirely nonthreatening behavior in almost every case.

In March 2011, Tashkent region's Ohangaron District Police raided a Sunday worship service for elderly residents in the Sakhovat ("Kindness") home in Ohangaron. Six Baptists were leading the service.

"Police unexpectedly broke into the foyer of the nursing home during the service, and halted it, saying that they were carrying out an anti-terror operation," local Baptists told Forum 18, whose religious freedom reporting is the primary source of news about the former Soviet Union. "The raid was led by Bakhtiyar Salibayev, Head of Ohangaron District Administration, and Major Sofar Fayziyev, Deputy Head of the District Police, accompanied by District Police criminal investigators."

During the next four hours at the seniors' home, police officers repeatedly insulted the Baptist men and women and threatened them with punishment. The officials filmed all those present with cameras and cell phones. They went on to search the Baptists' car, from which they seized Christian musical CDs and tapes, songbooks, a Bible, and other personal belongings. After the prolonged "investigation," the six Baptists were driven to the police department. Frail as they were, the elderly residents insisted on going along with them, sorrowful that these generous friends had suffered daylong abuse for simply trying to provide them with a Sunday morning Christian service.

When interviewed later, the police refused to answer questions about the legality of their raid, or why a Christian service at a nursing home was the target of an "anti-terrorism operation."[20]

Uzbekistan's constitution technically provides for religious freedom, but more recent laws demand that all religious groups be registered, while also making registration difficult if not impossible for most groups. Meanwhile, many Christian congregations refuse to register because of security concerns or simply on principle.

Proselytizing, or in Christian terms, sharing the gospel with others, is banned, as is teaching religious subjects in public schools, or even private instruction in religious principles. Religious literature cannot be printed or distributed without a license, which is, of course, nearly impossible to get. Those who violate the religion law's numerous bans and restrictions are subject to criminal penalties, including up to twenty years of imprisonment.

TURKMENISTAN

In 2011, a group of government officials broke into a worship service in Turkmenabad and arrested seventeen frightened Protestants for practicing their faith without a license. Despite their evident poverty, they were fined as much as US$140 for their "crime"—a small fortune to them. They were told the money was supposed to cover the "administrative offense of participating in unregistered religious activity." The city judge went on to say that a local imam had reported them, avowing that their faith was "against the state."[21]

On December 20, 2010, in the city of Dashoguz, the chief mufti Rovshen Allaberdiev, who is imam of the region, led a police raid that broke into the Path of Faith Baptist Church while twenty-two Christians were gathered for Sunday prayer. The alarmed congregants watched helplessly as officers took photographs of everyone present. They also confiscated more than one hundred Bibles and other Christian books. All the Christians were taken to the local police station, where they endured hours of interrogation. Some were afraid not to sign an agreement stating they would no longer attend Christian meetings.[22]

Turkmenistan, like Uzbekistan, has been an independent republic since 1991. Its former leader, "President for Life" Saparmurat Niyazov, established a quasi-religious personality cult when he came to power in 1991 and, although he died in 2006, his writings are still preserved in a book called the *Ruhnama*—a collection of his "spiritual thoughts"—which is still required reading in public schools. In 2003, Niyazov set in place a religious law that stifles religious communities.

IMPOSSIBLE REGISTRATION

Today's president, Gurbanguly Berdimuhamedov, who came to power in 2007, has made small gestures toward reform, but the draconian religious law remains. The only two religions recognized by the government are Sunni Islam and the Russian Orthodox Church. They both wield power over smaller religious groups and make the registration process nearly impossible, forcing minority believers to practice their various faiths illegally.

Applications for registration have been repeatedly filed and rejected with respect to the Armenian Apostolic Church, an assortment of Protestant groups, and the Jehovah's Witnesses. The Peace to the World Pentecostal Church in the town of Mary has persistently sought to register since 2007. Not only has it been rejected but its pastor, Ilmurad Nurliev, has been imprisoned since 2010 on trumped-up charges—a common means of repressing religious leaders in Turkmenistan.[23]

After police in the capital Ashgabad found Bibles in the possessions of three guests at a local Protestant's home, all four were taken to the government's Council for Religious Affairs for questioning, and then taken to court. Although the judge refused to try them without proper documentation, they were brought back and fined by the same judge a week later for "violation of the law on religious organisations."[24]

The family of Pentecostal pastor Ilmurad Nurliev expresses real fear that "he and Jehovah's Witness Ahmet Hudaybergenov, also convicted, will be sent to Seydi labour camp, where there is evidence of torture against Baptist Christians and Jehovah's Witnesses prisoners with psychotropic drugs." Nurliev's trial was held behind closed doors, and a representative of the US Embassy was not allowed to attend. After his imprisonment, he has not been permitted to appeal his case.[25]

USCIRF's 2011 report confirms the worst fears of the besieged pastor's loved ones. Ilmurad Nurliev "has been denied the right to appeal his case and is being held at the notorious Seydi prison camp, where he reportedly has been put in a cell with an inmate with tuberculosis and denied his diabetes medication and a Bible. . . . His requests to be transferred to Mary, to be closer to his family, have been rejected, and his wife [was] denied her scheduled visit in February 2011."[26]

AZERBAIJAN

Pastor Zaur Balaev heads up a Baptist congregation that meets in his home. On April 13, 2010, police knocked on his door. They told him that because his church was unregistered, he could no longer host meetings for religious worship. They warned him that if the church continued to meet, he would face "unpleasantness with the law."[27]

On December 22, 2011, a Baptist worship service was broken up in the town of Neftechala. The church was then declared to be "closed," and the pastor and parishioners were all sent to the police station for interrogation. When the officer in charge was asked to explain the government's actions, he responded, "Without registration, you can't pray. We close any place of worship that isn't registered, including mosques."[28]

NO MEETINGS WITHOUT PERMISSION

Approximately 96 percent of Azerbaijan's nine million people is nominally Muslim; the other 4 percent includes Roman Catholics, Protestants, Jehovah's Witnesses, Armenian Orthodox, Jews, and nonbelievers. Although the constitution guarantees religious freedom, like many other former Soviet republics, Azerbaijan keeps virtually every aspect of religious practice under its scrutiny.

The country's laws are becoming more oppressive. In December 2011, the legislature (known as the *Milli Mejlis*) passed a law that increased the range of religious conduct considered criminal, such as the distribution of unauthorized religious materials, and added even more civil offenses to its administrative code.

Under Azerbaijani law, all religious organizations must register with the State Committee on Work with Religious Structures (SCWRS), which also regulates the import and distribution of religious literature. Without registering, a group cannot bring in foreign guests, maintain a bank account, or rent property. Groups that operate without registration are subject to significant harassment.[29]

Jehovah's Witnesses are particularly prone to persecution because of their refusal to serve in the armed forces and their proselytization methods. Because the country has begun deporting Jehovah's Witnesses who are not Azerbaijani citizens, foreign Christians are anticipating similar treatment.

In September 2009, a Baptist foreigner named Javid Shingarov opened his home to his friends and neighbors for religious events. The following day he was fined by the local police. According to Shingarov, the officers "turned everything upside down in my house and accused me of holding illegal books." After the officers confiscated many of his books, including Bibles, they detained him. While he was in jail, the police called upon a journalist to write a hostile news item about him. Shingarov is almost certain that he will be deported, based in part on the experience of a man named Elguja Khutsishvilli.[30]

Elguja Khutsishvilli is a Jehovah's Witness. On July 15, 2009, police raided his home. They ordered him to hand over "the weapons," and when he replied that he had none, they confiscated every scrap of religious literature they found. They then ordered him to report to the police station the next day. He did, and the police forced him to sign documents he could not understand. Without a hearing, a local judge ruled that Khutsishvilli should be expelled from Azerbaijan. On July 23, he was put on a plane and deported. In 2007, four Jehovah's Witnesses were kicked out of the country because they "violated the ban on religious agitation." They were expelled using administrative deportation orders, which do not require any court proceeding.[31]

TAJIKISTAN

Twenty-four-year-old Parviz Davlatbekov dressed up in a "Father Frost" costume in preparation for a visit with family friends celebrating the traditional—and secular—New Year, a beloved holiday in Tajikistan. On the holiday, a Santa Claus–like character delivers colorfully wrapped packages at family gatherings and parties.

Davlatbekov never made it to the family celebration. He was attacked by assailants who shouted "Infidel!" as they brutally beat him and ultimately stabbed him to death. RT News reported that the attackers were "Muslim radicals who had targeted Davlatbekov for wearing a Father Frost outfit. Some reports claimed that thirty people participated in the killing." The police, however, denied that the motive was religious.[32]

Located in a scenic panorama of lakes and mountains, the largely Persian-speaking country of Tajikistan shares long borders with Afghanistan and China. This smallest of Central Asian countries lies in a tough neighborhood that rightly raises security concerns about what are commonly identified as "extremist elements." But, in response, the Tajik government thuggishly crushes not only extremist Muslim groups but other Muslims, and virtually all other minority faiths.

Most of the roughly 150,000 Christians in the country are Russian Orthodox, with a small scattering of others, mainly Baptists, Seventh-day Adventists, Lutherans, Roman Catholics, and Korean Christians. There are small groups of Baha'is and Jews. Jehovah's Witnesses have been banned since 2007.

SUPPRESSION AND PUNISHMENT

According to USCIRF's 2012 report, the religious freedom situation is worsening and "The state suppresses and punishes all religious activity independent of state control."[33] Although the repression is aimed at the Muslim majority, it also targets minority communities viewed as foreign-influenced, particularly Protestants and Jehovah's Witnesses.

In April 2009, Dushanbe's Protestant Grace Sunmin Church was given an eviction notice that required the congregation to vacate their property in only ten days. "Claiming they didn't want to 'disturb' the church over Easter, the authorities subsequently extended the deadline to the end of April. Church members strongly dispute the authorities' claim that they do not own their own church, and are scandalized by the 'ridiculous amount offered' as compensation."[34]

Besides closing more than seventy mosques, fifty of them in early 2011, the government has demolished a synagogue and a church. But far more damage is done by the regime's draconian laws than by wrecking balls. Radio Free Europe reported that Russian Orthodox Christians in the south were appalled by a proposed new law on "parental responsibility" that would not allow children under eighteen to take part in worship services in churches.

Nikolay Golub, pastor of the Russian Orthodox Church in Qurghonteppa, said of the ban on those under eighteen attending church: "Even the authorities in the officially atheist Soviet Union did not impose such harsh restrictions." Golub added that if the law about parental responsibility is passed, many Christians will leave Tajikistan and return to Russia. "Svetlana Bugakova, another member of the Russian Orthodox congregation in Qurghonteppa, said if the law is passed she will leave Tajikistan with her children because she wants them to grow up as good Christians."[35]

BELARUS

On February 13, 2011, a Baptist congregation in the southeastern railroad town of Gomel started their Sunday worship service with singing and prayer, but fell silent when twenty police officers suddenly appeared in a chilling invasion. One officer in civilian clothes claimed the raid was routine: they "came to see what was going on."

The officers filmed the rest of the service and searched the building. They continued their investigation in adjacent private premises where two families lived. While tearing through cupboards and closets, they confiscated CDs, audiocassettes containing sermons and personal testimonies, and religious literature. The church belongs to the Baptist Council of Churches, which as a matter of principle does not register its churches.

The congregation's leader, Nikolai Varushin, is awaiting trial for "holding an unauthorised religious service." He believes he has done nothing wrong. Their "Baptist meetings," he explained to an interviewer, "are always peaceful and can't be referred to as mass events." He also protested that confiscated religious literature and other materials have not been returned.[36]

It's not just the Baptists who have their property stolen. Old Believers are Orthodox dissenters who refused to accept liturgical reforms imposed on the Russian Orthodox Church in the seventeenth century. They continue the older liturgies and have often been persecuted. Even though the Russian Orthodox Church accepted the validity of their rites in 1971, they still face persecution, especially in one of the most repressive remnants of the Soviet Union, Belarus.

Scores of beautiful and often historic icons have been stolen from Belarus's Old Believers' churches. For non-Orthodox, it is hard to appreciate how important these icons can be—but they are central to worship for the Orthodox.[37] Although repeated efforts have been made for church leaders to reclaim their property, stolen icons are rarely returned, even if they are recovered. According to Forum 18, most of the time they are confiscated by the State Customs Committee and given to museums, or to churches affiliated with the Moscow Patriarchate. This is done by the "Expert Commission for Distributing Historic and Cultural Valuables," working under the auspices of the Minsk Department of Culture.[38]

EUROPE'S LAST DICTATORSHIP

The state of Belarus has often been referred to as Europe's last dictatorship, and is a throwback to the Soviet era. The authoritarian regime of President Aleksandr Lukashenko has had a vicelike grip on power since his election in 1994. He uses hardcore Soviet tactics to maintain his stranglehold on the country.

A 2002 law ostensibly guarantees freedom of religion, but in practice such freedom does not exist. The government has created an environment where members of minority religions can be harassed and persecuted with no protection whatsoever.

Unlike those of neighboring Russia, Belarus's restrictions are usually not enacted with a claim that they are needed to prevent extremism (although in 2009, the Interior Ministry established a unit on "countering extremism and preventing terrorism"[39]). Instead, the government maintains that it wants to protect the purity of "traditional" Belarus as understood by Lukashenko and his circle. They block any organizations the paranoid regime perceives as a potential threat to its power.

Only 59 percent of the population claim to be religious, with around 83 percent of believers belonging to the Belarusian Orthodox Church, which is under the governance of the Moscow patriarchate of the Russian Orthodox Church. Roman Catholics make up 12 percent of the religious population, 3 percent belongs to Eastern religions, and 2 percent belong to Protestant or other Christian groups, including Old Believers. The Jewish community numbers about thirty thousand to fifty thousand people.[40]

The 2002 religion law is one of the most oppressive in Europe, with stringently enforced registration required for all religious activity. As elsewhere, registration is complex and difficult to obtain. Officials routinely and arbitrarily deny "disfavored organizations" the rights to worship.[41] Religious activity is only allowed inside official worship sites designated by registration. That means that one-on-one evangelism (or even conversation), public religious gatherings, and Bible studies in private homes are illegal. The extensive bureaucracy monitoring religion is headed, as in Russia, with authorities bearing pompously bureaucratic titles as the "Office of the Plenipotentiary for Religious and Ethnic Affairs," and the "Presidential Administration Head of Ideology."

"Ideology officers" sit in on religious services, question locals about the activities of religious groups, and work with law enforcement to crack down on groups in alleged violation of the law. They focus particularly on those seen to have foreign or political agendas; such people are nearly always involved in nontraditional religious groups.

In July 2010, a Pentecostal pastor was fined three times in the same day for "sharing his faith," which included singing and handing out leaflets outside the official area of registration—in his case, outdoors in a local village.[42]

On February 13, 2011, police stormed a Belarus Baptist church and warned three members that if they continued to worship without state registration they would face criminal prosecution. That could mean a two-year prison term in one of Belarus's notorious penal facilities—cruel and unusual punishment for worship, prayer, and Bible study in an "unauthorized" setting. Such sentencing does not seem cruel or unusual to people like Svetlana Starovoitova, who joined other KGB officers in disrupting the congregation's worship. She shrugs it off, reiterating that the Baptists' worship was illegal.[43]

OUSTING FOREIGN INFLUENCE

To make matters worse, in January 2008, a decree was issued that gave the Office of the Plenipotentiary for Religious and Ethnic Affairs total discretion in admitting foreign religious workers—and the legal right to reject a visit or deport a worker already in Belarus without providing a reason. Shortly after these measures were passed, a coalition of civil society organizations gathered fifty thousand signatures—the minimum required for submission to the Constitutional Court—on a petition asking the government to change the highly restrictive 2002 Religion Law. The authorities arrested the activists who gathered the signatures, and then confiscated their materials. The petition, not surprisingly, was rejected.[44]

Restrictions on foreign workers have particularly hampered the Roman Catholic Church, since the country's Catholics have been short of local priests due to state regulations regarding local seminaries. It has also been denied church property seized by the former Soviet government, and has been seeking the return of a former Bernardine monastery in Minsk since 2005. In August 2010, a month after government officials promised the property would be returned, a private real estate developer announced it would be redeveloped into a hotel in advance of the World Hockey Championships in Minsk in 2014.[45]

A Belarusian documentary exposing Soviet-era persecution of churches is titled *Forbidden Christ*. The Office of the Plenipotentiary for Religious and Ethnic Affairs recently banned it from a Catholic film festival. The film was seized from film director Aleksei Shein and sent to the KGB for an "expert analysis." When asked why he thought the film had been banned and seized, the director offered a more-than-reasonable explanation. "Perhaps," he said, "the authorities fear that some believers will see a parallel with what is happening in our country now."[46]

KAZAKHSTAN

On January 24, 2010, Kazakh police videotaped a religious service at Grace Church in Ayagoz. They interrogated worshippers after scrutinizing their personal identification documents. This wasn't the first time the authorities had acted against Grace Church. In August 2009, the secret police raided the church's headquarters in Karaganda, as well as another Grace church in Ust Kamenogorsk. They also raided church-owned private homes in January 2008, as well as the Almaty Grace Presbyterian Church. The US Department of State reported that an officer of the Zhambyl regional department argued that the church posed a threat to national security because it promotes pro-American ideology and aims to discredit local and federal authorities.[47]

In Kazakhstan, as in many former Soviet Republics, state-sponsored Islam and the Russian Orthodox Church have privileged positions, while other groups face restriction and repression. Kazakhstan metes out harsh treatment to minority religions, including smaller Christian communities and Muslim groups such as Ahmadis.

The country's already harsh religious regulations became even worse in late 2011, when two new laws were passed requiring re-registration of all religious communities—a formidable and at times impossible task for small communities that can't meet the criteria demanded by the registration process. Felix Corley, editor of Forum 18, explained: "We have two faiths. We've got the majority Muslim faith, we've got the minority Russian Orthodox faith, and anyone outside that is somehow a danger, a threat, a traitor to their ethnic origins, or ancestral faiths, or whatever."[48]

KYRGYZSTAN

Baptists in the Issyk-Kul region of Kyrgyzstan, living in Ak-Terek village, were attacked by an angry mob several times in the spring of 2011. Their assailants demanded they either renounce their Christian faith or move away. There are only ten believers in the little church, all Kyrgyz by nationality, and all born in Kak-Terek. In May 2011 the police held a meeting with the village elders and the Baptists, and said local people should stop disturbing the Baptists, and that the Baptists must seek state registration. There have been no further disturbances. But the Baptists say that if the church had been registered—an impossibility owing to the requirement to have two hundred founders—"those mobs would not have been so bold in harassing the Church."[49]

After being threatened by local Muslims in a dispute over burial grounds, a grieving Christian family in Kyrgyzstan had to dig up the remains of a beloved relative. Only forty-eight hours after the deceased's burial, a group of irate Muslims confronted the family. They would get a bulldozer, they threatened, and dig up the grave and throw the corpse away if the family didn't take him to the Christian cemetery.

Sympathetic Christian friends organized a meeting with the

mayor to try to find a solution. Although the family pleaded with the local imam to allow the old man to rest in peace, the Muslim leader refused to consider their appeal. The body was in a plot that was considered Islamic, he explained. The body of the Christian would have to be exhumed, transported to someplace else, and reburied. The mayor and other authorities submitted to the imam's demands.[50]

Kyrgyzstan, south of Kazakhstan, is a photographer's dream and a tourist destination of amazing natural beauty and colorful cultural charms. It is not, however, a haven for Christian believers who belong to small churches or communities. It is a Muslim-majority country, with 20 percent of the population Russian Orthodox. There are also communities of Roman Catholics, Jews, Jehovah's Witnesses, Baha'is, and an assortment of Protestants, the largest of which is the Church of Jesus Christ.

In 2005, when President Bakiyev took power, both registered and unregistered religious communities could function freely, despite a 1996 presidential decree requiring religious communities to register. Occasional problems, such as pressure against schoolgirls wearing hijabs, were ascribed to the attitudes of local officials. The exceptions were the official banning of Falun Gong, which occurred under Chinese pressure in February 2005, and social pressure, including violent attacks, against non-Muslims manifesting their beliefs in the south.

However, in January 2009 a highly restrictive new Religion Law came into force, breaking the constitutional guarantee of freedom of "thought, speech and press, as well as to unimpeded expression of those thoughts and beliefs."

"Abai" is the founder and director of a Christian school in a small Kyrgyz community, an outreach of the Church of Jesus Christ that he attends. He started the school in the hope that it would provide a quality "secular" education for children from Christian families as well as give some Christian instruction. He was confronted with a bureaucratic nightmare.

"We executed all the necessary conditions, constructed a new building, and provided it with all the required equipment and furniture, but for three years the government didn't give us permission for educational activity because under the law Christian churches can't provide the base for a school." He pointed out that numerous Muslim schools are established by mosques and are financed from abroad by countries like Turkey and Iran. "At those schools the children live away from their parents five days a week and study Islam."

Once Abai agreed to provide only secular courses, the school received permits. But he has now added Bible classes, although it is risky, and contrary to the state's rules. "Even so," he says, "Muslim families send their children to our school because it is such a pleasant place to learn, and it has a clearly moral atmosphere."[51]

ARMENIA AND GEORGIA

On July 10, 2009, the authors of a study titled "Religious Tolerance in Armenia" interviewed priests and public officials about the Armenian educational system. One public-school principal commented that their curriculum is designed to "keep our children away from erroneous, empty, dangerous religious tendencies. We have one church, our Holy Armenian Apostolic Church, and we have our God; we are a Christian people."

When asked about children who might not belong to the Armenian Apostolic Church, she replied that such children "have been well taught at home to hide their convictions." Indeed, she said, such children often do not speak up because they "suffer from an inferiority complex," and "they prefer not to be subjected to a derisive attitude or get offensive nicknames. . . . That is natural because those who are not for us are against us, and we know how to fight those who are against us."[52]

Apart from the countries on Open Doors' list of the worst persecutors of Christians, the former Soviet republics include others who have severe problems. Two of these are Armenia and Georgia, ancient Christian countries where the long-established church fears competition from newcomers.

Although Armenia claims to protect freedom of religion, the state creates difficulties for religious minorities, particularly Christian minorities, through a combination of laws, policies, and practices. Religiously, Armenia is about 90 percent Armenian Orthodox (Armenian Apostolic) and 5 percent religious minorities, including Catholics, Protestants, Jehovah's Witnesses, Shia and Sunni Muslims, and Jews, with the rest atheist or agnostic.[53]

Although Armenia's Constitution declares there is a strict separation between church and state, it recognizes the Armenian Apostolic Church (AAC) as the official church. Religious groups need not register in order to meet together and practice their religion, but unless they register, they are not allowed to publish more than a thousand copies of a newspaper or magazine, rent meeting places for worship, broadcast television and radio programs, or sponsor visitors' visas.

Although few religious groups have been turned down for registration, any religious group seeking to register must have more than two hundred members and must subscribe to a doctrine "based on 'historically recognized holy scriptures.' "[54] A plethora of laws and bylaws inhibit the freedom of minority Christian groups. One law specifically prohibits "soul hunting." Though this conjures up eerie imagery and science-fiction programs, its legal meaning is "forced conversion" and "proselytism." Some Armenian groups maintain that, since everyone born in the country is born into the Armenian Apostolic Church, then any other groups that propagate their faith are by definition "soul hunting."[55]

CONCLUSIONS

While not as severe as those of Iran (chapter 6) or North Korea (chapter 2), the laws of the former Soviet republics are often both harsh and ambiguous, and those in authority often act arbitrarily.

Believers know that at any moment there may be a knock on the door. They brace for an unprovoked raid on a wedding or reunion or baptism. They fear the arrest and disappearance of a loved one.

Although the intensity of control varies from one country to another, the tactics are remarkably similar. Religious groups are required to register, but the terms of registration often cripple both small and large communities of believers. Sometimes they are impossible to meet.

Religious communities are often required to have a minimum number of members, and to have already been in existence for years, sometimes decades—a very difficult requirement for a group that is still desperately trying to gain a legal existence. It can be a crippling kind of catch-22: in order to meet, you must be registered; in order to register, you must prove that you have been meeting for years.

A small Christian congregation had been unsuccessfully trying for two years to register its Kyrgyzstan church. "How can we collect 200 signatures if we are not allowed to function normally?" In order to get the signatures, they had to meet together as a group; but to do so was illegal.[56]

Often the names, addresses, and ID or passport numbers of members are required. A specific location for gatherings is demanded. Because of these and many other rules and regulations, or because they will simply not submit to state power in such matters, many church groups refuse to register.

Even those that try to register are frequently rejected, or their applications are held for prolonged periods without explanation. This means that the groups are operating "illegally" while their applications are in limbo. Meanwhile, religious literature and Bibles are strictly limited if not entirely banned, with confiscations taking place at transit stops and during raids on churches and homes.

It is often difficult to get personal stories from these countries. Forum 18, the news service and religious freedom organization we rely on, provides a large portion of the information that is available.

It does a marvelous job and we are grateful for its diligence and accuracy, and for the low-profile ministries and individuals who also provide information. Yet, there is still much about religious restrictions in these countries that is not known to the outside world.

FOUR

SOUTH ASIA'S CHRISTIAN OUTCASTES

India / Nepal / Sri Lanka / Bhutan

IN 2008, THERE WAS AN EXPLOSION OF VIOLENCE AGAINST Christians in the Indian state of Orissa. It began on August 23, when Swami Lakshmanananda, a local leader of the Hindu nationalist group Vishwa Hindu Parishad (VHP), was murdered. He had fomented violence against Christians, so although his killers were probably Maoist extremists who were engaged in guerilla warfare in the area, many local radical Hindu groups accused Christians of the murder. They proceeded to attack them throughout the state. Indian paramilitary forces did not respond until August 27, and, even after they arrived, they could not penetrate the most violent areas because of trees that had been felled to block the roads.

Among those killed were a schoolteacher named Gullu in the Kandhamal area, a pastor who was burned in Padmapur Bargarh, and seven villagers in Digi, Raikia, and Kandhamal. A nun named Mina Barua was raped in Nuagaon. Father Edward of the Bargarh Orphanage House was doused with gasoline in an attempt to set him aflame in Padampur. Reverend U. C. Pattnayak, president of the Orissa Missionary Movement, was attacked by a mob of five hundred, who burned his office and church in Koraput.[1] Catholic schools, such as St. Anne's Convent in Padangi and St. Joseph's Convent in Sankharkhole, were destroyed. Among the thousands of devastated church properties and homes were a Catholic church, a Baptist church—all of its furniture was torched—a Lutheran church in Koraput, and a diocesan pastoral center in Bargarh.

The mobs killed at least forty people and burned thousands of houses, hundreds of churches, and thirteen educational institutions. During the attacks, a large number of women and girls were victims of sexual violence. Nearly two years later, about sixty of the area's women were found in Delhi. They had been sold into sexual slavery.[2] The attacks led to ten thousand fleeing from their homes.

In one of hundreds of cases, Rajendra Digal described what happened to his father after his parents fled their village and took shelter in the state capital, Bhubaneswar. The father returned to his village to check on his house and livestock, but, when he tried to get on the bus to return to Bhubaneswar on September 24, some assailants stopped the bus and dragged the elder Digal out, breaking his leg. The attackers looted his shop and took him and eight of his goats to a nearby forest, where they feasted on the goat meat throughout the night. When Rajendra Digal heard about it, he told the police, who ignored him. Twelve days later, his father's body, naked and burned with acid, was found twenty-five miles from the village. His genitals had also been cut off.[3]

Subsequent investigations and arrests did not touch most of the Orissa perpetrators. "According to information provided to USCIRF from the All India Catholic Union, 3,232 complaints were filed, but only 831 cases were registered and, after preliminary investigations, 133 cases were dropped. Further, according to Compass Direct, among those accused in the violence were 85 members of the RSS, 321 members of the VHP, and 118 members of Bajrang Dal, all militant Hindu organizations."[4]

In September 2010, Manoj Pradhan, a leader in the Hindu-nationalist BJP (or Bharatiya Janata Party), was charged with the murder of eleven people during the riots. "However, the state's high court convicted him only for the culpable homicide of one person and gave him a small fine. Despite this conviction and pending charges for seven other crimes associated with the Orissa violence,

Pradhan was released on bail and remains a member of the Orissa state legislature."[5]

Because of the failure of the authorities to adequately investigate and prosecute the Orissa massacre, in 2011 the National People's Tribunal held public hearings and took expert testimony on the carnage. Its report concluded that the violence was a crime against humanity under international law, and strongly criticized the police, the judiciary, and state authorities for their failure to defend the Christians, for blocking NGOs during the rescue and rehabilitation phase, for creating relief camps that denied inmates the right to a life of dignity, and in some cases for their collusion with extremists responsible for the violence. Two senior Orissa State officials testified that the violence was not spontaneous but preplanned, including the cutting down of trees to disrupt movement by the police.[6]

SOUTH ASIA: THE BIG PICTURE

If asked to name those areas where Christians are heavily persecuted, perhaps few would name South Asia—India, Sri Lanka, Nepal, and Bhutan. These countries are predominantly Hindu and Buddhist, and their people have a reputation, in many cases well deserved, for peaceful religious coexistence with their stunningly varied neighbors. But both these religious groups have some followers who are all too willing to repress others. Both Hindus and Buddhists also have strong militant traditions in these countries, including intolerant and violent movements. While these countries can be strikingly different—India has more than one thousand times as many people as Bhutan, for instance—there are common patterns in religious repression.

One pattern is that in each of these states, strains within both religions maintain they are the only indigenous, authentic, and legitimate religion in the country, and that the country belongs to them in some sense. They then denigrate and may even physically attack members of other religions. Sometimes Hindus attack Buddhists, and vice versa, but frequently much of the violence is aimed at the Christian and Muslim minorities. There have also been attacks by Muslims on Christians, especially in Kashmir. Often the violence is ongoing and endemic.

Christianity is sometimes treated as a foreign faith, although in South Asia it has roots that go back farther than in most of Europe. Sometimes the Christian faith is pilloried as a British colonial import, even though Christianity is older in India than it is in Britain. In India, the most ancient churches trace their founding to the ministry of the apostle Thomas, the "doubting Thomas" who was at first skeptical of Jesus' resurrection and who is believed to have arrived in Kerala (in southwest India) around AD 52.

Christianity is also attacked because it is an evangelizing religion, urging others to trust in Jesus. For religions that suppose their people and lands are tied to a particular faith, evangelism is treated as invasion, imperialism, and usurpation, even if it is done by their long-time neighbors. Often the violence has political overtones as local strongmen try to preserve positions of power rooted in local customs. Abusive incidents often spike during election periods as vying political candidates try to gather nationalist support by vilifying supposed outsiders. Even political leaders of the majority faith—for example, Mohandas Gandhi in India and S. W. R. D. Bandaranaike in Sri Lanka—have been assassinated by radicals who thought them too conciliatory to minorities.

Again, it must be emphasized that this is not the majority pattern within these religious cultures or in these countries. The results of these attitudes, however, are pervasive discrimination, harassment, and hundreds of episodes of religious violence.

INDIA

On November 8, 2011, Bashir-ud-Din, the grand mufti of Kashmir, accused Reverend Chander Mani Khanna of All Saints Anglican

Church of converting people for money. The mufti demanded that Khanna appear before the Kashmir sharia court to explain why he had baptized seven Muslims. The summons had no legal basis, since sharia courts don't have any general legal authority, much less jurisdiction over non-Muslims.

Nonetheless, the police arrested Reverend Khanna. Kashmir has no anticonversion law, and the converts were all willing adults who said they had asked to be baptized. But the authorities took a different course—they charged him under the penal code articles 153A (promoting enmity between different groups on ground of religion) and 295A (malicious acts intended to outrage religious feelings). Police also arrested the seven new Christians and tortured them to get them to testify against the pastor; their beards were ripped out and their feet were beaten. One of those baptized was arrested three days after the birth of his twin daughters, one of whom died less than a month later. In early February 2012, the High Court of the state of Jammu and Kashmir stayed the proceedings against Reverend Khanna as police had failed to produce sufficient evidence to press charges.[7]

India is huge, sprawling, chaotic, colorful, and energetic. With more than 1.2 billion people, it is the world's second most populous country, and will soon outstrip China as the most populous.[8] It is also, by far, the world's largest democracy. Its politics is plagued by infighting, pervasive criminality, and widespread corruption, but it also has an active civil society, competing political parties, an independent judiciary, and a vibrant press, as well as the world's largest movie industry. While some 80 percent of its people are Hindu, it may have the world's second-largest Muslim population, as well as some thirty million Christians, along with Sikhs, Buddhists, Jains, Parsis (Zoroastrians), Jews, and Baha'is. For the most part, its religiously diverse citizens live freely and coexist peacefully. India has had several Muslim presidents and, as we write, its current prime minister is a Sikh, Manmohan Singh.

The constitution describes it as a "secular democratic republic" and contains detailed provisions for religious freedom. Article

19 provides for freedom of speech, expression, and association, and Article 25 provides for freedom of conscience, free profession and practice of religion, as well as the right to propagate religion. Articles 28 and 30 protect religious freedom in relation to religious instruction, while Article 51A imposes a positive duty on citizens to promote harmony and the spirit of common brotherhood transcending religious boundaries.

However, alongside and despite all these virtues, not only does India have widespread religious discrimination but is also the site of hundreds of vicious religious attacks annually. Christians and other religious minorities face three major sets of problems: discrimination, especially against lower-caste Christians; vague anticonversion laws and restrictions on changing one's religion; and communal violence.

ANTICONVERSION LAWS AND VIOLENCE

One means of official repression is state-level anticonversion laws. There are such laws in various Indian states, though the degree to which they are implemented varies.[9] Ostensibly, these laws are aimed only at conversions carried out by "forcible" or "fraudulent" means, but these categories are defined vaguely and very broadly, and can include "any temptation in the form of any gift or gratification . . . or any benefit either pecuniary or otherwise," which could include peace of mind or forgiveness of sins.[10] Claims to any spiritual benefit could be illegal.

This would be laughable if the results were not so tragic. Priests have been convicted of forcibly converting people even though the converted testified they did so voluntarily. In one case, Father L. Bridget and Sister Vridhi Ekka were sentenced to six months of "rigorous imprisonment" for allegedly "forcibly converting" ninety-four people. The court did not explain how two people could forcibly convert ninety-four people, especially when all ninety-four denied that they had been forcibly converted.[11]

The prescribed penalties are also disproportionate, with the Rajasthan and Gujarat conversion laws carrying punishments greater than those for causing death by negligence. Some states have harsher penalties with respect to the conversion of scheduled castes and scheduled tribes, who are people in the lower castes, or even outside the caste system. Since the majority of Hindu converts to Christianity come from these groups, there is suspicion that the goal of anticonversion laws is preservation of the caste system (which has been officially abolished) and thereby maintaining a pool of unpaid or poorly paid workers for higher castes to exploit.

The anticonversion laws also foster a climate that encourages violent attacks on Christians, and especially clergy. States that have such laws have a higher incidence of intimidation and violence against religious minorities. The vague laws give a green light to religious extremists to attack those whom they allege to have been fraudulently or forcibly converting people. Often the police ignore the assault and instead arrest the brutalized or threatened clergy on suspicion of forcible conversion.

On July 3, 2011, near the village of Munugodu, Pentecostal pastor G. N. Paul was returning home from leading the service at Independent Baptist Church, which is attended by about twenty families. Four radical Hindus suddenly attacked him. They accused him of forcibly converting people to Christianity, and they repeatedly stabbed him. Paul sustained serious wounds to his stomach and head and was taken to a hospital in Nalgonda; he was later transferred to one in Hyderabad where he underwent surgery for his injuries.

On January 21, 2011, in the case of the murder of Graham Staines and his two sons, described below, the Indian Supreme Court said a reduced sentence was justified because the murder was an act of passion against "proselytization": "Though Graham Staines and his two minor sons were burnt to death while they were sleeping . . . the intention was to teach a lesson to Staines about his religious activities, namely, converting poor tribals to Christianity."[12]

On March 8, 2009, twenty-five-year-old Rajesh Singh attacked

Prarthana Bhawan (House of Prayer), a church in the eastern state of Bihar. Singh threw a crude bomb through a church window and then walked in and shot the pastor, thirty-five-year-old Vinod Kumar, at point-blank range. According to police inspector Hari Krishna Mandal, Singh "was personally against Christian conversions and wanted to kill the pastor to stop conversions." Church members stopped Singh before his plan was completed and Pastor Kumar, married with three children, was taken to a nearby hospital in Varanasi.[13]

On March 11, 2009, at approximately 6:00 p.m., Pastor Erra Krupanamdam was returning from a prayer meeting in Andhra Pradesh State when a group of thirty to forty Hindu militants attacked him. While they beat him, the pastor's assailants decried his faith and told him to stop conducting prayer meetings. He suffered fractures to his spine and ribs that resulted in permanent injury.[14]

ONGOING VIOLENCE

It is difficult to recount the sheer number of religiously motivated attacks in India. Most violence is not on the massive scale of Orissa, but there are hundreds of violent attacks each year. Here are some summaries of reports from just one month—December 2011—from just one source, Compass Direct News:[15]

- MADHYA PRADESH: On December 2, police arrested Pastor Titus of the Indian Pentecostal Church and other Christians after Hindu extremists filed a complaint of forceful conversion against him. About twenty men from a radical Hindu organization stormed into the police station demanding the arrest of the pastor. Police seized the vehicle the Christians were using as well as CDs and Bibles.
- TAMIL NADU: On December 3, Hindu extremists destroyed the Christu Sabha church building after threatening a pastor in Hosur. The extremists had attacked twice before, stealing the pastor's meager savings and destroying a small

shed in which he held worship services as well as beating him and stabbing him with a screwdriver. They also made threats to kidnap his four daughters and hurt his son if he continues teaching Christianity in the village. Police have refused to file charges.

- ORISSA: On December 8, Hindu extremists attacked three Christian families from tribal areas, beat them, and accused them of forceful conversion. When Christians complained to the police, they were detained.
- MADHYA PRADESH: On December 9, about a hundred members of the radical RSS (Rashtriya Swayamsevak Sangh) and VHP (World Hindu Council) groups attacked and stoned Pastor Ramesh V. Asnia's house, beating another pastor unconscious, destroying Bibles, and stealing gold and silver jewelry, a TV, and a cross. They assaulted the pastor's fifty-year-old mother, breaking one of her legs. Other women escaped and alerted the pastor. When Pastor Ramesh returned, about twenty RSS and VHP members severely beat him, alleging he forcibly and fraudulently converted Hindus. The beating continued even after he was bleeding and unconscious.
- TAMIL NADU: On December 9, after local officials demolished their church building, which was under renovation, police arrested Reverend Arul Saiju and Reverend Stanley Baburaj, along with ten Christians from the Malankara Catholic Church. "Saiju and Baburaj provided the original title deeds to establish the ownership and legitimacy of the church, but Hindu extremists attacked them, took them to the police station, and alleged they had obstructed civil servants from discharging their responsibility."
- ANDHRA PRADESH: On December 11, masked men stormed into a Sunday service in the New Fellowship Gospel Church and stoned Pastor Bangariah. The pastor bled heavily and received fourteen stitches on his head and face.

- MAHARASHTRA: On December 14, Hindu extremists demolished a church building and beat Pastor Prabhakaran Kaviraj of the Apostolic Christian Assembly in Mumbai, after he complained that the church's worship site had been omitted on an area development plan map.
- KARNATAKA: On December 16, police arrested a pastor and other Christians after Hindu extremists went into the house of Venketesh, of Badhravathy Baptist Church. The attackers beat six women, four elders, and the assistant pastor, and accused the Christians of forcible conversions. The Christians were held for two days before being released on bail.
- ANDHRA PRADESH: On December 16, Hindu extremists at the Mahabubnagar railway station attacked and beat Pastor R. Prasad as he was distributing Christian literature. They then took him to a Hindu temple, burned the literature, and beat him again.
- KARNATAKA: On December 18, in Pillanna Garden, near Bangalore, about two hundred Hindu extremists barged into the Agape Bible Church Sunday service and beat pastors Reuben Sathyaraj and Perumal Fernandes. The pastors were accused of forcible conversions, and police arrested them. After questioning some twenty allegedly forced convertees, who denied the accusation, the police nevertheless charged the pastors with "promoting enmity between different groups on grounds of religion."
- MADHYA PRADESH: On December 21, "Pastor Dilip Wadia of Light Giving Church went to the house of Kailash Gormeys for a prayer meeting and to watch the Jesus Film. One of the twenty-four people present belonged to the RSS and soon informed other extremists, who attacked the house and beat its occupants. Police filed forcible conversion charges against the Christians."
- TAMIL NADU: On December 22, Hindu extremists threatened Pastor K. Solomon and other church members and burned down a church building in Kadaloor district in order to

> stop Christmas and New Year's celebrations. A week later, on December 30, in Nagarcoil, police arrested "Sagaya Dass after Hindu extremists accused him of forceful conversion when he and students from a local Hindu college organized a Christmas program."

Some attacks did not make even this brief survey. For example, on Christmas Day 2011, Pastor Suresh of the New Life Church was having dinner in Surathkal with his family and other believers when about twenty people forced their way into the house with stones, sticks, and clubs and assaulted everyone, including women and children. The attackers repeatedly shouted, "Are there Hindus here?" A man named Jason had his leg fractured by a club. The pastor's wife, Latha, was beaten on her chest and wounded severely. When the police came, they did not inquire about the attackers, but interrogated the people in the house about forced conversions.[16]

Individually, few of these local attacks are reported other than in regional news outlets, and none are likely to draw the attention of international observers, but their cumulative effect is devastating.

THE SANGH PARIVAR

Many of these religious tensions can be attributed to the rise of Hindu nationalist movements, usually collectively known as the Sangh Parivar ("family of organizations"). Fr. Cedric Prakash of Gujarat told us that their core ideology is targeting minorities, particularly Christians. Hinduism is a tremendously varied faith, or perhaps even faiths, and its forms can be starkly different and opposed. The popular imagination often identifies political Hinduism with the nonviolence of Mohandas Gandhi, a view that contains a large measure of truth. There are, however, other very different political expressions of the faith—Gandhi was killed by a Hindu radical who thought he gave too many concessions to non-Hindus.

The Sangh Parivar includes the Bharatiya Janata Party (BJP), which formed the government of India in 1998 at the head of a coalition of mostly centrist parties. Its allies include the Rashtriya

Swayamsevak Sangh (RSS), the Bajrang Dal, and the Vishwa Hindu Parishad (VHP), some of which engage in virulent hate campaigns and sometimes acts of violence against religious minorities. Gandhi's assassin, Nathuram Godse, was from the RSS. In 1998, Godse said, "If you ask me, did I feel any repentance, my reply is no—not in the least. . . . We knew if we allowed this person to live any longer, he would do more and more harm to Hindus, and that we could not allow it."[17]

The Sangh Parivar's ideology of *Hindutva* is directed at ensuring the predominance of Hinduism in Indian society, politics, and culture. Some members want to subjugate or drive out Christians and Muslims. They label them as foreign elements, even though Indian Christians trace their origins to the first century, and Islam came to India as early as the seventh or eighth century. M. S. Golwalkar, the Sangh Parivar's senior leader from 1940 to 1973, supported Hitler's racial laws and in 1938 declared that "the non-Hindu . . . must either adopt the Hindu culture and language, must learn to respect and revere Hindu religion . . . [o]r [they] may stay in the country wholly subordinated to the Hindu nation, claiming nothing, deserving no privileges, far less any preferential treatment, not even citizen's rights."[18]

The RSS has several million activists and, despite the backlash against radical Hinduism after Gandhi's assassination, has thrived largely by urging cultural renewal and avoiding electoral politics. Because its activities are frequently associated with violence, it has been banned three times, first after Gandhi's assassination in 1948, then in the State of Emergency from 1975 to 1977, and after the destruction of the Babri mosque in 1992.[19]

The Gospel for Asia Bible School in Kutabaga (in Orissa State) was attacked by a mob of nearly four hundred people stirred up by Hindu extremists belonging to the Bajrang Dal on February 28, 2007. The mob was armed with sticks, axes, and swords; it cut electric wires on campus, damaged the roof, and left five people hospitalized. The group also ransacked the Believers Church Bible College campus at Jharsuguda and beat up both students and staff.[20] The militants scattered once the authorities arrived, but soon afterward another group of Hindu extremists belonging to the Sangh Parivar came to the site and shouted slogans, terrorizing the Christians.[21]

On December 9, 2010, ten Bajrang Dal activists stormed into the house of eight Christian coolie workers on a coffee estate in Karnataka State. As the Christians were praying, the militants insulted them, beat them, and then dragged them to the Gonikoppa police station. Two of the victims were bleeding profusely and had to be taken to the Gonikoppa government hospital. One could not urinate after repeated kicks to his groin. The police reportedly advised the victims to "stop praying in their own houses in the future," as they could not give any protection.[22]

The BJP, particularly at the federal level, has distanced itself from violence and has had to compromise with partners in parliamentary and government coalitions, which has produced a mellowing effect. But former prime minister Atal Bihari Vajpayee publicly praised the RSS, attended their functions, and feted the organization's leadership at his residence. Other senior BJP officials, including former home affairs minister L. K. Advani, were RSS associates. The BJP has tried to Hinduize the school curriculum, restrict minority religious groups' international contacts, reduce their rights to build places of worship, pass state anticonversion laws, and alter personal laws that govern marriages, adoptions, and inheritance.

DALITS AND DISCRIMINATION

India's notorious caste system has been abolished by law, yet such traditions die hard. Dalits, formerly called "untouchables," and scheduled castes (usually lower castes) continue to suffer from discrimination that, though illegal, is widespread, intense, and humiliating. They are often barred from entering temples and may be denied access to water supplies used by higher-caste Hindus. These problems are compounded by physical persecution, with thousands of atrocities registered against Dalits and indigenous tribal groups.

Many Indian Christians are Dalits, or from scheduled castes or scheduled tribes. Discrimination, while affecting all Dalits, can be compounded for Christian Dalits. Some argue that the 2001 census underestimated the number of such Christians (which may be 14 million), by linking class and religion so that the lower castes were limited to marking their religion only as Hinduism, or Buddhism or Sikhism, which are legally regarded as part of Hinduism.[23]

Because of the crushing problems and suffering faced by Dalits and similar castes, Indian governments have affirmative-action programs that set aside a percentage of educational opportunities and government jobs for them. However, Christians and Muslims are usually excluded from these programs with the argument that caste matters are really internal to Hinduism. Hence Christian Dalits suffer in two ways: their status means they are subject to pervasive social oppression, sometimes by high-caste Christians, while at the same time they are excluded from government programs that help those from minority religions.[24] This also means any Hindu who converts to Christianity loses these benefits.

Christians who aid Dalits or people with leprosy often suffer particular persecution. Retired Indian army corporal Henry Baptist Robey had been visiting a village in Tamil Nadu State twice a year to bring clothing, medicine, and food to leprosy-affected people in the village. On Sunday, June 12, 2011, he invited about eighty of the leprosy patients to his home in Bangalore, Karnataka State, to celebrate Pentecost.

While they were meeting, Hindu extremists, allegedly from the nationalist Jai Karnataka group, forcibly entered the house and beat some of the leprosy patients. After the police arrived, they took all those present to the police station. Two hours later, everyone was released except Robey and two Hindu lepers accused of aiding him. That night they were taken to the Hennur police station and officially arrested under Section 295(A), which bans the "deliberate and malicious intention of outraging the religious feelings of others."

Robey said he believed the charge stemmed from the false belief that he was forcibly converting the leprosy patients, and said,

"All the leprosy patients who had come for the prayer function told the police that they were Hindu, and that they were not being converted, but the police still registered a complaint against us." Indeed, the two men with Robey and charged with forcible conversion were in fact Hindus who had not converted to Christianity. The three were released on bail two days later.[25]

TOLERATING VIOLENCE: "NO ARRESTS WERE MADE"

On September 26, 2010, a Pentecostal pastor, Shivanda Siddi, forty-five, was conducting a worship service at Gnanodaya Assemblies of God Church in the state of Karnataka. Five people belonging to a Hindu extremist organization disrupted the service and attacked the pastor. They tore his clothes and, after beating him for about half an hour in front of the congregation, they called the police at the Yellapur station and beat him again in front of police officials. "The pastor, as well as seven women, including two girls aged ten and eleven, were reportedly arrested by the police," and the pastor was charged with forcible conversion under Section 295 of the Penal Code. He was sent to Sirsi jail.[26]

At the state level, governments are sometimes complicit in violence against religious minorities, or, more commonly, they refuse or fail to give adequate protection to them. For example, in the largest attack on a minority in recent Indian history, in February 2002 about two thousand Muslims were killed in Gujarat. This happened after claims that Muslims had burned a train carrying Hindu volunteers who had helped build the controversial Ram Janmabhoomi temple on the site of the demolished Babri mosque. VHP international president Ashok Singhal described the Gujarat carnage as a "successful experiment" and warned it would be repeated all over India.[27] Subsequent official inquiries concluded the Gujarat government was negligent or complicit in the killings, so much so that the then–chief minister of Gujarat, Narendra Modi, was denied admission to the United States. In February 2012, the Gujarat High Court chastised the Gujarat government for its conduct and ordered it to pay compensation to the victims.[28]

Most of this violence is between Hindus and Muslims, but the country's Christians have also become particular targets. Assaults on Christians have increased significantly since 1998, fueled by antiminority propaganda from radical Hindus, and despite the defeat of the BJP in federal elections in 2004. These assaults are more common in election periods, as Hindu radicals and others resort to hate-rhetoric and violence in calculated political moves to solidify their support. One of the most troubling aspects of this violence is police complicity, demonstrated either by failing to prevent or investigate attacks, or by arresting those who have been attacked rather than their assailants, sometimes even with the authorities themselves joining in the attack. The lack of official response is felt most acutely in BJP states, where political sympathies tend to be reflected in the police.

On June 4, 2011, Pastor Shantilal Ninama of the Believers Church in Rajasthan was repairing his motorcycle when Khatiya Pitakaniya, a villager, attacked him. The pastor said that Pitakaniya "told me that he did not want to see my face in the early morning as it will bring bad luck to him because I am a Christian. . . . He . . . called his wife to bring a knife to kill me." The pastor escaped, but later Pitakaniya returned with his wife, Devali, and two of Pastor Ninama's relatives (his older brother and cousin), and they began to curse and stone him.

On June 6, the village authorities called a meeting with Pastor Ninama, and the village leader attempted to reconvert the pastor back to Hinduism. He was ordered not only to reconvert but also to burn his Bible and all Christian literature in front of the group. After he refused, his father's electricity was cut off and, on June 8, he signed an agreement with the extremists that he would withdraw his complaint to the police if they would do no further harm to him. That same night, however, they burst into his house and beat and stoned his sister, wife, and three children. His father was beaten unconscious. The police initially refused to help him, but eventually they came and the extremists left after seeing the police. No arrests were made.[29]

REMEMBERING GRAHAM STAINES

While the Sangh Parivar often claims it is attacking foreign influences, almost every victim in India of anti-Christian persecution is one of India's more than thirty million and growing indigenous Christian population. The charge is ludicrous, since Christianity has been in India for almost two millennia, and the ratio of indigenous Indian Christians to foreign missionaries is more than twenty thousand to one.

In this sense, the story of Graham Staines and his family is atypical. But since it has increased international attention to the persecution of Christians in India, and since it reveals some of the dynamics of the Sangh Parivar, and, most importantly, since it reveals the life of a remarkable man and his family, it is worth recounting.

Graham Staines was born in Brisbane, Australia, in 1941. He became a pen pal with Santanu Satpathy who lived in Baripada, in eastern India. In 1965, Staines went to India to meet Satpathy and he never returned to Australia. Instead, he dedicated himself for the next thirty-four years to serving leprosy patients in the area. He became a fixture in Baripada and was usually known as Saibo or "Dada." Eventually, he became the superintendent of the Leprosy Mission of Australia and director of the Evangelical Missionaries Society.

In 1983, he married Gladys and the couple had two boys, Philip and Timothy, and a daughter. In 1996 a fire burned much of Baripada, leaving nearly one hundred dead, and the Staineses spent many nights caring for the wounded. A local government official, V. V. Yadav, said, "Mr. Graham Staines had lost his identity as an Australian. He was a true citizen of Baripada . . . he was a light in this town."[30]

Graham had been organizing training camps in the town of Manoharpur for fourteen years. On the night of January 22, 1999, he and his sons, Philip, nine, and Timothy, six, slept in their vehicle after a visit there. While they were sleeping, a group of about fifty people poured gasoline on the vehicle and set it on fire. The three tried to escape the flames, but the armed mob stopped them and watched as they burned to death. The local Hindu villagers, among whom Staines was well-known and very popular, tried to help him, but were driven off by the violent attackers.[31]

While there had already been many attacks on native Indian Christians, the international media were especially shocked and reported the Staines murders widely. Many were stunned at the barbarity of this killing, targeting children and their father—a man who had labored with leprosy-affected people in India for more than thirty years. Immediately after the incident, Subhas Chouhan, convenor of the state unit of the Hindu Jagran Samukhya (Awareness Program for Hindus), attempted to defend Staines's murder by alleging he had been "proselytising" and that people may have "killed him in a fit of rage."[32] However, according to a Central Bureau of Investigation report, Staines was not in fact inducing people to convert, and, of course, even if he had been engaged in such unlawful activity, there were no grounds to kill him.[33]

Abkhay Mokashi, political editor of *Mid-Day*, wrote, "The Hindu fundamentalists responsible for the killing of Staines and his two sons should know that the loss of these three lives is not to Christianity, but to humanity at large. The Hindu leprosy patients, for whom he devoted his life, have lost their savior." One of the Staines's former patients, Sarida, recounted: "We were untouchable. . . . And we were left to die in the jungle all alone, like worms. . . . Dada and his wife would personally wash our sores and dress the wounds with medicines, and when we were cured, they would teach us some skills—and give jobs to us. . . . What did he do that he should be burned alive?"[34]

Ten thousand people from the area gathered for the funeral procession in Baripada.

STAINES: THE AFTERMATH

After Staines's murder, Orissa State police arrested forty-seven militants associated with the nationalist Bajrang Dal group, who alleged the family was using leprosy as a cover for conversion activities.[35] However, the main suspect in the murder, Dara Singh, was not apprehended. Singh's real name is Rabindra Kumar Pal; he had been a Bajrang Dal activist in the Manoharpur area for ten years, and several criminal cases were pending against him, most for the murder of Muslim truck drivers. He went into hiding for almost a year, during which time he was implicated in the August 1999 murder of a Muslim shopkeeper, Sheikh Rehman, and the September 1, 1999, murder of a Catholic priest, Father Arul Doss. Singh was eventually convicted of killing Father Doss, who, as he fled his burning church, was shot with arrows until he was dead.[36]

Dara Singh was finally arrested on February 1, 2000, but, on March 21, 2001, he and eleven others were acquitted because neither the complainants nor the witnesses were willing to identify him as the perpetrator.[37] Despite the barbarity of the acts of which he has been accused—Sheikh Rehman was also burned alive—some Hindu extremists treated Singh as a hero, and pamphlets praised his act as "an effort to save Hinduism." Pro–Dara Singh organizations spread and *Dara Sena* (Dara's Army) congratulated Dara Singh's parents for having "saved Hinduism" by producing such a son. The VHP honored his mother and awarded her 25,000 rupees. An inflammatory booklet propagating Dara Singh's beliefs became a bestseller in areas of Orissa.[38]

On September 23, 2003, a court in Bhubaneswar, the capital of Orissa, convicted and sentenced Singh to death. The court also sentenced twelve accomplices to life terms. On May 19, 2005, the Orissa High Court commuted Singh's sentence to life in prison and released eleven of the twelve accomplices.[39]

As noted above, on January 21, 2011, the Indian Supreme Court upheld the Orissa High Court's decisions, saying that the reduced sentence was justified because the murder was an act of passion against "proselytization": "Though Graham Staines and his two minor sons were burnt to death while they were sleeping . . . the intention was to teach a lesson to Staines about his religious activities, namely, converting poor tribals to Christianity." The Court also said there was "no justification for interfering in someone's belief."[40]

Following protests, the Court deleted the phrase "to teach a lesson to Staines," but even today, India's Christians remain worried. John Dayal, secretary general of the All India Christian Council, asked, "Is talking about your own religion 'interference'?"[41]

More hopeful, and more typical of the Indian response, were the words of the Indian president K. R. Narayanan, who lamented at the time of the Staineses' deaths:

> That someone who spent years caring for patients of leprosy, instead of being thanked and appreciated as a role model should be done to death in this manner is a monumental aberration from the traditions of tolerance and humanity for which India is known. A crime that belongs to the world's inventory of black deeds.[42]

On the tenth anniversary of the murder, Gladys Staines, who continued her husband's work, said, "I cannot express how I felt when I got the news of my husband and sons being burnt alive. I told my daughter Esther that though we had been left alone, we would forgive and my daughter replied, 'Yes, we will.' "[43]

NEPAL

The Pashupatinath Temple is one of Nepalese Hinduism's most sacred shrines. In 2009, Christians, as well as Hindus and Muslims, were given permission to bury their dead in the Sleshmantak forest, which is in the hills surrounding the temple. But in early 2011, officials began enforcing a ban on Christian burials in the forest, which had been issued by the Pashupatinath Area Development Trust.

Christians fasted for a month, then marched with empty coffins in front of government offices. In March 2011, the Supreme Court lifted the ban, but temple authorities still refused to permit further Christian burials.[44] Meanwhile, the Christian tombs are being dug up, and temple authorities are reclaiming the forested land, home to at least two hundred Christian graves. Gamala Guide, widow of Narayan Guide—a former captain in the Nepal army—fears the destruction of her husband's grave. "What kind of strange country is this that doesn't allow its own citizens to rest in peace? Please do something to stop the desecration, or my husband will die a second death."[45]

Another majority Hindu land is Nepal, which was, for almost 240 years, the world's only Hindu kingdom. About 75 percent of its thirty million people are Hindu, about 16 percent Buddhist, 4 percent Muslim, and 3 percent Christian. After a brief period of constitutional monarchy from 1990 to 1996, an ongoing conflict with a Maoist insurgency led to the abolition of the cabinet and parliament and provided the king with absolute power. In 2006, after ten years of civil war, the Maoists signed a peace agreement with the government.[46] In 2008, the country elected a Constituent Assembly, which declared Nepal a secular republic and abolished the monarchy, and is considering two drafts for a permanent constitution, both of which make it illegal to convert someone from one religion to another.[47]

Article 160 of the proposed penal code also prohibits abetting a person to change religions, and would carry a fine of up to 50,000 Nepali rupees (US$700) and five years in jail. Offenders who are not Nepali citizens could be deported immediately after their sentence is finished.[48] These provisions are likely to be used against Christians, who, like Buddhists and Muslims, are not adherents to a recognized religion. Nepal's approximately four thousand churches cannot register as religious trusts and are not tax exempt as are Hindu temples.[49] Christians are also frequent victims of discrimination and violence.

In Christianity, as in most religions, the treatment of the dead is tied to sacred ritual. Hindus and Buddhists customarily cremate the dead, while Christians commonly prefer burial. Yet, because Christianity is not legally recognized, churches are denied the right to buy land for cemeteries.[50] The government says the problem is one of insufficient land, though it does find land for other religious purposes. When Christians do attempt to bury their dead on private land, they are often blocked by Hindu protests. At times the bodies are even dug up and thrown away.

Christians may also be attacked by extremist Hindu groups. On November 22, 2011, a crude bomb was detonated outside the Christian charity United Mission to Nepal in Kathmandu, though fortunately there were no injuries or damage to buildings. Since 1954, the United Mission, funded from sixty countries, has built hospitals, schools, hydroelectric plants, and training institutions in Nepal. Six days later, security personnel defused a powerful bomb outside the Assemblies of God Navajiwan Church, also in Kathmandu.

The Nepal Defence Army (NDA), a militant armed group pushing for a Hindu state and with a history of violence against Christians and Muslims, claimed responsibility for the first attack. The NDA chief, Ram Prasad Mainali, is serving a life sentence for three deaths in the bombing of the Catholic Church of the Assumption in Kathmandu on May 23, 2009. Six days after that bombing, the NDA released a statement declaring, "We want all the one million Christians out of the country, if not we will plant one million bombs in all of the houses where Christians live and detonate them."[51]

Nepal's government has begun negotiations with the NDA, offering amnesty for Mainali and others if the NDA agrees to stop violence. As the Constituent Assembly comes closer to enacting a constitution, there is increased persecution as priests, pastors, and worshippers are victims of random mob violence.[52]

SRI LANKA

Just thirty-eight years old, Reverend Nallathamby Gnanaseelan was the pastor of the Tamil Mission Church in Jaffna and the father of four children. On January 13, 2007, he took his wife and daughter to the hospital on his motorcycle and then rode toward his church to conduct a fasting and prayer service. On the way, he was shot in the stomach by government security forces. As he lay in the street, he was fatally shot in the head.

The killers took the pastor's Bible, identity card, and motorcycle, and left his corpse lying in the road. At first, the security forces claimed that Gnanaseelan was carrying explosives, but then later said he was shot because he did not stop when they told him to, even though the fatal shot came as he was lying on the ground. The World Evangelical Alliance called this "a deliberate attempt to frame Rev. Gnanaseelan," a man who "was not involved in any political activity."[53]

In South Asia, factions of both Hindus and Buddhists have melded their religion with a chauvinistic, violent nationalism, in this case Sinhalese nationalism. Sri Lanka's dominant Theravada Buddhism has features distinct from the better-known (in the West) Tibetan or Chinese Mahayana Buddhism. Many in the Sinhalese religious and ethnic majority, which accounts for about 70 percent of the population, believe they have been entrusted with the future of a particularly pure form of Buddhism. This melding of ethnic, religious, and political identity has given birth to religious militancy, even justifying violence in the name of protecting Buddhism from corruption, and especially from foreign peoples and foreign religions.

In 1956, the parliament made Sinhala the sole official language and ushered an era of widespread discrimination against minority Tamils, who make up about 11 percent of the population, are largely Hindu, and are linguistically and ethnically distinct. In 1959, a Buddhist monk assassinated Prime Minister S. W. R. D. Bandaranaike for not protecting the privileged place of Sinhala Buddhism. In 1978, Article IX of the new constitution granted Buddhism "the foremost place" and required the state to "protect and foster" it. Although Article X guarantees freedom of thought and religion, including "the right to have or adopt a religion of one's choice" and manifest it "in public or private," the harsh reality is ongoing legal discrimination against non-Buddhists and violence against religious minorities, including Christians.

CIVIL WAR

Some members of the Tamil ethnic group sought independence and supported the militant Liberation Tigers of Tamil Eelam (LTTE), which waged a violent campaign to create an independent country in the north and east, where most Tamils live. The outnumbered LTTE frequently employed child soldiers, perpetrated brutal assassinations, and pioneered the use of suicide bombing. In turn, the Sri Lankan government committed widespread human rights violations, including extrajudicial killings by paramilitaries and indiscriminate artillery and air attacks. The civil war claimed tens of thousands of lives and ran from 1983 until 2009, when the LTTE was defeated.

Since then, most of the conflict has been between Hindus and Buddhists. But Christians, who make up 8 percent of the population and are mostly Catholic, also suffered in the war. Since Christians include both Tamils and Sinhalese, some were simply general war victims. For example, on January 2, 2007, sixteen Tamil Christians were killed by government bombing at Padahu Thurai, in the district of Mannar. The bombing destroyed twenty-five houses and about sixty people were injured, including loss of limbs; among the dead were seven children under ten years old.[54]

On other occasions, however, Christians appear to have been specifically targeted. Father Thiruchelvam Nihal Jim Brown was ordained in 2004. In July 2006, he was appointed the parish priest of St. Philip Neri Church in the Jaffna district. The previous priest, Father Amal Raj, had been transferred; he had received death threats after gunmen murdered a Christian family in Allaipiddy village. Jim Brown's uncle, Manuel Aseervathampillai, described Father Jim as "a Samaritan." As he recounted: "During the war period, [Fr. Brown] fetched bundles of essential goods for his laypeople, carrying them on his shoulders for several kilometers on foot through the no man's land between the rival forces."[55] During one clash on August 12, 2006, between the navy and the LTTE, naval artillery destroyed a church, and twenty people were killed and many more injured. Father Jim gathered up about eight hundred of his parishioners and took them to a shelter in St. Mary's church in Kayts, a neighboring town. He successfully begged navy troops at the checkpoint to allow them to escape the violence.[56]

On August 20, Father Jim Brown left Kayts with his assistant, Wenceslaus Vincent Vimalan. Later they were met by another priest on the road, Father Peter Thurairatnam. They were stopped at a military checkpoint and told they could not go further. After they separated at the Allaipiddy checkpoint, Father Brown and Mr. Vimalan disappeared.[57] On March 14, 2007, a fisherman found a weighted sandbag holding a "mutilated torso" off the coast of the Jaffna peninsula, near Pungudutheevu. Unofficial hospital sources say that its DNA matched Father Brown's.[58]

LEGAL WOES

Sri Lanka's Christians also suffer targeted legal discrimination. In 2003, a Catholic order, the Sisters of the Holy Cross, who provide education and social services, sought to be legally incorporated. Some Buddhists objected that this would violate the constitution's protection of Buddhism. Eventually, the Supreme Court denied there was a "fundamental right to propagate a religion" and asserted "the propagation [and spreading of Christianity] . . . would impair the very existence of Buddhism." Even after the United Nations Human Rights Council said the decision violated Sri Lanka's international human rights obligations, the Supreme Court explicitly reaffirmed its decision. Hence, basic Christian activities have been legally labeled as contrary to the constitution and a threat to the very existence of Buddhism.[59] Meanwhile, school textbooks make defamatory remarks about the pope and the Catholic Church, and the Ministry of Religious Affairs declares all construction and maintenance of places of worship must have its permission.[60]

The year 2003 also saw the death of Gangodawila Soma Thero,

a popular anti-Christian monk who had long railed against Buddhist conversions to other religions. Although his death was proven to be from natural causes, many monks claimed Christian forces backed by foreign NGOs assassinated him. His burial on Christmas Eve sparked an unprecedented wave of anti-Christian violence and church burnings. There were nearly two hundred violent attacks on churches and Christian communities, including dozens of church fire-bombings and desecrations. More than 140 churches were forced to close due to attack, intimidation, and threats. Nonetheless, there were few arrests of perpetrators and fewer prosecutions.[61]

Radical Buddhists connected to the Jathika Hela Urumaya (JHU) party have introduced legislation that outlaws "inducing" voluntary conversion out of Buddhism, which can carry a punishment of five to seven years in prison for "spreading the faith," a goal common to Christianity, Islam, and many other religions. The bill is purportedly designed to stop people from being forced to convert from one religion to another under duress or when enticed by money or economic advantage. However, as in India, the law's sweeping language renders it liable to abuse. Help to the poor could be seen as a form of coercion. Also, as in India, the proposed law creates a climate and pretext for attacks on Christians.

AN EPIDEMIC OF VIOLENCE

At around 9:00 p.m. on February 17, 2008, Samson Neil Edirisinghe, the thirty-seven-year-old pastor of a church in Ampara, was returning home from a meal at a friend's house. His thirty-one-year-old wife, Shiromi, and their two-year-old son accompanied him. Two men drove by on a motorcycle and shot the pastor in the back, killing him instantly. They also shot his wife, leaving her in critical condition; their son sustained minor injuries but was in shock after seeing his parents shot.[62] The police took the child to a YMCA before taking the couple to the Ampara hospital where the pastor was pronounced dead. Witnesses say the two murderers wore the uniform of Home Guard troops—a security force established to assist the police and military. Early the next morning, police arrested two men wearing Home Guard uniforms who then confessed to killing the pastor.[63]

There are indications the killing was contracted by a husband whose wife had converted to Christianity. The killers said they had been offered 100,000 rupees (about US$900) by a rich businessman in Ampara for the pastor's murder. This was not the first attack against the pastor for his evangelism. In November 2007, arsonists tried to burn down his house.[64]

On March 2, 2008, masked men on motorbikes attacked ten Believers Church Bible College students in Lunuwila, Puttlam district, and beat, kicked, and hit them with rods. Two weeks later, on March 15, a Provincial Council member, Winton Appuhamy, carrying a gun, assaulted a security guard at the school.[65] On June 23, 2008, in Uhana, three men asked Reverend Fernando from the Methodist church in Ampara to follow them to a house where they claimed three people wanted to become Christians. When the pastor sensed a trap and instead invited them to church, the men beat him severely and warned him not to return to the village. Allegedly, the attackers were members of the Gramarakshaka Niladhari or "Home Guards."[66] On March 25, 2009, a man carrying a machete entered Vineyard Community Church Pannala in Kurunegala district and attacked the assistant pastor and a coworker, who were cut on their heads, lips, and hands.[67]

After Tamil separatists were defeated in May 2009, there was an upsurge of violence against Christians. On July 28, a mob set fire to an Assemblies of God church in Norachcholai, destroying the building, which had replaced the one that had been burned to the ground the year before. Also that July, the pastor of a Foursquare Gospel church and his wife were stopped on the street in Radawana by a mob shouting they would not tolerate Christian activities in Norachcholai. During the attack, they caned the pastor and dumped cow dung on him. In the same village on June 28, a mob, including Buddhist monks, vandalized the home of a female pastor of a Foursquare Gospel church. The pastor was forced to sign a document stating she would not host worship services for non-family members. The following month, three masked men attacked the pastor of another Foursquare Church in Polonnaruwa district as he returned from a prayer meeting. As they tried to cut his throat, they shouted, "If we let you live, you will convert the whole town!"[68] The pastor escaped with severe cuts; his arms were wounded as he tried to protect his throat.[69]

The Rosa Mystica Catholic Church at Crooswatta, ten miles north of Colombo, Sri Lanka's capital, serves more than three hundred families. Its sanctuary was constructed in 2003 and the church started extension work in February 2007. This extension led to tension with some local Buddhists. On September 28, 2007, a group of extremists went to the site and threatened that "if building does not stop by tomorrow, you'll lose 10 to 15 lives." For fear of violence, many parishioners did not celebrate mass.

The dispute was temporarily settled when Father Susith Silva agreed to delay the extension. However, on October 6, police interrupted mass, ordered the priests to stop the liturgy, and sent worshippers home. The church went to court again and was allowed to hold mass, catechism, and other religious activities, but construction remained suspended.

Local Buddhists continued to protest the church, saying its presence insulted Buddhist families in the area. Uddamitta Buddahsiri, the senior monk at the local Kotugoda Boddhirukkaramaya Buddhist Temple, who led the initial protests, said locals "don't want a church here. Catholics can go to the other two or three churches in the area. We are not going to let them finish the building. If it restarts the whole village is going to rise up." Father Silva countered that most of the Catholics "are poor people and cannot pay for a taxi to the nearest church, which is several kilometres away."[70]

On July 28, 2008, the Supreme Court allowed the church to continue construction. But, on December 6, 2009, a mob of about a thousand people invaded the church. Father Jude Lakshman, a priest at the church, recounted the violence: "I can still hear the shouting in my ears: 'Kill him!' . . . A mob of about a thousand people with sticks, swords and stones stormed the church when I and my parishioners were still inside. I had just finished the 7 o'clock Mass. . . . They destroyed everything."[71] One of the attackers attempted to hit Father Lakshman with a sword, and six parishioners had to be hospitalized after being beaten with swords and batons. The enraged mob burned cars, and destroyed religious statues and the altar.[72]

BHUTAN

The Himalayan country of Bhutan, remote, mountainous, largely Buddhist, and never colonized, has sometimes appeared in the West's imagination as a Shangri-La, a beautiful, peaceful land, isolated from the outside world, bestowed with mystic wisdom. Beautiful though it is, in recent decades it has seen little peace, and has also been highly repressive, especially of religious minorities. Happily there are promising indications of change, though as yet they remain unfulfilled.

PRESERVING AND PROTECTING BUDDHISM

About three-quarters of Bhutan's seven hundred thousand people are Buddhist, and most of the rest are Hindu: Christians make up only 1 to 2 percent of the population. It is the only Vajrayana Buddhist country in the world (Vajrayana is an offshoot of Mahayana, one of two main branches of Buddhism), and many of its people, like those in Sri Lanka, believe they have a national calling to preserve, protect, and promote Vajrayana beliefs as the core of their culture and sovereignty. With these concerns in mind, there is even government-mandated dress, language, and architectural style.

In this small country wedged between mammoths China and India, the preservation of culture is also seen as essential to national security. Prior to 1950, Bhutan had two other neighbors, Tibet and

Sikkim, also both small Buddhist countries. China invaded Tibet in 1950, and Sikkim, after a large influx of Hindu immigrants, voted to become an Indian state in 1975. The Bhutanese Minister of Home and Culture, significantly also the Minister of National Security, has stated, "If we lose our culture we lose everything."[73] The constitution describes Buddhism as the "spiritual heritage" of the country, and one of the primary purposes of the Religious Organizations Act is to "protect the spiritual heritage of Bhutan."[74]

An absolute monarchy for more than one hundred years, in the 1980s and 1990s the government stripped many Hindus of their citizenship, and almost one hundred thousand of them fled to Nepal, where in 2010 an estimated seventy thousand were still left in refugee camps. This made Bhutan one of the world's highest per capita creators of refugees, a dubious notoriety that included extensive human rights violations.

In recent years, however, there have been major changes. In 2008, Bhutan held its first democratic elections and became a constitutional monarchy. Article 7 of the 2008 constitution protects "the right to freedom of thought, conscience and religion."[75] The king says he will be the protector of all religions, not just Buddhism, and the government has expressly approved of freedom of Christian worship. Numerous Buddhist organizations and one Hindu federation have been granted legal registration under the Religious Organization Act.[76]

However, the National Security Act prohibits words or acts that promote "on grounds of religion, race, language, caste, or community, or any other ground whatsoever, feelings of enmity or hatred between different religious . . . communities." The government believes "proselytizing" might lead to enmity, and also threatens the culture. Hence, Article 7 of the constitution declares: "No person shall be compelled to belong to another faith by means of coercion or inducement."[77] Proposed Section 643 of the penal code bans using "coercion or other forms of inducement to cause the conversion of a person from one religion or faith to another."[78] While almost everybody would agree with banning attempts to "coerce" a religious change, the definition of "inducement" is, as elsewhere, vague.

On October 6, 2010, Prem Singh Gurung, a forty-year-old Christian, was sentenced to three years in prison for showing Christian films in two Bhutanese villages. He was charged with "attempting to promote civil unrest" and with violating the Bhutan Information, Communication and Media Act of 2006, which requires prior examination of all films by public authorities before public screening.[79]

PRAYING FOR CHANGE

The government remains suspicious of conversions, and of Christian conversions in particular. Prime Minister Jigmi Yoser Thinley has acknowledged that Section 643 is designed to deter evangelism, particularly by Christians, who practice it more often than Buddhists or Hindus, since it is part of their religious mission. Further, government officials acknowledge harboring the belief that many Christians induce conversions through promises of economic, social, and spiritual advantage.

While Thinley acknowledges Christians must have rights equal to Buddhists and Hindus, and while Christian leaders affirm their opposition to unethical conversions, and express distress at the government's misperceptions of Christianity, the association of Christianity with "proselytism" still leads to restrictions on Christians' practice of their faith. Christianity does not yet have legal status, which means that, while Christians are permitted to worship openly in homes, they are not allowed to have church buildings, bookstores, or cemeteries.

Despite high expectations and stated government support for registering a Christian federation, no action has yet been taken. However, the Bhutanese government retains a high level of trust from its people, including Christians, who sympathize with the need for social and religious harmony. The prime minister, partly raised as a Christian, has called Christianity "a good moral and ethical framework for the functioning of a good society."[80]

Therefore, while they are frustrated by restrictions and delays, most Christians are patient and do not expect a return to the types of violence seen in Sri Lanka or India.[81]

CHANGES: BEARING SEEDS OF FREEDOM

Each of these countries is undergoing momentous changes. India is experiencing sustained economic growth that may make it one of the world's great powers. At the federal level, the Hindu nationalist BJP party has been out of power on the national level since its defeat in 2004, and suffered further losses in 2009. Sri Lanka's civil war effectively ended in 2009. In 2008, Nepal's conflict with Maoists ended, the Hindu monarchy was abolished, and the country was declared a secular republic. That same year, Bhutan held its first democratic elections and became a constitutional monarchy, and the new constitution promised "freedom of thought, conscience, and religion."[82]

So far these changes have not often produced increased freedom from persecution for Christians or other religious minorities. In India, conversion to Christianity is frequently restricted, especially at the provincial level, de facto if not de jure, by radical elements within the majority religions. Repression by several states, coupled with endemic violent local attacks, continues. In Nepal, Christianity is still not legally recognized, while reactionary Hindu militias such as the Nepal Defense Army threaten to bomb every Christian household. Similarly, in Bhutan, Christians cannot have church buildings or cemeteries since Christianity is not legally recognized, and promised changes are slow in coming. The end of Sri Lanka's war led not to harmony but to an upsurge of violence against Christians and others.

But these changes bear seeds of freedom, and are reasons for real hope of lessened violence and increased freedom for all these peoples. In these countries, political leaders committed to reform, religious leaders committed to peaceful relations, church leadership that is both forceful and careful, and judicious advocacy and support by others all have made a difference. If continued and supported, these things will increasingly change things for the better in the coming years.

FIVE

THE MUSLIM WORLD: A WEIGHT OF REPRESSION

Malaysia / Turkey / Area Administered by Turkish Cypriots or Turkish Military in Cyprus / Morocco / Algeria / Jordan / Yemen / Palestinian Territories

IN JORDAN IN SEPTEMBER 2004, MOHAMED ABBAD, A CONVERT to Christianity, was arrested on charges of apostasy. He refused to renounce his Christian faith and was found guilty and stripped of his civil rights. The court ruling stated that he no longer had a legal religious identity and therefore possessed no property rights and could not be legally employed; it also declared his marriage annulled and that he could only remarry his wife if he converted back to Islam; potentially he could lose custody of his children. Having received death threats from his brothers, he fled the country.[1]

The most widespread persecution of Christians today takes place in the Muslim world, and it is spreading and intensifying. Of course, there are very different degrees of repression and harassment. The countries we discuss in this chapter—Malaysia, Turkey, the Area Administered by Turkish Cypriots or Turkish Military in Cyprus (as it is officially known), Morocco, Algeria, Jordan, Yemen, and the Palestinian Territories—are clearly not as dangerous and deadly for Christians as Saudi Arabia and Iran. Nonetheless, in varying degrees, they discriminate against Christians and at times Christians are subject to acts of persecution, which result in restricting Christian practice.[2] With the exception of Malaysia, in Southeast Asia, these countries are concentrated in the Middle East and around the Mediterranean Sea.

MALAYSIA

In December 2007, the Malaysian Chinese Muslim Association, together with the Islamic religious councils of seven states, filed a lawsuit against the Malay-language weekly, the *Catholic Herald* (published by the Catholic diocese of Kuala Lumpur) for using the word *Allah*. While the *Herald* is usually distributed only in Catholic churches, some Muslims complained that the offending word could also be found on the newspaper's website. The federal government agreed, saying that the word "Allah . . . could increase tension and create confusion among Muslims," and also ordered the *Herald* to print the word *terhad*—"restricted"—on its front page, meaning it could be distributed only to Christians.[3]

On December 31, 2009, a High Court ruled that Christians had a constitutional right to use the word *Allah*, although only because the *Herald* was focused on reaching Christians. This caused an uproar. The government called for calm, but quickly said it would appeal and, on January 6, 2010, the judge suspended her ruling pending an appeals-court decision.

In the uproar over these decisions, eleven churches were vandalized (some of them firebombed), a Sikh temple was attacked, pigs' heads were found in two mosques, and two young Muslims desecrated a holy communion wafer. There were also attacks on the Catholic *Herald*'s legal team, whose offices were vandalized.[4]

IMPEDING CHRISTIANITY

Malaysian governmental authorities are proud of the country's economic success, and its political leaders, such as former prime minister Abdullah Badawi, emphasize that the country is developing a modern Islam, a "Civilizational Islam" (*Islam Hadhar'i*). Article 3 of the constitution makes Islam "the religion of the Federation," while "other religions may be practiced in peace and harmony." Article 11 gives everyone "the right to profess and practice his religion and . . . to propagate it." In practice, however, systematic government restrictions and discrimination undercut this promise.

While Malaysia is more open than many other Muslim countries, and religious violence is rare, state and local governments are trying to shore up their electoral position by appealing to the majority Muslim population. One tactic increasingly in use is to discriminate against the 40 percent of the population who are not Muslim, as well as non-Sunni Muslims.

State governments frequently use their authority over the construction of non-Muslim places of worship and over land for non-Muslim cemeteries to impede or block Christian activity. The Selangor State government took twenty-eight years to approve the construction of the Roman Catholic Church of the Divine Mercy, and, even then, it was consigned to the grim Glenmarie Industrial Estate in the city of Shah Allam. In some new towns, such as Putrajaya, no non-Muslim religious centers have been allowed to be built.[5]

In Malaysia, religion is often closely related with ethnicity. The 10 percent of Malaysia's twenty-six million people who are Christians are mostly from the country's ethnic Chinese minority and, on the island of Borneo, the indigenous Orang Asli population, and this leads to discrimination. The state discriminates in housing, education, and employment in favor of ethnic Malays, who are legally defined as Muslims. Ethnic Malays, "Bumiputeras," are by law given special economic preferences: when selling homes, developers must allocate at least 30 percent of the units to Bumiputeras, and also give them a 10 percent discount. There is similar discrimination in education and business. Since ethnic Malays are defined as Muslim, the result is pervasive discrimination in favor of Muslims. There are also reports that government agencies are pressuring Orang Asli to convert to Islam.

Another general grievance is that religious authorities can confiscate bodies of the deceased before families can bury them, and may then bury the bodies according to Muslim practice if a sharia (Islamic) judge rules they were Muslim—a decision that requires only the word of one Muslim witness.[6]

BIBLES: "NOT FOR MUSLIMS"

The Malaysian government uses Section 7(1) of the 1984 Printing Presses and Publications Act to restrict or ban publications it believes contradict the official version of Islam. Between 2000 and July 2009, 397 books were banned, including *Islam at the Crossroads*, coauthored by Paul Marshall and Lela Gilbert, along with Roberta Green. In 2003, the government banned publication of a Bible in Iban, an indigenous language, ostensibly to prevent Christians from proselytizing, although the ban was later lifted. In 2005, Prime Minister Badawi proposed that Malay-language Bibles have "Not for Muslims" stamped on the front, be distributed only by churches or Christian bookshops, and be banned for use in Malay homes.[7]

In 1986, the Interior Security Ministry had prohibited the use of the word *Allah* in non-Islamic publications (the same law of which the *Catholic Herald* ran afoul). The claim is that its use could confuse Muslims. While this ban was rarely observed until 2007, the restriction was still highly unusual since *Allah* is the Arabic word for God. Arabic-speaking Christians have used it for centuries, as have Christians in neighboring Indonesia. No other country has such a ban, and even the restrictive Malaysian Islamic Party (PAS) says it opposes one. Apparently, the government thinks the Malay population is very easily confused; a position at odds with its claim that it represents an open, modern Islam. Worse, it insults Malaysia's energetic and increasingly educated population, implying they are not capable of dealing with different thoughts and ideas.

In March 2009, customs officials began seizing Christian books that contained the word *Allah*. Since neighboring Indonesia, whose language is similar to Malay, has Bibles with *Allah* in them, Indonesian Bibles and other Christian literature couldn't be imported to Malaysia. Eventually about thirty-five thousand Bibles were impounded, and the government said they could be released only if serial numbers and "For Christians Only" were stamped on the cover. Later the government said the Bibles would be released without serial numbers but with the words "For Christianity" on the cover, and that all future shipments must conform, and also bear an official seal and the words "by order of the Minister of Home Affairs." In March 2011, the government announced it would release the Bibles only if they said, "The Good News Bible is for the use of Christians only."[8]

Meanwhile, in 2010, Selangor State, using its sharia Criminal Offences Enactment of 1995, which carries prison sentences of up to two years, declared that non-Muslims could not use thirty-five "Islamic" terms, including *Allah*, *Firman Allah* (Allah's decree), *solat* (daily prayers), *Rasul* (prophet), *mubaligh* (missionary), *iman* (faith), and *haji* (Muslims who have done the pilgrimage).[9]

FORBIDDEN TO LEAVE ISLAM

Lina Joy was born into a Malaysian Muslim family in 1964 and named Azlina binti Jailani. In 1990, she began attending mass and, on May 11, 1998, was baptized into the Catholic Church. Soon after, she tried to marry a Catholic, but Malaysia's Civil Registry of Marriages denied her request because a registered Muslim could not marry a non-Muslim.

She then applied to change the name and religion on her identity card, but, although her name change to Lina Joy was granted, she could not change her official religion without the permission of an Islamic sharia court. Since the sharia courts had never granted such a request, and protesting that, as a Catholic, she was not under the sharia court's jurisdiction, she appealed to the civil courts. On April 18, 2001, a tribunal of the High Court ruled against her, saying that Malaysian Muslims were forbidden to renounce Islam. Although the constitution's Article 11 guarantees freedom of religion, the court ruled that this freedom must be construed harmoniously with other provisions, including the Islamic ban on apostasy. On September 15, 2005, the court of appeals also denied her request. Finally, on May 30, 2007, the Malaysian Federal Court upheld the verdicts.

Lina Joy was disowned by her family and fired from her sales job. She and her boyfriend, whom she is not allowed to marry, fled into hiding out of fear of Muslim extremists who have threatened her.[10]

Malaysia faces increasing controversy over conversions from Islam, whether to Christianity, Hinduism, Buddhism, or Sikhism. While there have been threats and detentions, these cases are usually addressed through a legal process. As a result, Muslims are usually barred from converting. Ten states—Terengganu, Kelantan, Selangor, Perak, Kedah, Malacca, Pahang, Negeri Sembilan, Johor, and Perlis—also have laws limiting the spread of other religions to Muslims. In Negeri Sembilan, a mufti must counsel applicants for conversion for a year and, if they still want to convert, a sharia judge might permit it. No other states have procedures to leave Islam; in some, attempted conversion is punishable by a fine or jail term. Sharia courts have ordered that applicants for conversion be detained for "rehabilitation."[11]

DANGEROUS POLITICAL TRENDS

These court cases and bans on words and Bibles have increased tensions, and radical Islamist groups are seeking to foment unrest. In 2008, after a court ruling that a Buddhist woman had never really become a Muslim and was still a Buddhist, Hizbut Tahrir Malaysia, an extremist Islamic group, protested outside the court and its president, Abdul Hakim Othman, declared, "In Islam, a person who insists on leaving the religion must be punished with death."[12]

In August 2011, the Damansara Utama Methodist Church (DUMC) in Petaling Jaya held a thanksgiving dinner for a charity that worked with HIV patients. In support of pan-Malaysian unity, the dinner included citizens of different races and religions. The Selangor State Islamic Religious Department found this deeply suspicious and the police raided the event. They gave no official explanation for the raid, but its defenders say it was undertaken to defend Islam, for fear there would be attempts to convert Muslims. Even though the Sultan of Selangor, Sharafuddin Idris Shah, concluded there was "insufficient" evidence of "proselytization," he nevertheless commanded Islamic officials to "provide counseling to Muslims who were involved in the said dinner, to restore their belief and faith in the religion of Islam."[13]

In 2011, there were signs that the governing parties, worried about losing Muslim support, were sowing suspicion of non-Muslims, especially Christians. On May 14, after the *Utusan Malaysia* newspaper claimed there was a conspiracy to turn Malaysia into a Christian state, Ibrahim Ali, leader of the three-hundred-thousand-member Pertubuhan Pribumi Perkasa Malaysia, which has ties to the governing coalition, threatened to wage a campaign against Christians.[14] Hasan Ali, executive councilor in charge of Islamic affairs in the state of Petaling Jaya, denounced apostasy and declared that Christians were using "solar-powered, talking Bibles to proselytize" Muslims.[15]

TURKEY

On April 18, 2007, three Protestant men were found tied up, tortured, stabbed, and strangled inside the office of Zirve Christian publishing house in Malatya. The victims were Necati Aydin and Ugur Yuksel, both Turkish Protestants who had converted from Islam, and Tilmann Geske, a German Protestant missionary. Their killers were five youths who were arrested as they ran from the crime scene.

The murder trial, which has dragged on since November 2007, has been explosive, not for any revelations about the actual crime but for what it has uncovered about connections between the crime, ultranationalist groups (called "Ergenekon") within the government, and those outside it. Court hearings have exposed a pervasive anti-Christian paranoia in both Turkish society and government. In December 2010, a defense lawyer stated in court that the victims were "planning to eliminate our religion, dividing up our country, bribing our people and financially supporting terror organizations," and shouted at the judges, "This is a Protestant court."[16] Mehmet Ulger, the gendarmerie commander at the time of the murders, admitted that while proselytism is legal in Turkey, the gendarmerie considered it to be an "extreme right-wing" activity, "the same as radical Islamic activity."[17] In March 2011, twenty people were detained in connection with the Malatya murders and the Ergenekon conspiracy.[18]

In his January 2007 column for the Armenian weekly newspaper *Agos*, editor in chief Hrant Dink wrote that he was made to feel like an "enemy of the Turkish state." His writings criticizing Turkey's treatment of Christians and other minorities had subjected the Turkish-Armenian writer to criminal charges and a conviction under Article 301 of the criminal code for "insulting Turkishness." During the previous year alone, he had received more than six thousand death threats. Dink did not stress Armenian nationalism and opposed European legislation criminalizing denial of the Armenian genocide. His writings did refer, however, to Turkey's 1915 "genocide" of Armenian Christians, and aimed to begin a national discussion on the cultural contribution of Turkey's Christian and Jewish architects, writers, and physicians—generally taboo subjects. His column concluded that "2007 is likely to be a hard year. . . . Who knows what other injustices I will be up against."[19]

This column was to be his last. Days later, on January 19, as he walked from his office onto a busy Istanbul street, he was shot in the head point-blank and died.

Five years later, Dink's murder case finally ended. On January 17, 2012, the Istanbul court handed down its verdict, acquitting all nineteen defendants accused of being part of an ideological criminal organization. No state involvement was found. Earlier, a juvenile court had convicted seventeen-year-old Ogun Samast for the murder. Before fleeing the scene, he had shouted, "I killed the non-Muslim," and "I shot him after saying the Friday prayers. I'm not sorry."[20]

He will likely complete his sentence by the time he is thirty.

During the investigation, it was discovered that an informant had provided police with information on the plot to kill Dink, but the police never followed up. Moreover, upon Samast's initial arrest, police detained him in a tearoom rather than a prison cell. There they lined up to have their photos taken with him, holding a calendar that read, "The soil of the motherland is holy, and it will not be abandoned."[21] Many in the international human rights community concluded that the failure of the court to find a broader plot defied the evidence. While many say this murder stemmed from nationalistic rather than religious motives, in Turkey, the two overlap.[22]

Straddling Europe and Asia, Turkey has an ancient Christian presence that has long struggled to survive in the midst of an overwhelmingly Muslim population. Beginning with the apostles, the church flourished for fourteen centuries in what today is Turkey, before suffering conquest, genocide, brutal population exchanges, pogroms, and many other persecutions. Then, roughly one hundred years ago, Turkey became a radically secular republic that stifled religion across the board and saw continued bloodshed.

Now a prosperous democracy under the rule of an Islamist party, modern Turkey is home to remnant Christian communities who find themselves at risk of being extinguished altogether. They suffer not so much from violence—though, as seen by the Dink and the Zirve publishing house murders, violence can occur—as from more sophisticated measures. They confront a dense web of legal regulations that thwart the ability of churches to survive and, in some cases, even to meet together for worship. These laws, aimed at promoting an extreme secular nationalism, also encourage a climate of animosity toward Christians, who are seen to defy "Turkishness," despite Christianity's two-thousand-year presence there.

HISTORICAL BACKGROUND

To grasp the plight of Turkey's Christian minorities, it is important to understand a little of this complex country's history.

With its fabled city of Istanbul—formerly known as Constantinople—Turkey has been the seat of both Christian and Muslim empires. Within its borders lie the ruins of Ephesus, the city of antiquity where Paul addressed the early Christians. For a thousand years, Constantinople was the preeminent center of Eastern Christianity and, for centuries after the Western Roman Empire collapsed, it was an ecclesial center for the Christian world.

In 1453, Constantinople city fell to the invading Sultan's armies, consolidating Muslim rule and civilization throughout Turkey. In the nearly five centuries of Islamic Ottoman rule that followed, Islam dominated all areas of life. Under the Ottoman *dhimmi* system, Christians and Jews were legally and socially subordinate to Muslims, but allowed to worship and to manage their personal affairs under their own religious courts.

As Ottoman rule collapsed between 1914 and 1923, a radically secular movement of "Young Turks" rose up and set in motion a "Turkification" program that dealt the Christian populations a devastating blow. Between them and the remnant Ottoman Empire, several million Armenian, Greek, and Assyrian Christians were targeted and eliminated from their ancestral homelands in Asia Minor. They were destroyed by genocide, massacres, and ruthlessly executed population exchanges. The Turkey subsequently founded in 1923 by Mustafa Kemal Ataturk, the "father of the Turks," rested on a rigid secular nationalism in which Turkishness became the defining feature of the state and all religious faiths were repressed.

In 2002, Turkey embarked on a new direction with the election of the Islamist Justice and Development Party (Adalet ve Kalkınma Partisi or AKP). Its popularity stems from its undoubted success in modernizing the country's economy, as well as its openness to public religious expression, which has especially helped Sunni Islam. But, after ten years in power, it has not fundamentally expanded religious freedom for Turkey's Christians or lifted the onerous state regulations that are dimming their prospects for survival.

Turkey's Christians—including Greek, Armenian, and Syriac Orthodox Christians, as well as Catholics and Protestants—have collectively dwindled to just 0.15 percent of the country's population of some 78 million people. As one Turkish church leader who requested anonymity told us, the Christian minority is an "endangered species."

TODAY'S DOUBLE THREATS

In today's Turkey, Christian communities confront two interrelated threats: First, they are suppressed by all-encompassing state restrictions on internal governance, education, houses of worship, and wider property rights, and the denial of legal status. They are in practice barred from operating seminaries and directly owning property. Largely through its Directorate of Religious Foundations, the state supervises and tries to control all Christian activity—meddling even in the title of the Greek Orthodox Church's ecumenical patriarch by refusing to recognize the term "ecumenical," and in elections for the acting Armenian patriarch.[23]

While Muslim women have recently won the freedom to wear headscarves in university classrooms, the state still forbids all Christians, with the exception of one leader from each faith tradition, from wearing religious garb anywhere in public. The Syriac metropolitan, Yusuf Cetin, told us that even the retired metropolitan was prohibited from wearing his religious dress in public.[24] Designed by radical secularists in the early twentieth century, such restrictive laws are now being systematically employed by Islamists to suppress Christianity.

Second, as confirmed by the Pew Forum on Religion and Public Life, social hostilities against Turkey's religious minorities run high. Such bigotry is reinforced by the official attitude of suspicion toward Christians. It is difficult even to have a frank national discussion about the plight of Christians in Turkey; those who have tried, like Hrant Dink, can face charges for insulting Turkishness. In commenting on the unlawful destruction by city officials of an Armenian house of worship in Malatya in February 2012, a Turkish writer observed:

> I am seriously concerned about the attitude of the Malatya Municipality. Most probably this is "local" retaliation against the French bill [criminalizing denial of the Armenian genocide]. Intolerance always operates like this. When your prime minister reacts strongly to something, then local authorities take a cue from it and act accordingly. And when local authorities do something, locals also get a message from their actions and act accordingly. This is quite dangerous.[25]

TRAINING OF CLERGY AND RELIGIOUS EDUCATION FOR THE YOUNG

A prime example of Turkey's oppressive regulatory regime is the government's refusal to allow Christian clergy to be trained in Turkey and, generally, its interference in religious education. Without the right to form leaders and educate the young, religious communities struggle to pass the faith from one generation to the next.

The Turkish state's forcible shuttering in 1971 of the Greek Orthodox Theological School of Halki—once the educational center for global Orthodox Christianity—is a case in point. Nestled in the Princes' Islands, it is built on the site of a Byzantine monastery belonging to the church for more than a thousand years. A four-decade-long international campaign to obtain its return, including appeals from several American presidents, has been to no avail. The fortieth year of its closing passed without the AKP returning it, despite high expectations that it would. The Orthodox, like Turkey's other Christian groups, have had no seminary within the country for more than forty years. A state regulation that the patriarch must have Turkish nationality complicates this problem. These policies threaten the very survival of the ecumenical patriarchate and its flock in Turkey, now numbering only seventeen hundred.[26]

Turkey's largest Christian community, the Armenian Orthodox Church, has only twenty-six priests to minister to its sixty-five thousand faithful. Because it also is barred from having a seminary, in 2006 the Armenian patriarch petitioned the education minister to allow the establishment of a state university faculty on Christian theology, including instruction by the patriarchate. The request was ignored. Seminary students must go to Lebanon or Armenia to study. There appears to be no political will on the part of Turkey's rulers to allow the training of Christian clergy and pastors.[27] Armenians and Greek Orthodox may have schools that meet strict state regulations, but other Christian groups may not have such schools. Muslim religion courses in state schools are mandatory—even Christians have difficulty getting exemptions—and Turkish history textbooks are antagonistic toward Armenian, Greek, and Syriac Christians.[28]

Even though missionary activities are legal, some government bodies criminalize missionary work and declare it a threat to society. The government's colossal Directorate of Religious Affairs (*Diyanet*)—with a $1.6 billion budget supported by all taxpayers, including Christians—supervises all the personnel and religious activities of the Muslim majority, including the content of Friday mosque sermons. It issued a sermon to be preached at seventy-five thousand mosques across Turkey on March 11, 2005, advising Muslims that Christian missionaries presented a clear danger to Turkey's national unity and integrity and that they were essentially agents of crusading powers that exploited weaknesses in Turkish society in order to destroy the state.[29]

The respected news service Forum 18 reported that the Directorate of Religious Affairs has stated:

> Today, rather than Christian priests, missionary activities are conducted by doctors, nurses, engineers, Red Cross workers, human rights defenders, volunteers for peace, language teachers, computer instructors, sports organizers, etc. . . . The Diyanet considers these activities as separatist and destructive

> since they may create a basis for a spiritual and cultural gap and distort our religious/national integrity in the long run, and considers it necessary that our citizens notify the Diyanet and all relevant government institutions about such activities.[30]

STATE DEPRIVES CHRISTIANS OF CHURCHES

The state's denial of property to churches goes to the heart of freedom of worship and religious practice. In thousands of cases, the government retains churches, seminaries, hospitals, schools, orphanages, and monasteries that were seized long ago. At times the state denies permission to acquire new church buildings. At other times it is still actively confiscating or destroying church property.

According to Turkish law, religious services can only take place in the house of worship of a legal religious group, as designated by the government. But other Turkish laws make it impossible for a Christian community to obtain recognition as a legal group. As in the Communist countries, Christians find themselves in a catch-22.

Turkey's five thousand Protestants have very few church buildings and frequently worship in house churches. In a 2012 interview, Protestant Association chair Zekai Tanyar expressed his frustrations in trying to get government permission for a place of worship:

> There has been dialogue several times but with no result. There is need for more talk. However, these visits do not go beyond polite stalling. . . . Churches find themselves shuttled between municipalities and governorships in their search for a solution to this problem. Even if one municipality responds positively, often the state Governor does not give approval. Sometimes the authorities respond with ridiculous excuses saying "there are not enough Christians in the neighbourhood." So are we supposed to do head counts and form ghettos?[31]

Under a new regulation, Turkey has established a legal process for reclaiming confiscated properties for the ecumenical patriarchate and for the Armenians, who, along with the Jews, are the only three non-Muslim minorities that Turkey is required to recognize (under the 1923 Lausanne Treaty that ended the post-World War I conflicts). Other Christian groups are simply not eligible. But even these two specially protected Christian groups cannot apply for properties confiscated between 1923 and 1936. And only a small fraction of the some fourteen hundred applications filed for churches, schools, and monasteries seized after 1936 have resulted in property returns so far.[32]

The ecumenical patriarch is waiting to hear about his requests to reclaim many of his community's churches, especially the Halki seminary and other religious properties, including twenty-three monasteries.[33] For a thousand years, his predecessors' cathedral was the magnificent Church of Hagia Sophia in Istanbul, built by the Byzantine emperor Justinian I in the sixth century, which many regard as the most inspiring Christian church in the world, and which, like Turkey's other churches, the Ottomans converted into a mosque. Ataturk then turned it into a museum, and its grandeur continues to awe thousands of visitors every day. Since it is a state museum, worship in this great church is forbidden. The patriarch must now lead services in a decidedly smaller and undistinguished church attached to the crowded compound where he lives in a run-down Istanbul neighborhood. The state bars the Greek Orthodox Church from acquiring other property.

Meanwhile, in an ominous sign, in November 2011, another Hagia Sophia church was converted by the state into a mosque. This church, in Iznik, south of Istanbul, rests on no ordinary site. The place was formerly called Nicaea, which is where the first Christian ecumenical council met, at the Hagia Sophia church in 325. This is where the Nicene creed was formulated. Like Istanbul's Hagia Sophia, the church at Iznik had been a museum for the past one hundred years, though not formally registered as such.[34]

The ecumenical patriarchate has won a property transfer in recent years: in November 2010, when Turkey returned the rights of the Buyukada orphanage on the Princes' Islands. Originally deeded to the patriarchate in 1902, the orphanage was expropriated by the state in 1999, resulting in a lengthy legal battle, which the government eventually lost in the European Court of Human Rights. It, however, was a largely symbolic victory for the patriarchate, since there are no orphans now in need of such shelter. The facility will be turned into an interreligious studies center and an environmental protection observatory.[35]

In an incident just days earlier, seventy-eight graves were desecrated in a Greek Orthodox cemetery on the island of Gokceada, where the current ecumenical patriarch, Bartholomew I, was born and raised. He linked the two events, seeing "a ray of hope in the solution of our problems, and now these sad events occur again. . . . Whenever we want to breathe in peace, something like this happens. But the Church . . . won't cease to fight for her survival in Turkey."[36]

In a meeting with USCIRF in February 2011, the Syriac Orthodox metropolitan Yusuf Cetin verified that his community has only one church in Istanbul, where almost 90 percent of Turkey's twenty thousand Syriacs now live, having been driven by violence from their ancestral areas in the southeast. Also known as Arameans, the Syriacs still speak Aramaic, the language of Jesus. Their former lands have been seized and resettled by locals who mostly are unwilling to return it. That their problem has not ended is demonstrated by the recent Turkish government seizure of property from the sixteen-hundred-year-old Mor Gabriel Monastery, the world's oldest Syriac Orthodox monastery and an important pilgrimage site—a second Jerusalem—for the Syriacs. In January 2010, Turkey's Supreme Court granted the state's treasury parts of the monastery's land.[37]

The Istanbul Syriac Orthodox community's sole church, which we have visited, is average-sized and grossly inadequate to meet the community's needs. It depends on other faith groups to lend them space to hold services and perform marriages, baptisms, and funerals, which, as the metropolitan bishop pointed out, are difficult to reserve far in advance. Bishop Cetin said that an application is pending with the government to build a second church, but the community was told that it requires approval by the Defense Ministry because the site is near the airport. The bishop told USCIRF he fears that, without more space in Istanbul to perform baptisms and marriages, the faithful will lose touch with their rituals and will drift away from the church. Thus, red tape continues to suffocate the church's ministry.[38]

In July 2011, Turkey's government permitted, for the first time in ninety years, the Syriac community to hold a service at Mor Petrus and Mor Paulos Church in the eastern province of Adiyaman, which drew hundreds of Syriac Christians from across Turkey. Similarly, the ecumenical patriarch of the Greek Orthodox Church was allowed to celebrate the divine liturgy at the Sumela monastery near Trabzon in August 2010, and again in 2011. And the Armenian Orthodox were allowed to hold services in their one-thousand-year-old church on Lake Van in September 2010 and in September 2011. These changes are to be welcomed; but still, each church was permitted one liturgy, once a year. This falls far short of any definition of freedom of worship.[39]

AN UNDERCURRENT OF VIOLENCE

Violence against Christians has been rare in recent years, but some recent high-profile murders and plots, by ultranationalists but with Islamist undertones, have also come to light.

In 2006, Father Andrea Santoro of Trabzon was shot to death as he prayed in church. Convicted in the murder was a fifteen-year-old boy, who claimed he was avenging a Danish newspaper's publication of caricatures of Muhammad.[40] Bishop Luigi Padovese, who served as the Vicar Apostolic for Anatolia and had previously expressed concern over rising anti-Christian sentiment, spoke during his memorial mass, saying, "As long as television programs and newspaper articles produce material that shine a bad light on Christians and show them as enemies of Islam (and vice versa), how can we imagine a climate of peace?"[41]

Several weeks later a priest in Izmir was attacked by so-called nationalist youths, barely escaping with his life. Another priest was attacked in Mersin, causing Bishop Padovese to exclaim, "We are no longer safe here."[42] Several months later, another Roman Catholic priest was attacked, this time in Samsun.[43]

Four years later, just a day after meeting with Turkish authorities to discuss the problems of Turkey's Christians, Bishop Padovese was stabbed to death and nearly decapitated by his driver, who reportedly shouted "Allah Akhbar!" He then reportedly boasted that he had killed "the great Satan!"[44] Authorities rushed to conclude that the driver was mentally unstable. Turkish authorities labeled the confessed killer, Murat Altun, as psychologically disturbed, and not motivated by political or religious agendas. Soon after, reports were leaked to the media suggesting the driver was not a Muslim but a convert to Catholicism and that Padovese had forced Altun into a homosexual relationship. Izmir's Archbishop Ruggero Franceschini, who succeeded Padovese as head of Turkey's Catholic Church, angrily rejected these "pious lies" as "intolerable rumors circulated by the very instigators of the crime."[45]

Archbishop Franceschini stated that he believes Padovese's murder, like attacks on other Christians in Turkey, was orchestrated by ultranationalist, often secular groups. Attacks on Catholic priests have continued. In April 2011, Reverend Francis Dondu of Aziz Pavlus Latin Italian Catholic Church in Adana narrowly escaped an attempt on his life by two sword-wielding suspects.[46]

Having arrived with Western missionaries in the nineteenth century, Protestantism is regarded as a foreign presence on Turkish soil, so much so that Protestant Christians are placed in a different legal category entirely, one with even fewer rights than other Christians. Although evangelization is legal in Turkey, Christians—even Turkish citizens—who seek to spread their faith are often regarded as subversive threats. Antimissionary rhetoric increased in 2005, when the wife of the late prime minister Bulent Ecevit was quoted claiming that the infiltration of Christians into Turkey was part of a Western plot to destroy the state: "Our citizens are being Christianised through various means. America tops the list of those who await the increase of Christian population in

Turkey. America thinks that if the Christian population increases, it would be easier to dismantle Turkey."[47]

Of the nearly five hundred thousand Syriacs in southeastern Turkey in the early twentieth century, only twenty-five hundred remain in that area. More than sixty unsolved murders of local Syriacs from the 1970s to the early 2000s caused the population to flee.[48] Murder plots have also been uncovered against the ecumenical patriarch. In June 2010, authorities arrested Ismet Rençber for plotting his assassination.[49] Murat-Yetkin, editor-in-chief of Turkey's leading *Hürriyet Daily News*, upon hearing the verdict in the murder case of Hrant Dink, wrote:

> It is important that Dink's murderer has been convicted. It is no less important to try to deal with this atmosphere of hatred—that will take more time and effort.[50]

THE AREA ADMINISTERED BY TURKISH CYPRIOTS OR TURKISH MILITARY IN CYPRUS

In 1974, Turkey invaded and occupied the northern third of the Republic of Cyprus—the only Christian majority country left in the Eastern Mediterranean and a member of the European Union. Turkey's army of about forty thousand troops still presides over a relentless eradication of all traces of Christian civilization in northern Cyprus.

Apart from a few Greek Orthodox enclaves with about 350 residents in all, the north, once religiously diverse, is now entirely Muslim. Few traces of the two-thousand-year-old presence of Christianity remain intact. The Turkish military fails to protect either the northern churches or the cemeteries and monasteries left behind when the Christian communities fled to the south after the invasion, from looting, destruction, and decay.[51]

In the north, five hundred Greek Orthodox, Armenian, and Maronite churches and monasteries, some dating to the fourth century and with innumerable sacred and sometimes priceless mosaics, frescoes, icons, vessels, and other objects within them, have been lost or desecrated. Byzantine art pieces by the thousands have been stolen and sold on the international black market.[52]

We have walked through some of these churches, including St. George and St. Andronikas, and found them in ruins. Filled with trash, stripped of their religious frescoes, and overgrown with weeds, it is only a matter of time before they are erased completely. With their roofs and windows broken, they are open to the elements and have become roosting places for pigeons and secret hangouts for teenagers. Some are used for nonreligious purposes—one as a Turkish bath, another as a storage place, and yet another as a barn for livestock. The great cathedral of St. Sophia has been converted into a mosque.

These sacred sites belong to the churches based in the southern part of Cyprus, but northern controlling authorities prevent their members from returning to restore them or even to hold worship services in them. The Turkish military only allows access to churches in military areas on a limited basis, generally once a year for specific religious festivals.[53]

An Armenian representative told us that his community had recently been allowed to visit their major monastery in the north on its August 15 feast day, but only on that day and only to hold a picnic on its grounds, not to hold communal prayer. Other Christian Cypriots told us that, though they were married in one of the north's now-decaying churches and their parents are buried in its now-broken cemetery, they cannot get permission to do maintenance work.[54] Apostolos Andreas Monastery, a UNESCO-designated site on the very tip of the Karpaz Peninsula in northern Cyprus, is still allowed to be used for services, but it also badly needs repairs to its leaking roof. Northern authorities have created impediments blocking the Orthodox Church from fixing the roof, much less going ahead with the overall restoration, for which the United States government and others have offered funding.[55]

May 2, 2011, saw the demolition of the two-hundred-year-old

Greek Orthodox Chapel of Saint Thekla in the northern village of Vokolida. "Local Turkish Cypriot authorities have generally failed to take adequate measures to protect religious places of worship from vandals and looters," said USCIRF chair, Leonard Leo. He went on to emphasize, "Allowing the demolition of the Saint Thekla chapel exemplifies the ongoing disrespect and violations by Turkish troops and local Turkish Cypriot authorities for the religious freedom and heritage of Greek Orthodox and other religious minority communities in the northern part of Cyprus."[56]

There is greater access to religious sites in the northern areas not directly controlled by the Turkish military, but wide restrictions, including some against worshipping, still exist. On Christmas Day 2010, Father Zacharias, the only Greek Cypriot priest who is permitted by northern authorities to reside in the northern part, was stopped in the midst of the Christmas Liturgy at St. Sinesios Church, which serves the enclave Christian community. The local authorities forced the congregation out of the building, claiming that special permission was needed since Christmas did not fall on a Sunday that year. Father Zacharias told us this was the first time in thirty-six years that they were unable to hold a service at the church and the first time the church was required to seek permission.[57]

USCIRF raised this issue with northern authorities and the permission requirement was changed. Authorities decreed that Greek Orthodox Cypriots could henceforth hold services on any day and at any time in the few churches already in use. Permission to hold a worship service is still required—and exceedingly difficult to obtain—for the churches and monasteries that are not in use, or for priests other than the *two* state-authorized ones to serve the north, or for congregations coming from the south.[58]

With its flag conspicuously planted and its troops ever present, Turkey, which alone recognizes the north as a separate country from the rest of Cyprus, is the looming reality in northern Cyprus. On its watch, Christian practice is being suppressed, sometimes directly by strict prohibitions and sometimes by a frustrating and shifting regime of bureaucratic regulations. All vestiges of

Christianity's rich cultural history there are being destroyed, dismantled, and erased.

MOROCCO

Thirty-three Christian foreign residents were deported from Morocco in March 2010. At the same time the Moroccan government also declared at least eighty-one other Christians personae non gratae. Many of those arrested were long-term residents. Among the foreigners ejected, fourteen adults and eleven children were from the Village of Hope (VOH) Orphanage in Ain Leuh, a village near Ifrane. This unprecedented government intervention effectively closed down the facility.

In this process, the authorities seized thirty-three Moroccan children, tearing them away from their foreign guardians—the only parents they had ever known. These boys and girls were reportedly interrogated for two days about their faith. Subsequently, they were permanently removed from the custody of their guardians, including three with special needs.

In total in the 2010 incident, the Moroccan government deported or declared personae non gratae, without due process, approximately one hundred and fifty Christian foreign residents from nineteen countries, all for alleged proselytizing.[59]

Morocco has a population of 34.8 million of which 98.7 percent are Muslim, 1.1 percent are Christian, and 0.2 percent are Jewish.[60] It is one of the most religiously open countries in the Muslim world and the first to recognize American independence. The current government has explained that in the 2010 deportations it was simply cracking down on legally forbidden proselytizing by foreign residents. But many of those forced to leave were deported on the grounds of "threatening public order," a charge requiring no documentation of illegal activities under the state's Immigration Act. On April 17, 2010, the High Council of Ulema, consisting of seven thousand Muslim religious leaders, supported the deportations by signing a document that termed the work of Christians in Morocco as "moral rape" and "religious terrorism."[61]

During that same year Christians—both citizens and foreign residents—reported harassment, surveillance, and detention and interrogation by the government, along with social persecution. During the period of heightened suppression, the government also confiscated Bibles and other Christian literature from libraries and bookstores throughout the country.[62] Christians who come for business or as tourists, residents, and students are generally welcome and can feel secure in Morocco as long as they keep their Christian faith to themselves.

ALGERIA

Siaghi Krimo, an Algerian Christian, was arrested on April 14, 2011, for allegedly proselytizing a neighbor, who complained to police that Krimo had tried to convert him to Christianity by giving him a CD. The police searched Krimo's house and confiscated his Bible, CDs, and computer. The prosecutor requested that the suspect be sentenced to two years in prison and fined fifty thousand dinars (US$690).

The Christian community was stunned on May 4, when the judge sentenced Siaghi—without a witness or any evidence whatsoever—to the maximum sentence possible: five years in prison and a fine of 200,000 dinars (US$2,760). On December 15, 2011, Siaghi's appeal was postponed indefinitely due to lack of evidence. Fortunately, he is not required to serve the lower court's sentence unless the appellate court affirms his conviction, but his future is uncertain.[63]

Algeria's history is bloodstained. A war during the 1990s, in which the government ultimately prevailed over several indigenous Islamist groups, took more than one hundred thousand lives, mostly those of Muslims. The powerful film *Of Gods and Men* relates the story of seven Trappist monks who were brutally murdered for their faith by Algerian Islamist terrorists in 1996, during this period. The church has deep roots in the area; it was once home to St. Augustine of Hippo. Today, the state's constitution declares Islam the state religion, but it also provides for freedom of belief and opinion and for the right of citizens to establish institutions whose aims include protecting fundamental liberties. However, the constitution also prohibits institutions from engaging in behavior incompatible with Islamic morality.

Additional laws limit freedom for non-Muslims, who include somewhere from ten thousand to fifty thousand Christians of a total population of thirty-six million, 99 percent of whom are Sunni Muslims. One ordinance requires all religious activity to be regulated by the state, and it mandates that worship by members of non-Muslim faiths be practiced only in state-approved locations. A request for non-Muslim worship must be submitted to the governor at least five days before any such event, and must be held in a building that is open to the public. Additionally, all religious faiths are required to register with the state through the government's National Commission for Non-Muslim Religious Services.[64]

On October 29, 2011, six Algerian Christians were arrested before their morning prayer service in a private apartment. They were accused of worshipping in an unregistered location, and of proselytizing and blasphemy. The arrests took place in a village near Bougous; the Christians were reportedly part of the Protestant Church of Algeria. Although this denomination is registered with the state, many small local congregations are not separately registered. The six Christians' legal situation is not clear at the time of this writing.[65]

Proselytizing is a criminal offense. It carries a punishment of one to three years' imprisonment and fines for non-clergy, and three to five years in jail and double fines for religious leaders. The law applies to anyone who "incites, constrains, or utilizes any means of seduction tending to convert a Muslim to another religion."[66]

JORDAN

In March 2008, relatives who then reported him to the authorities savagely beat Jordanian Christian Muhammad Abbad Abbad, who had converted from Islam fifteen years before. He was taken to the Sweilih Islamic court without legal representation and charged with apostasy. Sentenced to one week of imprisonment for contempt of court, Muhammad and his immediate family fled the country. On April 22, 2008, the court found Muhammad guilty of apostasy. It annulled his marriage and declared him to be without any religious identity. Despite the fact the family had left the country, Jordan issued arrests orders against them. As of November 2010, the family remained in another location.[67]

The Hashemite Kingdom of Jordan, as it is officially known, is a constitutional monarchy, with King Abdullah II holding broad executive powers. Precariously situated between Iraq to the east, Israel and the West Bank to the west, Syria to the north, and Egypt to the southwest, Jordan vacillates between autocracy and semi-democratic rule. The constitution provides the freedom to practice religious rites unless they violate public order or morality and also bans discrimination based on religion. It also establishes Islam as the state religion and mandates that the king be Muslim. The Christian community, comprising 1.5 to 3 percent of a total population of 6.3 million mostly Sunni Muslims, is relatively free for the region: the major problems occur around the conversion of Muslims.

Neither the constitution nor the penal code nor civil legislation explicitly bans conversion from Islam or evangelizing Muslims. However, for Muslims, laws concerning religion, marriage, divorce, child custody, and inheritance are under the exclusive jurisdiction of sharia Islamic courts. Other religious groups, including Christians, have their own special religious tribunals. The Islamic courts have always ruled against the right of Muslims to adopt a different religion or belief, and the consequences for conversion include societal discrimination, mental and physical abuse by family members, and the loss of civil rights.

At least twenty-seven foreign individuals and families suspected of evangelical activities were deported or denied residence permits in 2007 alone. Two Egyptian pastors, from officially recognized Christian denominations, were among the many expelled. One, Sadeq Abde, married to a Jordanian woman and father of two children, was handcuffed, blindfolded, and placed on a ferry to Egypt. The other, also married to a Jordanian woman and father of three, was arrested, held for three days, and put on a boat to Egypt.[68]

YEMEN

In 2009, armed Islamist extremists kidnapped nine Christian foreigners working at the Protestant-run Jumhuri hospital near Saada. Three women—a Korean and two Germans—were killed immediately. The six remaining hostages included a British man named Anthony and a German family—two parents and three young children between the ages of two and six. Some Yemeni officials attributed the kidnappings and murders to forces linked to an Al-Qaeda group working with Shia rebels.

In May 2010, the two girls from the German family, Lydia Hentschel and her younger sister Anna, were found and rescued by Saudi and Yemeni security forces during a Saudi border raid in a disputed border region between Yemen and Saudi Arabia. The girls were quickly taken back to Germany. However, the whereabouts of the girls' parents, Johannes and Sabine Hentschel, and of their two-year-old brother Simon, as well as the Briton Anthony, remain unknown. A family spokesperson has said that Simon is probably dead since he was not found with his sisters.

Reports have suggested extremists targeted the foreigners based on rumors that they were missionaries engaged in proselytizing.[69]

Yemen has long been torn asunder by religious, political, and tribal unrest between Muslim groups, including Shia Zaydis and Sunni Salafis, a dozen rival political parties, and southern secessionists. Recently, during the Arab Spring uprisings in 2011, tensions escalated further, with protests and violent demonstrations taking place between the government and opposition groups, including Al-Qaeda in the Arabian Peninsula, which makes its base in Yemen. In late November 2011, President Ali Abdullah Saleh agreed to step down, transfer some powers to the vice president, and call for an election in February 2012. On February 21, 2012, acting president Abd Rabbuh Mansur al-Hadi—the only candidate—was elected president; meanwhile, the country remains fragmented and violent.

The constitution declares Islam as the state religion and Islamic law the source of all legislation. Overwhelmingly its twenty-three million people are Muslim, with an estimated three thousand Christians who are largely refugees and temporary foreign residents. While the government allows the possession of non-Islamic religious literature, quantities deemed too large for personal use are confiscated. The government detains those who own the literature on the grounds of proselytizing Muslims, which is prohibited; and under Islamic law, as interpreted in Yemen, conversion by a Muslim is punishable by death.[70]

PALESTINIAN TERRITORIES

Ahmad El-Achwal was a Christian convert from Islam, a father of eight who lived in the West Bank near Nablus. He was first arrested on false charges of possessing stolen gold. Although the only gold in the house was Ahmad's daughter's tiny necklace—a gift from her grandfather—the Palestinian Authority officers who stormed his house were not convinced. The PA imprisoned Ahmad in a small cell, where he was left for days without food or water. Meanwhile, he was tortured so severely that he required prolonged treatment in a hospital. Photos of his abuses revealed severe burns on his back, buttocks, and legs.

Still Ahmad's enthusiasm about his new Christian life was unabated. After his release from the hospital, he started a small house church in his home, where he distributed Bibles and Christian literature. Sometimes Muslims attended. Over a seven-year period, Ahmad was arrested repeatedly, and his Bibles and Christian publications confiscated. He lost his business and continued to receive death threats. He eventually moved to Jerusalem for employment and safety. But, whenever he returned to visit his family in the West Bank, his enemies sought him out, beat him, torched his car, and firebombed a relative's home.

Ultimately, Ahmad's story had a tragic ending. He was shot dead by masked gunmen in January 2004. His killers have never been brought to justice.[71]

The Palestinian Territories include the West Bank and the Gaza Strip. The West Bank has a population of 2.7 million, including approximately 300,000 Israelis, while Gaza is home to about 1.5 million. East Jerusalem has been under Israeli control since 1967 and, in 1980, Israel formally annexed East Jerusalem and Israeli law applies there.[72] Together these three areas—West Bank, Gaza, and East Jerusalem—are thought to have some 50,000 to 55,000 Christians.

The primary threat to religious freedom is not the political authorities per se, but rather the near anarchy due to violence instigated by individuals and mobs—sometimes called the "Muslim mafia"—who operate undeterred by Palestinian policing.[73] Clans, militias, and families, as well as religious and political factions, battle for power, prestige, and financial support. Because they are not Muslim, Christians are sometimes used as scapegoats, labeled as "Zionist collaborators" and accused of cooperation with the Israelis. Such incidents have contributed to large numbers of Christians fleeing the territories, resulting in a dramatic decline in the Christian population. Up to the mid-2000s, Christians faced serious harassment, sometimes even torture and imprisonment, from both the Palestinian Authority and Hamas officials. Though violence appears to have declined since the Second

Intifada, brutal attacks on Christians continue and are frequently not reported.[74]

In October 2007, Rami Ayyad, who operated a Christian bookstore in Gaza, was abducted and murdered. Before the attack, Ayyad had been publicly accused of engaging in missionary activities.[75] Since Hamas seized power in Gaza in 2007 and as word spread of Rami Ayyad's murder and of other abuses, many Christians fled Gaza, and the Christian population there has declined considerably.

CONCLUSION

Malaysia has long prided itself on developing a modern Islam and is indeed among the most open Muslim countries. There is little violence directed against Christians and other minorities there. However, this situation has been faltering, and intolerance is increasing. As mentioned, Malaysia is now in the ignominious position of being the only country in the world to try to ban Christians from using the name Allah and other "Islamic" words. Politics is also becoming more polarizing. On November 29, 2011, Ahmad Maslan, a deputy minister from the United Malays National Organization, the dominant party in the governing coalition, claimed Islam would be "lost" if the opposition advanced in the upcoming election: "Say goodbye to Islam, because they are agents of Christianization."[76] If some Malaysian politicians provoke further division while striving for political gain, the future will indeed be bleak for the religious minorities, including the Christians, and for the country.

Turkey is admired for its growing economy and stable democracy, and is often upheld as a model for other Muslim nations, particularly those in the Arab world. Yet it is also known for its regulatory oppression of Christian minorities, pervasive controls on all religions, and culture of impunity, which are all contributing to the decline in the numbers of Turkey's Christians. These, as well as other factors, prompted USCIRF to recommend in 2012 that

Turkey be added to the US government's list of the world's worst violators of religious freedom, as a Country of Particular Concern.[77]

To be sure, the AKP government has ushered in some improvements for Christians, including additional permission for worship services, citizenship for denominational leaders, and accurate national identity cards for converts. But Christians are still deeply burdened by state restrictions on having churches, seminaries, and schools; on wearing religious garb; on their ability to even talk about their cultural contributions; and on governing themselves. Their leaders have been threatened and some even murdered in recent years, leaving their fragile and historically traumatized communities insecure and increasingly pessimistic about their future. Turkey's Christian communities struggle for survival even into the next generation. Turkey is a member of NATO and the Council of Europe, and a US ally. Western churches should use this leverage to help preserve Turkey's Christian communities and Cyprus's Christian patrimony.

At the time of writing, when the Near East region is politically unstable, Morocco, Algeria, Jordan, Yemen, and the Palestinian territories all face uncertain futures. Meanwhile, Libya, Tunisia, and Syria have been roiled by popular uprisings, civil wars, violence, and, in the first two countries, regime change, as well as the possibility of further bloodshed. It is likely that radicalized Islamists will gain greater influence in some of these countries, as has already taken place in Egypt. These profound changes in government and the rise of Islamist groups undoubtedly foretell difficult times ahead for Christian minorities.

SIX

THE MUSLIM WORLD: POLICIES OF PERSECUTION

Saudi Arabia / Iran

IN MAY 2008, IRAN ARRESTED TEN PEOPLE IN CONNECTION WITH conversions to Christianity, including Mohsen Namvar, who had been arrested and tortured in 2007 for baptizing a Muslim who wanted to become Christian. He was arrested again in May 2008 and so severely tortured that he continued to suffer fever, severe back pain, high blood pressure, uncontrollable shaking of his limbs, and short-term memory loss. He and his family have subsequently found refuge in Turkey, a country that is almost entirely Muslim but whose courts, unlike Iran's, do not punish converts to Christianity. Eight other converts were also arrested in Shiraz that month and later released.[1]

On November 16, 2008, a Saudi sharia court sentenced to death a Filipino man identified only as "Pablo," who had been arrested on March 24, 2007, for blasphemy, based on accusations of "mocking the name of the Prophet Mohammad." In July 2010, the court commuted his sentence to five years' imprisonment and five hundred lashes. Eventually, the former trailer driver received a royal pardon and was deported, arriving back in Manila on October 10, 2011. What kind of horrors he suffered in the interim can only be guessed.[2]

On July 26, 2008, Iran's Ministry of Intelligence and Security agents attacked a house-church in the town of Malek, in the suburbs of Isfahan, arresting eight men, six women, and two children. The detainees included a couple in their sixties, who were savagely beaten and had to be taken to intensive care in Shariati Hospital in Isfahan. They both died shortly thereafter.[3] On August 9, 2008, a Christian Kurd, Shahin Zanboori, was arrested in the southwestern city of Arak. To obtain information on other converts, Zanboori says police hung him from the ceiling and beat his feet. His arm and leg were broken during interrogations.[4] One young woman convert, who used the pseudonym Caty, was beaten so severely by her family that she is at risk of permanent disability from spinal injury.[5]

When surveying stories such as these, it should not surprise us that the respected Pew Research Center found that most of the countries with the highest levels of religious persecution are Muslim majority states.[6] The story of current persecution of Christians in the Muslim world is indeed extensive. It is so widespread in fact that we have had to devote four chapters to it.

The previous chapter looked at general repression by Muslim governments. This chapter covers only two countries, Saudi Arabia and Iran, which are bitter enemies and compete for religious influence within the Muslim world, with Saudi Arabia pushing its reactionary Wahhabi Sunni tradition and Iran its strict Twelver Shia beliefs. A leaked 2008 State Department cable reported that the Saudi ambassador, quoting the Saudi king, urged America's General Petraeus to "cut off the head of the snake," meaning Iran. A bomb plot by Iran to kill the Saudi ambassador in a Washington restaurant, which was thwarted in 2011, illustrates the two states' high-stakes rivalry.

Saudi Arabia allows no churches or non-Muslim places of worship of any kind within its borders, and requires all Saudis be Muslims. The kingdom's continuous religious cleansing means that its Christian community consists almost entirely of foreign workers and diplomats.

For its part, Iran subjects Christians, as well as other minorities, to severe state pressures. As a result, the numbers of Christians, as well as Jews, Baha'is, and Zoroastrians, have plummeted over the last several decades. There are reports of an increasing number of Iranian Muslims converting to Christianity, for which they face risk of execution.

Since 1979, both of these states have used their petrodollars to try to influence Muslim communities abroad to be similarly intolerant. Because of its greater wealth and the fact Sunnis constitute some 90 percent of the Muslim world, Saudi Arabia is making a significant impact in spreading its wrathful brand of Wahhabi Islam.

SAUDI ARABIA

For ten years, Pastor Yemane Gebriel led a three-hundred-member underground house church in Riyadh. A father of eight, the native Eritrean had also worked as a private driver in Saudi Arabia for twenty-five years. Gebriel reported to Compass Direct News that on January 10, 2009, he found an unsigned note on his vehicle threatening to kill him unless he left the country. Three days later, Saudi religious policeman Abdul Aziz, who is also a sheikh at the local mosque, accompanied by other men, forced him from his van and told him to get out of the country.

On January 15, Aziz again approached Gebriel, berating him for being a Christian and trying to convert Muslims. "He finished by telling Yemane to get out of the country or 'measures' would be taken," said a Compass Direct News source, who requested anonymity for security reasons. That night, four masked men in a car cut off the van he was driving, and again warned, "We will kill you if you don't go away from this place—you must leave here or we will kill you."

After consulting consular officials, the pastor quickly made an escape from Riyadh. A local Christian source thought it was no idle threat: "The . . . circumstances remind me very much of the machine-gun murder of Irish Roman Catholic layman Tony Higgins right here in Riyadh in August 2004."[7]

Professor Camille Eid of the University of Milan said in a 2011 interview that, despite the kingdom's strict law that all Saudis be Muslim, there were some converts. He follows Arabic media call-in programs that broadcast into the region and noted that many calls come from Saudi Arabia. About the Saudi converts, he observed:

> Those converts who travel to Morocco and Egypt talk about their experience but do not mention their names and request only that the Christian community pray for them because they desire to see the day when they will be allowed to go to a church, to be able to have access to the Gospels and to be able to share their new faith with their own family. If a convert informs his/her brother or father of his/her new faith, he or she faces the danger of being charged with treason by the family; a treason not only of one's family but also to the nation and society in general. Apostasy is a question of honor and as such it is considered treason.[8]

SAUDI CHURCHES BANNED

Saudi Arabia bans all churches and public manifestations of Christianity, as well as other non-Muslim religions. It does not even permit churches that are state regulated. Moreover, secret congregations that pray together in private homes risk being raided and shut down, and seeing their members flogged, beaten, jailed, deported, or even killed. The only secure prayer services are ones quietly held in US and various European embassies for their nationals, or those hidden deep within the gated compounds of Western oil companies for their employees. In March 2012, Saudi Arabia's Grand Mufti Abdulaziz ibn Abdullah Al al-Sheikh, who holds his high cabinet level post by appointment from the king, issued a religious fatwa declaring it "necessary to destroy all the churches" in the region, including those outside of Saudi Arabia itself.[9]

The entire country has long been "cleansed" of its historical indigenous Christian community, and no trace of its old churches exists. Christian and Western leaders have repeatedly asked for a church in Saudi Arabia. At the Saudi monarch's behest, Pope John Paul II petitioned Rome's city council to permit the construction of a mosque there, which it subsequently did, and moreover donated 7.5 acres of woodland on which it could be built. Saudi Arabia put up 80 percent of the costs of construction and, in 1995, Rome's mosque, Europe's largest, opened to wide publicity.[10] Yet, despite repeated papal appeals, Riyadh has never reciprocated. Nor has it even so much as allowed a Catholic priest to permanently reside in order to administer the sacraments to the large foreign population.

Bibles cannot be distributed. Christian signs and symbols cannot be displayed; religious garb, rosaries, crosses, and even red roses on St. Valentine's Day all are prohibited. When an Italian soccer team came to play a game in the kingdom, they had to blot out part of the cross—the logo on the team's uniform—turning it into a stroke instead. One year, in the American school, a Santa Claus was almost arrested; he only managed to escape through a window. Overhead highway signs indicate "Muslim only" roads to warn non-Muslims that they are prohibited from entering the Muslim holy cities of Mecca and Medina.

Islam, specifically the hard-line Sunni Wahhabi version, has been the official religion and ruling ideology of the Saudi state since its founding in 1932. All Saudis are required to be Muslim. A strict monarchy, Saudi Arabia defines itself as an Islamic state; its law is sharia along with royal decrees, and the Qur'an is declared to be the constitution. The monarchy-funded Wahhabi religious establishment controls the court system and much of the policing.

In court cases, compensation for Christian plaintiffs is legally required to be half that awarded to Muslims.

Camille Eid recounted:

> All residents are subjected to this [sharia] law and you cannot object because it is tantamount to objecting to Islam. Upon arrival at the airport you are informed immediately that you are to abide by the strict Islamic laws. I as a Christian, for instance, had a Pepsi in my hand during Ramadan. I noticed

> that everybody was looking at me in a certain way and they could have beaten me. You cannot eat outside or in public during the fast. You can only eat in secret. So you have to observe the fast even if you are not Muslim because that is the law.[11]

RELIGIOUS BIGOTRY AND INCITEMENT TO VIOLENCE

Some state-sponsored imams regularly incite violence against Christians and Jews in their sermons. In 2011, Sheikh Salman Al-Oudah denounced these imams for praying for "the destruction and total annihilation of non-Muslims," and said such calls were against Islamic law.[12] Nevertheless, mosque speakers continue to pray for the death of Christians and Jews, including at Mecca's Grand Mosque and at the Prophet's Mosque in Medina, where they serve at the pleasure of King Abdullah, whose official title is "Custodian of the Two Holy Mosques." The State Department reports it is "common for preachers in mosques, including the mosques of Mecca and Medina, to end Friday sermons with a prayer for the well-being of Muslims and for the humiliation of polytheism and polytheists," Christians being included among "polytheists" because of their belief in the Trinity.[13]

State schools teach students to "hate" Christians as "infidels" and to view them as "enemies." National textbooks instruct, "The struggle of this [Muslim] nation with the Jews and Christians has endured, and it will continue as long as God wills." An official 2011 eighth-grade textbook teaches, "The Apes are the people of the Sabbath, the Jews; and the Swine are the infidels of the communion of Jesus, the Christians."[14]

These texts teach that Christians and their property are to be protected from murder and robbery, but only if there exists a protection covenant with Muslims, and even then converts from Islam can be killed. Converts can be executed either by the state or by individual Muslims, who can do so with impunity. By way of example, *Gulf News* reported in August 2008 that a Saudi religious policeman had murdered his daughter because she converted to Christianity. Blogging under the name "Rania," Fatima Al-Mutairi had stated in an online posting several days earlier that she was being pressured by her family; her brother found a cross on her computer screen and Christian poems and articles she had written. The paper reported that she was burned to death and her tongue had been cut out.[15]

It seems the mere presence of Christians is deemed a threat. An eleventh-grade text teaches there is a "New Approach in the Crusader Wars," through the establishment of schools and universities, and that "these include: The American Universities in Beirut and Cairo, The Jesuit University, Robert College in Istanbul, and Gordon College in Khartoum."[16] "Zionists and Crusaders" was also a common phrase in the rambling diatribes of Osama bin Laden, who, himself, was educated in Saudi Arabia, as were most of the 9/11 hijackers.[17]

Since 1979, Saudi Arabia has poured much of its enormous oil wealth into exporting such teachings, as well as funding mosques, schools, libraries, and academic centers in America and elsewhere. This ideological export is changing mainstream expressions of Islam in places such as Pakistan, Egypt, Afghanistan, and northern Nigeria. The US Congressional Research Service states that Wahhabism is now "arguably the most pervasive revivalist movement in the Islamic world." As Abdurrahman Wahid, the late former president of Indonesia, and ex-president of the world's largest Muslim organization, lamented, it is making "inroads" even in his tolerant part of the world.[18]

It is not difficult to understand why some senior American intelligence directors call such education "kindling for Usama Bin Laden's match." Although each year since 9/11 the Saudi government has assured the US government that it has cleaned up its curriculum, the state's hateful middle- and upper-school religion textbooks, as the Center for Religious Freedom at Hudson Institute has shown, have not been substantially revised.[19] The Saudi Minister of Education explained to us in a meeting in his office in Riyadh in 2011 that he is "not concerned" by the need to reform the high school curriculum since the king has made higher education the priority instead.[20]

BESIEGED FOREIGN WORKERS

Of the twenty-seven million people in Saudi Arabia, up to ten million are foreign workers and, of them, one million or more are Christians from the Philippines, Lebanon, Ethiopia, Eritrea, Pakistan, Egypt, and India, as well as from Western countries. Some have lived and worked in the kingdom for as long as thirty years, but they have no rights as citizens, they cannot marry Saudis without converting to Islam, and their bodies cannot be buried in Saudi Arabia should they die there.

As noted, Christians are prohibited from having churches. The Saudi government maintains that they may worship privately in their houses but, as the US Department of State delicately puts it, "[t]his right was not always respected in practice and is not defined in law."[21] In other words, police even hunt down and punish Christians praying together privately.

Under Saudi law, Christians may enter the kingdom on visas for work, for diplomacy, or when specifically invited by the government, but not as tourists; foreign journalists are strictly controlled. As professor Camille Eid described:

> You have 5,000 religious police divided among 100 districts, but any Muslim can enforce the law by denouncing the individual. I spent two and half years in Jeddah; I was afraid to extend the Easter and Christmas greetings even via phone because I was afraid that someone might be listening. The religious police control everything including the bookshops because it is prohibited to sell any card with non-Muslim themes.[22]

Although information is strictly controlled, there are reports of persecution. The agents are usually the *mutawwa'in*—the religious police of the presumptuously named "Committee to Promote Virtue and Prevent Vice." This religious police force caused an international outcry in 2002, when, during a fire at a girls' school in Mecca, they pushed fleeing girls back into the blazing building because, in their panic, the girls had rushed out without their veils and abayas. Fifteen of the girls died. In 2005, the *mutawwa'in*'s treatment of Christians was so oppressive that India's Ambassador in Riyadh sent a circular to his nationals, warning them that Indians were being increasingly detained for religious activities. He advised Indians not to preach in any way or organize prayer meetings in private homes. He also told the Indian government to warn everyone leaving for the Saudi Kingdom to leave behind religious books, Bibles, photos, and icons.[23]

Compass Direct News reports that in April and May of 2005, the *mutawwa'in* arrested seventeen pastors; ten were Indian, two Pakistani, two Eritrean (including Yemane Gebriel, mentioned above), and three Ethiopian. They were jailed for several weeks until the quiet efforts of US and other foreign embassies resulted in their release.[24]

On February 12, 2011, Eyob Mussie, an Eritrean in his early thirties, was arrested for proselytizing. After psychiatric tests confirmed Mussie's sanity, there were reports that he would receive the death penalty. Instead, Saudi authorities deported him to Eritrea, where he would meet an uncertain fate at the hands of that repressive regime.[25]

In 2006, after years of listing it among the world's worst persecutors as a Country of Particular Concern, the US State Department sought with the Saudis a new diplomatic initiative on religious freedom. This resulted in a publicized (in the United States, if not in Saudi Arabia) agreement confirming with the Saudis that they would allow private worship in house churches, approve the import of one Bible per person for personal use, and restrain the vigilante-like religious police, as well as reform their textbooks within two years. The agreement was largely honored in the breach, though church crackdowns seemed to ease that year and the next.[26]

However, by 2008, the US Department of State International Religious Freedom Report noted continuing abuses by the religious police. "Mutawwa'in continued to conduct raids of private non-Muslim religious gatherings," the report states. "There were also charges of harassment, abuse, and killings at the hands of the mutawwa'in. . . . These incidents caused many non-Muslims to worship in fear of, and in such a manner as to avoid discovery by, the police and mutawwa'in."[27]

In 2008, two raids by the mutawwa'in resulted in arrests of both men and women. Compass Direct News observed: "Every three or four years, there is a clamp-down in Riyadh. . . . However, the underground church here is far better placed than heretofore to manage any such persecution."[28] Some house churches, such as Gebriel's, one of those targeted, had a backup pastor ready to take over when Gebriel had to flee; the church could continue praying in community, albeit clandestinely.

In October 2010, more than 150 foreign Catholics were detained for taking part in an underground mass with a French priest. Twelve Filipinos and the priest were reportedly charged with proselytizing, and conditionally released into the custody of their employers. The rest of the group detained with them were released due to a shortage of space in the police jail.[29] The Philippine embassy in Riyadh confirmed it had arranged a kafala—a bail bond that can only be arranged by an embassy—to obtain the temporary release of the priest and twelve Filipinos.[30]

Fides reported that an unnamed thirty-two-year-old Catholic factory worker, originally from the Philippines' Laguna Province, was arrested for blasphemy on October 14, 2011. His company's supervisor complained to the religious police that he had an illustration that was "offensive" toward the prophet Muhammad. He reportedly "sketched a 'dirty finger' sign and with it was the word 'Mohamad,'" according to the group Brotherhood in the Middle East.[31] Apparently, the complaint was filed following an argument about a work assignment between the man and his supervisor, and the Bishops of the Philippines appealed for the man's release. They stated: "The context for thousands of Filipino Catholic workers is very difficult in all countries, with an Islamic majority pervaded by fundamentalism. Our appeal is crucial to religious freedom and the fundamental respect toward all human beings."[32]

On December 15, 2011, thirty-five Ethiopian Christians working in Saudi Arabia were arrested and detained by the kingdom's religious police for holding a private prayer gathering in Jeddah. The official charge was that they were "mixing with the opposite sex"—a crime for unrelated people, but the real reason is that they were praying as Christians. On the day of their arrest, the six men and twenty-nine women were holding their regular prayer meeting.[33]

A Christian leader from Saudi Arabia explained: "The Saudi officials are accusing the Christians of committing the crime of mixing of sexes because if they charge them with meeting for practicing Christianity, they will come under pressure from the international human rights organizations as well as Western countries. In fact, when an employer of one of the detainees asked for the reason for their employee's arrest, the Saudi official told him that it was for practicing Christianity."[34]

Saudi officials strip-searched all the women and subjected them to an abusive body-cavity search, and assaulted the men. In a remarkable prison interview with the Voice of America's Amharic-language service, one of the women, who contracted an infection from the search, attested: "We are traumatized by the strip search. They treated us like dogs because of our Christian faith. While talking about me during a recent visit to the prison medical center, I overheard a nurse telling a doctor 'if she dies, we will put her in a trash bin.'"[35]

The Christians remained in Saudi prisons for many months; the last of the thirty-five were finally deported back to Ethiopia on August 1, 2012, according to confirmation provided by International Christian Concern (ICC),[36] the nondenominational human-rights group that first broke the story about the arrest. One of the prisoners told ICC: "A high-ranking security official insulted us, saying, 'You are non-believers and animals.' He also said, 'You are pro-Jews and supporters of America.' We then responded, 'We love everyone. Our God tells us to love everyone.'"[37]

THE DANGERS OF CONVERSION

Christian converts, such as the Christian martyr Fatima Al-Mutairi described above, do exist in Saudi Arabia. In February 2011, while in Riyadh on US diplomatic business, Nina Shea was able to meet with another Saudi convert, Hamoud Bin Saleh al-Amri:

A slight man, wearing a white robe and the checkered keffiyeh (headdress) of Saudi men, the thirtysomething Bin Saleh al-Amri said he had converted after reading the Bible when he was twenty-four, while on a study abroad program in Jordan. In 2004, in Lebanon, he applied for refugee status on the basis of his conversion but was denied by the United Nations refugee office that screened him, and he was involuntarily returned to Saudi Arabia. A Saudi military official was sent to bring him back and, upon landing in Riyadh, he was immediately arrested and detained for nine months. He was then left alone for two years, but was rearrested and jailed for about a month in late 2008, after he started a blog about his views on Islam, Saudi Arabia, and Christianity.

His most recent arrest was on January 13, 2009, again for comments posted on his blog criticizing the Saudi judiciary and discussing his conversion to Christianity. Released again on March 29, 2009, he stated that he had been severely mistreated while in prison and threatened with harm to his family. He attributes his freedom to outside pressure on the Saudi authorities and to the fact that a relative has connections in the government.

Authorities blocked his blog, which Google subsequently locked on the basis that it violated terms of service. Due to popular outcry, the company reactivated his site.[38] Bin Saleh al-Amri defiantly continued to blog until it was shuttered again. He refuses to be silenced and has sent interviews outside the country where they can be viewed on the Internet.

When we met in 2011, Bin Saleh, as he is called, was free, and some have remarked that Saudi authorities have treated him with relative leniency.[39] But it is important to recognize that, even when he was not in prison, he existed in a bubble of almost complete social isolation. He was not part of a church community, something he longs for but dares not pursue. He had lost his job and supported himself as a freelance chauffeur. His family has all but cut off relations with him. He is not married and has no real friends in Riyadh, where he lives. He was under tight police surveillance and believed his telephone was monitored. His passport has been confiscated and he cannot escape Saudi Arabia. In March 2012, there were reports that he had been rearrested.

Bin Saleh is fearless in his faith. He asked for prayers that he may one day "revive the church of Mecca," which, he pointed out, has been suppressed for fourteen hundred years. His parting words were: "My goal is to be recognized as a Christian. I don't want to live as a hypocrite."

Other than Bin Saleh, only one other Saudi convert is publicly known. On November 29, 2004, the religious police imprisoned Emad Alaabadi on charges he had converted to Christianity two years earlier. There are reports that other unidentified Saudi Christians were arrested at the same time. Reportedly, Alaabadi has since been released and lives in Saudi Arabia under heavy restrictions.[40]

MODERATE SAUDIS' EXCEPTIONAL COURAGE

A word of acknowledgment is needed for those Saudis who do try to foster greater tolerance toward Christians within Saudi Arabia. This takes exceptional courage. Saudi state instructions, backed by violent enforcement measures, assert that freedom of thought must be rejected since "[f]reedom of thinking requires permitting the denial of faith."[41]

Some Saudi moderates have faced harrowing ordeals for advocating tolerance. In the opening fatwa of a government booklet distributed in 2005 by the Saudi embassy in the United States, the late Grand Mufti Bin Baz pronounced an unnamed European Muslim cleric an infidel or apostate for stating that Jews and Christians were not infidels. Bin Baz's fatwa, held out by Saudi Arabia as authoritative even after his death, implies that the moderate European Muslim preacher, and others like him, can be killed with impunity and stripped of property if they do not repent three days after being warned.[42]

In November 2005, Mohammed Al-Harbi, a Saudi high school teacher, was sentenced to three years in prison and 750 lashes on charges of blasphemy and insulting Islam because he had discussed the Bible, among other things, in positive terms. He was pardoned by the monarchy in December 2005, but nevertheless lost his job and suffered other repercussions.[43]

Another well-known case is Hassan al-Maliki, a theologian, who lost his job at the Ministry of Education, was threatened with death, had his books banned, and spent time under virtual house arrest after challenging Wahhabi teachings. In 2007, he lamented that the Saudi educational system taught "whoever disagrees with Wahhabism is either an infidel or a deviant—and should repent or be killed."[44] Sheikh Saleh Al-Fawzan, who authored the portions of the curriculum that al-Maliki criticized, responded to the criticism by threatening to behead him.[45]

QATAR TAKES A STEP FORWARD

Will Saudi Arabia ever open up and allow churches? At the moment, it seems impossible that Christians will ever be permitted to gather publicly to pray in Saudi Arabia. However, the example of the tiny neighboring country of Qatar offers some hope.

Qatar shares a border with Saudi Arabia on the Arabian Peninsula. It also shares its literalist Wahhabi brand of Islam and, for fourteen centuries, like Saudi Arabia, it had banned the practice of Christianity. In 1988, Qatar abruptly dropped this prohibition and allowed a Christian service for foreign workers to publicly take place.

The then-American-envoy to Qatar, Ambassador Joseph Ghougassian, gave the following account of that path-breaking event:

> Friday, September 13, 1988, will long be remembered in the history of Qatar, the history of the Catholic Church in Qatar, and

> the history of all Christian denominations in Qatar. For the first time since the seventh century AD, the days when Prophet Mohamed converted Qatar to Islam, the first ever Catholic Holy Mass and Christian service was publicly celebrated. . . . To my amazement as we were approaching the vicinity of the [American] school, I saw several traffic police and secret agents directing the flow of traffic. . . . Their foresight was wise. I wasn't prepared for the sight that awaited me, and even today I still vividly see the image of countless men, women and children, well-dressed Westerners and poorly clothed Asians, flocking to the big hall of the school to occupy the best seats near the makeshift altar.[46]

That worship service was followed by at least one every week thereafter; later more services for a variety of foreign Christian denominations were added. Twenty years afterward, Qatar's first Catholic church, Our Lady of the Rosary, opened on government-provided land, with fifteen thousand people in attendance. Now there are five more legally recognized Christian denominations in Qatar, including Protestant, Coptic, Orthodox, and others, each with a church building or the right to build one on government-leased land. The churches are permitted to display crosses, bells, and other symbols, albeit only within their interiors. A two-thousand-seat Catholic community center is also allowed. Instead of attacking and arresting the foreign congregants as they used to do, the police now protect them and help direct churchgoing traffic. Qatar still restricts religious freedom for native Qataris, but this is a big step in the right direction.

This astonishing reform was largely due to the efforts of one man, Ambassador Joseph Ghougassian. The American ambassador, born in Egypt, used his fluency in Arabic and, more importantly, his fluency in Islam, to reach out to the head of Qatar's Sharia Court. Over a period of months, the ambassador engaged him on points of both religion and history, as recounted in his book *The Knight and the Falcon*.

His extraordinary experience deserves examination. Among other questions, he challenged the principal rationale Saudi Arabia offers today for why it bans churches—that all the country is sacred ground that "infidels" like Christians and Jews must not defile with their prayers. The ambassador pointed out this applied only to Mecca and Medina, which are only a small part of the country, a country whose national borders did not exist at the time of Islam's prophet Muhammad.[47]

Ambassador Ghougassian made another argument that appealed directly to the Sheikh's religious sensibilities and helped him see the issue in a new light. The Ambassador said to the Sheikh of Qatar's Sharia Court:

> Well, Allah forbid, if you were to die tomorrow, and you appeared in front of Allah, do you think Allah would be pleased with you? Do you think that Allah might complain by telling you, "My son, what have you done to those hundreds of thousands of Christian souls who lived and worked in Qatar when you were the head of the Sharia Court? Look in the Gehennam. There they are. Because you prohibited them from openly professing their faith and performing their religious duties toward me, they forgot me, stopped worshipping me, and went astray on the wrong path."[48]

Eventually, the ambassador posed the matter directly: "We have a simple request, which should not be offensive to you. We want to be able to gather as a Christian community and pray to Allah." (It should be noted that *Allah* is an Arabic term for God that is not distinctly Muslim; in fact, it was used by Arab Christians long before the rise of Islam.) The Sheikh agreed and, with his influential backing, the US envoy helped reverse fourteen hundred years of history. Not only the international community's Christians but Hindus and Buddhists are now permitted to hold worship services in Qatar.

Ambassador Ghougassian was never instructed by the US Department of State to help the expatriate Christians, who, as in

Saudi Arabia, comprise a sizable minority in Qatar. In fact, before his posting, he was never even briefed on the religious situation there. Nor was he ever recognized by the State Department after his tour of duty for what he achieved for the cause of religious freedom, though he did receive a knighthood from Pope John Paul II. It is unfortunate, because the lessons from his experience could help American diplomacy achieve its goal of fostering greater religious freedom in Saudi Arabia—a goal that, after 9/11, has never been so pressing.

IRAN

On December 5, 2010, Iranian Supreme Court judges Morteza Fazel and Azizoallah Razaghi issued the following ruling:

> Mr. Youcef Nadarkhani, son of Byrom, 32 years old, married, born in Rasht in the state of Gilan, is convicted of turning his back on Islam, the greatest religion, the prophecy of Muhammad, at the age of 19. He has often participated in Christian worship and organized home church services, evangelizing and has been baptized and baptized others, converting Muslims to Christianity. He has been accused of breaking Islamic Law [in] that from puberty (15 years according to Islamic law) until the age of 19 the year 1996, he was raised a Muslim in a Muslim home. During court trials, he denied the prophecy of Muhammad and the authority of Islam. He has stated that he is a Christian and no longer Muslim.
>
> During many sessions in court with the presence of his attorney and a judge, he has been sentenced to execution by hanging according to article 8 of Tahrir-ol Vasileh. . . . He must repent his Christian faith . . . if it can be proved that he was a practicing Muslim as an adult and has not repented, the execution will be carried out.[49]

Pastor Youcef Nadarkhani is married to Fatemeh Pasandideh, and has two young sons.[50] He became a Christian as a teenager and was never a practicing Muslim. In 2009, he discovered a recent change in Iranian educational policy that forced all students, including his own children, to read from the Qur'an. He went to the school and protested this requirement on the basis that the Iranian constitution guarantees freedom of religion. Nadarkhani's protest was reported to the police, who arrested him on October 12, 2009. Only then was it discovered that he had Muslim parents.

On September 21 and 22, 2010, the Eleventh Chamber of the Assizes Court of Gilan Province declared that, since Nadarkhani's parents were Muslims, he must necessarily have been Muslim also. The court therefore found him guilty of apostasy and sentenced him to death for leaving Islam. Apostasy is not a crime under any Iranian statute—the court simply decided to follow the late Ayatollah Khomeini's book *Tahrir-ol Vasile*, section 8, where he wrote: "A national apostate will be caused to repent and in case of refusing to repent will be executed. And it is preferable to give a three-day reprieve and to execute him on the fourth day if he refused."

After the verdict was appealed, the Supreme Court ordered the lower court to review whether Pastor Nadarkhani had in fact previously been a Muslim. The court again decided that he had been one and, following Khomeini's writings, demanded on three consecutive days that the pastor renounce his Christian faith. On September 28, 2011, the final demand was made and he once again refused. Consequently, his death sentence for apostasy could be carried out. (Two months previously, his lawyer, Mohammed Ali Dadkhah, had been sentenced to nine years in prison for "actions and propaganda against the Islamic regime.")[51]

This sentence led to an international outcry. In the United States, Republican House Leader John Boehner urged Iran's leaders to "abandon this dark path."[52] British foreign secretary William Hague said, "This demonstrates the Iranian regime's continued unwillingness to abide by its constitutional and international obligations to respect religious freedom. I pay tribute to the courage shown by Pastor Nadarkhani who has no case to answer and call on the Iranian authorities to overturn his sentence."[53] Faced with these and other declarations of support for the pastor, the Iranian regime began to backpedal, equivocate, obfuscate, and then lie, claiming there had been no verdict, and that in any case Nadarkhani was not on trial for apostasy but for rape, "Zionism," and other offenses.

However, the American Center for Law and Justice published part of the 2010 Iranian Supreme Court ruling, quoted above, which revealed exactly what the charges and verdict were. The courts then referred the matter to supreme leader Ayatollah Khamenei. In January 2012, Pastor Nadarkhani was given a further offer of release if he would state that the Muslim prophet Muhammad was a messenger sent by God. He refused to do so. International appeals were launched on his behalf. Finally, Iran's courts acquitted him of apostasy and convicted him of the lesser crime of evangelizing Muslims. He was sentenced to three years of imprisonment—time that he had already served—and released on September 8, 2012. He is now at serious risk of assassination at the hands of Islamist death squads.[54]

SYSTEMATIC DISCRIMINATION AND INCREASING REPRESSION

Iran is one of the world's worst religious persecutors. All religious groups suffer: Baha'is, Christians, Mandaeans, Jews, and Zoroastrians, as well as Sunnis, Sufis, and dissenting Shia Muslims. Many minorities are dwindling; the ancient Assyrians and Mandaeans have almost disappeared. Although Iran is a signatory to UN human rights conventions, senior Iranian leaders denounce them as Western aberrations.

The Iranian regime claims to be based on Shia Islam, particularly the doctrine of the Twelver (Shia) Jaafari School. According to the Fundamental Law, the government is an Islamic one in which the clergy have a prominent function.

The constitution officially recognizes Zoroastrianism, Judaism, and Christianity, but does not ban religious discrimination. Non-Muslims must state their religion on census forms. Zoroastrians, Jews, and Orthodox Christians are nominally free to practice rituals and educate their children, but cannot enter government service or hold commissions in the military. University applicants are screened for Islamic orthodoxy and must pass a test in Islamic theology, obviously restricting religious minorities.

The penalty for killing women, Christians, Jews, or Zoroastrians is less than that for killing a Muslim man. Murdering people of other, unrecognized religions, such as Baha'is, has no legal ramifications. Killing them, or killing those who leave Islam, carries no punishment. For even consensual sexual relations between a non-Muslim man and a Muslim woman, the non-Muslim faces death.

Christianity has a long history in Iran: the Church of St. Mary, in the northwest, is considered by some historians to be the world's second-oldest surviving church. Today, there are about three hundred thousand Iranian Christians, almost all ethnic Armenians belonging to the Armenian Apostolic Church. Of the smaller Christian bodies, the Assyrian Church of the East has about eleven thousand members, and the Chaldean Catholic Church about seven thousand. Protestants include Presbyterians, Anglicans, the Assyrian Evangelical Church, and the Assemblies of God. There are also newer churches such as the Church of Iran, many of them Pentecostal, and there are reports that they are growing rapidly. This is causing anger and fear in the government, leading to harassment, surveillance, arrests, and imprisonment.

Despite this long history, and the Iranian Constitution's recognition of Christian minority rights, the government often portrays Christianity as Western, interferes with and discourages Christian practices, and tries to bar any activity outside church walls. Christian worship must be in the Assyrian or Armenian languages. On February 7, 2012, plainclothes agents raided a house, arrested ten Christians gathered for prayer, took them to an unknown location, and refused to give the families any information. *Mohabat News* reported that one of those arrested was Mojtaba Hosseini, who had been arrested on May 11, 2008, along with eight others. Security officials had then asked him to renounce his faith and collaborate with the intelligence office. The authorities have also forcibly closed churches where services are held in Persian (Farsi), Iran's national language. In some other churches, the Intelligence Ministry has imposed the requirement of barring Farsi-speaking people.[55]

Since 1993, churches and their pastors have been required to declare publicly—and falsely—that they have full rights, as well as that they will not attempt to convert Muslims. Worshippers can be subject to identity checks by authorities standing watch outside congregational centers, church services are restricted to Sundays, and churches must inform the Ministry of Information and Islamic Guidance before admitting new members. In the mid-1990s, authorities closed down the 160-year-old Iranian Bible Society and all Christian bookshops, prohibited the printing of Bibles or other Christian literature in the Farsi language, banned Christian conferences, and shut down Protestant churches in Gorgan, Mashhad, Saari, and Ahvaz.

Ever since the 1979 revolution, the regime has persecuted Christians, other minorities, and even many Muslims. But in recent years, arrests of Christians have accelerated and the regime is demonizing them as conspirators and so-called parasites. Ayatollah Ahmed Jannati, chairman of the Council of Guardians and adviser to President Ahmadinejad, has denounced non-Muslims as "animals who roam the Earth and engage in corruption." Since Ahmadinejad's rise to power, repression of Christians has been directed mostly against those involved with the conversion of Muslims. There is no specific law stating that Muslims cannot convert, but Article 167 of the constitution requires that if there is no codified law the judge "has to deliver his judgment on the basis of authoritative Islamic sources and authentic [fatawas]."[56] This was the basis for Youcef Nadarkhani's death sentence. In the aftermath of its violent attacks on the democratic opposition following the 2009 elections, the regime has been increasing arrests not only of political opponents but also of those who differ from the regime's religious dogmas.

ATTACKS ON CONVERTS

In 2009, one Christian leader reported, "[T]here are more arrests, of Christians as well as Baha'i, in the last several months... [than] maybe the whole 30 years before." But this was only the beginning of a wave of repression. There is a pattern of leaders being imprisoned, beaten to get information on other converts, and released after a few weeks. The summer of 2009 saw a wave of arrests of Christians. Ten Christian converts were arrested in Shiraz in June 2009, eight were arrested in Rasht on July 29 and 30, and twenty-four in Amameh on July 31.[57]

In May 2008, there were ten arrests in Iran in connection with converts, including Mohsen Namvar, who had been arrested and tortured in 2007 for baptizing Muslim converts. He was re-arrested on May 31, 2008, by a branch of *Sepah*, the Revolutionary Guards, and was held for several weeks. He was so severely tortured that he continued to suffer fever, severe back pain, high blood pressure, uncontrollable shaking of his limbs and short-term memory loss. He and his family subsequently fled to Turkey on July 2, 2008.[58]

On March 5, 2009, two Christian converts, Maryam Rostampour, twenty-seven, and Marzieh Amirizadeh Esmaeilabad, thirty, were jailed in the notorious Evin prison on charges of "acting against state security" and "taking part in illegal gatherings." On August 9, a judge asked them to renounce their Christian faith and, when they refused, he ordered them returned to their cells to consider it. Esmaeilabad, who suffered from spinal pain, an infected tooth, and severe headaches, was denied medical care. On October 7, 2009, the two were acquitted of "anti-state activities" but charges of apostasy and propagating Christianity remained pending. On November 18, 2009, they were released without bail, an unusual development in such a case, and, in May 2010, acquitted of all charges. However, they were told that if they continued with Christian activities, they would be punished. On May 22, they fled the country.[59]

RECENT INCREASES IN ABUSE

On June 3, 2008, twenty-eight-year-old Tina Rad was arrested and charged with "activities against the holy religion of Islam" for reading the Bible with Muslims in her home. Her husband, thirty-one-year-old Makan Arya, was charged with "activities against national security." Security officials confiscated their personal computer, satellite dish, and television set, as well as all their books, videos, CDs, DVDs, and a photo album. They were jailed for four days and tortured so severely that Rad was unable to walk when she was released. Security officials also told them that in the future they would be charged with apostasy and that their four-year-old daughter would be taken away from them and placed in an institution.[60]

It is impossible in any brief space to cover all the recent cases of discrimination, assaults, attacks, and imprisonments, so we will merely give some examples from the last few years. As is becoming common in the region, repression often surges around a Christian holy day: Christmas. Beginning on December 26, 2010, security forces raided Christian homes in Tehran and elsewhere, abused and handcuffed their occupants, and dragged twenty-five people off to prison and interrogation. Among those taken were married couples, at least two of whom were forced to leave babies behind.

When police raided another dozen houses where the occupants were not at home, the homes were ransacked, looted, and sealed. In the following weeks, the regime arrested another thirty or forty Christians in a series of ongoing raids—some sources say as many as six hundred. This was the largest targeted Iranian violence against Christians since the government assassination campaign against Protestant leaders in the mid-1990s, and perhaps since the earliest years of the revolution.[61]

Elam Ministries, which works closely with churches in Iran, reported the release of some of those imprisoned. Not only had they spent more than a month in prison, most of them in solitary confinement, solely for being Christians, they were also released on bail, which meant they could still be tried. In keeping with common regime practice, the bail for one of those released, Sara Akhavan, included her family's trade license, which means their livelihood would be destroyed if the authorities decided that bail had been broken.[62]

In early March 2011, Pastor Behrouz Sadegh-Khandjani, Mehdi Furutan, Mohammad Beliad, Parviz Khalaj and Nazly Beliad, all members of the Church of Iran—a charismatic denomination—were sentenced to one year's imprisonment for "Crimes against the Islamic Order."[63] On March 15, 2011, the government suspended Mohabat News, one of the best news sites for information on Iranian Christians, and its staff was threatened. Mohabat had just reported that the previous month the government had confiscated and burned six hundred New Testaments discovered on a bus during a border inspection in Salmas. This occurred at the same time the Iranian government was condemning the burning of a Qur'an by preachers Terry Jones and Wayne Sapp in Florida. In August 2011, a consignment of sixty-five hundred Bibles was seized as it was being shipped between the cities of Zanjan and Ahbar in the northwestern province of Zanjan.[64]

In April 2010, Pastor Behnam Irani, a member of Youcef Nadarkhani's church, was leading a house church service when he was assaulted and arrested. He was tried on January 16, 2011, on charges of apostasy and "action against the [Islamic] order." He was found guilty of the latter charge and was sentenced to one year in prison. Following a failed appeal, on May 31, 2011, Pastor Irani was again violently put under arrest and taken to Hesar prison in Karaj to serve the one-year term.

Days before he was due to be released, he was informed on October 18, 2011, that he would remain in prison to serve a suspended five-year sentence for "action against national security," handed down by a revolutionary court in 2007. That verdict also described Pastor Irani as an apostate and reiterated that apostates "can be killed." In late 2011 he was held in a cell with criminals who regularly beat him, and was having difficulty walking due to injuries. "During his first months of imprisonment, the pastor was held incommunicado in a small cell, where guards would repeatedly wake him as a form of psychological torture." He was moved into a cramped room where inmates could not lie down to sleep before being transferred to his current cell.[65]

Christian Solidarity Worldwide (CSW) also reports that, on September 14, 2011, eleven Iranian Christians who had previously fled Iran received e-mailed threats from a group calling itself "The Unknown Soldiers of the Hidden Imam." These messages demanded they forsake their Christian faith or face extrajudicial execution. The "unknown soldiers" are thought to have links with the Iranian security services. The e-mail concluded with a demand that the Christians take "the opportunity to repent and ask forgiveness from the presence of the Hidden Imam and the Great Allah" or "according to the Fatwa given by Mehdi the Hidden Imam, they must be killed."[66]

BENDING THE LAWS

In January 2012, the Guardian Council approved a new Islamic Penal Code. Penal sentences such as stoning, dismemberment, and the execution of minors, as well as religious and gender discrimination, continue as in the old code. It does drop provisions from earlier drafts that carried the death penalty for apostasy, but that penalty can still be drawn from other sources, since the code instructs:

> The judge is duty bound to make all efforts to find the proper sentence in the codified laws. If he fails to do so he should issue the sentence in accordance with the valid Islamic sources or valid fatwas. . . . The judge cannot use the absence or insufficiency or brevity or conflict of the codified laws as an excuse to refuse to issue a verdict.[67]

It was on the grounds of such "valid Islamic sources" that Youcef Nadarkhani was initially sentenced to death. The regime can also charge people with many other offenses, such as "friendship with the enemies of God," "fighting against God," "dissension from religious dogma," "insulting Islam," or "promoting pluralism." But such ideological charges can rebound on the ideologues. Iran's president Mahmoud Ahmadinejad has himself recently been accused of "witchcraft," "experimenting with exorcism," and "communicating with genies."[68] Mullahs have denounced his administration as containing "deviants, devils and evil spirits." At the same time, the disgust that many Iranians feel for their rulers seems to be one reason many Iranians have expressed the desire to leave Islam.[69]

WHAT LIES AHEAD?

In Saudi Arabia and Iran, Christians face egregious and systematic persecution. Both states are designated by the US Department of State as "Countries of Particular Concern" under the International Religious Freedom Act.

Because Saudi Arabia supplies one-quarter of the world's oil, and is considered a strategic ally, the United States and other governments have been reluctant to press it harder to end its demonization of and incitement to violence against Christians and other non-Muslims, as well as other Muslims, both within the kingdom and throughout the world. This reluctance exists despite the financial and other support for terrorism that emanates from the kingdom—terrorism that is based on Wahhabi doctrines of religious hatred and jihad.

The United States sees Iran as a strategic threat to the West, and most immediately to Israel, which Iran's rulers have repeatedly threatened to annihilate. Thus, US and other government policies in recent years have been focused, through economic sanctions and diplomacy, in stopping Iran from developing nuclear weapons.

This means there has been little sustained external attention to either of these countries' religious freedom violations. While there are some congregations in Iran that are growing, in the short to medium term, prospects for religious freedom in these countries look dim.

SEVEN

THE MUSLIM WORLD: SPREADING REPRESSION

Egypt / Pakistan /Afghanistan / Sudan

MOST OF CAIRO'S GARBAGE COLLECTION IS DONE PRIVATELY BY Christians, known as the *zabaleen*, who pick up refuse in trucks and carts, take it back to where they live, and sort through it for anything valuable, which they sell. The zabaleen literally live amid the garbage.

On the night of March 9, 2011, Christians in Cairo's Christian neighborhood of Mokatam—often called "Garbage City"—were viciously attacked. Gangs, some armed with guns, roved through Mokatam into the early morning hours. Homes were looted and set on fire using combustible propane tanks, and garbage recycling plants and trucks were destroyed. One long-time resident wrote, "Although over 130 people were injured, most through gun shots and some very seriously, no ambulances or fire engines arrived at the Village until early the next morning. . . . So far, ten have died, nine of them young Christians and one a Muslim who lives at the Village and was defending his home there."

She added it was "obvious that this was a well-organized and deliberate attack on Christians in general and Garbage People in particular."[1]

In August 2009, in Pakistan's Punjab village of Gojra, a rumor began to circulate; it quickly spread like the deadly wildfire that was soon to follow. The story was that three Christian men had desecrated a Qur'an during a wedding ceremony. Enraged by this story of blasphemy, an angry mob gathered, incited by members of a radical Sunni faction. Armed with clubs and petrol, they attacked Gojra. After assaulting the supposed perpetrators of the "crime" against Islam, they torched forty homes and a church. Eight people were burned to death and eighteen others were injured. An investigation later revealed that, although local officials knew about the attack in advance, they made no effort to prevent it.

Mukhtar Masih (Masih is a common Christian surname in Pakistan, a form of "Messiah"), one of the three so-called blasphemers, later explained that during a quiet wedding in his home, local Muslim youths had wadded up several pages of the Qur'an and tossed them over the wall of his family home. Later the same young troublemakers retrieved them as evidence, and accused the Christians of defiling Islam's holy book and, thus, of blasphemy. Masih and several other family members were brutally beaten prior to the arson; they fled for their lives. But after the fires were extinguished, Masih learned his young daughter had died in the flames. His surviving three sons and three daughters were, in his words, "left with nothing." The dozens of suspects in the case have been released, according to news sources.[2]

Shoaib Assadullah became a Christian in Afghanistan in 2005. He was arrested on October 21, 2010, after giving a man a copy of the New Testament, and imprisoned in the northern city of Mazar-e-Sharif. On January 3, 2011, a judge told Shoaib that if he did not renounce his Christian faith within one week, he would be imprisoned for up to twenty years or possibly sentenced to death.

As in other Christian cases, no Afghan lawyer agreed to defend Assadullah. While he was in prison, his mother died, perhaps because of her son's situation. In a February 17, 2011, letter, Shoaib wrote, "Several times I have been attacked physically and threatened to death by fellow prisoners, especially Taliban and anti-government prisoners who are in jail."[3]

Shoaib was taken in chains and bare feet to the hospital, where the doctor said he was incoherent and needed to be hospitalized. Perhaps this was meant to show he was insane, both in order to explain his conversion and to justify a more lenient sentence, thus easing international pressure. In late March 2011, he was released and fled the country.[4]

US Representative Frank Wolf, who has had a twenty-year-long interest in Sudan, traveled with Samaritan's Purse to a refugee camp for twenty-five thousand in Nuba in February 2012. His report, based on refugee interviews, is a heart-wrenching description of indiscriminate bombings, killings, and manipulated famine by the North Sudan Armed Forces. A refugee woman gave the Virginia congressman an account of the continued targeting of Christians:

> [She] raised the issue of religion, saying that soldiers armed with AK47s would come to their villages in trucks with machine guns in the back and say "we don't want anyone who says they are a Christian in this village." She spoke of rapes and brutal attacks carried out by uniformed Sudanese soldiers. These government soldiers would tie people up and then execute them, she said.[5]

VIA CRUCIS

Egypt, Pakistan, Afghanistan, and Sudan vary widely in geography, culture, and degree of Christian presence.[6] Egypt is home to the largest and one of the most ancient Christian communities in the greater Middle East. Not a single church remains in Afghanistan; its tiny Christian population consists of recent converts. Christians, who account for small fractions of the populations of Pakistan and North Sudan, can, for the most part, openly operate churches. But, while their circumstances differ, the Christians in these four countries constitute severely persecuted minorities whose very survival depends on a constant struggle in the face of ever-increasing Islamic extremism.

These Christians are subject to states, even nominally secular ones, that favor Islam and repress Christianity and other non-Muslim religions, and they are also subject to violently intolerant Islamists, including terrorists. These two forces usually operate independently but on occasion work together, especially at the lower ranks of the security services.

Northern Sudan is waging a bombing campaign and enforcing starvation against the Nuba people and others along its southern border because they are suspected of sympathizing with largely Christian and non-Muslim South Sudan. In its capital of Khartoum, Christians are treated as second-class citizens and repressed. With increasing frequency in Egypt and Pakistan, attacks take the form of pogroms against vulnerable Christian villagers. State laws that suppress Christians' rights exacerbate this situation. This includes, in Egypt, their ability to repair or build churches. Time and again, these governments have failed to protect Christian minorities from violence and denied them justice in the wake of attacks. In Egypt and Pakistan, Christians are sometimes arrested along with, or instead of, their attackers.

Bishop Macram Gassis, the Catholic bishop of Sudan's Nuba people, wrote an anxious plea to us right before Christmas in 2011, "Please keep us in your prayers. My flock is on the *via crucis*." He meant that the powerless tribal Christians of central Sudan were experiencing their own Calvary.

Those words could be said for the Christians in each of the four countries described below. They face states that mix sharia restrictions with pragmatic measures, and they encounter widespread social violence, including from terrorists.

EGYPT

On October 9, 2011, Egypt's armed forces ruthlessly crushed a largely Coptic protest in the Maspero area of Cairo.[7] The October demonstration had been organized by the Maspero Youth Group to protest a string of church burnings and the failure of authorities to protect Christians from attacks over the previous months. When the demonstrators passed through the El Qolaly and Abdeen neighborhoods, the marchers were pelted with stones thrown by some of the Muslim residents. As they assembled near Maspero, Egypt's army swept in to disperse the gathering. More than twenty Copts were killed and three hundred wounded. The army appeared to have moved from its earlier practice of passivity in the face of attacks on Copts to a position of overt hostility against them. This resulted in unrestrained violence. According to forensic reports for the slain protesters, a third of the twenty-seven victims were killed when they were run over by armored vehicles; while the others were shot with live ammunition. There is no evidence the Coptic protestors were armed.

Meanwhile, Egyptian state *Nile News* falsely broadcast that Copts were shooting at the army and called on Egyptians to come to the army's defense. This report, which was retracted by the station the following day, immediately inflamed many Muslims, who went to Maspero and clashed with the protesters, including some who were Muslim. Salafi TV stations also broadcast that Christians had burned a Qur'an at Maspero, stoking further attacks on Copts, and against the Coptic hospital where many of the wounded had been taken.[8]

On October 11, armed Muslims assaulted funeral processions for several of the murdered Copts, blocking their way and hurling stones and Molotov cocktails at them. The besieged mourners sought shelter and called the army emergency phone line for help. For several hours, there was no response.

Then–prime minister Essam Sharaf blamed the Maspero violence on "invisible hands," implying American or Israeli influence. At an October 12 press conference, the military blamed Christian protesters and "enemies of the revolution." Major General Adel Emara denied that troops opened fire on protesters, claiming their weapons did not have live ammunition. He said it was "[not in] the dictionary of the armed forces to run over bodies . . . even when battling our enemy." The forensic evidence and graphic photographs posted on the Internet showed otherwise. On October 15, twenty-eight persons, almost all of them Copts, were arrested for the violence and held for several months before being released. No Egyptian official was held responsible. Investigations were dropped and the case closed after a panel of judges appointed by the justice ministry decided there was a lack of evidence.[9]

The al-Qidiseen church (Church of the Two Saints) in Alexandria was bombed shortly after midnight on January 1, 2011, as worshipers were leaving a midnight service for the New Year. Twenty-one Copts were killed and almost a hundred injured, as were some Muslim bystanders. The death toll was the highest for a single incident since the massacre of Copts at the village of El-Kosheh on January 1, 2000. Most attacks on Copts are not precisely planned but rather carried out by local vigilantes or mobs enraged by inflammatory accusations broadcast by radical preachers. In contrast, the bombing in Alexandria, likely a suicide bombing, bore the hallmarks of an Al-Qaeda or some other jihadist group attack. At about the same time, an Al-Qaeda–affiliated website published a "death list" naming two hundred Coptic Christians, most of them living overseas, over half in Canada.[10]

Christianity in Egypt is ancient. Church tradition says it was founded by St. Mark, the gospel writer. Copts, as the Christians are called from the ancient form of the word *Egypt*, number between 6 and 10 million, or about 10 percent of Egypt's 83 million people. They are by far the Middle East's largest Christian community. More than 90 percent are Coptic Orthodox, but they also include Greek Orthodox, Catholics, evangelicals, and others. The rest of Egypt's population is Sunni Muslim, with small Shia and Baha'i communities and about two dozen indigenous Jews.

Prolonged massive demonstrations forced out Egypt's longtime authoritarian president Hosni Mubarak on February 11, 2011, turning power over to the armed forces. After parliamentary elections concluding in January 2012, the Muslim Brotherhood took 47 percent of the seats of the lower house. Salafists, whose version of Islam is similar to Saudi Arabia's, gained a further 26 percent. These groups did even better in the less-powerful upper-house elections, thus giving Islamists a dominant position in the new government and control in appointing the drafters of a new constitution. On June 14, 2012, Egypt's supreme court unexpectedly ordered the parliament dissolved due to irregularites in the elections for the seats set aside for independents. A leading figure in the Islamist Muslim Brotherhood, Mohammed Morsi, was elected president and assumed office on June 30, 2012. In mid-August 2012, he took steps to consolidate his power by replacing the country's top ranking military officials. Most Copts fear that the empowered Muslim Brotherhood and Salafists will be more repressive of the Copts than was Mubarak. Many of the attacks on Copts described here have been carried out by Salafists. Copts who were able to do so began fleeing Egypt in 2011.[11]

While the situation was bad before, attacks on Copts from extremists and from security forces have markedly increased since Mubarak's resignation. Christians have long suffered from lack of state protection thanks to police who don't assist them, judges who don't prosecute their abusers, and discriminatory and restrictive Egyptian government policies. Taxes pay for mosques, Muslim schools and universities, and for imams' salaries, but not for Christian functions. Copts are underrepresented in the governmental media, public schools, and other government jobs. Discriminatory laws restrict the construction and repair of churches; and laws on marriage, inheritance, and conversion discriminate against Christians.[12]

Egyptian authorities routinely downplay or cover up violence against Christians and refuse to investigate such incidents properly. Judges and law enforcement officials also have a tactic of arranging "reconciliation" sessions between Christians and their Muslim attackers. While proper reconciliation is good, authorities use this enforced reconciliation as a cosmetic substitute for trying and punishing the attackers and compensating the victims. The culprits escape, secure in the knowledge that attacking Copts, their church, or their property brings little or no penalty. Often such cases result in even greater injury to the Copts, because they are sometimes expelled from the areas—their homes and workplaces—where they were victimized.[13]

On April 28, 2011, the United States Commission on International Religious Freedom recommended for the first time to Secretary of State Hillary Clinton that Egypt be officially designated a Country of Particular Concern (CPC). Commission chair Leonard Leo stated that "severe religious freedom violations engaged in or tolerated by the government have increased dramatically since . . . President Mubarak's resignation."[14]

FORBIDDEN: CHURCH CONSTRUCTION AND INSULTS

The government enforces cumbersome and frequently arbitrary restrictions on building or repairing churches, restrictions that do not apply to mosques. Such laws are carried over from Ottoman rule. In Decree 291 of 2005, then-President Mubarak delegated authority to the state governors to authorize the expanding or rebuilding of existing churches, but in practice the security forces can block any work, and the approval process for church construction is delayed sometimes for decades. Churches have collapsed while their congregation awaits approval to restore them. By some estimates, about one-third of recent attacks on Copts have been on those who tried to repair or expand churches in the face of unjustifiable restrictions.

In November 2010, for instance, state authorities attempted to stop the construction of an addition to St. Mary's Coptic Church in Giza. At about 3:00 a.m. on November 24, police surrounded the site while men were working on the roof, with two hundred worshippers keeping vigil inside the church. Security forces, using tear gas, rubber bullets, and live ammunition, killed four Copts and wounded at least fifty, many seriously. At least two hundred Christians were arrested at or near the scene, and were denied access to lawyers. Church leaders insisted they had a permit for the construction, but the authorities disputed this.[15]

Copts without churches may pray at home, but this also has its dangers—sometimes leading to attacks on houses, pressure to drive believers from their homes, and the detention of the owners and guests on charges of "sedition" or "prayer in an unauthorized place."[16]

Copts, as well as other Egyptians, can be attacked for "insulting Islam." In October 2005, a mob of at least five thousand people surrounded St. George's Church in Alexandria after the newspaper *Al-Midan* reported on October 13 that a play had "insulted Islam" by featuring a Copt who resisted becoming a Muslim. In the riots, four people died and ninety were injured. There were attacks on seven other churches in Alexandria, as well as on cars and Coptic businesses, and a mob surrounded another church as far away as Cairo. In the days following, anonymous taggers marked Coptic houses in Alexandria with crosses, in what was generally assumed to be a sign to aid future attackers. Many Christians remained home in fear. Death threats against Alexandria priests and against Coptic Pope Shenouda III also appeared on extremist websites.[17]

DANGEROUS LIAISONS AND DEADLY CONVERSIONS

Under Egyptian law, a Muslim woman is forbidden to marry a Christian man (though a Muslim man may marry a Christian woman). If a Christian man becomes romantically or sexually involved with a Muslim woman, violence is aimed not only at him or his family but also at the entire local Christian community. Such incidents are not infrequent.

On March 4, 2011, a mob several thousand strong attacked and burned the church of St. Mina and St. George in the village of Soul, about nineteen miles from Cairo. The mob pulled down the church's cross and detonated gas cylinders. The ensuing fire destroyed the church and all its contents, including centuries-old relics. The fire department and the armed forces initially failed to respond to Coptic pleas for help. The incident appeared to stem from a romantic relationship between a Christian man and a Muslim woman and the refusal of the woman's father to kill her to restore the community's "honor." Subsequently, more than a thousand Copts fled the area. The army rebuilt the church by Easter, but no one was prosecuted for the attack.[18]

Copts who convert from Islam or who assist converts or who are implicated in proselytism, evangelism, or witnessing to Muslims face their own set of problems. While no law specifically forbids evangelism or apostasy, Article 98(f) of the penal code, which prohibits "ridiculing or insulting heavenly religions" or "inciting sectarian strife," functions as a de facto apostasy law.[19]

The late Sheik Muhammad Tantawi of Al-Azhar University told one of us: "It is forbidden for any Muslim to change his religion in Egypt." On May 1, 2007, the *Sout el Oma* newspaper reported that Interior Minister Habib el-Adly had sent a memo to the Administrative Court arguing that Islam, as the state religion, demands the death of any Muslim man who leaves the faith, while a female apostate "should be imprisoned and beaten every three days until she returns to Islam."[20]

In early July 2010, Sheikh Youssef Al-Badri, a member of the Supreme Council for Islamic Affairs, an affiliate of the Egyptian Ministry of Islamic Endowments, declared on state television that converts from Islam "should be killed."[21] On December 2, 2010, the Pew Research Center, a respected US-based research center on religion and society, released its Middle East survey report, which found that 84 percent of Egyptians favor executing any Muslim who changes his religion.[22] Even if he is not killed, a convert's marriage may be annulled, his children taken away, and he may face arrest and torture.

Gasir Mohammed Mahmoud converted to Christianity in 2003. When his family found out, his adoptive father sought the help of local Muslim sheikhs, who issued death threats against Gasir for apostasy. His mother asked the police to protect her son from being killed, but her pleas fell on deaf ears. Instead, Gasir was detained by security officials and tortured, including reportedly by having his toenails ripped out. On January 10, 2005, he was forcibly confined to Cairo's El-Khanka mental hospital and kept in solitary confinement. Mahmoud recalled, "They filled the room with water, to prevent me from sleeping." After international publicity, he was released on June 9, 2005, and then went into hiding.[23]

One of the major problems faced by converts is the government's refusal to change their religion on their identity cards. That means Christians are treated as if they are Muslims. And that's a problem because Egyptian family law is based on religion, and sharia applies to any family in which at least one parent is Muslim.[24] Since sharia law forbids Muslim women to marry outside their religion, Christian women identified as Muslim cannot marry Christian men.[25] Desperate to marry, they may acquire forged Christian identification documents, but if the police discover this, they have the authority to forcibly divorce such women from their husbands. Some have been arrested and tortured. Recently, Egypt has been cracking down on marriages with forged documents.

On December 17, 2008, twenty-two-year-old Martha Samuel Makkar was arrested at Cairo's airport on charges of forging official documents as she attempted to leave for Russia with her husband and two sons, aged four and two. Five years earlier, she had converted to Christianity, changed her name from Zainab Said Abdel-Aziz, and married a Christian, Fadel Thabet. Subsequently, police tracked her down and her family attempted to kill her. There are reports that Makkar was sexually assaulted by Egyptian police at El-Nozha police station; she was assaulted by other prisoners while in detention; she was also tortured to force her to return to Islam.[26] On January 24, 2009, she was released on bail, but not before the judge expressed his informal opinion that she should be killed for leaving Islam.[27]

Since the government refuses to recognize converts, and because they often live in hiding, there are no reliable figures on how many people convert from Islam to Christianity in Egypt. There may well be thousands. But many are afraid to speak of their new beliefs, while others relocate in the hope of beginning a new life where they're not known. Unfortunately, Egypt's identity cards make religious anonymity nearly impossible—they are publicly marked as Muslims—and government officials are thus able to abuse converts when they attend church, marry, and give birth to children who are in turn issued IDs marking them as Muslim, wherever they go.[28]

Some Egyptian Christians may not realize the government considers them Muslim until years after their conversion. Sisters Shadia and Bahia El-Sisi were convicted forty-five years after their alleged offense of apostasy. In 1962, their father had left home and converted to Islam. Three years later, he moved back, reconverted to Christianity, and obtained forged documents stating that he was Christian. In 1996 police discovered this, detained him, and told him that he was a Muslim and therefore his daughters were also Muslim. Neither sister knew of their father's doings decades before, and their identity documents had always listed them as Christians. Shadia, who had been married to a Christian for twenty-five years, was threatened with forced divorce.

In November 2007, she was sentenced to three years in jail, purportedly for committing fraud on her identity documents since, in 1982, she had listed "Christian" on her marriage certificate. In early 2008, she was released when the attorney general determined the judgment was based on false information. Bahia, who went into hiding when Shadia was detained and came out when her sister was released, was then put on trial and convicted for identifying herself as Christian on her marriage certificate. She was freed pending an appeal. If she continues to be regarded as Muslim, then her husband will be forced to convert to Islam or their marriage will be annulled by the court. In that case, her children will be reregistered as Muslim, with her daughters also facing possible involuntary marriage annulment.[29] In principle, this procedure of retroactive forcible conversion could carry on through generations.

Despite the dangers they face, in recent years several Christian converts have challenged the Egyptian government's refusal to recognize their conversions. Most of these are people who were born

Christian, converted to Islam—often for reasons of marriage—and then decided to reconvert back. Some recent judicial rulings have been made in their favor, but the authorities often fail to implement such rulings. As distinct from "reconverts," no Muslim-born convert has yet won the right to have his or her new religion recognized.

Mohammed Ahmed Hegazy converted to Christianity in 1998 and shortly after was tortured by the police for three days. He was held again for ten weeks in 2002 in conditions he describes as being like a "concentration camp." On August 2, 2007, when his wife was expecting a baby (who would have to be raised as a Muslim) Hegazy filed a court case challenging the government's refusal to recognize his conversion. After receiving death threats, he went into hiding. The Minister of Religious Endowments, Mahmoud Hamdi Zakzouk, publicly stressed the legality of capital punishment for converts, and Hegazy's lawyer, Mamdouh Nakhla, withdrew from the case after receiving death threats and being told by Egyptian State Security that he might be killed.[30]

At a January 15, 2008, hearing, a dozen Islamist lawyers tried to attack Hegazy's attorneys. Hegazy's father said, "I will kill him with my own hands. I will shed his blood publicly."[31] On January 29, 2008, the Supreme Administrative Court ruled that Hegazy could not have his conversion recognized since "monotheistic religions were sent by God in chronological order" and, therefore, one cannot convert to "an older religion."[32] Hegazy tried to flee the country but was unable to get a passport, and he went into hiding.[33]

Maher El-Gohary, now named Peter Ethnasios, filed on August 4, 2008, to change his official religion from Islam to Christianity. He had converted some thirty years previously, and his main motive for going to court was that his fourteen-year-old daughter would, at age sixteen, be issued an identity card designating her faith as Muslim, which would make it illegal for her to marry a Christian.[34] Because of threats, El-Gohary could not attend the court hearing; when he sought to get documents to authorize his lawyer to act on his behalf, registry office employees beat him.[35] The court asked him to provide a conversion certificate from the Coptic Orthodox Church, something almost impossible to do. El-Gohary then traveled to Cyprus, returning with a conversion certificate from a Cypriot church that the Coptic Orthodox Church officially accepted.[36] Despite the certificate, the judge rejected his appeal.[37] Near the end of March 2010, his fifteen-year-old daughter, Dina, ventured out of hiding in Alexandria to get some water and had acid thrown on her; it damaged only her jacket.[38] In December 2010, a court revoked a Ministry of the Interior travel ban on El-Gohary, and in March 2011, he fled from Egypt.

AN INCREASING DANGER OF ABDUCTION

The kidnapping of Coptic girls for purposes of forced conversion to Islam is also on the rise. Even though one has to be over sixteen to legally convert to Islam, local authorities do not always uphold this. Sometimes they have permitted custody of a minor Christian female who "converts" to Islam to be transferred to a Muslim custodian, who then grants approval for an underage marriage. Not all the claimed cases are bona fide kidnappings, as many represent instances of young Christian girls falling in love and converting willingly, but actual abductions are real enough.

A report released November 10, 2009, by Christian Solidarity International and the Coptic Foundation for Human Rights documents twenty-five cases of abductions.[39] One priest reported that more than fifty women in his parish alone had fallen victim to this crime in the previous year.

On April 19, 2010, a bipartisan group of eighteen members of the US Congress wrote to Ambassador Luis C. de Baca, director of the State department's Trafficking in Persons (TIP) Office, saying they had received disturbing reports concerning Coptic girls documenting "a criminal phenomenon that includes fraud, physical and sexual violence, captivity, forced marriage, and exploitation in forced domestic servitude or commercial sexual exploitation, and financial benefit to the individuals who secure the forced conversion of the victim."[40]

AFTER THE ARAB SPRING

Egypt's future after Mubarak's resignation is uncertain, and we certainly do not know what the future might bring. But the first two years of the Arab Spring, with the empowerment of the Muslim Brotherhood and the Salafis, have been bleak for Egypt's Christians. The number and scale of attacks on them has increased.

Incited by a rumor that a woman who had converted to Islam was being held there, on May 7, 2011, a Salafist mob attacked St. Mina Church, one of the oldest churches in Egypt. They then firebombed the church of the Virgin Mary in Imbaba, in the same area. There was also shooting, some from the rooftops. Coptic homes and shops were firebombed. The clashes led to ten deaths, both Muslim and Christian, and more than two hundred were injured: the military then surrounded the churches and detained about 190 people.

Anba Theodosius, bishop of Giza, where Imbaba is located, said, "We have no law or security, we are in a jungle. We are in a state of chaos. One rumor burns the whole area. Everyday we have a catastrophe." Subsequently, police arrested twenty-three Salafists and the military said it would assist in rebuilding the churches. Egypt's National Council for Human Rights stated on May 9, 2011, that its report on the violence would hold security forces largely responsible, citing their slow response. According to its report, assailants targeting the Coptic community walked the mile and a quarter between the St. Mina Church and the Virgin Mary Church, carrying shotguns, knives, and Molotov cocktails, without being stopped by the police. It also states the Virgin Mary Church was set on fire amid a total absence of security.[41]

A few days after the infamous Maspero massacre, on October 16, 2011, a wrathful teacher and his class murdered a Coptic boy. Ayman Nabil Labib, a seventeen-year-old Coptic high school student in the Upper Egyptian town of Mallawi, was murdered because of the cross tattooed on his wrist. His Arabic-language teacher, Usama Mahmud Hasan, began insulting and harassing the teenager during class by telling him to wipe off the cross. When Ayman responded that the cross was a tattoo and therefore impossible to remove and then added that under his shirt he was also wearing a necklace with a cross, the teacher became incensed and asked the class, "What are we going to do with him?" Two students in the class, Mustafa Walid Sayyid and Mustafa Hasanayn 'Issam, beat Ayman and led about fifteen students who chased him as he struggled to escape. Two school supervisors, Tahir Husayn and Muhammad Sayyid, reportedly then forced Ayman into a teacher's room. There the group beat him to death. The two student ringleaders, Sayyid and 'Issam, have been charged with murder, but no action has been taken against the school personnel.[42]

PAKISTAN

In the waning months of 2009, a forty-five-year-old Christian woman and mother of five children named Asia Bibi (also known as Asia Noreen) was working in the fields near her home in Ittan Wali, located in Pakistan's Sheikhupura district. It was a scorching day, and Bibi and her coworkers were thirsty. Someone asked her to bring water for them all. When she returned, several of the women refused to drink the water she offered them. Because they were Muslims and Bibi was a Christian, they pronounced the water to be "unclean."[43]

An argument ensued. During the increasingly angry exchange, Asia Bibi was accused of having blasphemed Islam's prophet Muhammad—a capital crime, according to Pakistan's unforgiving blasphemy laws. The argument died down, but a few days later, she was assaulted by a mob of radical Islamists. Local police intervened—and arrested her.

It is noteworthy that at the time of the incident, there was reportedly an ongoing argument about property damage between Bibi and one of her neighbors, who was also one of the coworkers who accused her of blasphemy.[44] According to the *Daily Telegraph*, "The police were under pressure from this Muslim mob, including clerics, asking for Asia to be killed because she had spoken ill of the Prophet Mohammed. So after the police saved her life they then registered a blasphemy case against her."[45]

Bibi was held without being charged for more than a year. Because the sharia court gives the testimony of an infidel half the weight of the testimony of a Muslim, she didn't stand a chance. In November 2010, she was tried and convicted of blasphemy and sentenced to death by hanging. In April 2011, reports emerged that she was in deteriorating health.[46] This was said to be due to the filthy conditions in her Lahore jail cell. She remains on death row.

PERSECUTED BY THE STATE

> You are free; free to go to your temples, you are free to go to your mosques or to any other places of worship in this state of Pakistan. You may belong to any religion or caste or creed—that has nothing to do with the business of the state. . . . Minorities, to whichever community they may belong, will be safeguarded. Their religion, faith or belief will be secure. There will be no interference of any kind with their freedom of worship.

So declared Muhammad Ali Jinnah, the "father of the state" of Pakistan in a 1947 speech, shortly after the nation's founding.[47]

Jinnah's words were well intentioned and even liberating at the time. And, if they were put to good use today, they would be doubly comforting to Pakistan's religious minorities—including 3 million Christians out of the 174 million people of this overwhelmingly Muslim nation. Unfortunately, due to the increasing radicalization of Islam in the region, Pakistan's Christians live a precarious existence, victimized by extremists, officially discriminated against in the sharia courts, terrorized under draconian blasphemy laws, demonized in classrooms, and often denied protection by law enforcement and the criminal justice system.

And in 2011, the assassination of two prominent Pakistani leaders, one Muslim and one Christian, who sought to defend abused

Christians and other Pakistani minorities, focused world attention more than ever on the country's egregious religious injustices.

Today, Pakistan's Christians face innumerable pressures, particularly from the state's severe Islamic laws that are stacked against them. Police forces and courts are unwilling to protect Christians' interests or to treat them equally, and they suffer pervasive economic and legal discrimination. They are left with high illiteracy rates—even by Pakistani standards—and with menial and low-wage jobs.

Christians are disadvantaged in public university admissions because "they do not know the Koran by heart," a condition that prompted the Pakistani Catholic Bishops' Justice and Peace Commission to submit a formal complaint against the government to the High Court of Lahore in early 2012. As the international Catholic news agency *Fides* reported, the case arose because Christian student Aroon Arif was highly qualified in his field but denied admission because he had not memorized the Qur'an. On the medical school entrance exam for the State University of Sciences in Lahore, out of 1100 possible points, he scored 930 in one section, and 860 in the other. Muslims applicants were able to score 20 points higher since the medical admissions exam also tested for "knowledge of the Koran."[48]

On November 9, 2011, USCIRF released its study finding that Pakistan's public schools and madrassas (Islamic schools that teach exclusively the Qur'an and other Islamic texts) negatively portray the country's Christians and other religious minorities, and "reinforce biases which fuel acts of discrimination, and possibly violence, against these communities."[49] "[Public school textbooks] used by all children often had a strong Islamic orientation, and Pakistan's religious minorities were referenced derogatorily or omitted altogether"; "[Teachers] were divided on whether religious minorities were citizens"; and, "[T]eachers often expressed very negative views about . . . Christians." The study also made an additional startling finding: all the public school teachers interviewed believed the concept of jihad to refer to violent struggle, compulsory for Muslims to engage in against the enemies of Islam.

Only a small number of teachers extended the meaning of jihad to include both violent and nonviolent struggle. Aside from the generalized belief that "enemies of Islam" should be targeted, the overwhelming majority of public school teachers held the view that an individual decides when and against whom jihad is appropriate. It is important to note that upward of 80 percent of the public school teachers viewed non-Muslims as enemies of Islam in some form or another, despite contradictory views expressed in other parts of the interviews.[50]

EXTREMISM WITH GOVERNMENT SUPPORT

Such official views signal to extremists within the society that Christians are not equal citizens, that their property is not fully protected, and that they can be targeted with impunity.

The extremism within Pakistani society, of which the presence of Osama bin Laden in an army garrison town was a potent reminder, is daunting and intensifying. However, the state has played an important role in permitting such radicalism to gain ground. Bowing to radical pressures, it demands that Christians, along with other Pakistanis, follow harsh, though vague, Islamic laws banning blasphemy against Islam.

Pakistani government policies, along with its failure in the education sector, have allowed the country to become a breeding ground for Islamist factions, and radical elements have worked their way into the country's military and intelligence communities. The NATO war against Afghanistan's Taliban has also driven alarming numbers of terrorist groups into Pakistan, and has exacerbated strife between the government and US-led forces. In 2011, USCIRF reported, "Pakistan continues to be responsible for systematic, ongoing, and egregious violations of freedom of religion or belief. . . . Growing religious extremism threatens the freedoms of religion and expression, as well as other human rights."[51]

TARGETED ATTACKS ON POLITICAL LEADERS

Following the killing of Osama bin Laden in the Abbotabad area, local Christians were specifically targeted. One group was attacked in a park near bin Laden's compound as they gathered to watch a film depicting the life of Jesus. Local parish priest Father Javed Akram Gill was reported asserting: "The situation in Abbotabad remains 'critical' for religious minorities, who are 'fasting and praying for peace in the region'; bin Laden's death has raised fears within the Christian community."[52]

A few weeks after bin Laden's death, on May 30, 2011, Protestant clergyman Reverend Nadeem John and three other Christians in his car were shot at by Muslim extremists as they were leaving a seminar organized by the Catholic Church in Gojra, Punjab. They abandoned the car and, bolting across a field, were chased by the terrorists, who continued to fire at them. They found refuge in a predominantly Muslim village, where some local residents fired back at the attackers who fled. Speaking to AsiaNews, the pastor said, "The attackers wanted to kill Christian voices. . . . Extremists have a habit of waiting for cars to leave Christian villages before shooting at them."[53]

Beside ubiquitous Taliban elements and the terrorist Haqqani network, another similar extremist group, Lashkar-e-Taiba (LeT), has sponsored numerous terrorist attacks, including the massacre in Mumbai in November 2008. Pakistan's former ambassador to the United States, Husain Haqqani, wrote in the Hudson Institute journal *Current Trends in Islamist Ideology* in 2005 that LeT is Pakistan's "most significant jihadi group of Wahhabi persuasion" and is "backed by Saudi money and protected by Pakistani intelligence services."[54]

It was only as recently as 1973—twenty-six years after Pakistan gained independence from Britain and became a state—that Islam formally became Pakistan's state religion. Since that declaration, various sects and individuals have sought to conform Pakistan's public life to Islamist ideology. Despite the efforts of legislators who attempted to protect minorities in the constitution during the regime of military ruler Muhammad Zia ul-Haq (1978–1988), Islamization in Pakistan went from bad to worse for Christians and other minorities. Among other things, those years saw the creation of Pakistan's draconian blasphemy laws.

FORBIDDEN SPEECH

Pakistan's most notorious abuses emanate from the country's infamous blasphemy codes. A close look at their wording reveals why the country's abuses of religious freedom are virtually unmatched in the world. Consider the implications of severe and vague rules like: "Whoever by words, either spoken or written, or by visible representation, or by any imputation, innuendo or insinuation, directly or indirectly, defiles the sacred name of any wife, or members of the family of the Holy Prophet (peace be upon him) or any of the righteous Caliphs or companions of the Holy Prophet (peace be upon him) shall be punished with death, or imprisonment for life, and shall also be liable to fine."[55] Further, anyone who "damages or desecrates" a Qur'an faces a life sentence. If one is a Christian, just touching a Qur'an can bring punishment. Ruqqiya Bibi, a Christian woman, not to be confused with Asia Bibi, was sentenced in October 2011 to a twenty-five-year prison term for blasphemy based on an accusation that she defiled a Qur'an by handling it with unclean hands.[56]

Intent is irrelevant, leading to improbable accusations. On July 28, 2001, for instance, five Christian boys and a Muslim boy in Okara were arrested on charges of blasphemy. The boys, who were between ten and fifteen years old, were caught trying to treat a wounded donkey. The medicine they used to place over the wounds streamed in different shapes down its body. A small group of Muslims declared the boys had written the names of holy personalities on the donkey. Some extremists in the community accused the Christians of insulting Islam and demanded they be arrested. The boys were arrested and the wounded donkey detained (due to a complaint lodged by one Maulana Abdulmanan). After the investigation, the police released the children. This was due, at least in part, to many people in the area who had submitted written affidavits testifying to the innocence of the accused.[57] On August 16,

2012, as this book goes to print, a young Christian child, Rimsha Masih from a neighborhood near the capital of Islamabad, was jailed on accusations of burning a Qur'an, and a local mosque leader called for her to be burned to death; she is mentally disabled. After a public outcry over the injustices surrounding the case, Rimsha was released on bail three weeks later, but, fearing vigilante attacks, she and her family were then forced into hiding.[58]

Any person can file a complaint of blasphemy against another, and once it is lodged, there is typically no turning back. Even those who are acquitted, or their neighbors, have been targeted by vigilante violence, often carried out with utter impunity. On November 11, 2005, Yousuf Masih, a Christian, won several thousand rupees in a card game with his Muslim neighbor. The sore loser, seeking revenge, informed the police that Yousuf had set fire to a copy of the Qur'an. On February 18, 2006, the neighbor withdrew the charge and Yousuf was released on bail. But that wasn't enough for local Muslim clerics. They called on their followers to "avenge the insult." An inflamed mob of more than two thousand attacked the town's minority Christian community, set fire to three churches, and vandalized a Catholic convent and a Christian elementary school.[59]

Despite their mortal penalties, the laws do not clearly spell out what "blasphemy" actually is. Nor do they provide protection for those who are falsely accused. This, of course, makes room for shocking abuses and frequent false accusations. Blasphemy allegations are often motivated not by religious offenses but by business rivalries, personal grudges, property disputes, ill-fated love affairs, and a host of other self-centered reasons.

Although no one in Pakistan has yet officially been executed for blasphemy, it is likely that hundreds of those accused have been put to death by other means. These victims typically die at the hands of vigilantes, local thugs and mobs, or the police. Extremists engage in witch hunts to murder the accused before, during, or after adjudication. Many other victims have endured brutal rapes and beatings; churches, homes, and businesses have been ransacked, looted, and burned.

Even if exonerated by the courts, those accused of blasphemy are targeted by vigilantes and must go into hiding to save their lives. Aslam Masih, an illiterate Christian from Faisalabad, was said to have hung verses from the Qur'an around the neck of a dog. The reasons for this supposed action remain unclear; the verses seemed to have been encased in some sort of a charm. Illogical as the charges were, Masih was arrested in 1998. As the prosecution presented the case against him, additional testimony exposed angry rivalries between him and his Muslim neighbors. Jealousy had inspired the neighbors to refuse to pay for farm animals they had at first agreed to purchase. They later stole the animals from Masih, then hauled him to the police station, declaring him to be a blasphemer. At the time of his arrest, he was violently assaulted both by his neighbors and the police, and the beatings caused permanent injuries. More than three years after his arrest, he was sentenced to two life sentences—all based on secondhand evidence. A higher court later exonerated Masih, but by then he was physically broken and his life ruined. Meanwhile, since his release he has been forced to remain in hiding due to ongoing death threats.[60]

All Pakistanis are liable under the blasphemy laws, but Christians and Ahmadis (an offshoot of Islam considered heretical by many Muslims) are targeted disproportionately. According to the Jinnah Institute's 2011 report, "Since 1986, nearly a thousand cases of blasphemy have been registered in Pakistan. Of these, 476 have been registered against Muslims, 479 against Ahmadis and 180 against Christians. In 2010, over 32 people were killed extra-judicially by angry mobs or individuals on the basis of allegations of blasphemy and 64 people were charged under the blasphemy law."[61]

In a May 2011 report, Compass Direct News stated that an entire generation of Pakistani Christians is growing up without a clear understanding of their faith because parents are afraid that instructing their children in basic Christian beliefs "will lead to potentially disastrous schoolyard talk." Moreover, children required to take Islamic studies in school are in danger with a single misstep. " 'If they write anything or misspell anything to do with the prophet Muhammad, they can be in serious danger,' a source said. 'In fact, the other side of this is that they are made to answer questions saying what a wonderful man he was.' "[62]

TWO MURDERED HEROES

The discriminatory blasphemy law, which protects only Islam, gives a platform to extremists by allowing them to determine what ideas are acceptable or banned. As part of their agenda, they also use the blasphemy laws to target Muslims who espouse toleration.

Starting in the late 1990s, international pressure to rescind or revise Pakistan's blasphemy laws has increased. This movement began with the tragic 1998 death of Catholic bishop John Joseph, who died under questionable circumstances as he was protesting a blasphemy verdict against one of his parishioners. Today, other courageous Pakistani political leaders and diplomats continue to speak out about the need for reforms in the laws and for the establishment of greater religious freedom in Pakistan. In at least two recent cases, it has cost them their lives.

In January 2011, Salman Taseer, the Muslim governor of Punjab, was gunned down by one of his bodyguards, shot repeatedly at close range with a submachine gun. Taseer was a senior member of the Pakistan People's Party (PPP). He had defended Asia Bibi, who was awaiting execution, and had openly opposed the blasphemy charges against her.[63]

Although members of the PPP mourned Taseer's death and demonstrated against it in the streets of Lahore, his murderer, twenty-six-year-old Malik Mumtaz Hussain Qadri, attracted far more media attention. He was celebrated as a folk hero when he arrived at an Islamabad court to plead guilty. Qadri was embraced exuberantly by a crowd of well-wishers from the lawyers' bar association, kissing his cheeks and showering him with flower petals. Of this tragic scenario Pakistani observer Mosharraf Zaidi wrote in *Foreign Policy*:

> As an advocate of realistic optimism, Taseer's assassination for me, and many among the small English-speaking urban community

> in Pakistan, is gut-wrenching and heart-breaking. It is a reminder that the realities of Pakistan . . . are stark and intimidating . . . Pakistan is in desperate need of a viable counter-weight to the irrational and frankly un-Islamic voices of religious extremism that dominate religious discourse in the country. That is not a year-long fight. It is an intergenerational struggle.[64]

Qadri was eventually convicted following a difficult effort to find a lawyer willing to prosecute the case. After the verdict, the judge had to go into hiding.

On March 2, 2011, Shahbaz Bhatti, a Roman Catholic and the minister of minorities affairs, and the only Christian member of Pakistan's cabinet, was ambushed and assassinated by gunmen as he sat in a car outside his mother's house. Like Taseer, he had championed Asia Bibi. He had waged a strong campaign—inside the government as a minister and outside it in cooperation with human-rights groups—for the blasphemy laws' repeal. He was also the longtime head of the All Pakistan Minorities Alliance, a nongovernmental organization promoting national unity, interfaith harmony, and human equality. His work was his life; at the end of each day, he left his government cabinet office and headed over to his office at the Alliance, where he continued to help Pakistan's persecuted minorities until late into the night.[65]

His death was not unforeseen. He even left a video-taped message with AP and other news agencies to be broadcast if he were murdered, in which he says that threats by Al-Qaeda and the Taliban would not change his views or stop him from speaking out for "oppressed and marginalized persecuted Christians and other minorities" in Pakistan.[66]

We had the privilege of knowing and working with Shahbaz Bhatti. The forty-two-year-old once told us that he had never married because he did not think it would be fair to a wife and children to subject them to this concern.

In a pantheon of human rights heroes, Shahbaz Bhatti's commitment stands out. In September 2009, he was presented with

USCIRF's first religious freedom medallion. He vowed again to reform the blasphemy law: "They are using this law to victimize minorities as well as Muslims of Pakistan. This law is creating disharmony and intolerance in our society. . . . I personally stand for religious freedom, even if I will pay the price of my life."[67]

According to Reuters, the Pakistani Taliban claimed responsibility for Bhatti's killing, but no one has yet been charged with his murder.

KIDNAPPING

There are persistent reports of Christian (as well as Hindu) girls and women being abducted and forced to marry Muslim men and convert to Islam. In many cases, there is no recourse for the women or their marginalized families. Police too often sympathize with the kidnappers and rapists. Also, in Pakistan, a rape victim can be imprisoned for unlawful sex, and may be released on the condition that she marry her rapist. In its sharia courts, the testimony of a non-Muslim is worth less than that of a Muslim, and a woman's is worth less yet. This whole system is rigged against the Christian woman.

Describing the fate of Amariah Masih, Father Khalid Rashid Asi, general vicar of the Catholic diocese of Faisalabad, emphasized that "cases like these occur daily in Punjab. . . . It is very sad [that] Christians, often girls, are helpless victims."[68]

Eighteen-year-old Amariah Masih (also reported as Mariah Manisha), a Catholic girl from the village of Tehsil Samundari near Faisalabad, was shot dead on November 27, 2011, after putting up resistance when a Muslim man abducted her with the intent to rape her.

The girl's mother, Razia Bibi, fifty, said she and her daughter were riding on a motorbike on their way to pick up drinking water, which is not available in their village. A man seized the motorbike, grabbed the young woman, and tried to drag her away at gunpoint. As she tried to pull away, the man opened fire, killing her instantly. Twenty-eight-year-old Muslim Arif Gujjar, the son of a wealthy local landowner, was reportedly in police custody for questioning for the murder of Amariah.

Amariah's funeral was presided over by Father Zafal Iqbal, who said to the Catholic press: "She is a martyr. . . . The girl resisted, she did not want to convert to Islam and she did not marry the man, who killed her for this." He explained: "Wealthy and influential landowners often take aim at those who are marginalized and vulnerable, for their dirty interests."[69]

Anna, a twelve-year-old Christian girl, was visited by a Muslim friend at her home in Lahore and invited to do some last-minute Christmas shopping on Christmas Eve 2010. Instead, when she got into the friend's car, the friend's relatives abducted her. She was reportedly taken to a house in another city where she was held for eight months and repeatedly raped, beaten, and ordered to convert to Islam. Her family did not know what had happened to her, and her father, Arif Masih, filed a complaint with police. They took no action.

In September 2011, Anna managed to escape and run to a bus station where she called her frantic family, who drove to retrieve her. Her kidnappers then petitioned police for her return, asserting she had converted to Islam and was now married to one of her rapists. The police told the family it would be better to hand over Anna to the rapist, who was also a member of the extremist group LeT, since he was now her husband and they would face a criminal case if they refused. Appalled at the suggestion and terrified their daughter would be taken again, the family has gone into hiding. The human rights defenders reporting this case point out that under Pakistan's Child Marriage Restraint Act of 1929, the legal age of marriage for girls without parental consent is 16.[70]

AFGHANISTAN

Abdul Latif was killed after being abducted from his village outside Enjeel, a town south of Heart, by four militants claiming to be Taliban. A two-minute video clip shows the militants reciting a death sentence against the Christian convert in his forties. At least two of the killers carry automatic weapons, and all wear suicide explosive vests. Scarves cover their faces.

Latif was pinned to the ground, his feet bound, and his hands tied behind his back. One of the killers read aloud in Arabic from the Qur'an: As a "warning to other infidels," he intoned, "You who are joined with pagans . . . your sentence [is] to be beheaded . . . whoever changes his religion should be executed." Latif struggled, crying out, "For God's sake, I have children," until one of his murderers thrust a knife in his neck. While he bled, the killers shouted, "Allahu Akhbar" repeatedly until his head was cut off and placed on his chest.[71]

On May 27, 2010, an Afghani TV show called *Sarzamin-e-man (My Homeland)* broadcast a two-year-old video of indigenous Afghan Christians holding a worship service. Days later, some twenty-five Christians were arrested, and many others fled. One who had converted to Christianity eight years previously, Said Musa, was arrested when he sought asylum at the German embassy. Having lost his leg after stepping on a landmine while serving in the Afghan army, he now wears a prosthetic limb. He is the father of six young children, the oldest then eight and another who is disabled. He worked for the Red Cross/Red Crescent as an orthopedic therapist, giving advice to other amputees and fitting patients for prosthetic limbs.

In early June, the deputy secretary of the Afghan parliament, Abdul Sattar Khawasi, said, "[T]hose Afghans that appeared on this video film should be executed in public." The authorities forced Musa to renounce Christianity on television, but he continued to say he was a Christian.

His wife only learned his whereabouts from a released inmate who had shared his jail cell, and she first saw her husband on July 27. He was forced to appear before the court without a lawyer and without knowing the charges against him. "When I said 'I am a Christian man,' he [a potential defense lawyer] immediately spat on me and abused me and mocked me. . . . I am alone between 400 people with terrible values in the jail, like a sheep." No Afghan lawyer would defend him, and authorities denied him access to a foreign lawyer.

In a letter smuggled to the West, he described the first months of his detention: "The authority and prisoners in jail did many bad behavior with me about my faith in the Lord Jesus Christ. For example, they did sexual things with me, beat me by wood, by hands, by legs, put some things on my head. [They] mocked me 'He's Jesus Christ,' spat on me, nobody let me for sleep night and day." He added that he would be willing to sacrifice his life so "other believers will take courage and be strong in their faith. Please my English writing is not enough good. If I did some mistake please forgive me! From Kabul Provincial jail."[72]

After this letter was publicized, the US embassy and others successfully pressured Afghan officials to move Musa to the Kabul Detention Center, where he received better treatment but had to sleep in a corridor to avoid further beatings. NATO sources reported that General David Petraeus—then US commander in Afghanistan—raised the case in an early December meeting with President Karzai. US and other diplomats and international NGOs pressured the Afghan government to discharge Musa and, on February 21, 2011, he was released and quickly smuggled out of Afghanistan.[73]

TALIBAN ATROCITIES

After Soviet forces retreated from Afghanistan in 1989, there was a vicious civil war and the highly repressive Taliban ("students") militia took control of most of the country. In response to the September 11, 2001, Al-Qaeda terrorist attack, the United States led an invasion that toppled the Taliban and thereby eliminated Al-Qaeda's safe haven. Afghanistan adopted a new constitution and government, which has been led by Hamid Karzai, but the Taliban and other Islamist militias have continued fighting and control parts of the country.

The population of about thirty million is overwhelmingly Muslim, and only 1 percent is "other," including Sikhs, Hindus, Christians, and, in 2011, one remaining Jew. Estimates of the number of Afghan Christians vary from five hundred to eight thousand persons. In 2010, the country's single church building was torn down despite the congregation's frantic opposition. The US Department of State's 2011 Religious Freedom report states: "There is no longer a public Christian church; the courts have not upheld the church's claim to its 99-year lease, and the landowner destroyed the building in March [2010]," though there are hidden worship places for the international community.[74]

When it ruled most of Afghanistan, the Taliban persecuted Christians and many others; and when it can, it still does. On January 8, 2001, Taliban leader Mullah Mohammed Omar announced they would execute apostates from Islam and any non-Muslims involved with them. He also decreed that owners of bookshops containing texts that criticized Islam, or that even discussed other religions, would receive a five-year jail sentence.[75]

In August of that year, Taliban officials arrested eight foreign Christians working for the Shelter Now International (SNI) aid organization, claiming they had been "trying to convert Afghan Muslims to Christianity."[76] Sixteen of the organization's Afghan employees were also arrested, although their friends and coworkers maintained they were all firmly Muslim. Unlike the foreigners, the incarcerated Afghans were not allowed visitors, and Taliban representatives said they might face death or life imprisonment. The Taliban even detained sixty-four children who had been in contact with the aid workers, holding them until any possible "Christian influences" on them could be eradicated.

Asserting there was a "larger conspiracy" behind SNI's alleged proselytism, the Taliban closed two more Christian relief agencies, SERVE and the International Assistance Mission (IAM).[77] Thirty-five Afghan employees of IAM were later arrested. When the Taliban evacuated Kabul on November 13, 2001, they confined their foreign prisoners in a steel container and drove them south. They were freed two days later by Northern Alliance troops.[78]

Even after its collapse as a government, the Taliban continued its vicious repression wherever it could. On July 1, 15, 23, and 28, and August 7, 2004, Taliban supporters murdered a total of five Afghan converts to Christianity by stabbing or beating them to death. In the first case, a Taliban representative, Abdul Latif Hakimi, announced to Reuters news agency that "Taliban dragged out Assad Ullah and slit his throat with a knife because he was propagating Christianity." Hakimi warned foreign aid workers—whom he accused of proselytizing—that "they face the same destiny."[79]

On July 19, 2007, Taliban forces kidnapped twenty-three South Korean Christians visiting Afghanistan as short-term volunteers. They killed two then freed two others when the South Korean government agreed to negotiate directly with them. On August 28, as a condition for the release of the remaining hostages, South Korea agreed to remove its two hundred military support personnel from Afghanistan by the end of 2007 and block any missionary activities by South Korean Evangelical groups. South Korea's government later claimed it had merely confirmed the existing timetable to withdraw troops and an existing agreement to withdraw South Korean volunteers and missionaries.[80] South Korea's troops, more than two hundred military medics and engineers, were in fact removed from Afghanistan in 2007.

In August 2010, members of the Taliban shot to death ten members of a Christian medical team. They had provided eye treatment and other health care in remote villages in northern Afghanistan as part of International Assistance Mission (IAM), the longest serving nongovernmental organization in Afghanistan, which is registered as a nonprofit Christian organization focused on medical care, not evangelism. The team had been on a three-week trip to Nuristan Province. After driving, they had left their vehicles and hiked with packhorses over mountain ridges to reach the remote Parun valley in the province's northwest. The *New York Times* reported,

"Taliban spokesman Zabiullah Mujahid said the medical team was killed because they were 'spying for the Americans' and 'preaching Christianity.' "[81]

OFFICIAL ABUSE OF CHRISTIANS

The areas controlled by Afghanistan's government, which the United States heavily supports financially and defends militarily both through American and NATO troops, are better for Afghan Christians than those controlled by the Taliban, but that is not saying much; conditions there are among the world's most repressive. Afghans are assumed to be Muslims, so that an Afghan who professes to be a Christian will be condemned by locals as an apostate. There are no public churches in the entire country, so Christians must hold services in private, and, to throw off suspicion, do so on days other than Sundays, frequently shift locations, and not possess Bibles because of the constant fear their homes will be searched.

The utter dearth of religious freedom in Afghanistan is reflected in an episode showing a panicked American response to a shipment of Bibles. In May 2009, when a year-old video surfaced showing US troops in Afghanistan receiving boxes of Bibles in Pashto and Dari languages, there was an immediate outcry that they were "proselytizing," a violation of the US military code of conduct. The soldiers denied the accusation and said a church in the United States had sent the Bibles—unsolicited.

US Colonel Greg Julian insisted the video footage was taken out of context and the Bibles were never distributed. The US military quickly confiscated and destroyed the Bibles: "The decision was made that it was a 'force protection' measure to throw them away."[82] The implication was that mayhem would result if Afghans were given Bibles, even when supplied and distributed by private sources. The United States gave no apology to Christians for destroying hundreds of Bibles.

The Afghan Constitution, adopted in January 2004 under American auspices, contains some human rights guarantees, but it also specifies, in Article 3, that "no law can be contrary to the sacred religion of Islam."[83] The president, cabinet, and Supreme Court judges must swear to "support justice and righteousness in accord with the provisions of the sacred religion of Islam."[84] The constitution does not say what the principles of Islam are, but Article 130 says that, in the absence of an explicit statute, the courts should decide "in accord with Hanafi jurisprudence," one of the four main Sunni schools of Islamic sharia law. Traditional versions of Hanafi jurisprudence specify the death penalty for apostasy.[85]

The 2004 constitution's first major interpreter was Afghanistan's first post-Taliban Supreme Court Chief Justice, Fazul Hadi Shinwari, who added his own unique perspectives to the justice system. Of non-Muslims he said, "We can punish them for propagating other religions—such as threaten them, expel them and, as a last resort, execute them, but only with evidence."[86] While in office, he told an American National Public Radio correspondent that Islam has three essential rules. First, a man should be politely invited to accept Islam; second, if he does not convert, he should obey Islam. The third option, if he refuses, is "to behead him."[87]

CONVERTS

Currently, under the Karzai government, "Male citizens over age 18 or female citizens over age 16 of sound mind who converted from Islam had three days to recant their conversion or be subject to death by stoning, deprivation of all property and possessions, and the invalidation of their marriage."[88] The iconic example of this was a case that riveted world attention in 2006.

Abdul Rahman became a Christian in 1990 while working for a Christian relief agency assisting Afghan refugees. His wife divorced him and his parents took custody of his two young daughters. He then traveled for nine years seeking asylum in Europe before being deported back to Afghanistan in 2002. After several years, he tried to regain custody of his children. He was arrested in February 2006 when he went to the local police station carrying a Bible and admitted to being a Christian.

The prosecutor, Abdul Wasi, said he would drop the case if Rahman reconverted to Islam, but, when he refused, Wasi called him "a microbe in society, and he should be cut off and removed from the rest of Muslim society and should be killed." A prison employee told reporters, "We will cut him into little pieces. . . . There's no need to see him." Because of threats from other inmates, he was transferred to the high-security Policharki prison. For his part, Rahman said, "I am serene. I have full awareness of what I have chosen. If I must die, I will die."

After the case drew international attention and pressure, Afghan officials said Rahman might not be mentally fit to stand trial but this would be difficult to determine since, if he were taken to an Afghan hospital, "he would be killed immediately." He was released on March 27.

After his release, protestors, including many clerics, chanted "Death to Christians," "Death to America," and "Abdul Rahman must be executed!" Without a formal vote, the lower chamber of Parliament demanded that he not be allowed to leave the country, but on March 29, he fled to Italy, whose government had offered him asylum. There were repeated calls for him to be brought back and/or be killed.[89]

The Abdul Rahman case drew wide attention, but he wasn't the only Christian convert in danger. Similar cases often attract little notice, sometimes because they occur in remote areas. Also, those targeted may ask that their cases not be publicized for their own protection. *Spiegel Online* interviewed a Christian, using the pseudonym Hashim Kabar, who reported that at the time of his conversion, "[T]here were a lot of churches," and Afghans could practice Christianity above ground. However, this ended when the Taliban took power. Kabar survived by pretending to be a Muslim when questioned by the police or visited by Muslim associates.[90] Compass Direct News reports that while the Rahman case proceeded, police raided other Afghan Christians. Two were arrested, and one was beaten unconscious by six men. Others received threats.[91]

If Afghanistan's Christians do manage to flee the country, they are not guaranteed asylum elsewhere. In 2011, the United Nations agency in charge of processing international refugees refused to protect at least eight Afghan Christians and their families who had fled to India. All face deportation back to Afghanistan, even though their fellow believers have faced death sentences. One of them, Amin Ali, had become a Christian eleven years before but fled after the May 2010 video of an Afghan worship service was broadcast, feeling certain he and his family would be arrested. Afghan Christians exiled in New Delhi published an open letter: "We do not know how the whole world and especially the global church is silent and closing their eyes while thousands of their brothers and sisters are in pain, facing life danger and death penalty and are tortured, persecuted and called criminals."[92]

"Ahmed," a recent Christian, met secretly with US troops at the Kabul Afghanistan International Airport in order to join Christians with whom he could pray. He first learned of Christian teachings when his English instructor offered him an English-Dari Bible. Ahmed hid the Bible under his mattress, where his mother later found it. He was thrown out of his parents' home and forced to marry a relative in hopes the marriage might renew his Muslim faith. During weekly services he prays "for a day to come in which there is freedom of religion in Afghanistan and each and every person can practice what they believe."[93]

SUDAN

Militiamen loyal to the Islamist government of North Sudan kidnapped two Catholic priests from St. Josephine Bakhita Catholic Church in South Sudan on January 15, 2012. They were released two weeks later; apparently, no ransom was paid for them, though details of their release are not available. Their capture and abuse represent a crackdown against Christians in South Sudan following the new state's inauguration in July 2011. "The two Catholic priests were mistreated," Auxiliary Bishop Daniel Adwok Kur reported to Compass Direct News. The kidnappers reportedly tortured the two clergymen both physically and psychologically.[94]

When Howida Ali started having visions of Jesus in 2004, she didn't know what to think, and when Jesus spoke to her in those visions, she didn't know what to say. Howida had always been a Muslim, so she asked one of her friends, also a Muslim, what the visions might mean. Her friend told her that she had heard about similar visions and dreams from other Christians, so Howida sought out a South Sudanese Christian for advice.

The Christian woman told Howida who Jesus is, and she prayed with her. Howida's dreams and visions increased. But before long, despite the fact that she tried to keep her new faith a secret, word of her conversion got back to her family. She fled from Sudan to Egypt in 2007, in fear for her own and her son's life.

Howida had divorced her husband in 2001 because of his addiction to drugs, but now she discovered that he and her brother—both of them now strict Muslims—were looking for her and her son, who was ten at the time. By 2011 she realized that, because she had converted to Christianity, her ex-husband wasn't just trying to take her son away from her. He wanted to kill her because she was an apostate and had disgraced her family's honor.

Compass Direct reported, "The Reverend Emmanuel S. Bennsion of All Saints' Cathedral confirmed that Ali's ex-husband and brother were acting on a tip from one of Ali's relatives when they came searching for her in Cairo. They went to her son's school to take him back to Sudan. It was a Christian school, and the director refused to hand the boy over to them." Bennsion said, "Since that time, she has started hiding and become afraid."

Howida Ali says, "We have stopped going out of the apartment or even going to church," and adds, "My son can no longer go to school daily as before. We cannot live our lives as before. I cannot now participate in the Bible study or fellowships—I'm now depending only on myself for growing spiritually, and for prayer and Bible study."[95]

CHRISTIANITY IN SUDAN

Christianity arrived in Sudan, in Nubia, in the Meroe area about 125 miles northeast of Khartoum, in AD 37 with the eunuch minister of Queen Candice. In Phyle, there were monasteries by AD 284, and the first bishop was appointed there in 325, a sign of a mature church.[96]

However, since the arrival of Islam, the Sudanese Church has been driven to the borders or eradicated several times. Christianity was revitalized there in the nineteenth century and became widespread in the south during the twentieth. In 2011, as separation of the country became imminent and President al-Bashir threatened to impose a strict form of sharia, thousands of the estimated half a million to a million and a half Christians in the North fled back to the South.[97] And, even now, some northern Muslims convert to Christianity, though the persecutions and pressures are severe.

When Mohammed Saeed Omer's Sudanese parents learned their son had become a Christian while attending university in New Delhi, India, they were horrified. Faithful Muslims themselves, they demanded he immediately return home. They also informed him that he would face disownment and disinheritance if he didn't change his mind about his religion.

Omer returned to Sudan on July 17, 2001. Perhaps he underestimated his parents' determination, because their wrath knew no bounds. They confiscated his passport and vowed to call in the Sudan's formidable Islamist security police unless he returned to Islam and gave up his newfound Christian faith.

Despite the danger, however, Omer was unrepentant. He found courage and hope in his new beliefs, and faithfully attended church services and Bible studies notwithstanding his family's rage and attempts at intimidation. When one of Omer's uncles vowed to kill Omer as an apostate, the young man finally fled his parents' home and moved in with a friend. His parents reported him to security forces, who apprehended him following a meeting he'd had with a Christian pastor. After ripping out his fingernails with pliers, the police handed him over to his parents, who kept him under strict surveillance, monitoring his phone calls and Internet use.

Thanks to the help he received from the Christian community, Omer finally escaped. In 2004, he found a way to leave Sudan and has since begun a new life in a different country.[98]

SOUTHERN INDEPENDENCE AND ITS COSTS

On July 9, 2011, there was great rejoicing in Juba, South Sudan. Flags flew, prayers were offered, and speeches were made before an ecstatic throng, who spent many hours singing, dancing, and applauding in celebration. Tens of thousands gathered to mark the culmination of their long march to freedom. On that scorching summer day, South Sudan was formally separated from the Islamist North and officially became the Republic of South Sudan, the world's newest nation.

Sudan straddles Africa's religious fault line between a Muslim north and a Christian and animist south. For decades, Sudan's South has been bloodied by one of the most protracted and brutal civil wars in world history, a war that was, as the West was slow to recognize, essentially over religious freedom. The war began in 1983 when the Khartoum regime forcibly imposed sharia law on the entire country and the South's Christians and animists rebelled. The North's attacks against the South intensified after 1989, when General Omar al-Bashir, who has been indicted for genocide for later attacks in Darfur, seized power in Khartoum. In all, a staggering two million South Sudanese died, many of them Christians; some four million others were displaced, many to squalid refugee camps, while thousands of others were abducted into slavery in Muslim households in the North.

Joyful as the Independence Day festivities were, the agony of Sudanese Christians is still not over. Persecution of the Christian population in the region along the North-South border continues to be perpetrated by loyalists to the North, through attacks on churches and Bible schools and villages, and through bombings, abductions, rapes, murders and door-to-door evictions. There are twin motives for the continued violence: Khartoum's thirst for southern oil and its self-proclaimed ongoing jihad, intended to Islamize South Sudan.

In 2005, the conflict between North and South Sudan was supposed to have formally ended with a US-brokered peace treaty. John Garang, leader of the Sudan People's Liberation Army (SPLA), had helped negotiate the 2005 Comprehensive Peace Agreement (CPA) on behalf of the Southern Sudanese government. Garang, who had led the South Sudanese army for many years, became vice president of a unified Sudan under the CPA's terms, and many expected him to be elected the independent South's first president. However, to the dismay of the South Sudanese, he died in a helicopter crash just two weeks after signing the CPA documents.

Without Garang's leadership, and thanks to the duplicity of Khartoum's murderous President al-Bashir, the North's regime continued to enforce its radicalized interpretation of Islam on Christians, animists, and Muslims alike. And it brutally sought to take possession of the South's treasure trove of oil.

Nonetheless, the South Sudanese persevered in their quest for freedom. As agreed upon in the CPA, in February 2011, they went to the polls. When the referendum commission published the final results, 98.83 percent of South Sudanese had voted in favor of independence.[99] The summer celebration of freedom and independence marked a new beginning for war-torn South Sudan.

ATTACKS ON THE BORDERLANDS

Today, Christians and others in the Republic of South Sudan enjoy religious freedom. However, the well-being of the area's people, mostly Christian, is increasingly precarious because of ongoing bombing attacks by the North on the oil-rich border regions of Abyei and South Kordofan. President al-Bashir continues to ferociously target the one million Nuba tribespeople in central Sudan, which remains formally part of the North, as well as other groups in those areas.

Though it had sided with South Sudan in the civil war that raged from 1983 to 2005, the state of South Kordofan was, under the CPA, left behind when the South formerly separated from the North. On June 5, 2011, fighting broke out in South Kordofan. Khartoum made it impossible for foreign aid groups to investigate reported atrocities and massacres. Only glimpses of the violence were possible, thanks to leaked UN reports and intermittent accounts by NGOs, church representatives, and actor George Clooney, who, after visiting the area in March 2012 with the stalwart activist on Sudan John Prendergast, presented testimony to Congress.[100]

One such leaked report from late June 2011 describes al-Bashir's regime conducting "aerial bombardments resulting in destruction of property, forced displacement, significant loss of civilian lives, including of women, children and the elderly; abductions; house-to-house searches; arbitrary arrests and detentions; targeted killings; summary executions; . . . mass graves; systematic destruction of dwellings and attacks on churches."[101] Indefatigable and indispensable veteran Sudan analyst Eric Reeves wrote:

> Strong evidence is growing of house-to-house searches for Nuba people and those sympathizing with the northern wing of the Sudan People's Liberation Army [SPLA]. Also, compelling evidence points to roadblocks that have similarly targeted Nuba. Most Nuba found were arrested or summarily executed. This has occurred primarily in the Kadugli area, capital of South Kordofan. . . . Most disturbingly, a great many eyewitness accounts of mass gravesites are being reported.[102]

Christians are singled out because they are presumed to oppose Bashir's government. Brad Phillips of the Persecution Project and Voice of the Martyrs, who entered the region in July 2011 in a privately chartered plane (one of the few outsiders to enter the area during this period), attested to this development before an emergency hearing of the US House of Representatives Foreign Affairs Committee's Subcommittee on Africa, Global Health, and Human Rights:

> I spoke with Reverend Luka Bolis, an Episcopal priest and Western Regional Chairman of the Sudan Council of Churches, who escaped from Kadugli and told me, "The NCP [National Congress Party—Bashir's party] is targeting the church in this war." Rev. Luka received a call from some friends in Kadugli warning him not to return. They told him the SAF [Sudan Armed Forces] had a list of all church leaders and suspected SPLM [Sudan People's Liberation Movement] sympathizers.

Phillips also testified:

> The daily bombings have terrorized the local population to the degree that normal cultivation is not taking place during this crucial planting season. The Nuba Mountains are isolated, cut off, and facing a humanitarian crisis within 60 days unless relief flights are allowed to recommence. And this will not happen while [Sudanese Air Force] MiGs and Antonov bombers and gunships patrol the skies.[103]

THE NUBA STILL ATTACKED

Bishop Macram Gassis, Catholic bishop for the Nuba, leads a church that remains active in the war-wracked area. He told us the attacks now underway amount to ethnic cleansing and that Khartoum is now bringing the Janjaweed—the same genocidal militias that ravaged Darfur—to his diocese from across the border in Chad and Niger. He went on to say the government is preparing to import mercenaries from among Somalia's Al-Shabab terrorists.

Ahmad Haroun—an accused war criminal wanted for arrest by the International Criminal Court for having managed the Janjaweed's systematic murder, rape, and mass deportation of Darfur's Fur people in 2003—is the new governor of South Kordofan, in north Sudan. Bishop Gassis reported that Haroun has threatened to use chemical weapons on his Nuba constituents if SPLA troops do not turn over their guns and equipment. The bishop wrote, "In the Nuba Mountains, in Abyei, in Darfur and in Blue Nile, our crucifixion continues unabated."[104]

In early February 2012, at least eight bombs were dropped in the area near a Bible school during its first day of classes, reported Samaritan's Purse, the American ministry that supports the school. "Two bombs landed inside the compound—located in the region's Nuba Mountains—destroying two Heiban Bible college buildings and igniting grass fires across the area," the group said. "It was a miracle that no one was injured."[105]

Though the Nuba are mostly Muslim, they refused to wage Bashir's proclaimed jihad against South Sudan. For their resistance, a 1993 fatwa sponsored by the government declared they were "apostates," which meant that it was deemed permissible to kill them along with non-Muslims. As a consequence, tens of thousands of Nuba people were starved to death under the regime's two-pronged strategy of conducting saturation bombing and banning international relief flights—the same strategy being used now.

None of this bodes well for peace any time soon. In February 2012, our colleague Andrew Natsios, formerly the US Special Envoy to Sudan, wrote in *Foreign Affairs*:

> Despite the mediation of former South African President Thabo Mbeki, negotiations before independence (and since) left several unresolved issues to fester: How much the South would pay to transport oil through the North, where the actual border would lie (especially the status of the disputed region of Abyei), debt sharing, and what the citizenship status of South Sudanese remaining in the North, and vice versa, would be. In addition to tension surrounding these questions, a wider opposition that includes the three major Darfur rebel movements, the Northern arm of the Southern political movement, is growing.[106]

Despite its embattled northern border, the new Republic of South Sudan protects religious freedom. In the US State

Department's 2012 report on religious freedom, it stood out as a country where "[t]here were no reports of societal abuses or discrimination based on religious affiliation, belief, or practice"[107] and moreover that the "laws and policies protect religious freedom and, in practice, the government generally respects religious freedom." Meanwhile, in al-Bashir's North Sudan, the persecution of Christians accelerates.

KHARTOUM'S BESIEGED CHRISTIANS

All Sudanese in the north, including Christians, are subject to sharia law. The US Department of State continues to designate north Sudan as a Country of Particular Concern, that is, one of the world's worst religious persecutors. USCIRF's 2012 Annual Report states:

> In meetings in Khartoum in December 2009, both Christians and Muslims told USCIRF that they felt their religious freedoms were infringed by the government's imposition of its own particular Islamic ideology on the entire population, including its enforcement of religiously-based morality codes and corporal punishment.[108]

Christian women are flogged if they do not conform to Islamic dress codes and wear headscarves. Under Sudanese law, conversion from Islam is a capital crime, though Muslims are free to proselytize for Islam. Building new churches is difficult, and a Christian's testimony is weighed less than a Muslim's in the country's sharia court system. Christians are denied airtime on the media, which is government controlled, and are discriminated against in education and in receiving government services. They are portrayed negatively in school textbooks.

USCIRF reported that, on November 14, 2010, hundreds of police officers, arriving in a convoy of seven trucks, stormed into the Khartoum building housing the Sudan Council of Churches, a body that represents Orthodox, Protestant, and Roman Catholic churches. The police ransacked the Council offices, claiming they were looking for weapons, though none were found.[109]

Christianity Today reported that Northern Christians are living under "a blanket of fear" since the South seceded. It continued:

> Just one month after the South voted for independence from the predominantly Islamic North, pressures on churches and Christians have increased, with Muslim groups threatening to destroy churches, kill Christians and purge the country of Christianity.

It cited the example of a Presbyterian church, led by Reverend Maubark Hamad, in Wad Madani, eighty-five miles southeast of Khartoum, which was burned down on January 15, 2011, following extremist threats. "Christian sources said they are increasingly fearful as Muslim extremists pose more threats against Christians in an attempt to rid what they call Dar al Islam, the 'Land of Islam,' of Christianity."[110]

THE POWER TO CHANGE THINGS

A source in Afghanistan who is close to Said Musa—the Christian convert spared from execution—praised the efforts of the international community:

> We feel that the release reveals that when many, many people come together trying to enforce justice, in some case like for our friend Said Musa, good things happen, even though it looks impossible. The voices of the people outside Afghanistan who put pressure on the Afghan government and on the international diplomats have been heard. . . . [When local churches and international bodies advocate for the persecuted in faith] they have the power to change things.[111]

If raising our voices can make a difference even in so Islamicized a country as Afghanistan, where not one church is allowed to exist openly, then we can bring moral comfort and political and material help to other persecuted Christians as well—in Sudan, Egypt, Pakistan, and Afghanistan—in this time of their great suffering.

We opened this chapter by describing the Christian garbage people of Cairo, the zabaleen, of Mokatam, "Garbage City." Apart from the murders in March 2011, they have suffered many other atrocities and indignities. In what was said to be a swine-flu precaution, the Egyptian government announced in April 2009 a mass cull of pigs. Since Islam holds pigs to be unclean, Copts owned nearly all the pigs, especially in Garbage City. Hundreds of Mokatam's pig farmers clashed with police as the latter sought to destroy the animals. Many dirt-poor Christians—in the most literal sense possible—lost what little livelihood they had. Egypt is the only country to have engaged in such a killing of pigs; the World Health Organization has said it is unnecessary to combat the A H1N1 flu strain by such measures.[112]

Mokatam is also the site of one of the Middle East's most unusual churches: the Church of St. Samaan (Simon) the Tanner, popularly known as the "cave church." Despite its huge Coptic population, Garbage City had no church at first and, for many years, the government refused to permit one to be built. To compensate, the Copts then deepened the caves in the hill overshadowing their streets and began to meet and worship in them. Now Mokatam is a warren of meeting places that draws tourists, including Muslim ones. The largest of the caves regularly holds more than ten thousand worshipers.

EIGHT

THE MUSLIM WORLD: WAR AND TERRORISM

Iraq / Nigeria / Indonesia / Bangladesh / Somalia

SALAT SEKONDO, A SOMALI WHO LIVED IN A REFUGEE CAMP IN Dadaab in northeastern Kenya, was attacked by Muslim youths in October 2008. He and his twenty-two-year-old son were able to overpower the youths. But weeks later, Salat discovered that local Islamist groups had fined him twenty thousand Kenyan shillings for dishonoring Islam and the prophet Muhammad by converting to Christianity.

In November, his home was attacked again, by a mob threatening to "teach him a lesson" for converting from Islam. He tried to escape by crawling out of a window, but was shot several times in the shoulder and left for dead. He later recovered, but others in his family were not so fortunate. The previous July, his relative Nur Osman Muhiji was dragged from his vehicle by Islamic extremists and stabbed to death while the ten Christians he was attempting to secretly rescue from Kismayo, Somalia, remained hidden. Muhiji's home was set on fire, but neighbors were able to save his young children.[1]

Welhelmina Holle had dedicated her life to teaching elementary mathematics and the Indonesian language in Masohi, in the Maluku islands. When religious conflict flared up in Maluku in 1999, resulting in more than ten thousand deaths, she was the only

Christian teacher who remained at the school. She had taught there for twenty-five years.

In December 2008, Welhelmina was accused of blaspheming—insulting Islam—in a comment she made while tutoring a sixth-grade student. Rumors spread quickly through the community, and the local chapter of the Indonesian Ulema Council lodged a complaint with the police.[2] Soon, five hundred Muslims rampaged through the area, clashing with police and Christian residents. They burned two churches, a health clinic, and sixty-seven homes, including some owned by Muslims, resulting in injuries to at least six people.

The police arrested Welhelmina and named her, along with Muslim leader Asmara Wasahua, as a suspect in sparking the riots. She was also charged with blasphemy and "public insult."

Welhelmina was found innocent of blasphemy since the judges did not think the testimony of the young students was reliable. But she was found guilty of public insult for allegedly insulting, then apologizing to, a student who kicked a ball at her chest in 2007. Even though no one had filed a charge in the intervening time, and the case had passed the one-year statute of limitations, she was sentenced to a year in prison. Even the head of the Masohi prison essentially agreed it was unfair, saying that she was imprisoned to contain "the anger of the townspeople."[3]

Paulos Faraj Rahho, the popular Catholic Chaldean archbishop of Mosul, Iraq, was abducted after he prayed the Lenten stations of the cross in Aramaic at the Church of the Holy Spirit on February 29, 2008. The sixty-five-year-old prelate was found dead two weeks later in a shallow grave. Islamists, possibly working with criminal gangs, were thought to be behind his death. Archbishop Rahho had been a dynamic leader and a man of great hope. Despite the odds, he had recently founded the new parish of St. Paul in Mosul, started a "Youth Week" in his diocese, and founded the Fraternity of Charity and Joy, with the aim of assisting sick people and guaranteeing them a dignified life.

For many Iraqi Christians, Catholic or not, the archbishop's murder felt like a defining moment. Johan Candalin, the executive director of the World Evangelical Alliance's Religious Liberty Commission, commented, "An archbishop is more than one ordinary clergyman. He is a symbol of the whole church. And when he is killed in this brutal way it is a very clear signal to all Christians that this is what could happen to any one of you."[4]

EXTREMISTS AND TERRORISTS

In the Muslim majority countries we have described so far, the main source of repression and persecution has been, as in Saudi Arabia and Iran, Islamist governments, or, as in Afghanistan and Pakistan, a vicious mixture of governments, mobs, and vigilantes, often acting in concert. There is another set of countries where the persecution of Christians does not usually come directly from the government—at least not the central government—but rather from extremists in society, including terrorists. The problem with these countries' governments is that they cannot, or at least they do not, control or stop this violence.

In some cases, as in Indonesia and Bangladesh, the central government is not strong enough to maintain security, or it is simply unwilling to risk political unpopularity by effectively countering extremists. At the other end of the spectrum is Somalia, which is in the midst of a brutal civil war and has been without an effective central government since 1991. As a result, militias such as Al-Shabab wreak havoc in the areas where they operate, and deliberately seek to exterminate Christians. Between these two cases are Iraq and Nigeria, where, in large parts of the country, militias and terrorist groups are comparatively undeterred as they target religious minorities.

In several of these countries, the major persecutors have Al-Qaeda links. In Iraq, the attack described below on Baghdad's Church of Our Lady of Perpetual Help, which killed fifty-eight Christians, was carried out by a branch of Al-Qaeda. In North

Africa, Al-Qaeda's affiliate there has declared its willingness to arm and train the Nigeria militia and terrorist group Boko Haram, which is massacring Christians as part of a deliberate policy to drive them out of Northern Nigeria. About Somalia's Al-Shabab, Ayman Al-Zawahiri, who took over the leadership of Al-Qaeda after Osama bin Laden was killed, declared, "[T]he Shabab movement has joined Al-Qaeda," while Al-Shabab's leader, Ahmed Abdi Godane, replied, "We will move along with you as faithful soldiers." These complex scenarios result in some of the worst situations in the world for Christians.

IRAQ

On October 31, 2010, Al-Qaeda in Mesopotamia laid siege to Our Lady of Perpetual Help, a Syrian Catholic church in Baghdad, while 120 local worshippers attended Sunday mass inside. Nearly everyone in the church was killed or wounded. Among the some 58 dead were two priests, Father Wasim Sabih and Father Thaier Saad Abdal, while a third, Father Qatin, was wounded by a bullet lodged in his head. The Islamist attackers pushed Father Sabih to the ground and, as he clutched a crucifix and pleaded with them to spare the parishioners, shot him dead in a hail of bullets. Three-year-old Adam Udai also begged one of the terrorists to "please stop" and was summarily murdered.

The suicide attackers posted numerous Internet threats against infidels "everywhere they can be reached" and demanded the release of two Christian women who they alleged had converted to Islam and were being held against their will in Egyptian monasteries—allegations that the women in question later denied. The massacre, now known as "Black Sunday" by Iraqi Christians, tore at the fabric of the community. " 'We've lost part of our soul now,' said Rudy Khalid, a sixteen-year-old Christian who lived across the street from the church. 'Our destiny, no one knows what to say of it.' "[5]

On August 18, 2009, a Christian doctor, Sameer Gorgees Youssif, was kidnapped in a presumably safe section district of Kirkuk and held in captivity for twenty-nine days. Christians are a particular target for Iraqi kidnappers. His release came thanks to his twenty-three-year-old daughter's negotiations with the kidnappers. Initially the hostage takers demanded $500,000, but finally dropped the amount to $100,000. "They were threatening us all the time, and we were living in hell," Youssif's daughter said. "We just stayed and prayed and fasted and closed the doors and locked them. We were afraid that maybe they would come here and kill all of us. God was our only hope." Dr. Youssif was dumped in front of a Kirkuk mosque a month later, hours after the ransom money was delivered. He was in critical condition; his body bore signs of torture and he had been starved beyond recognition. He had been bound, gagged, and blindfolded and had lain on his side for twenty-nine days, developing severe ulcers on his right thigh and arm. He was covered with bruises and his forehead and nose showed signs of repeated beatings.[6]

RUTHLESS RELIGIOUS CLEANSING

The Iraqi church is in acute crisis after a decade of vicious persecution. The 2003 overthrow of secular Baath Party dictator Saddam Hussein unleashed a ruthless religious cleansing campaign against Iraq's ancient Christian communities. Relentless waves of targeted, religiously motivated bombings, assassinations, kidnappings, extortions, and rapes have triggered a mass exodus of Christians. Since 2003, up to two-thirds of the estimated 1.5 million Iraqi Chaldean and Syriac Catholics; Assyrian, Syriac and Armenian Orthodox; as well as some Protestants, have fled to Syria, Jordan, and farther-flung places.

Christians still remain the largest non-Muslim minority in the country, but church leaders voice a real fear that the light of the faith in Iraq, said to have been kindled personally by Thomas, one of Jesus' twelve apostles, could soon be extinguished. Iraq's other non-Muslim religions, the much smaller groups of Mandaeans (followers of

John the Baptist), Yezidis (an ancient angel-centered religion), and Baha'is are also all being violently driven out. Religious persecution in Iraq is so egregious that the country has now been included as one of the world's worst places for religious persecution on a recommended short list of "Countries of Particular Concern" by the United States Commission on International Religious Freedom (USCIRF), under its mandate given by the International Religious Freedom Act.

No Iraqi group, Muslim or non-Muslim, has been spared massive and appalling religiously motivated violence. However, as the commission found, the one-two punch of Sunni and Shia extremism, combined with deep governmental discrimination and indifference, now threatens the very existence of Iraq's ancient Christian churches. Some of these still pray in Aramaic, the language of Jesus of Nazareth.

Christians and other smaller minorities are not, as many secular news reports declare, simply caught in the middle of a Muslim sectarian power struggle. They are not simply collateral damage. They suffer from violence that is much more focused. While the purpose of attacks on the Shia majority is to trigger a civil war and bring down the government, the goal of the attacks against Iraq's Christian minorities is to rid the nation of their presence. The refugee branches of both the UN and the US Conference of Catholic Bishops have, after extensive research, separately concluded that these minorities are being "obliterated" (the bishops' term)[7] because of specifically targeted violence. Wijdan Michael, Iraq's human rights minister and herself a Christian, summed it up succinctly when she said it was an attempt "to empty Iraq of Christians."[8]

Sustained violence against Christians began in August 2004 with the coordinated bombing of several churches. Since then, documentation shows that some seventy churches have been bombed, mostly in Baghdad and Mosul.[9] On Sunday, July 12, 2009, six churches were bombed in coordinated attacks in Baghdad, killing three Christians and one Muslim, and leaving dozens injured. Attacks on five of the churches were carried out with minor explosives, but the car bomb that exploded near the Church of Mariam Al-Adra, as parishioners were leaving mass, was extremely powerful and resulted in the heaviest casualties.[10]

The most catastrophic incident, described above, occurred at Our Lady of Perpetual Help Catholic Church in Baghdad at Sunday mass in October 2010. On December 30 of that year, one week after an Islamic group threatened violence against Christians, ten bombs exploded in Baghdad, claiming the lives of two people and injuring twenty more—all Christian. These would not be the last such attacks. On August 2, 2011, a car bomb exploded outside the Holy Family Church in central Kirkuk, wounding at least twenty-three people.[11]

Christians remember that similar bombings of synagogues and other violence in 1948 prompted Iraq's Jewish community to flee. Iraq's Jewish population today amounts to about eight souls; Jews made up one-third of Baghdad's population in the 1940s.[12]

"ALL OF MY LEADERSHIP . . . ALL DEAD."

Religious leaders have been targeted. On October 9, 2006, Father Paulos Iskander, a prominent Syriac Orthodox priest, was kidnapped for ransom and three days later beheaded and dismembered, with a message from his captors linking the murder to the pope's speech at Regensburg, which seemed critical of Islam. On November 30, 2006, Father Mundhir al-Dayr was kidnapped from his Mosul Protestant church and found later dead of a gunshot wound to the head. As they went about their ministry on June 3, 2007, "Chaldean Catholic Friar Ragheed Ganni and three deacons were gunned down in their car, which was rigged with explosives to prevent anybody retrieving their bodies."[13] Anglican Canon Andrew White, who leads a Baghdad ecumenical congregation, reported "All of my leadership were . . . taken and killed—all dead."[14]

During the 2006 American military occupation, Sunni militants operating from a mosque in Baghdad's religiously integrated Dora neighborhood conducted a religious cleansing of the area.

They issued a fatwa specifically commanding the two thousand Christian families residing there to convert, or pay an Islamic protection tax, or be killed. Most left Dora and have never returned. The Chaldean Federation of America provided the following example of a death threat received by the Dora Christians:

> To the traitor, apostate Amir XX, after we warned you more than once to quit working with the American occupiers, but you did not learn from what happened to others, and you continued, you and your infidel wife Rina XX by opening a women hair cutting place and this is among the forbidden things for us, and therefore we are telling you and your wife to quit these deeds and to pay the amount of (20,000) thousand dollars in protective tax for your violation and within only one week or we will kill you and your family, member by member, and those who have warned are excused.

The notice was signed "Al-Mujahideen Battalions."[15] The fate of these particular recipients is not known but the majority of those receiving such threats fled their homes and did not return.

The US Catholic Bishops report that some Christian children have been tortured to death. Islamic fanatics broke into one Chaldean home near Mosul and killed a ten-year-old boy while shouting, "We've come to exterminate you. This is the end for you Christians!" Christian women have been hit hard as well. At Mosul University some young Christian women were raped and killed for offending some Muslims by wearing jeans and having a picnic with male colleagues.[16]

Both Sunni and Shia extremists who seek to impose their codes of behavior have been ruthless toward Christians, throwing acid in the faces of women without the hijab (veil). Flyers were posted at Mosul University declaring that "in cases where non-Muslims do not conform to wearing the hijab and are not conservative with their attire in accordance with the Islamic way, the violators will have the Sharia and the Islamic law applied to them."[17] Men who operate liquor stores, hair salons, and cinemas have also been gunned down for their "un-Islamic" businesses.

From southern Basra to northern Kirkuk, all across Iraq, Christians have suffered bloody reprisals for failing to conform to the fanatics' version of Islamic behavior—in their dress, their social patterns, and their occupations, as well as in their worship. Sunni terrorists and insurgents have targeted the Chaldean and Assyrian Christians with particular ferocity, linking them to the West and accusing them of collaborating with the American occupation. Criminal gangs of Sunnis, as well as those of the majority Shia population, have found easy prey in the religious minorities, who, faced with indifferent security forces and lacking militias of their own, are utterly defenseless.

The Assyrian Christian news agency AINA.org reported "thousands of Christians have been taken hostage, with ransom payments averaging $100,000 each. One who could not afford the payment, twenty-nine-year-old Laith Antar Khanno, was found beheaded in Mosul on December 2, 2004, two weeks after his kidnapping."[18]

Cold-blooded assassinations of Christians also began to make their appearance in 2004. Prominent Assyrian surgeon and professor Ra'aad Augustine Qoryaqos was shot dead by three terrorists while making his rounds in a Ramadi clinic on December 8, 2004. That same week two Christian businessmen from Baghdad, Fawzi Luqa and Haitham Saka, were abducted from work and murdered. High-ranking government officials have not been spared.[19]

Pascale Warda, an Assyrian Christian from the Chaldean Catholic Church, served in the transitional government of Iraq as the Minister of Migration and Displacement in 2004. Since 2004, there have been four different assassination attempts on her life, and in 2005, four of her Christian bodyguards were killed during an assassination attempt.[20]

The list of victims is long, and it continues to lengthen. Iraq's shocking and potentially destabilizing Sunni-Shia violence rightly concerned the United States, but the military surge that was devised to alleviate it overlooked the unique plight of the Christians.

Evidence suggests it may have even made things far worse for them by flushing terrorists northward into the ancestral Christian areas around Mosul, the northern Nineveh Plains, as well as the northern city of Kirkuk. Many of the recent attacks on Christians occurred in those areas and came at the hands of Sunni terrorists. Some were killed after failing to pay ransom demands or what could be considered an Islamic tax, *jizya*, on non-Muslims. Others were targeted for elimination simply because they were Christians. A small sample of the many cases follows.

A nongovernmental group reported the 2008 religiously motivated attacks on Zaya Toma, a twenty-two-year-old engineering student, and his cousin Ramsin Shmael, a twenty-one-year-old pharmacy student. As the two waited at a bus stop in Mosul's al-Tahrir district on their way to class, assailants impersonating police officers asked them for their identity cards. Their names gave them away as being Christians. After producing his ID, Toma was shot point-blank in the head, killing him instantly. Ramsin began to run but was shot at twice, with one bullet shattering his teeth; but he survived. The murderers fled, and family members arrived on the scene to find Toma lying in a pool of blood, his books and ID card scattered nearby. His family told the investigators they wanted to leave Iraq because "our only crime is that we are Christian."[21]

Aziz Rizko Nissan al-Bidari, the director general of the Financial Directorate in Kirkuk, was shot and killed by gunmen on July 12, 2009. He had been the most senior Christian government official in that city at the time of his death. The following month, sixty-year-old Mosul Christian businessman Salem Barjjo was abducted; he was found dead on September 7, 2009, after his family had failed to pay the large ransom. He was closely tied to the local church. Imad Elias Abdul Karim, a fifty-five-year-old Christian nurse who was kidnapped on October 3, 2009, in Kirkuk, was found dead the following day. Police found the body "thrown" by the side of the road, and according to medical reports, it bore "obvious signs of torture."[22]

Arkan Jihad Yacob, an Orthodox Christian, was killed on

May 30, 2011, leaving behind a wife and four children. Yacob had been the victim of two previous attempted ransom abductions from which he had been able to escape. This time, however, the attackers ambushed him as he went to work, shooting him several times in an "execution-style cold-blooded murder." The sixty-three-year-old Yacob was employed as the vice director of a cement factory, which, along with his religion, made him a prime target for criminals; not only did he have some measure of wealth but he was not a member of a tribe or militia that would seek retribution. And he, as a religious minority, had lost the protection of the state.[23]

NO PROTECTION AND NO JUSTICE

In 2005, in a national referendum, Iraq adopted a new constitution, heralded as establishing the first electoral democracy in the Arab Middle East. However, the constitution gave a major role to Islam, which Christians fear negates its positive language on religious freedom and other human rights. It specifically requires the Supreme Court to include sharia experts. Article 2 bars any law that "contradicts the established provisions of Islam," and it guarantees "the Islamic identity of the majority of the Iraqi people." The actual status of basic rights is left to future decisions by sharia judges, who may decide that these rights conflict with their version of Islam and so are null and void. These provisions reinforce the perception of Iraq's already beleaguered Christian community: that they are second-class citizens denied real hope for a better future in their ancestral homeland.

Though Iraq's president, prime minister, and Shia leader Grand Ayatollah Sistani all denounced attacks on Christians, the persecution did not abate. The Chaldo-Assyrians have endured much throughout the last century in Iraq, including brutal Arabization and Islamization campaigns. Those who survived through the Saddam Hussein era, when dozens of their northern villages were obliterated, were die-hards; they held out because of their devotion to their unique churches, culture, and Aramaic language. But they may be seeing their last stand as a cohesive community.

Iraq's government has made no serious attempt to ensure either justice or adequate security for the besieged Christians. The United States Commission on International Religious Freedom has pointed to the general indifference of Iraq's government, which "creates a climate of impunity" for the attackers of Christians and the other small minorities. The Iraqi government also discriminates against and marginalizes these victims in the provision of essential government services, including American-supported reconstruction projects.

"PEOPLE ARE LEFT WITH NO CHOICE BUT TO FLEE"

Hundreds of thousands of Christians have fled to escape violence in Iraqi cities, particularly in Baghdad, Basra, and Mosul. Many have moved north, mainly to the rural Nineveh Plains. This is their last hope for staying in Iraq. Nineveh is the traditional home of the Assyrian Christians, who trace their civilization to Nimrod, Noah's great-grandson, and their faith to the prophet Jonah and the apostle Thomas, both of whom preached there, with Thomas establishing the church in Nineveh. Isaac the Syrian, a seventh-century bishop of Nineveh, is regarded by many as one of the greatest spiritual and monastic writers in the history of the church.

Others have fled to semi-autonomous Kurdistan. Still others have gone abroad. This mass exodus accelerated after the October 31, 2010, Baghdad church bombing.

On the night of November 22, 2010, thirty-five-year-old Diana Gorgiz heard screams and saw that her neighbor's garden had been set aflame. When the Iraqi army arrived, they told Diana's family they were no longer safe. "When the army comes and says, 'We cannot protect you,' " Diana explained, "what else can you believe?" The following day, three generations of the Gorgiz family—fifteen in total—fled to a monastery in Qosh where they crowded into a single room.[24]

The town of Ankawa, a predominantly Christian community in Iraq's north, which has several churches, has also become a safe haven for many of the refugees. One Christian woman, Jabir

Hikmet Al Sammak, said at the funeral of her seventy-eight-year-old father and seventy-six-year-old mother, "Baghdad has too many evils . . . it is a city of guns." Extremists had beheaded both her parents. But, despite improved safety, Ankawa is still a place of extreme hardship. The family lives on money they made by selling their Baghdad home.[25]

Since Christians are not a majority, they are at the mercy of dominant governmental groups who seize their property, businesses, and villages, and have at times withheld American reconstruction aid. In the north, local Kurdish *Peshmerga* forces have confiscated Christian farms and villages. American reconstruction aid to establish roads, schools, clean water, electricity, and other vital infrastructure largely bypassed Chaldo-Assyrian communities. The US State Department distributed these funds exclusively to the Arab- and Kurdish-run governorates—part of the old Saddam Hussein power structure—who then failed to pass on the Chaldo-Assyrian's share.

On December 24, 2010, members of the Sacred Church of Jesus gathered to worship, celebrating the birth of Jesus. In a sanctuary built for four to five hundred members, only one hundred assembled; others stayed home for fear of violence. Many churches in Kirkuk, Mosul, and Basra cancelled Christmas observance altogether or called off any ceremonies due to be held after dark. Church leaders also advised Christians not to hold parties or display Christmas symbols.[26] As the US Department of State observed, Christian groups can no longer gather in safety, and many have stopped holding worship services altogether. Chaldean Archbishop Kassab of Basra—who says his prayers in Aramaic as is the Chaldean tradition—will not be celebrating Christmas mass with his diocese any longer: the church has transferred him to Australia. Today a mere few hundred Chaldean Catholics remain in Basra. These churches are not just lying low. They are being eradicated.

In late 2010, Joseph Kassab, executive director of the Chaldean Federation of America and brother of the former archbishop of

Basra, wrote to our office: "Things are deteriorating very fast in Iraq; our people are left with no choice but to flee because they are losing hope and there is no serious action taken to protect them as of today."

A MESSAGE OF ETERNAL HOPE

Lebanese Catholic scholar Habib Malik wrote in the Center for Religious Freedom's 2008 survey, Religious Freedom in the World, that the Middle East's Christians have historically served as moderating influences. The presence of Iraq's ancient Christian communities highlights pluralism, and they have served as a bridge to the West and its values of individual rights. They have sponsored schools with modern curricula, benefiting all. One prime example was Baghdad's Jesuit College, whose past students include three Muslim presidential candidates in Iraq's 2005 election. Without the experience of living alongside Christians and other non-Muslims, the Muslim Middle East loses the experience of peacefully coexisting with others. Western governments and Western churches need to consider this carefully.

With the Christian community absorbing one shattering blow after another, Iraq's Reverend Meyassr al-Qaspotros, a Chaldean Catholic priest, delivered a message of eternal hope: "We are threatened, but we will not stop praying." He added, alluding to the words of Jesus before his crucifixion, "Be careful not to hate the ones killing us because they know not what they are doing. God forgive them."[27]

NIGERIA

On June 12, 2006, Joshua Lai, a Christian high school teacher in Keffi, in Nasarawa, was teaching an English class when a Muslim student, Abdullahi Yusuf, arrived late. Yusuf's excuse for his tardiness was that he just was coming from prayers at the mosque. As a former Muslim, Lai knew that morning prayers could not have delayed Yusuf until 9:00 a.m., so he caned him—a common punishment in Nigeria. Yusuf later accused Lai of saying he would "flog the prophet Muhammad." That night, students burned down Lai's school residence as well as his home. He was moved to Abuja for his protection and, on October 16, 2006, put on trial for blasphemy.[28]

On February 20, 2006, in Bauchi State, a student accused Christian high school teacher Florence Chuckwu of blasphemy, and she was nearly killed. When she noticed that one of her students was reading a book during her lecture and ignoring her requests to stop, she confiscated his book until after class. She was unaware that his book was the Qur'an. Muslim students began to throw books at her and one shouted, "Kill her!" She received serious head injuries. Students began to riot, and before the mob scene ended, more than twenty Christians were killed and two churches burned down. Chuckwu fled, and her present whereabouts are unknown.[29]

Recent news images from Nigeria have been disturbing: photographs of burned villages, blown-up cars and churches, and charred human remains. The country has some 162 million people, by far the largest population in Africa, and more than 250 ethnic groups. With such diversity, Nigeria would face dramatic tensions even without its profound religious differences. But in this sharply divided land, those religious differences are often deadly.

Nigeria's population is about equally apportioned between Muslims and Christians, with another 10 percent retaining traditional African beliefs. Christians are the majority in the south, Muslims in the north, and the two are mixed in the middle belt, the scene of frequent violent conflict. Usually these conflicts also have ethnic characteristics and are often tied to disputes over land and resources. Still, there is an inescapable religious dimension.

In recent decades, Nigeria has been ripped apart by violence between Muslims and Christians at the cost of thousands of lives. These groups' already troubled relations have been exacerbated by the increased influence of radical Islam, manifested especially in two trends. One has been the overt attempt to apply Islamic law nationwide; the other, which is overlapping, is the growth of Islamic militias.[30]

EFFECTS OF SHARIA

Since the governor of Zamfara State, Alhaji Ahmed Sani, introduced a draconian version of Islamist sharia law in 1999, eleven of Nigeria's thirty-six states followed suit. Under these dictates, Muslims, and especially Muslim women, also suffer. But the Christian population has borne much of the brunt. Their taxes pay for Islamic preachers, while local government orders have closed hundreds of churches.

Conflict over sharia has also led to riots, mob attacks, and vigilantes, producing the largest death toll in Nigeria since the civil war over Biafra in the 1960s. The authorities have been largely ineffectual in preventing attacks, which, though stemming mainly from Muslim elements, are sometimes initiated by Christians. Those who change their religion from Islam are threatened with death. The Catholic and Anglican churches have had to set up protected centers for converts. A similar fate awaits those accused of blasphemy, and blasphemy charges can also lead to generalized violence.[31]

On September 29, 2007, a Christian teacher allegedly posted an insulting caricature of Muhammad in his classroom, and nine people were killed in the ensuing clash between Christian and Muslim youths. On October 5, 2007, another nine people, all Christians, were killed, and churches, shops, and houses were torched, in reaction to a cartoon purportedly defaming the Muslim Prophet.[32]

Two months later, hundreds rioted and attacked Christians over claims that a Christian had written an inscription on a wall disparaging Muhammad. On April 20, 2008, hundreds of Muslims in Kano attacked Christians and their shops and burned vehicles after claims that a Christian had blasphemed Muhammad. The rioters demanded that the accused shopkeeper be stoned to death, and, to escape being killed, he ran to the police station. He subsequently had to be moved to police headquarters for his own protection. "Thousands of Christians were trapped in churches until police dispersed rioters. Fearing that Muslims might attack again, many Christians have relocated to army and police barracks in the city."[33]

MILITIAS: "A HOLY WAR AGAINST CHRISTIANS"

In January 2004 in Yobe, Nigeria, a man calling himself Mullah Omar (after the Afghan Taliban's head) led an uprising by a militia identified as *al-Sunna Wal Jamma* and usually nicknamed "the Taliban." While the names had a comic-opera quality, their actions were brutal. Demanding an Islamic state governed by sharia law, they stormed police stations and other government buildings, pulled down the Nigerian flag, raised the old Afghan flag, stole large quantities of weapons, and declared they would kill all non-Muslims in a holy war against Christians. Tens of thousands of people were displaced. The uprising was not put down until hundreds of troops were rushed to the area. In early 2007, there were further attacks on the police in Kano by a group calling itself the Taliban, leaving dozens dead.

The "Taliban" group spawned a variety of vicious offspring. One is Jama'atu Ahlis Sunna Lidda'awati wal-Jihad, more usually known by its nickname, Boko Haram, which translates roughly as "Western education is forbidden," and is much easier to say. Even today, the majority of Muslim parents in Nigeria's northern states do not send their children to school for Western education. Instead, they either learn nothing or are graduates of Islamiyya schools, where they often learn simply to recite the Qur'an in a language they do not understand. We don't begrudge Muslims the opportunity to learn their own sacred texts. But since they often are taught little else, they have few work skills and end up unemployed and roaming the streets of northern towns. In turn, these angry, alienated youths become the lifeblood of groups like Boko Haram, who reject broader education, and so the cycle repeats itself.34

Boko Haram treats as infidels anyone—Christian or Muslim—who does not conform to its views. In July 2009, in the northeastern city of Maiduguri, it attacked police stations, prisons, schools, churches, and homes, burning almost everything in its path. Its violence spread through Borno, Kano, and Yobe states, particularly targeting Christians. Many were abducted and forced, under threat of death, to renounce their faith. The riots continued for five days before police were able to stop them, and seven hundred people were killed in Maiduguri alone. On August 9, 2009, the group released a statement aligning itself with Al-Qaeda and calling for jihad in response to the killing of its leader, Mallam Mohammed Yusuf. There are also reports that some of its members have trained with militants in Mali linked to the organization Al-Qaeda in the Islamic Maghreb (AQIM).[35]

Boko Haram's leader, Mallam Mohammed Yusuf, declared before his demise that his militia would "hunt and gun down those who oppose the rule of sharia in Nigeria and ensure that the infidel does not go unpunished."[36] In March 2010, the group promised to continue its "holy struggle to oust the secular regime and entrench a just Islamic government."[37]

In August 2011, Boko Haram carried out a suicide bombing of the UN headquarters in Abuja, Nigeria's capital, which killed twenty-four people. It continues to attack security forces but is focusing its attention on displacing or killing Nigeria's Christian population, which, at some 70 million, is in the list of the top ten largest in the world. When the group stormed the town of Damaturu in Yobe State, at the end of their four-hour rampage, some 150 people had been killed, at least 130 of them Christians.[38]

Boko Haram also has picked Christmas as a focal time for attacks, a practice followed by its international allies. In 2010 and 2011, it pitilessly bombed five churches in Jos as congregations were celebrating Christmas. One blast targeted congregants as they left Christmas-morning mass in 2011 at St. Theresa Catholic Church in Madalla, a suburb of Nigeria's capital, Abuja. Thirty-five bodies were recovered and many others were wounded as the explosion ripped through the church, leaving a crater.[39]

On consecutive Sundays in June 2012, militants attacked multiple churches, killing and wounding scores and triggering retaliatory violence by Christians, which church leaders tried to stop. The BBC reported: "Recently, hardly a Sunday has gone by without reports of churches being attacked in Nigeria."[40]

On January 1, 2012, Boko Haram followed up its attacks by warning the millions of Christians living in the north that they had three days to leave or they would be attacked. In 2011, Boko Haram had killed about five hundred people; in just the first month of 2012 it killed more than half as many. Gun and bomb attacks in Kano killed at least 178 people. Thousands have fled.[41] Meanwhile Al-Qaeda in the Islamic Maghreb has declared, "We are ready to train your people in weapons, and give you whatever support we can in men, arms and munitions to enable you to defend our people in Nigeria."[42]

Nigeria's conflicts, like those everywhere in the world, can be complex, but the anti-Christian element is undeniable. Boko Haram's leader, Abubakar Shekau, has declared: "Everyone knows that democracy and the constitution is paganism. . . . [Y]ou Christians should know that Jesus . . . is not the Son of God. This religion of Christianity you are practicing is not a religion of God—it is Paganism. . . . We are trying to coerce you to embrace Islam, because that is what God instructed us to do."[43]

INDONESIA

On May 2, 2008, a mob from the predominantly Muslim village of Saleman attacked the mainly Christian village of Horale. They burned one hundred and twenty houses, three churches, and the village school, and injured fifty-six Christians and killed four. Three of the four murdered had their throats slit. Welhelmina Pattiasina, aged forty-seven, was tortured before she was killed. Her granddaughter,

Yola, aged six, had her stomach cut open. Edward Unwaru, aged eighty-four, and Josef Laumahina, aged thirty-nine, were burned after their throats had been cut.[44]

On May 13, 2005, three Christian women were arrested and charged under the 2002 Child Protection Act with attempting to force children into changing their religion. The charge has a maximum penalty of five years in prison and a fine of one hundred million rupiah.[45] The local chapter of the Indonesian Ulema Council (MUI) accused Rebekka Zakaria, Eti Pangesti, and Ratna Bangun of bribing Muslim children to participate in a church Sunday school program and trying to convert them to Christianity. The court recognized that the three had not converted any children and that, in fact, they had told children to go home if they did not have their parents' permission to attend.

The women showed photographs of Muslim children together with their parents at the Sunday school, proving they had attended with full parental knowledge and consent. However, hundreds of Islamic extremists gathered outside the court, chanting, carrying a coffin, and threatening to kill the teachers and the judge if they were not found guilty. This violent environment made it difficult for the judges to acquit the defendants. When they found the three guilty of using "deceitful conduct, a series of lies and enticements to seduce children to change their religion against their wills," the large crowd in the courtroom yelled and screamed.[46] On September 1, 2005, the three women were each sentenced to three years in prison. Feelings about the case were so intense that even two years later, the defendants were released in the early morning hours to avoid possible violence.[47]

Indonesia is often celebrated for its widespread religious tolerance. This forbearance is very real, and myriad religious and ethnic populations usually live harmoniously in this, the world's largest, Muslim-majority democracy with its some 240 million people. But despite some Indonesians' pride in saying, "Islam came to us on a breeze, not with a bullet," extremist Muslim organizations are growing, becoming more active and more violent. Between 1999 and 2002, there was widespread religious violence in the eastern Indonesian areas. The conflict between local Muslims and Christians was exacerbated by the intervention of Islamist militias such as Laskar Jihad: thousands of people were injured or killed, and hundreds of thousands of others were displaced. After peace agreements were accepted, the major killing stopped, but the area remains the site of continuing upheaval.

The Indonesian Protestant Church Union reports that religious violence against Christians almost doubled between 2010 and 2011. The Setara Institute for Democracy and Peace noted that governments and social groups were responsible for most incidents, and the main violators were religious extremist organizations such as the Islamic Defenders Front (FPI). The Wahid Institute, a Muslim organization that promotes tolerance, says that "the worst is perhaps yet to come if authorities continue to overlook the threat of extremism."[48]

For the 10 to 13 percent of the Indonesian population that is Christian, the greatest challenges to religious freedom come from social pressure, vigilantes, militias, and local government. Aceh is the only province with officially recognized Islamic law, but other local governments pass laws discriminating against religious minorities, and mobs and other forms of violence sometimes implement them. At least thirty-six regulations to ban religious practices deemed deviant from Islam were reportedly drafted or implemented in the country in 2011. Meanwhile, the problem centers on the fact that, at higher levels of government, law enforcement is weak and the rule of law founders.

RADICALIZATION AND FORCIBLE CHURCH CLOSURES

On Sunday, June 20, 2010, a group of Muslim organizations met in Bekasi to oppose "ongoing attempts to convert people to Christianity." They jointly called on the local government to instate sharia law and created a paramilitary force, the Laskar Pemuda, for potential conflict with local Christians.[49]

Bekasi, east of the capital Jakarta, is a site of ongoing conflict: it is a new town with new industry and jobs, and draws a growing population of Muslims and Christians. However, in Indonesia, houses of worship can be built only with the approval of the surrounding community, and this has been denied to Bekasi's Christians.

The Batak Christian Protestant Church (HKBP) community has been in Bekasi for twenty years and, in 2007, bought a house for Sunday prayers. But in December 2009, residents, incited by the radical Islamic Defenders Front, declared that the Christians could not use the house. The fifteen-hundred-member congregation then began worshipping in an empty lot, while extremists behind a police barricade tried to drown out the hymn singing with their own Arabic chants.

On August 1, 2010, at least three hundred members of the FPI and other groups, and as many as six hundred protestors in total, broke through a police barricade, and ordered the congregation to leave. As the members dispersed many were attacked with clubs and stones, leaving several in need of medical attention.

The following month, while going to a service on September 12, Hasian Lumbuan Sihombing, a church elder, was stabbed in his heart and stomach. The church's pastor, Luspida Simanjuntak, was beaten on her back and face with a wooden plank. In February 2011, three were jailed for the attack, including the head of the Bekasi branch of the FPI.[50]

Indonesia has recently been plagued by attacks on churches. It is impossible even to recap them all, so here are some examples from just the first part of 2010, as summarized by the United States Commission on International Religious Freedom.[51]

On January 22, 2010, local residents joined with members of radical groups to torch both the Batak Protestant Church building (HKBP) and the pastor's residence in Sibuhuan, North Sumatra. Also that day, the Pentecostal Church (Gereja Pantekosta di Indonesia) of Sibuhun, Tapanuli Selatan, North Sumatra Province, was also set afire, probably by arsonists from outside the area. The Reverend S. Lubis of the HKBP said, "It was a quiet day when suddenly hundreds of people arrived on motorcycles and burned the empty church. . . . When we asked our neighbors, they didn't know them either, and they did not help burn the church."[52]

USCIRF's 2011 report on Indonesia stated, "In March 2010, the Indonesian Christian Church (Gereja Kristen Indonesia) in Taman Yasmin, Bogor, West Java Province, was attacked by a mob and later closed down by authorities citing opposition from the local community." It was still closed in 2012.

Santa Maria Immaculata Catholic Church in Kali Deras, Jakarta, was under construction and had posted the building permit in plain view when demonstrators closed the access road to the site of the church on March 12, 2010. The protests, which were led by the United Islam Forum (FUIB) claimed the new construction did not have approval of locals. Church leader Albertus Suriata commented about the neighbors, "We have had good relations. I don't think anyone near the church had objections. We suspect outsiders."[53]

USCIRF also reported:

> In April 2010, 200 people gathered and disrupted Good Friday activities of the John the Baptist Catholic Church in Bogor, West Java. According to press reports, members of the Parung Ulema Forum protested the existence of the congregation, which had been meeting in tents on vacant land since 1990. . . . Also in April 2010, a mob burned a building under construction in Cibereum, Cisarua, Bogor, West Java, believing it to be a church; the building belonged to Penabur, a Christian educational organization. That same month, unknown assailants burned the Java Christian Church in Sukorejo, Kendal, Central Java. . . . [At the same time,] authorities closed a Catholic pilgrimage location in Jati Mulya, Rangkas Bitung, Lebak, Banten, because of public protest by a local extremist organization. . . .
>
> In May 2010, members of radical groups attacked a Catholic secondary school, Saint Bellarminus in Jatibening, Bekasi, purportedly in reaction to a student's anti-Islamic Internet posting. The 16-year-old student faces blasphemy charges, with

a maximum penalty of two years of imprisonment. In July 2010, local authorities destroyed a Pentecostal church in Jalan Raya Naragong, Bogor, West Java.

Many other similar church attacks, over several years, have been reported. These incidents are often permanent setbacks for the Christian minority communities. For example, on consecutive nights, July 26 and 27, 2008, students from the Arastamar Evangelical School of Theology were besieged by a mob of militant Islamists. Many of the protestors wielded machetes, sharpened bamboo, and acid. Attackers injured at least twenty students. Two and a half years after the attack, the school is still without a permanent facility.[54]

CONVERTS AND BLASPHEMY

Converts from Islam face increasing threats, as do those thought to be involved in evangelizing. On October 17, 2006, Muslim extremists in West Java kidnapped, brutally beat, and attempted to strangle a convert to Christianity from Islam. The Christian man, who was a lecturer at local religious institutions, was approached by one of his students who said he was interested in learning more about Christianity and asked the lecturer to accompany him and others on a trip to Lembang, a town near Bandung, and to bring along Christian books and cassettes. After getting into a van, he was strangled and hit in the head with a hammer before escaping and rushing to the nearest police station. The police later apprehended one of the extremists, who had been delayed in a traffic accident.[55]

Article 156(a) of the criminal code states, “Those, who purposely express their views or commit an act that principally disseminates hatred, misuses or defames a religion recognized in Indonesia, face at maximum five years’ imprisonment.” This provision has been enforced almost exclusively in cases of alleged heresy or blasphemy against Islam. Extremist Islamic groups and courts often use Indonesia’s “Blasphemy Law” as a pretense for violence and punishment against Christians and other religious minorities.

In April 2007, police arrested forty-two Christians in Malang for distributing a blasphemous video. The video was made by members of the East Java branch of the Indonesian Students Service Agency (LPMI), an umbrella organization of Protestants. The tape shows LPMI members praying as Christian songs play in the background. The pastor leading the prayer points to the Qur'an and calls it "the source of all evil in Indonesia, from violence to terror." In September 2007, all forty-one were found guilty of "insulting religion" and sentenced to five years in prison. For unknown reasons, they were pardoned in August 2008, restoring hope that Indonesia's tolerant tradition has not been entirely lost.[56]

Radicalization and attacks on Christians are increasing in Indonesia. Christians, along with Muslims, suffered a great loss on December 30, 2009, with the death of Abdurrahman Wahid, the former president of Indonesia, head of the world's largest Muslim organization, Nahdlatul Ulema, and a renowned Islamic scholar who was an energetic champion of religious freedom. However, the country's large and moderate Muslim organizations have taken the lead in reporting on the violence, while the (Muslim) Parmadina Foundation has been working to identify and implement steps that will prevent attacks on churches. A "Movement for an FPI-free Indonesia" has also sprung up in several parts of the country, with the express purpose of ending religious violence. Thanks to these courageous groups, the situation for Christians remains hopeful.[57]

BANGLADESH

On April 12, 2008, while in Australia, Rashidul Amin Khandaker converted to Catholicism. He telephoned friends back home in Bangladesh to tell them, and the response from many was rage: several of them looted his house and then threatened to attack his family if he reported their assault to the police. Muslim leaders in his hometown of Dhaka, Bangladesh's capital, ordered his sixty-five-year-old father, Rahul Amin Khandaker, to disown his son and placed him under house arrest until his son could be punished.

The Muslim leaders told the father, "If he comes to Bangladesh, you must hand him over to us and we will punish him." The shock of this threat brought on a stroke, but no local doctor would treat Rahul. One neighbor demanded: "Why did you not sacrifice your son like cattle before telling the news to us?" Rashidul's brother wrote to him, asking him to break off contact since local Muslim authorities had warned they would ostracize the family.

Despite the threats and turmoil and disappointment, Rahul has not disowned his son: "If all of my property and wealth is destroyed, I can tolerate that, but one thing I cannot tolerate is to carry the coffin of my son on my shoulders. . . . My son changed his faith according to his will, and our constitution supports this kind of activity."[58]

Bangladesh's some 155 million people make it the world's third-largest Muslim-majority country: about 90 percent of the population is Muslim, 9 percent is Hindu, and Christians make up less than 1 percent. The constitution declares Islam the state religion but also guarantees the right to profess, practice, and propagate other religions. "Deliberately" or "maliciously" hurting religious sentiments can bring a prison sentence, while newspapers can be confiscated for publishing "anything that creates enmity and hatred among the citizens or denigrates religious beliefs."[59]

The religious holidays of the major religious groups are also national holidays, and the government threatens legal action against anyone who tries to disrupt others' celebrations. In school, children can attend religion classes specific to their own religious faiths. Despite these good government policies and programs, religious minorities still face discrimination in access to government jobs, including the military.[60]

Since 2001, Bangladesh's courts have refused to give state legal backing to rulings based solely on sharia law; and in 2010, the

Supreme Court reaffirmed secularism as a constitutional principle and banned Islamic political parties. The same year, the government ended requirements that women wear veils and men wear skullcaps in workplaces. At the same time, it reformed the school curriculum and monitored the content of religious education in state-sponsored Islamic religious schools, known as madrassas. It has also banned books by the late Abdul Ala Maududi (1903 to 1979), a major theorist of extremist Islam.[61]

A WEAK GOVERNMENT

Despite some deficiencies in government policy, the major problems for Christians and other minorities in Bangladesh do not come from government actions but rather from inaction. As in the other countries covered in this chapter, the central government is weak and incapable of consistently maintaining order, and so the gap between law and reality is jarring. While the government makes some attempts to prevent violence, extremist Muslim groups continue to attack Hindus, Christians, Buddhists, and often other Muslims. Despite increased security, the police are often slow to assist minority victims of harassment and violence.[62]

On July 23, 2011, Bablu Biswas, a Christian, stood by helplessly as his house was illegally seized and occupied by Sohel Miah, a Muslim and the son of the ruling Bangladesh Awami League district president. Biswas filed a complaint and a police official called both sides to the police station to resolve the issue. A dozen local Christians came, and Muslim members of the ruling party accompanied Miah. In the meeting, Miah punched an elderly church pastor in the nose, and the Christians left in protest, but not before Miah and his supporters beat another church elder.

Several hundred Christians demonstrated against these attacks on church leaders. Reverend Samuel S. Bala, president of the Gopalganj Christian Fellowship, asked: "If they can beat us in the police station, they can do anything on us—where will we get protection?" On August 2, police arrested Miah, but released him the same day. The land was returned, but Miah received no punishment for stealing Biswas's house and beating Christian pastors. This was not the first such incident; Miah's father, Batu, had also seized church property.[63]

Many Christians are victims of routine discrimination and persecution in Muslim-dominated villages, often with the consent of, or inadequate enforcement by, local Muslim officials.[64] As in other settings, and even when the communities are relatively tolerant on other matters, converts from Islam are condemned and subjected to the worst persecution.

In November 2008, in Chakaria, located in southeastern Bangladesh, forty-five-year-old Laila Begum, a convert from Islam to Christianity, was assisting a local NGO micro-credit agency. A group of Muslims demanded that a Muslim woman repay a loan even though Begum had already repaid it on her behalf. When Begum protested, the group attacked her with sticks, iron rods, knives, and machetes. Her husband and son sought to rescue her and she reported: "They thrust at my son with machetes and a sharp knife and stabbed him in his thigh. . . . They also beat the kneecap of my husband and other parts of his body." Her teenage daughter was assaulted and partially stripped in front of the crowd. One attacker warned, "Nobody will come to save you if we beat you, because you are converted to Christianity from Islam."[65]

SOMALIA

Sister Leonella Sgorbati, an Italian nun of the Consolata Order, lived and worked in Somalia for forty years. She was qualified as a nurse and took care of children's medical needs; she also trained medical workers to reach out to the very poor and ill. She was sixty-five years old when she was shot in the back four times outside an Austrian-run children's hospital north of Mogadishu.

It was Sister Leonella's dream of a lifetime to serve God as a Christian missionary, and her vision for herself had been fulfilled in her work, first in Kenya and then in Somalia. She was fluent in the Somali language, and her colleagues said she was "an outgoing person who would be committed to a goal to its end."[66]

When Pope Benedict gave his famous address about the church's historic view of Islam to an academic audience at Germany's Regensburg University on September 12, 2006, he referred to a comment made about Islam at the end of the fourteenth century by Manuel II Palaiologos, the Byzantine emperor. When the pope's remarks were broadcast and printed, an uproar erupted among Islamic scholars, religious leaders, and politicians. They claimed the pope had offered an inaccurate and insulting view of Islam. Some demanded a violent response to his words. Blood was quickly spilled across the world.

On September 17, 2006, less than a week after the pope's speech, Sister Leonella was murdered. Her bodyguard was also shot dead. Since they were near the hospital at the time of the shooting, the mortally wounded nun was rushed inside. She died, however, before surgery could save her life. Although she was in severe pain and near death, Sister Leonella spoke of forgiveness as she died. Her last words, according to several reports, were "Perdono, perdono" (I forgive, I forgive). She was buried at the Consolata Shrine in Kenya.[67]

Some Westerners first became aware of Somalia during a well-publicized famine that cost many lives in 1992. But the bloodstained anarchy that persists in that war-ravaged African country came into much greater public awareness following the 2001 screening of the popular film *Black Hawk Down*. The movie portrays a tragic and heroic 1993 episode in American military history, during which eighteen US troops were killed, along with more than one thousand Somalis, during the Battle of Mogadishu.

Two decades later, Somalia is even more violent and unstable than before. It is, in fact, one of the most dangerous places on earth, controlled in large part by power-hungry clans, warlords, and rival gangs contending for money, piracy, and political advantage. Worst of all is the radical enforcement of Islamic sharia law over a significant portion of Somalia and beyond by the Islamist terrorist group Al-Shabab.

"ALL SOMALI CHRISTIANS MUST BE KILLED"

The Transitional Federal Government, which has had military support from the UN and Ethiopian forces, was formed in 2004 after more than a decade of civil war. This fragile authority has been embroiled in a protracted struggle with the radical Union of Islamic Courts and its Al-Shabab fighters for control of the country ever since.

Their hostility toward religious freedom was formalized in October 2006, when Sheikh Nur Barud, vice chairman of the influential Somali Islamist group, Kulanka Culimada, declared "all Somali Christians must be killed according to the Islamic law."[68] Since that time, the killing of Christians, both Somali and foreign, has increased exponentially. Al-Shabab is engaged in a systematic campaign to assault and kill Christians.

In January 2012, it was reported that the previous November Al-Shabab terrorists had abducted Sofia Osman, a twenty-eight-year-old Somali Christian who had converted from Islam. During a public flogging on December 22, Sofia received forty lashes from her radical captors while being jeered by spectators. An eyewitness reported that the flogging left the victim bleeding. "I saw her faint. I thought she had died, but soon she regained consciousness and her family took her away."

The violence took place in front of hundreds of spectators, after which the young convert was released from a gruesome month of custody in Al-Shabab camps. "She didn't tell what other humiliations she had suffered while in the hands of the militants," a source said. But while nursing her injuries at her family's home, in the days after the punishment, "she would not talk to anyone and looked dazed."[69]

The justification Somalia's Muslim radicals give for their cruelty is that Islam is the only true religion of the country, and all Somalis are Muslims, therefore any Somali Christians must be apostates—and thus deserving of death sentences. Christians are relentlessly tracked down, assaulted, kidnapped, raped, flogged, and beheaded; they are tortured for information about other

Christians, and then murdered. Al-Shabab is ever-increasingly notorious for its bloodthirsty and merciless tactics.

In September 2008, members of Al-Shabab promised a feast to a group of villagers in Manyafulka, who gathered in expectation of the slaughter of the customary goat, sheep, or camel. Instead, armed, masked men brought Mansuur Mohammed, a twenty-five-year-old World Food Program worker, before the crowd. They declared him to be a *murtid*—an apostate—and beheaded him.[70]

USCIRF's 2010 report on Somalia paints a horrifying portrait of Al-Shabab's radical Islamist worldview, in which

> women are required to be fully covered while in public and are forbidden from engaging in commerce that brings them into contact with men, including traditional female occupations such as selling tea. Men are forbidden to shave their beards or wear their pants below their ankles; those with inappropriate hairstyles have had their heads shaved. The organization closes cinemas, sets fire to markets selling khat (a mild narcotic frequently chewed by Somalis), forbids cell phone ringtones unless they are verses from the Koran, bans all forms of smoking, as well as video games, dancing at weddings, watching soccer, and listening to non-Islamic music.

"In June 2010, two Somali men near Mogadishu, watching the World Cup, were reportedly killed by Al-Shabab; the insurgents had previously warned Somalis against such activities, explaining that football comes from Christian cultures and is incompatible with Islam."[71]

Christian non-Somalis also find themselves in grave danger. British Christian aid workers Richard and Enid Eyeington were murdered in October 2003 by militia fighters with possible links to Al-Qaeda.[72] In a more widely publicized story, in February 2010, four Americans were killed by Somali pirates who had hijacked their yacht, the *Quest.* The two couples had set sail on a personal mission to deliver Bibles throughout the world. Scott and Jean

Adam from Marina del Rey, California, and their friends Phyllis Macay and Robert Riggle of Seattle, Washington, were killed in the attack, which took place while negotiations were being carried out on a US Navy vessel for their release.

AL-QAEDA LINKS

Al-Shabab's connections with the radical Muslim community in the larger world was clarified in January 2012, when Al Jazeera reported that Ayman al-Zawahiri, who had taken over the leadership of Al-Qaeda after Osama bin Laden was killed, announced, "[T]he Shabab movement has joined Al-Qaeda. . . . The jihadist movement is, with the grace of Allah, growing and spreading within its Muslim nation despite facing the fiercest crusade campaign in history by the West."

In a related story from Al Jazeera, "Al-Shabab's leader, Ahmed Abdi Godane, also known as Mukhtar Abu Zubair, addressed Zawahiri, saying, 'We will move along with you as faithful soldiers.' Al-Shabab controlled much of southern and central Somalia and has claimed responsibility for numerous kidnappings and bombings in the country."[73]

Zakaria Hussein Omar was beheaded by Al-Shabab on January 2, 2012, near Mogadishu. He had converted from Islam to Christianity in Ethiopia seven years before. Omar had worked for a Christian humanitarian organization that Al-Shabab banned in 2011. His decapitated body was left at the murder site for nearly twenty-four hours before nomads found it and carried it to Mogadishu, where a friend identified him: "This is the young man who stayed in Ethiopia, and people have been saying that he left Islam and joined Christianity. . . . Last year he mentioned to me that his life was in danger when the NGO he worked for was banned by the Al-Shabab."[74]

On September 25, 2011, Al-Shabab also beheaded Guled Jama Muktar in his home near Deynile, about twelve miles from Mogadishu. Earlier that month Compass Direct News reported: "On the outskirts of Hudur City in Bakool region in southwestern

Somalia, a kidnapped Christian convert from Islam was found decapitated on Sept. 2. Juma Nuradin Kamil was forced into a car by three suspected Islamic extremists from the Al-Shabab terrorist group on Aug. 21, [2011], area sources said. After members of his community thoroughly combed the area looking for him, at 2 p.m. on Sept. 2 one of them found Kamil's body dumped on a street."[75]

CONCLUDING COMMENTS

It is striking that Al-Qaeda and its cohorts such as Al-Shabab have a deliberate policy to target Christians. This reflects their view that they are engaged in a religious war. As the late Osama bin Laden emphasized,

> This war is fundamentally religious. . . . Under no circumstances should we forget this enmity between us and the infidels. For, the enmity is based on creed. . . . It is a religious-economic war. . . . [T]he confrontation and conflict between us and them started centuries ago. The confrontation and conflict will continue because the conflict between right and falsehood will continue until Judgment Day.[76]

This most certainly does *not* mean that we should regard *ourselves* as in a religious war against all Muslims, but it does mean that we should be aware of how these extremists think. Their primary categories for their supposed enemies are not "American," or "Western," or "modern." Instead they are spoken of as "infidels," "unbelievers," "apostates," "Christians," "Jews," "Hindus," or some other religious group. The radicals are engaged in a feverish, ongoing campaign to kill or subjugate Christians and the religious "other."

NINE

CRUEL AND USUAL ABUSE

Burma / Ethiopia / Eritrea

ON SEPTEMBER 11, 2009, IN THE PREDOMINANTLY MUSLIM town of Senbete, Ethiopia, a three-hundred-strong Muslim mob rioted after hearing a rumor that two Christian men had desecrated the Qur'an. The mob torched two churches and severely injured three Christians. They first set fire to Mulu Wongel Evangelical Church and attacked the home of one of the church leaders, evangelist Gizachew, destroying his clothes and other property. They then charged into Kale Evangelical Church where they beat Christians celebrating the Ethiopian New Year. They broke Aberash Terefe's arm and seriously wounded Tefera Bati and Desaleghn Eyasu, all of whom had to be treated at a local hospital. Christian sources identified the two Muslim religious leaders and three prominent Muslim businessmen who had encouraged the attacks. They were thought to have had done so with the intention of eliminating Christians from the area. Despite the mayhem and destruction caused by some Muslims, it was only the two Christians accused of desecrating the Qur'an who were detained by the police.[1]

Yemane Kahasay Andom, forty-three, died in July 2009 at Eritrea's Mitire Military Confinement Center, and it was reported that he was buried secretly. Besides having endured repeated torture, Andom had been stricken with a severe form of malaria. Following his death, Open Doors International reported,

"[Andom] was allegedly further weakened by continuous physical torture and solitary confinement in an underground cell the two weeks prior to his death for his refusal to sign a recantation form. . . . It is not clear what the contents of the recantation form were, but most Christians interpret the signing of such a form as the denouncement of their faith in Christ." Two other Christians, Mogos Hagos Kiflom, thirty-seven, and Mehari Gebreneguse Asgedom, forty-two, were also reported as having died at Mitire camp in 2009.[2]

UNIQUE CASES

Throughout the world, Christians may experience various forms of discrimination, harassment, and outright persecution. Most persecution of Christians follows specific patterns: the hunger for universal control in the Communist and post-Communist countries, the desire to preserve privilege in South Asia, the urge to dominate in radical Islam. But there are anti-Christian abuses that do not fall neatly into these categories; indeed, there are few, if any, countries in the world that have no problems at all with religious freedom.[3]

For example, there is local repression in Mexico. Of course, the major problems for the churches there come from attacks and kidnapping by organized crime, especially drug cartels, but there are also threats more specifically religious. In Puebla, Hidalgo, and Chiapas states, local leaders, usually opposed by the Catholic hierarchy, promote and profit from festivals combining copious amounts of alcohol with indigenous and Catholic rituals. Evangelical Protestants usually refuse to help pay for or participate in these revels, and dozens have been driven from their villages by threats to burn down or otherwise destroy their homes, most recently in 2011 from San Rafael Tlanalapan.[4]

In another instance, in Israel, proselytism is legal as long as no material benefits are offered for conversion. But elements within the government sometimes act as though this isn't so. People suspected of being missionaries have been denied visas and sometimes detained and required to post bail and pledge not to evangelize. There are also occasional mob attacks on churches or other buildings hosting converts.

Baptist House in Jerusalem, home to three congregations, including Messianic Jews, has been attacked several times. On February 19, 2012, it was painted with anti-Christian slurs, as were three cars, which also had their tires slashed. Earlier attacks have included rocks, firebombs, Molotov cocktails, and the detonation of a paint can filled with nails. In the last five years, however, the only assaults have been vandalism. In each case, the Israeli government has acted quickly to support the church.[5]

One peculiarity occurs on the Temple Mount, which is under Israeli control and Jordanian management. Anyone, regardless of religious belief, can go to the holy site—the holiest of all sites to Jews—but only Muslims are allowed to pray there. Anyone else thought to be praying or reading Jewish or Christian Scripture will be removed.[6]

Some countries, however, such as Burma and Eritrea, are among the worst persecutors in the world. And the circumstances of their abuses are unusual: their common feature is that they are heavily militarized states with rulers determined to stamp out any kind of opposition or center of power other than their own. Ethiopia, meanwhile, is also exceptional in its dynamics, and is experiencing increasing violence against believers from a growing number of Salafi Muslims.

Christians, while not usually intending to make churches centers of political power, do insist on the independence of the church so they can serve the Divine authority. For this reason, they become major targets of political oppression. In Burma this has been exacerbated by the presence of Christians in many of the non-Burmese ethnic groups.

BURMA

In November and December 2010, Burma's military, known as the Tatmadaw, began shelling the outskirts of Palu village in Karen State. Hundreds of villagers fled to refugee camps on the border with Thailand, fearful they would be coerced into forced labor if they remained. Tatmadaw soldiers frequently force villagers to carry their supplies for them, and herd them into mined areas, making them walk in front of the troops. These human minesweepers discover and reveal the mines by being killed or maimed when they explode.[7]

Baroness Caroline Cox, who has visited Burma many times, reported a worsening situation for Christians there in the mid-2000s:

> [T]he Chin used to build crosses on hill-tops as a symbol of their faith, but in the past decade they have not only been forced to tear down those crosses, but are forced to build Buddhist pagodas in their place—often at gunpoint. I stood on the India side of the border and, looking across to Chin State, I could see a bright golden pagoda on the hill-top in the distance—where a cross had once stood.[8]

Burma, also called Myanmar, is driven by an unusual combination of political forces. It has been run for decades by a military junta that, from 1988 to 1997, was known as the State Law and Order Restoration Council (SLORC). Since then it has styled itself as the State Peace and Development Council (SPDC). The junta rejected the results of the 1990 election and kept the real winner, Aung San Suu Kyi, under house arrest until November 13, 2010. Since 2011 it has ruled through a nominal civilian president appointed from within its ranks.

The regime lacks electoral legitimacy and its economic performance has been dismal. Hence, it has copied the example of many other national security states, swathing itself in the twin banners of nationalism and religion. It claims to be protecting the interest of the country's majority Burman ethnic group, and to be defending and promoting Buddhism, which is followed by more than 80 percent of the population. And it persecutes Christians, and other minorities, such as the Muslim Rohingya people.

Most Buddhists, and others in Burma, oppose the regime. Buddhist monks led many of the 2007 mass demonstrations calling for democracy and were among the thousands arrested. But, even though it does not represent Burmese Buddhism, the regime, under the policy of *Amyo, Batha, Thatana*, "One Race, One Language, One Religion," uses Buddhist nationalism as a source of legitimacy and method of control over an ethnically and religiously pluralistic society.[9]

WAR ON ETHNIC CHRISTIANS

There is little room in this scheme for Christians, who account for about 9 percent of the country's some 50 to 55 million people. The situation for Christians is worsened because they not only are a minority religion but are also concentrated in the non-Burman ethnic groups, and so also fall afoul of the government's ethnic nationalism. The Chin people are about 90 percent Christian, the Kachin also 90 percent, and the Karen about 40 percent, with large though unknown percentages among the Karenni and Naga. About four-fifths of the country's Christians belong to Protestant churches established by American Baptists in the early nineteenth century; most of the rest are Catholics. Portuguese missionaries from Goa, now part of India, introduced Catholicism in the sixteenth century.

When Burma became independent from the British in 1948, the Panglong Agreement promised autonomy for the ethnic states in return for becoming part of a unified Burma. But the central government broke this promise and instead embarked on a Burmanization campaign that marginalized minorities, invaded their territories, and sought to eradicate Christian practice and convert the populations to Buddhism. This triggered rebellions in seven of the ethnic states that, collectively, constitute one of the world's longest running and most overlooked civil wars. The ruling military junta has engaged in extreme brutality in trying to suppress the minority rebels and stamp out Christianity. Although the regime oppresses all its population, the religious minorities suffer most.

Six decades of repressive dictatorship and conflict have produced an immense humanitarian crisis and crippling poverty in what was once one of Asia's richest countries. Refugees International reports there are currently three million refugees, many of whom live in squalid camps on the borders of China, India, Bangladesh, and Thailand; there are at least five hundred thousand internally displaced people.[10]

"PROGRAM TO DESTROY THE CHRISTIAN RELIGION IN BURMA"

Christians suffer under oppressive laws, clandestine state policies of persecution, and abusive practices by security officials, who act with impunity. Legal restrictions on religious activity include bans on house churches, evangelization, and imported literature. While churches are not banned outright, there is tight government surveillance and restriction even of legal churches and Christian schools along with Bibles, sermons, and religious literature. The regime has used fines, denial of foreign aid and essential services, imprisonment, forced labor, forced starvation, rape, and violence to oppress Christianity in favor of Buddhism, though the latter is also tightly controlled.

While the closed political system makes documentation of religious persecution difficult, organizations such as the Karen Human Rights Organisation and Christian Solidarity Worldwide (CSW) have produced invaluable eyewitness reports.

In 2007, a purported secret government memo surfaced, entitled "Program to destroy the Christian religion in Burma." It lists seventeen specific directives on how to repress Christianity, such as:

- There shall be no Christian preaching/evangelism on an organised basis.
- If anyone discovers Christians evangelising in the countryside they are to report it to the authorities and those caught evangelising will be put in prison.
- Buddhists should study the Christian Bible so that they can contradict those parts which are untrue and be able to resist the Christian message.
- Take care as the Christian religion is very gentle—identify and utilize its weaknesses.
- There shall be no home where the Christian religion is practiced.[11]

Although the government disavowed the document, it did not condemn the directives contained in it, which seem to accurately reflect recent practices.

CLOSING CHURCH DOORS

Permission to build new churches requires a formal application to the government and is rarely granted. In Chin State, no new churches have been approved for construction since 2003, and in 2010, the government ordered the tearing down of nine large public crosses.[12] Some have been replaced with Buddhist structures, built with forced labor from Christian villages. Reportedly, eight pagodas and fifty-six Buddhist monasteries have been built there by government agencies.[13]

Similarly, in Kachin State, the confiscation or destruction of Christian sites has been frequent and permits to rebuild them refused.[14] The SPDC deliberately has held staff meetings and training sessions for government employees on Sundays, forcing Christians to choose between the official meetings and attending church services. Workers who choose to attend church are fired and replaced with Buddhists.

Since they are denied churches, Christians often gather in

private homes. CSW reports that, in 2001, eighty "house churches" of varying denominations—Baptist, Presbyterian, and Pentecostal, among others—were closed down in Rangoon. In 2005, the Full Gospel Assembly in downtown Rangoon was closed and all its activities suspended. At least seventeen churches were closed in Rangoon and twenty-eight in Mandalay the same year. An official directive in late 2008, put into effect in 2009, ordered the closing of all "house churches," which affected an estimated 80 percent of churches in Rangoon. A Rangoon pastor, who spoke anonymously out of fear of reprisal, said they were warned "that we could be punished [and could be jailed] if we fail to obey the order and the church would be sealed off."[15]

Religious literature is heavily restricted. Ethnic language Bibles cannot legally be printed in or imported into Burma, though many Christians still do so. In 2000, the SPDC reportedly burned sixteen thousand Bibles printed in the Chin and other ethnic languages.

Censors must approve any Christian material published in Burma. More than one hundred words are prohibited from use in Christian material because they derive from Pali, the liturgical language of Buddhism; these include words used frequently in both Proverbs and Ecclesiastes. As a result, the Burma Bible Society stopped translating the Bible rather than altering its verses.[16]

A Chin man arrested for bringing Bibles into Burma described his detention in 1999: "I asked for a lawyer but the military intelligence officers told me I couldn't have a lawyer. Before we went to court, the soldiers covered my eyes and beat my legs. In the court, the judge just said, 'You are not allowed to bring Bibles into the country but you still did this. You don't respect our laws and our country.'" This Chin Christian was imprisoned for nearly three years.[17]

MILITARY ASSAULTS ON ETHNIC MINORITIES: THE KAREN

While religious repression occurs throughout the country, the tribes with large Christian populations—the Karen, Chin, Kachin, and Karenni—have suffered the harshest persecution. The military carries out scorched-earth warfare, making no distinction between combatants and civilians.[18] The plight of the Karens, Burma's largest ethnic minority and a widely Christian one, is one of the world's least reported humanitarian disasters.

Vision Beyond Borders president Patrick Klein described assaults in 2009:

> Villages are being surrounded, and rockets are lobbed in. The Myanmar regime then goes in with machine guns and mows down whoever is still alive, and then the evidence is burned. There are reports they're also blockading villages so the people can't go out and get food; it is also reported that women are being raped and men are being set on fire while they're alive. And, they're actually poisoning the water supplies now.[19]

In July 2010, as Burma's senior general Than Shwe visited India, where he made a symbolic pilgrimage to two Buddha shrines, his army attacked the Karen Christian village of Tha Dah Der, burning fifty homes, a school, and the state's largest church. Some six hundred villagers fled into the jungle to avoid the army.[20]

In late 2011, the Burmese military waged an offensive, targeting the village's Roman Catholic church, destroying its roof, icons, shrine, and statues. A villager gave this account of the devastation: "[T]hey destroyed our place of worship and our cultural items in the village. Moreover, they broke the statue of Mary into three pieces and shot all over the pictures on the wall."[21]

Such attacks have driven hundreds of thousands of Karen from their homes into refugee camps in Thailand. Others are forced into hiding within Burma. These internally displaced people must survive without aid from international agencies, which are forbidden by the government from helping them. They survive by camping out in the jungle or living in temporary shelters under the protection of ethnic militias. They travel by foot through the most remote regions, which are littered with land mines. They often travel only at night, afraid that, without the cover of darkness, government soldiers will spot them. They eat what they can scavenge in the jungle and flee when government forces get too close. Most live on less than one dollar a day, suffer from constant hunger and unspeakable deprivation, and fear the ever-present military.[22]

THE CHIN

The 1.5 million Chin are almost entirely Christian, but they are commonly forced to practice Buddhism under penalty of extreme hardship or threat of death. In 2008, a Chin pastor who served as a missionary on the Arakan-Chin border told an international human rights group:

> Twice while working in a village, SPDC (ruling junta) soldiers brought me to a pagoda and told me to pray as a Buddhist. They would try to force me to worship their god. I told them that I am a Christian missionary and like a monk so I couldn't worship in their temples. They said that this is a Buddhist country and that I should not practice Christianity. They said, "Why don't you worship Buddha? Why are you here if you are not Buddhist? This is a Buddhist country." When they said these things, they also threatened me with their guns.[23]

For many years Chin Christians have not been allowed to build churches. In some places, the SPDC has built Buddhist pagodas and moved large numbers of Buddhist monks to the region to shift the demographics in favor of Buddhism. In 2006, a Buddhist monastery with an attached orphanage was constructed in Chin State on land confiscated from villagers, without compensation. All staff and orphans were required to convert to Buddhism prior to admission.[24] Many Chin refugees have reported that they were offered material assistance if they agreed to convert to Buddhism—and threatened with forced labor and imprisonment if they refused.

Government soldiers are encouraged to marry Christian Chin women in order to convert them to Buddhism.

Converting to Christianity from Buddhism is also forbidden. A Chin pastor and his wife tell of a Buddhist couple who became Christian:

> [T]he SPDC local authorities called the couple that we converted at night and forced them to attend one week of USDA [Union Solidarity Development Association, an SPDC controlled "social welfare" organization] training as punishment for converting. The authorities told them, "You should not worship western gods. Only eastern gods are good for Burma." After that, the couple was afraid to come to the church for two to three months.[25]

In addition to direct attacks, Burma's government has engaged in more unusual attempts to crush Christianity. CSW reported on a 1992 campaign designed to "undermine the fabric of Chin society" by introducing liquor called OB, a highly addictive mix of methyl and ethyl alcohol—a toxic mixture that "would be completely forbidden in the West." Army and police sold the liquor to children on the street and addiction spread among poor villagers. It encourages "the breakdown of body, mind, spirit and society" of Chin Christians.[26]

THE KACHIN

After three decades of fighting, a 1994 ceasefire eased the plight of the overwhelmingly Christian Kachin people, but religious repression has continued. On June 9, 2011, conflict reignited after the Burmese government signed a deal with China for the construction of a multibillion-dollar dam in Kachin territory. The dam would flood traditional lands and displace thousands of Kachin people without compensation. Local resistance was met with violence by the Burmese army. Tens of thousands of Kachin, mostly Christian, have sought refuge along the Chinese border.[27]

Although the dam project is currently suspended, violence has continued. An explosion rocked a Kachin Christian-run orphanage on November 13, 2011, killing seven children and three adults and injuring dozens of others. Without conducting a transparent investigation, authorities subsequently arrested the Christian couple who ran the orphanage, alleging they had planted the explosives themselves, even though their two sons and a grandson were wounded in the blast.[28]

A December 2011 presidential order for the military to cease attacks in Kachin had little effect. On Christmas Day 2011, Maran Zau Ja was walking home from a sugar cane farm with a friend when the two men were sprayed with bullets from a military battalion who were reportedly shooting ethnic Kachins on sight. Zau Ja's friend survived; he did not. Subsequently, after this incident and others, in which churches and homes were torched by the military, hundreds of Kachin fled their homes. By January 2012, there were more than sixty thousand refugees in camps along the Chinese border.[29]

After shelling his village in October 2011, the army rounded up Tumai Nhkum, a young Kachin man, and four others and pressed them into service as porters. The *New York Times* reported the Tatmadaw burned and looted the village, killed a child, and slaughtered farm animals before moving on. The men were beaten and finally released twenty days later. Tumai Nhkum found his family and fled to the refugee camp, where they remain.[30]

EXPLOITING NATURAL DISASTERS

The regime has even used natural disasters as opportunities to eradicate Christian minorities. In May 2008, southern Burma was left devastated by Cyclone Nargis, which killed more than eighty-five thousand and caused massive destruction. For three weeks after the storm, the military junta denied access to international aid and relief organizations. When the government finally did grant access, it systematically denied aid to the Karen. The army guards blocked roadways and entrances to Karen villages, even though villagers were suffering from hunger, disease, and injury. Then the SPDC forcibly relocated survivors from temporary settlements to their homes even though many had been destroyed, their villages were flooded, and their land was uninhabitable.[31]

Similarly, in March 2011, a magnitude 7.0 earthquake shook the country, affecting forty Christian villages along with others. The official death toll was seventy-four, although many believe it to be higher, and thousands were made homeless. While providing relief to others, the Burmese government deliberately neglected Christian villages.[32] The death toll of such deprivations is not known but is likely to be in the thousands.

A NEW DIRECTION?

Recent years have given cause for cautious hope. In 2010, after years of house arrest, the political opposition leader and Nobel Laureate Aung San Suu Kyi was released from prison and the government began adopting a series of reforms that could prove significant if continued. In 2011, it freed two hundred political prisoners.[33] Within the first weeks of 2012, officials signed a cease-fire agreement with Karen rebels, mandated a cease-fire and peace negotiations in Kachin Province, released 651 more prisoners, including high-level dissidents and the Buddhist monk leader of the 2007 pro-democracy "saffron revolution." Parliamentary elections were held in April 2012, in which Aung San Suu Kyi won a seat in the lower house.[34]

In January 2012, the United States and Burma announced they would exchange ambassadors. On January 19, 2012, Burma's president, Thein Sein, gave an interview to the *Washington Post*, asserting, "My message is that we are on the right track to democracy. Because we are on the right track, we can only move forward, and we don't have any intention to draw back."[35]

We must not be too quick to declare that the state has shed its oppressive past. In early 2012, the *New York Times* named Burma one of its top tourist destinations, touting the nation's "strong sense of place, undiluted by mass tourism," and "deserted beaches."[36] But

Burma is far from being an unspoiled paradise: civil liberties are still tightly controlled and government military offensives against Christians and other ethnic minorities continue to result in massive human rights abuses and many refugees. Hope for religious freedom is greater than it has been for many decades, but it is far from being realized.

After Burma hosted US Secretary of State Hillary Clinton in December 2011—the first visit from an American diplomat in more than fifty years—the US indicated it would gradually lift its economic sanctions on the country, but only as reforms continued. It is vital that these reforms include religious freedom for its Christians, including those in ethnic minority areas, as well as for all Burmese.

ETHIOPIA

In Worabe in May 2011, six Muslim men with machetes ambushed Abraham Abera, an Evangelical church worker, together with his pregnant wife, Bertukan, as they were returning home from visiting a sick friend. The assailants beat Abraham to death and severely wounded Bertukan, leaving her lying unconscious in the street. Rushed to the hospital and given a transfusion, she and her unborn baby both survived. She reported that during the assault, the killers said, "You [Christians] are growing in number in our area. You are spreading your message. We will destroy you."[37]

NEWCOMERS TO AN ANCIENT RELIGIOUS CROSSROADS

Ethiopia stands at a religious crossroads, where ancient Orthodox Christians and Muslims have coexisted, albeit often tensely, for some thirteen hundred years. More recently, Evangelical Christianity has gained in popularity and challenged the old order. Another new and worrisome development is the appearance among Muslims of pockets of highly intolerant and sometimes violent Wahhabi or Salafi Muslims, who threaten the nation at large.

Christians—mostly Orthodox, with a newer population of

Evangelicals and Pentecostals—constitute about two-thirds of the total population of ninety million. The Ethiopian Orthodox Church, dating from the fourth century, is one of the world's oldest Christian national churches. It was served by the patriarchate for both Egypt and Ethiopia until 1959 and has had its own independent patriarchate since then. Evangelical and Pentecostal churches have experienced exponential growth throughout Ethiopia in the last twenty-five years, and now make up perhaps 20 percent of the population.[38] Orthodox Christians show signs of resenting these newer Christian groups as upstarts who steal their members, and have sometimes used their considerable influence in society and with the state to disadvantage the newer Christians.

Islam arrived in the eighth century and remains dominant in the east of the country, where it first began. Muslims are about one-third of the population, and most are Sunni Sufis, though an increasing number of Salafis, including some followers of Al-Qaeda, have appeared. The traditional Sufis stress spirituality, unlike the literalist Wahhabis, who seek to impose strict sharia law. The relatively recent rise of radical Muslim sects has heightened tensions throughout the country and led to increasing attacks on Christians.

STATE REGULATION AND DISCRIMINATION

Ethiopia's constitution affirms religious freedom rights and, though the state discriminates against newer Christian groups, it is not a major persecutor. The greater danger comes from societal hostilities based on religion.[39]

The government regulates religious groups and will use laws and restrictions to placate more influential religious groups, usually to the detriment of Evangelicals and Pentecostals. A law banning defamation of religion has been used against Evangelicals to protect Muslims' religious feelings.

In 2010, Tamirat Woldegorgis, a married father of two from Hagarmariam village, was sentenced to three years in prison for inscribing "Jesus is Lord" in a copy of the Qur'an.[40] In a separate incident, on May 2009, Bashir Musa Ahmed, a thirty-nine-year-old

Christian convert from Islam, was arrested for "malicious" distribution of Bibles whose covers resembled those of the Qur'an. Such arrests are troubling, but rare.[41]

A greater danger has been government discrimination combined with violent extremism. Together, they thwart Christian religious practice. Evangelicals in the Worabe area have been refused land for churches and burial space, barred from carrying out evangelism, and harassed by false accusations of causing noise pollution. They have been beaten and had their churches burned and confiscated. It took eight years, for example, for Abraham Abera's congregation to be granted a small plot of land for a church building, and even then the site was located on the outskirts of the town. These troubles may have been due to pressure from radical Muslims, some of whom later murdered Abera, as described above.[42]

The story of Tsehay Desta shows how government restrictions, in this case applied at the behest of the local Orthodox community and compounded by local social hostility, threaten religious freedom. After her evangelical cousin performed an exorcism on her, Desta, a teenager, joined the Evangelical church, much to the displeasure of her Orthodox husband. After several months of attempting to convert her back, her husband divorced her. She was pregnant at the time and, several months after giving birth to a son, she went to visit her mother in the small village of Luga. Several days later, on May 9, 2009, Desta's baby suddenly fell ill and died.

The Orthodox church refused to allow his burial on church property, but the Evangelical Kale Hiwot Church in Luga had been denied government permission to carry out funerals or any other religious services. Nevertheless the pastor agreed to bury the child within the church compound and the funeral was held without incident.

However, on May 11, the pastor found the baby's disinterred coffin on the church steps. The infant's body had reportedly been dug up by local Orthodox Christians in retaliation for Desta's conversion and out of anger at the pastor for giving the child a

Christian burial. Evangelical leaders from other parts of the country petitioned regional and national authorities and, while they received governmental assurances and several suspects were arrested, no burial permit was forthcoming and the suspects were released hours later.

The infant's body was reburied without problem in the former gravesite, but subsequently the pastor's house was stoned daily by unknown assailants. He has received verbal threats, and has even been beaten. He reported to Compass Direct News: "[A]fter this incident, things are changing. Even on my way home from the office, villagers are insulting and warning me for 'betraying' them."[43]

RADICAL MUSLIMS

The greatest threat to Ethiopia's Christians is increasing pressure from radical Islamists. Ethiopia has been relatively successful in repelling the influx of Islamic extremism that has plagued the Horn of Africa. This is due to centuries of more or less peaceful relations between Muslims and Christians, and a comparably strong governmental response to Al-Qaeda and other terrorist groups.[44] However, after a small but active population of Muslim extremists emerged, Ethiopia enacted an antiterrorism proclamation in 2009 that has been decried by human rights organizations as violating free speech and due process of law. Rather than preventing terrorists, it appears mainly to target journalists and the political opposition.[45]

Nonetheless, in 2011 the Ethiopian government reportedly uncovered a plot by Wahhabi-influenced extremists to make Ethiopia an Islamic state and drive out all non-Muslims. In a November press conference, Ministry of Federal Affairs director Mersessa Reda stated they had discovered literature "calling on the Muslim community to stand up against all non-Wahhabi Muslims and followers of other religions."[46] There were also increasing attacks on Christians by radical Islamists, especially in Muslim-majority areas.

In March 2011, Protestants in Asendabo, in the Jimma region, were assaulted by radical Muslims. In 2006, the same region had experienced religious violence, including the murder of dozens of Christians. But in 2011, in response to rumors that a Christian had desecrated the Qur'an, a group of Muslim extremists reportedly set fire to sixty-nine churches and dozens of homes. More than four thousand Christians fled the town, and one was killed. Abera Gutema narrowly survived the pogrom. Clutching his infant son, he managed to outrun a machete-wielding mob. He lost all his possessions and life savings when his home was looted and burned: "They were our friends, our neighbors with whom we shared everything . . . I never thought this day would ever come."[47]

The government took swift action, arresting and ultimately sentencing to prison more than five hundred people involved in the attacks. The displaced Christians have since returned and rebuilt their homes. The attacks shocked a nation that has prided itself on peaceful Christian-Muslim relations. There have been other recent attacks as well.

In July 2010, twenty-five Muslims rampaged through a village in the Goda district of Jimma, a predominantly Muslim city in southwestern Ethiopia. The mob burned down ten Christian homes, leaving eighty people homeless, set fire to their barns and harvests, and killed their livestock, thus stripping them of their livelihood. Afterward, they held the Christian villagers hostage for sixteen days and reportedly told them, "If you inform this to anyone, we will burn you the way we burn your homes." Despite the threat, one Christian escaped and reported the attack. Police arrested the assailants, but they were later released on bail.[48]

Further attempts by radical Muslims to "cleanse" areas of Christians' presence occurred in late 2010 and early 2011. Christians in the city of Besheno, an overwhelmingly Muslim town in the province of Alaba in Southern Ethiopia, for instance, woke up one day to find notes on their doors warning them to convert to Islam or leave the city, or they would be killed. Three Christian leaders fled the city, one of whom reported, "We were told by some Muslims that live in the city that there was already a plan to kill us and that the people who were assigned to kill us had already come from another city to do it."[49]

Reportedly, two Christians were forced to convert to Islam. On November 29, 2010, some Muslims beat evangelist Kassa Awano, who was left in critical condition for several days. Just days later, dozens of Muslims assaulted a vehicle in which several Christian leaders were, ironically, traveling to attend peace talks with Muslim leaders. Two of the leaders, Tesema Hirego and Niggusie Denano, were seriously wounded and others suffered lesser injuries. On January 2, 2011, after testifying in court about the attacks on Christians, Temesgen Peteros was stabbed by a Muslim man.[50]

For now, such violent incidents, horrific as they are, are the exception rather than the rule. However, violence can be expected to increase as Muslim extremists gain stronger holds over Ethiopia's Muslim communities. The government has developed civic programs in an attempt to combat sectarian violence. Minister Reda recognized the possible danger: "As such acts of Wahhabi Muslim extremists will lead the country in chaos, the government is forced to intervene."[51] For now, Ethiopian churches are flourishing and most Christians are free to practice their faith in peace. Time will tell whether this ancient crossroads of civilizations will be spared the Islamist radicalization and sectarian conflict suffered by some of its neighbors.

ERITREA

The *Christian Post* reported in October 2011 that Terhase Gebremichel Andu, twenty-eight, and Ferewine Genzabu Kifly, twenty-one, had "died as the result of starvation and untreated health problems," as reported by confidential sources inside Eritrea. Both had been arrested in 2009 during a prayer meeting in a private home. Subsequently they experienced "two years of physical torture and also were denied medical care inside Adersete Military Camp."

Angesom Teklom Habtemichel, a twenty-six-year-old Christian man, also died in late August 2011 while imprisoned at Adi Nefase Military Camp in Asab. Sources at Open Doors International reported that he, too, had suffered from severe malaria but was "denied medical treatment because of his written refusal to recant his Christian faith."[52]

ONE OF THE WORLD'S WORST PERSECUTORS

The tiny country of Eritrea—once part of Ethiopia—is an egregious religious persecutor. Although many people have heard little or nothing about Eritrea and aren't even sure where it is, those who focus on the persecution of Christians are well aware of its atrocious reputation. Violations of religious freedom in Eritrea are some of the most severe in the world.

With a population of around six million, Eritrea is approximately half Christian and half Muslim. Since 1993, when it achieved formal independence from Ethiopia after thirty years of civil war, the country has been crushed under the devastatingly oppressive rule of President Isaias Afwerki. Afwerki, who led the Eritrean People's Liberation Front during the war for independence, at first seemed to be a beacon of hope as Eritrea stood on its own for the first time. But any hope of democracy and freedom faded quickly as Afwerki, desperate to maintain his iron grip on power, refused to implement a constitution that had been ratified in 1997. He has recognized only one party—his own People's Front for Democracy and Justice.[53] Elections have been postponed indefinitely, ostensibly to prevent destabilization; in fact Afwerki stated in a televised interview that he would consider holding them in "three or four decades."[54]

As a result, Afwerki has managed in his twenty-year rule to consolidate one of the most ruthless dictatorships in the world, with complete control over the economy, media, and civil society. American diplomats have described him as "hard-hearted," "thin-skinned," "narcissistic," "paranoid," and "unhinged."[55] Djibouti's foreign minister referred to him outright as a "lunatic."[56] Afwerki uses the possibility of another war with Ethiopia to justify repression and, at this point, human rights are nearly nonexistent. There is no due process, arrests are often arbitrary, and detainees are held without charge indefinitely; imprisonment routinely involves beatings, torture, and death. Governmental repression is aimed at groups it perceives as potentially subversive, or even simply independent, making religious organizations a primary target—especially those that meet privately and are unregistered.

REPRESSION OF REGISTERED CHURCHES

The regime puts religious organizations in a double bind: registration is mandatory, but no registrations have been approved since 2002. Only four main religious groups are recognized: Islam, the Eritrean Orthodox Church, the Roman Catholic Church, and the Evangelical (Lutheran) Church of Eritrea.[57] Even though they are legally registered, these religious groups are tightly regulated by the state and subject to harassment.

In 2006, the government removed Orthodox patriarch Bune Antonios and replaced him with a government-approved priest to lead the church according to the regime's wishes. Patriarch Antonios was placed under house arrest following his removal, and he has remained there ever since. He has been prevented from communicating with the outside world and denied medical treatment, even though he reportedly suffers from diabetes. There has been no word on his condition. Since the patriarch's removal, more than seventeen hundred Orthodox clergy members have been removed from church service and at least twenty-three have been imprisoned.[58]

IMPRISONMENT AND TORTURE OF CHRISTIANS AND OTHERS

Clearly, although legislation gives religious groups the right to exist, their existence is devoid of freedom. Meanwhile, the greatest governmental persecution is aimed at members of nonregistered religious groups, predominantly Evangelical and Pentecostal Christians, as well as Baha'is, Seventh-Day Adventists, Baptists, and Jehovah's Witnesses.

Despite their relatively small number, Jehovah's Witnesses have the dubious distinction of suffering some of the worst persecution at the hands of the regime. It is generally believed that Afwerki's particular aversion is related to their refusal to serve in the military. Eritrea is one of the world's most militarized societies, with compulsory service required for an indefinite period of time that can span decades. Since 1994, Jehovah's Witnesses have been denied citizenship on the basis of their conscientious objection. Nearly sixty Jehovah's Witnesses are known to be imprisoned currently, held without charge. Three Jehovah's Witnesses have been imprisoned for more than fifteen years for refusing compulsory military service—thirteen years longer than the normal two-year sentence for such an offense.[59]

But military service aside, Eritreans of all religious affiliations are subject to persecution since they demonstrate loyalty to a higher power other than Eritrea's ruler. The regime offers little formal explanation for the ongoing persecution of Christians beyond Afwerki's fear, indeed paranoia, about possible subversion. With minimal release of information by the government and no judicial process for the detention and imprisonment of Christians, most of the evidence of this persecution comes from those Christians who have survived imprisonment and torture and fled the country.

Although it is impossible to obtain accurate numbers, it is estimated by both state and nongovernmental agencies that thousands of people are currently imprisoned for their religious affiliations, for "real or imagined opposition to the government."[60] The US State Department reports that 103 people belonging to unregistered religious groups were newly detained in the second half of 2010 alone.[61] Government forces routinely raid religious events such as weddings, baptisms, and church services. Christians are rounded up and arbitrarily detained without due process and often subjected to beatings. Some are released; some are temporarily detained while soldiers attempt to force them to recant their faith.

Prison conditions are some of the world's worst. Prisoners are packed into overflowing facilities, deep underground chambers, military camps, or even metal shipping containers, which magnify extremes in temperature. A prisoner reported being held in a forty by thirty-eight foot cell with six hundred other inmates, and American diplomats related the prison conditions in a diplomatic cable, saying that "although the physical abuse and deprivations took a toll on [the released prisoner's] body, it was the psychological abuse of being packed in with so many other people, of not knowing when the next beating would come, and believing he could be killed, that was the most damaging." They added, "[P]risoners were fed two pieces of bread three times a day. A bucket in the middle of the room served as a toilet between escorted bathroom breaks, but it constantly spilled and contaminated the room with urine and feces. Many prisoners could not talk due to the lack of water, their tongues stuck to the roofs of their mouth from thirst."[62]

Prisons are notoriously disease ridden, particularly the unventilated underground chambers contaminated with human waste and vermin. Inmates who contract treatable diseases such as tuberculosis and malaria are refused treatment. They experience torture, and specifically a technique called "the helicopter," in which detainees are contorted into an excruciating position with their feet and hands tied together behind their backs. Prisoners can be left in "the helicopter" for days at a time—one refugee told of being tied up for 136 hours—or even hung from trees in this position until they agree to sign a statement recanting Christianity. Lengthy use of the helicopter results in inmates being unable to use their arms or legs, relying on other prisoners to feed them.[63]

Hana Hagos Asgedom died in Alla military camp in January 2010, after being transferred from Wi'a where she had been held for three years. She was given a final chance to renounce Christianity when she was transferred and refused; she was then placed in solitary confinement. There she was beaten with an iron rod. As a result, she suffered a heart attack.[64]

Gospel singer Helen Berhane brought worldwide attention to

the atrocities taking place in Eritrea—both the targeted persecution of Christians and the unimaginably cruel prison conditions. Shortly after releasing a cassette tape of gospel songs in May 2004, Berhane was arrested in Asmara and imprisoned at the Mai Serwa prison camp outside the city. She spent much of her two and a half years of captivity in a metal shipping container and was routinely tortured in efforts to make her recant her faith.

Berhane was subjected to "the helicopter." She was also beaten repeatedly over the course of her imprisonment. By October 2006, she had been tortured so badly that prison authorities allowed her to be admitted to a local hospital. After being released from prison shortly thereafter, Berhane was confined to a wheelchair due to extensive damage to her feet and legs from beatings.

Berhane's story, which garnered international attention when nongovernmental organizations such as Amnesty International lobbied for her release, did not end in tragedy. Eventually she was able to flee the country with her young daughter, seeking refuge in Khartoum before being granted asylum in Denmark. Though suffering severe and lifelong damage from torture, she has been able to build a new life for herself and her child. She has since written a book, *Song of the Nightingale*, recounting her ordeal, and speaks out on behalf of imprisoned Christians in Eritrea.[65]

The US Department of State first declared Eritrea a Country of Particular Concern (CPC) in 2004 and has continued to do so every year since. It summarized the plight of imprisoned Christians in its 2010 Religious Freedom report:

> Dozens of short-term detainees were released, but only after recanting their faith or paying large fines. There continue to be reports of some religious prisoners being held in shipping containers in the desert subject to extreme temperature changes, in solitary confinement for extended periods of time, or in underground, unventilated bunkers with hundreds of other prisoners. Reports continue of religious prisoners being tied up for prolonged periods of time with their hands and feet

bound together behind their backs or from trees, forced to walk barefoot on sharp rocks or thorns, and beaten to confess or renounce their faith.[66]

REFUGEE CRISIS

Given the deadly conditions under which Christians struggle to survive in Eritrea, it is no surprise that a major refugee crisis has developed. Tens of thousands of Eritreans, the vast majority of whom are Christian, flee the country each year, preferring to risk life in refugee camps in Sudan and Ethiopia rather than to remain in their home country.

In a recent desperate development, many Christians now see their best chance for a new life in Israel, known for granting asylum to victims of religious persecution. In order to reach Israel, however, refugees must undertake a treacherous nine-hundred-mile trek across the Sinai Peninsula in Egypt. To navigate this dangerous journey, refugees are hiring smugglers to guide them to the Israeli border. These smugglers usually require a payment of $2,500 to $3,000 before departing.

Once inside Egypt, refugees face a host of potential abuses. Many are caught by authorities and imprisoned in deplorable conditions, only to be deported back to Eritrea where they face unspeakable punishments. Human rights organizations have pleaded with Egyptian authorities to show mercy to the estimated five hundred Eritrean refugees currently imprisoned in Egypt. Falling into the hands of human traffickers may be an even worse fate; they purchase the refugees from the smugglers and then resell them, or ransom them back to their families in Eritrea for sums as high as $20,000. There are estimates that at any given time five to six hundred Eritreans are being held for ransom.[67]

Traffickers mistreat refugees in any number of ways, subjecting them to slavery, sexual assault, starvation, dehydration, beatings, and torture. Undergoing treatment not unlike they experienced in Eritrea, they may be held underground or in shipping containers in blistering desert heat, and subjected to cruel torture, including electric shocks with cattle prods and burial in sand. Egyptian police have no compunctions about shooting those who are able to make it to the border into Israel, as evidenced by the recent shooting deaths of several Eritrean refugees being smuggled across the border; since July 2007, Egyptian officers have shot more than eighty-five people trying to cross into Israel. The cruelty has become so commonplace that Physicians for Human Rights has opened a clinic in Israel specifically designed to address the needs of those refugees who have survived their journey across the Sinai. Most of these refugees require extensive treatment for the effects of torture, including burns from electrical shocks, extreme dehydration, sores from chains, and pregnancies after repeated rape.[68]

The crisis of Christian Eritrean refugees will only worsen as persecution increases inside Eritrea. A new wave of emigration has swelled since an Eritrean governor ordered a purge of Christians in late 2010, leading to a mass exodus from that region.[69] Until the government of Isaias Afwerki ceases its relentless, violent persecution of people of faith, Christians will continue to see fleeing the country as the only alternative to harassment, imprisonment, and possibly death.

ABUSE IN THE NAME OF POWER AND PRIVILEGE

The crushing repression in Burma and Eritrea is proof that persecution need not necessarily stem from an overarching ideology or religion. These rulers' desire to protect their power and privilege by destroying all other centers of allegiance can by itself be enough, even if they dress up their lusts in the garb of national security and protection for their citizens and homeland.

Genuine efforts toward security and protection are a source of hope. In Ethiopia, inter-Christian conflict has been at a relatively low level, but a growing challenge is the government and local Muslim community combating increasing Wahhabi influence.

And, while we must always be cautious about proclamations of change in authoritarian regimes, recent events in Burma such as the release of opposition leader Aung San Suu Kyi and of political prisoners and a cease-fire with the Karen and perhaps with the Kachin, mean that realistic hopes for Christians to have religious freedom are higher than they have been in decades.

In Eritrea, President Isaias Afwerki's regime seems as entrenched as ever. But that also seemed true in Burma, where the regime's isolation, coupled with international pressure, has led to real changes. Meanwhile, faith remains alive in the midst of conflict and suffering.

A group of Karen Christians gave a new twist to Isaiah's verse of turning swords into plowshares. Baroness Cox, who has traveled to Karen State many times in the past fifteen years, described the following scene of Christian faith in the jungle:

> [W]e heard a strange sound, resembling a church bell. Puzzled, we went searching in the jungle to find the source. The sound got clearer and louder as we walked on until, eventually, we discovered a little Karen church in a bamboo hut in the middle of the jungle, where a worshipping community was singing hymns. We spoke to the pastor, who told us that the bell had been made from a Burmese bombshell which had been dropped on their village.[70]

TEN

A CALL TO ACTION

JUST BEFORE CHRISTMAS IN 2011, A CHRISTIAN WOMAN OF humble background from Ethiopia, who was working as a maid in Saudi Arabia, was imprisoned and sexually abused along with twenty-eight other Ethiopian Christians. During a raid by the Saudi government's religious police, they had been caught secretly praying in a house church in Jeddah. Christian prayer, even in private, is treated as a crime in Saudi Arabia.

In a phone call that managed to get through to an American advocacy group, the woman desperately pleaded: "We want you to help us to get out of prison in every way you can, including prayer. Please tell your governments about our plight, contact human rights organizations and others and inform them about us."[1]

From the first page until this final chapter of this book, we have focused on the underreported mistreatment of Christians, the most widely persecuted religious group in today's world. The repression falls on every type of Christian—Protestants and Catholics, Eastern Orthodox and Oriental Orthodox, Methodists and Mennonites, Charismatics and Calvinists, sacramental and simple, those of old churches and new, those who worship in cathedrals or churches steeped in millennia of history or house churches, in groups or alone and isolated. This broad panorama of abuse has prompted Cardinal Kurt Koch, president of the Vatican's Pontifical Council for Promoting Christian Unity, to adopt Pope John Paul II's apt phrase "Ecumenism of the Martyrs" to describe unfolding events.[2]

There is no single war against Christians; anti-Christian persecution has many instigators and intents. But most persecution comes from three sources: Communist or post-Communist governments, perverse nationalistic versions of Hinduism and Buddhism, and increasingly intolerant governments and societies in the Muslim world. Other religious minorities suffer grievous persecution in many of these same countries, but Christians are persecuted wherever there is religious persecution. Some types of Christians are particularly at risk.

FOREIGNERS, APOSTATES, AND BLASPHEMERS

When the subject of Christian persecution is raised, it is often associated with violence directed against missionaries. That certainly occurs, and many brave and dedicated Christians suffer, but, as we have shown, overwhelmingly, those who suffer most are indigenous Christians who outnumber missionaries by about ten thousand to one. In fact, the single largest destination for missionaries is the United States, to which churches throughout the world send pastors to help their growing immigrant flocks adjust to a new world.

In Burma, Laos, Vietnam, and elsewhere, although Christians are indigenous, they are often associated with the West and suspected as a fifth column, and may be forced to recant their faith. But Christianity is far older in these countries than is Communism or the dictatorship of the Burmese generals.

APOSTATES

A fifty-five-year-old Somali, Musa Mohammed Yusuf, was the leader of an underground church in Yonday village, located twenty miles from Kismayo. In February 2009, Musa was questioned in his home by a group of radicals from the notorious Al-Shabab. Well aware he was in grave danger, Yusuf fled to Kismayo.

When the radicals returned to Musa's home the following day, they were enraged to find that he had run away. As his wife, Batula Ali Arbow, watched, they roughly gathered up the couple's three sons: twelve-year-old Hussein Musa Yusuf, eleven-year-old Abdi Rahaman Musa Yusuf, and Abdulahi Musa Yusuf, age seven.

Batula fainted. She said later, "I knew they were going to be slaughtered. Just after some few minutes I heard a wailing cry from Abdulahi (who was) running towards the house. . . ." When she regained consciousness, Batula learned that Abdulahi had escaped the terrorists and survived the attack. But the Al-Shabab terrorists had beheaded her other two boys.[3]

Much violence is visited on those who choose to become Christians; they are often labeled as apostates or weak people subjected to "fraudulent" conversion. Conversion can be a punishable offense in places as diverse as Iran and India. In the Muslim world, converts can be punished, even killed, for leaving Islam.[4]

North Korea and Saudi Arabia are two very different countries, yet they share something in common: in both, all nationals must follow the state's official religion, a Kim dynasty personality cult in the former and Wahhabi Islam in the latter. In some Muslim-majority countries such as Iraq, Saudi Arabia, and Somalia, Christians and Muslims and everyone else can be attacked and even killed for violating what assailants perceive as Muslim dress and/or practices. In Africa, the young churches of Nigeria and Somalia are under grave threat. In Nigeria, the Muslim terror group Boko Haram explicitly aims to drive millions of Christians from the north and has killed thousands. The Al-Qaeda–linked Al-Shabab movement, which controls parts of Somalia, openly declares its intention to kill every Christian in the country and hunts down and beheads Christians on the grounds that they must at some point have left Islam. The *Economist* has concluded, "[M]ore Muslim leaders need to accept that changing creed is a legal right. On that one point, the West should not back down. Otherwise believers, whether Christian or not, remain in peril."[5]

In some Muslim-majority countries, persecution is extended to anyone thought to be involved in an act of apostasy, whether their own or another's. Even in generally moderate countries, conversion is forbidden. In Malaysia, converts have been sent to reeducation camps. Egypt's security forces have tortured converts. Even Morocco expelled dozens of expatriate Christians after accusations that they discussed their faith with Muslims.

Turkey's converts have greater rights than in Saudi Arabia and Iran, but pointing this out is "damning with faint praise," as one Turkish Christian leader put it. He recounted:

> [Converts] have to contest for every inch of legal territory. They are constantly surveilled by national security agencies. They have been threatened, attacked, hauled into court on bogus charges, and even brutally murdered by ultra-nationalists linked to a nationwide plot to destabilize the Turkish government. . . . Although many Turkish congregations meet quietly and safely on a Sunday, no group anywhere in the country meets without carefully taking the measure of each new person who walks through the door.[6]

BLASPHEMERS

Accusations of apostasy and blasphemy often overlap in the Muslim world, and Christians and other minorities are particularly at risk. In Pakistan, Christians and Ahmadis are disproportionately charged—typically with no evidence to support but the accusation itself—with defacing or burning the Qur'an or insulting the Muslim prophet. Like Asia Bibi, the Christian mother of five on death row for blasphemy, they are often convicted only on testimonial evidence. Christians cannot effectively counter such charges against them because their testimony is of less legal worth than a Muslim's in sharia courts. The testimony of a Christian woman is worth less again.

Christians in Sudan, Egypt, Malaysia, and a dozen other countries are also subject to blasphemy codes. In Pakistan, Afghanistan, Iraq, Nigeria, Turkey, and Somalia, Christians have been killed indiscriminately for "blasphemous" expressions that occurred in other countries, by other people: after Pope Benedict XVI's Regensburg speech, after a Florida pastor threatened to burn a Qur'an, and after a Danish newspaper printed cartoons depicting the prophet Muhammad.

ARAB SPRING, CHRISTIAN WINTER?

Other Christians also now face grave threats in Muslim-majority countries, especially the millennia-old Christian communities in the heart of the Middle East.

In early 2011, a revolutionary uprising, optimistically dubbed the Arab Spring, exploded in the Middle East and North Africa. While initially tinged with hope, it has brought great danger to indigenous Christians. The ancient churches of Iraq, and of Egypt, the Arab Spring's epicenter, are in dire peril. They are threatened with religious cleansing by Islamist forces acting with renewed violence now that repressive secular rulers have been removed.

These Christians have weathered much violence in the past and are long accustomed to severe discrimination. As the Vatican's senior official for dialogue with Muslims, Cardinal Jean-Louis Tauran, told Al Jazeera in March 2012, "I have been in the Middle East for many years . . . Christians feel they are second-class citizens in countries where Muslims are the majority."[7]

Since Saddam Hussein's dictatorship in Iraq was destroyed, up to two-thirds of that country's Christians have fled in less than a decade. These Christians are among the last to pray in Aramaic, the language Jesus spoke. They have emigrated due to the intense violence from Islamist extremists and common criminals, both of whom operate with impunity and who specifically target Christians. In 2006, Sunni death squads permanently drove out Christians from an entire Baghdad neighborhood, demanding conversion to Islam or death. Authorities in Baghdad have been slow to protect Christians and have watched passively as local authorities deprive Christians of essential services, including those provided through American reconstruction efforts.

Egypt's ancient Coptic community, about eight million souls, is the largest Christian and non-Muslim minority in the entire Middle East. They now suffer ruthless attacks by Salafi Muslims and by military troops, who have not been punished for abusing or using excessive force against Christians. Since the Arab Spring empowered Islamists, anti-Christian persecution has increased. Many Copts doubt the new Muslim Brotherhood leaders will protect them against even more radical and violent Salafis, who have been electorally proven to have sizable popular support. The Copts are acutely conscious of the fate of Iraq's Christian minorities; and tens, maybe hundreds, of thousands of Copts have fled the country since the beginning of 2011. Egyptian political scholar and Copt Samuel Tadros has said: "The Copts can only wonder today whether, after 2,000 years, the time has come for them to pack their belongings and leave, as Egypt looks less hospitable to them than ever."[8]

In Syria, the vicious Assad dictators drawn from the unorthodox Alawite Muslim minority have generally tolerated the Christian minority, which numbers about two million. Middle East Christian scholar Kurt Werthmuller recalled an Easter Sunday visit to Aleppo in Syria:

> I was visiting from Egypt, where I lived at the time and where Copts were typically seen but not heard, so I was amazed to hear the ringing of church bells and to find a Syriac Easter liturgy broadcasting over loudspeakers to overflow congregants in the city streets![9]

Now, with a change in the political order, the Christians "may incur the wrath of the Sunni majority striking back against all of Assad's traditional allies."[10] The perilous situation of Syria's Christians is all but ignored by Western foreign policymakers.

Native Christians were largely eradicated from the other Arab

Spring countries of Tunisia, Libya, and Yemen long ago. How the rest will fare remains to be seen.

The driving out of Christians from the region, after a two millennia presence there, should be a concern not only to Christians. Lebanese Christian scholar Habib Malik makes the point that Christian minorities have traditionally served as "moderators" and "mediators" in the Middle East.[11] They have often stressed Western-style education, individual freedoms, and women's rights. A case in point is his own father, Charles Malik, a major drafter of the Universal Declaration of Human Rights. Malik insisted:

> The existence of settled, stable, prosperous, and reasonably free and secure native Christian communities in the Middle East has served in many instances as a factor encouraging Islamic openness and moderation, creating an environment of pluralism that fosters acknowledgment of the different other.[12]

Without Christians, the Middle East will become even more radicalized and more estranged from the West. This will be a political problem for the West. As a Chaldean Catholic bishop lamented, "This is very sad and very dangerous for the church, for Iraq and even for Muslim people, because it means the end of an old experience of living together."[13]

HELPING CHRISTIANS HELPS OTHERS

Though our focus in this book is anti-Christian persecution, our concern and our work at the Center for Religious Freedom is not limited to Christians. Defending persecuted Christians and expanding religious freedom will also help other persecuted religious groups and minorities. Mandaeans and Yezidis in Iraq, Baha'is and Jews in Iran, Ahmadis and Hindus in Pakistan, Falun Gong in China, Buddhists in Vietnam, animists in Sudan, Shiites in Saudi Arabia, and Muslims in Burma all suffer imprisonment, exile, torture, and death at the hands of those who oppress Christians.

Many Muslims, as well as Christians, are persecuted under apostasy and blasphemy laws. In the Muslim world, blasphemy accusations and punishments are used not only against those who are deemed religiously insulting. They also are used to attack those, including Muslims, who express unpopular or dissenting views, especially views advocating political and religious freedoms. In recent years, people have been accused and punished for blasphemy because they have denounced stoning as a violation of women's rights (Afghanistan), opened girls' schools (Bangladesh), criticized rule by clergy (Iran), petitioned for a constitution (Saudi Arabia), rejected an order for violent jihad (Sudan), prayed at the graves of relatives (Saudi Arabia), translated the Qur'an into Dari (Afghanistan), opposed the blasphemy law itself (Pakistan), urged that the Qur'an be understood in its historical and cultural context (Indonesia), taught Shiism (Egypt), and called for a ban on child brides (Yemen). In all these cases, the victims were Muslims.

A prime example of the same forces persecuting Christians and other religious minorities is the case of South Sudan. When South Sudan became an independent nation in July 2011—a result of efforts by an American movement largely galvanized by Christians opposing persecution—all its citizens benefited equally. Now, as the US State Department validated in its 2012 annual report, Christians, animists, and Muslims alike enjoy religious freedom in the new Republic. Policy solutions that help Christians will usually benefit all religious minorities. Our cause is religious freedom.

"UNITE WITH THEM IN PRAYER"

Learning the stories of Christians facing religious persecution around the world should motivate Christians, among others, to, as Catholic theologian Michael Novak put it, "open ourselves to learn of them, and unite with them in prayer."[14] As we write, it is our hope that Christians living in freedom will prayerfully consider the people we have described and seek ways to aid them.

Faith McDonnell of the Institute on Religion and Democracy has developed some "Aids to Intercession" for churches.[15]

- Start a persecuted church prayer group and hold an all-night or all-day prayer vigil.
- Include the persecuted church during prayers at church every Sunday.
- Provide bulletin inserts with prayer points.
- During baptisms, pray for the persecuted Christian converts from Islam and the pastors who baptize them at great personal risk.
- Read testimonies from the persecuted church.
- Carry crosses in worship, and pray for the Dinka and other Sudanese who carry crosses.
- Observe the International Day of Prayer for the persecuted church each year.
- Collect and frequently update materials on the persecuted church for a church prayer chapel.
- Use a globe, world map, or newspaper in family prayer time.

CITIZENS AND FOREIGN POLICY

Since much of our focus in this book is on the action or inaction of governments, we will pay particular attention to the political dimensions of persecution. For Americans, religious freedom is an inalienable, God-given right, not a privilege or gift bestowed by governments. Religious freedom is the bedrock on which the United States was founded: it is enshrined in the first clause of the First Amendment of the US Constitution, and is also a fundamental freedom in every major international agreement on civil and political rights.

The United States and free countries generally can wield significant influence to help persecuted believers. Unfortunately our officials often miss or misunderstand the perilous circumstances of Christians and other religious minorities as they make foreign policy.

For example, while there were 130,000 American and NATO troops on the ground in Afghanistan, that country's last remaining church was razed in 2010 after its ninety-nine-year lease was cancelled. The US State Department knew of this, and even reported on it in September 2011, but took no effective measure to stop or reverse it. The destruction of Afghanistan's last church did not draw the international protest that accompanied the Taliban's destruction of the Bamiyan Buddhist statues in 2001, but it is equally emblematic and even more consequential because it deprived an existing religious community of its only house of worship. While the American people supported President Karzai's government financially and militarily, Afghanistan joined the infamous company of hard-line Saudi Arabia as a country that will not tolerate any churches. The Christians among America's own diplomats and contract workers in Afghanistan must now hide their worship services.

Pascale, a Christian woman whose name has been changed to protect her identity, has recounted her story of trying to escape Iraq because of religious persecution.

> My friend was stopped at a checkpoint on the road to Irbil from Baghdad. The people in the car had to show their ID cards to the masked men. They could see she was Christian from her name. They dragged her from the car, pushed her to her knees and put a gun to her head. They told her to convert to Islam, or die. She refused and started praying out loud. But they did not kill her, not straight away. They raped her and then she was shot in the head.[16]

Other examples occurred in Iraq from 2005 to 2008, when the United States was the occupying power and some one hundred thousand American troops were active there. During those years, Christians, Mandaeans (followers of John the Baptist), and Yezidis (an angel-centered religion related to Zoroastrianism) experienced horrific persecution that ultimately led to a nationwide "religious cleansing" campaign against non-Muslims. Christians now may number two-thirds fewer than in 2003 while the other smallest minorities have been similarly decimated.

American foreign policy officials seemed to believe that it would be "special pleading" to do anything to help the persecuted Christians, Mandeans, and Yezidis. When twenty thousand Christian families were being violently driven from Baghdad's Dora neighborhood in 2006–07, Secretary of State Condoleezza Rice maintained that the administration could not take effective action to protect them from being murdered and kidnapped because it did not want American policy to be seen as "sectarian."[17] But the United States was already up to its neck in sectarian considerations; Secretary Rice said this at the very time the United States was waging a military surge against Islamic Sunni extremists. The United States was engaged in intensive efforts to ensure that non-violent Sunnis gained positions in the Iraqi government, which, thanks to the overthrow of Saddam Hussein, was run largely by Shias, whom the administration had helped politically strengthen and unify.

Eventually, following the US military's surge, overall violence subsided, but violence against Christians did not. We are not asking for special privileges for Christians but for *equal* consideration; the problem is that US Iraq policy had many sectarian considerations—except when it came to Christians and other non-Muslims, whom, because they were peaceful, it consistently overlooked.

CHRISTIAN CITIZENS

We believe that all citizens of any or no religion should be equally concerned with the persecution of people of any or no religion. But, since Christians are the most widely persecuted group, the majority of Americans who profess to be Christians bear a particular responsibility to pay attention.

The two tragic developments in Afghanistan and Iraq took place under two different administrations, one Democratic and one

Republican. They happened without a significant policy response from the United States or any other Western country; the plain truth is that our governments do not usually take needed action simply because it is the right thing to do.

Democracies usually act based on the concerns expressed by their citizens. But, at that time, the American people, including Christians, were tragically disengaged. In invoking John Paul II's phrase "Ecumenism of the Martyrs," the Vatican's Cardinal Koch spoke of common concern and activism on behalf of persecuted Christians around the world. He urged:

> Today, as Christians, . . . we have to demonstrate this hope [of full unity of the Body of Christ] in a credible manner, by helping persecuted Christians, publicly denouncing situations of martyrdom and getting involved in efforts on behalf of respect for religious freedom and human dignity.[18]

Western Christians and other concerned people should use their citizenship rights to stand up for foreign policies that help alleviate and end religious persecution abroad—certainly not make it worse. We should join together and exercise our rights to speak, assemble, and petition on behalf of the religiously persecuted.

USING THE "BULLY PULPIT"

The "bully pulpit" is a shorthand term to describe political pressure exerted through speeches and other exhortations by the president and other influential government leaders. Though coined by Theodore Roosevelt, it is an unfortunate term—after all, who wants to be bullied, or known as a bully? But it is the term we have inherited, and public declarations by our elected officials play a large part in defining events. They can focus world attention, bolster the morale of those they champion, bring moral opprobrium upon those they denounce, and guide policymaking. We can and should petition our president and other elected officials to speak out on behalf of the persecuted. The president and cabinet members can help save a life, name and shame persecutors abroad, and more generally spotlight a pattern of severe persecution, serving as a blueprint for administration policies.

In his first few months in office in 2001, President Bush, briefed by Samaritan's Purse head Franklin Graham and pressed by a coalition of churches, charities, and activists, gave an important speech spotlighting the Sudanese regime's religious persecution of Christians. It was the first acknowledgment by an American president of that catastrophic persecution. It came at a time when the religious dimension of Khartoum's atrocities—we would say genocide—were missed by the major media. It was a powerful, detailed, and straightforward condemnation of Khartoum's crimes of bombing, enslaving, killing, and forcibly converting to Islam the Christians and animists of the Nuba and in Southern Sudan. In particular, President Bush asserted, "The right of conscience has been singled out for special abuse by the Sudanese authorities. Aid agencies report that food assistance is sometimes distributed only to those willing to undergo conversion to Islam."[19]

His later policies—encouraged and bolstered by Representative Frank Wolf, the late Representative Don Payne, then-Senator Sam Brownback, USCIRF, Jimmy Mulla and his nonprofit Voices for Sudan, the Institute on Religion and Democracy, the Center for Religious Freedom, many American Christians and their churches, and other activists of different religions and ideologies—resulted in a wonderfully successful chain of events. The president appointed a general special envoy for Sudan, which paved the way for the Comprehensive Peace Agreement of 2005. This, in turn, allowed South Sudan, through a referendum process, to become an independent country in 2011. President Bush's speech marked a turning point in American policy and for the future religious freedom of millions of South Sudanese.

THE SILENT BULLY PULPIT

In striking contrast to the speeches on Sudan from both the Bush and Obama administrations, the presidential bully pulpit has fallen silent regarding Middle Eastern Christians in their great hour of need.

On November 1, 2010, Islamist extremists assaulted Baghdad's Our Lady of Perpetual Help Catholic Church during a Sunday mass, killing or wounding virtually all the congregation. This atrocity occurred at a pivotal moment, when it was amply apparent that violence and the Baghdad government's failure to protect non-Muslims were leading to their eradication from Iraq. This is what the White House said:

> The United States strongly condemns this senseless act of hostage taking and violence by terrorists linked to Al-Qaeda in Iraq that occurred Sunday in Baghdad killing so many innocent Iraqis. Our hearts go out to the people of Iraq who have suffered so much from these attacks. We offer sincerest condolences to the families of the victims and to all the people of Iraq who are targeted by these cowardly acts of terrorism.[20]

This nowhere acknowledges that the "innocent Iraqis" targeted in this shocking incident were all Christians, that the massacre took place in a church, and that it occurred during Sunday worship. It mistakenly describes as "senseless" what was all too sensibly a deliberate and horrific act of religious cleansing against Christians targeted for their faith.

The White House's vague and generic condolences refused to describe the reality of the event. That church bombing, one of seventy in Iraq since 2004, was the watershed moment for Iraqi Christians; many then concluded there would be no future for them in Iraq, and en masse they abandoned their ancient homeland.

In contrast, on October 4, 2011, and on January 11, 2012, when two mosques were vandalized in Israel, the Department of State was specific about the victims and motives:

> The United States strongly condemns the dangerous and provocative attacks on a mosque in the northern Israeli town of

> Tuba-Zangariyye, which took place on October 3. Such hateful sectarian actions are never justified.[21]

And:

> The United States condemns in the strongest possible terms today's most recent vandalizing of a mosque, as well as the burning of three cars, in the West Bank village of Deir Istiya. Hateful, dangerous, and provocative actions such as these are never justified.[22]

In October 2011, Egyptian government forces massacred two dozen Copts as they were staging a peaceful street protest in Cairo's Maspero area. They were demonstrating precisely to demand religious freedom in the face of Salafi religious violence against Coptic churches and the failure of the Egyptian security forces to protect them. After the Maspero massacre, the White House stated: "Now is a time for restraint on all sides so that Egyptians can move forward together to forge a strong and united Egypt."[23]

The statement made no mention of the identity of those who were killed. Nor did it acknowledge they were attacked while demonstrating for religious freedom. Worse, in calling for restraint "on all sides," it drew a moral equivalency between the victims and their aggressors, who were not shadowy terrorists or vigilante groups but government troops supported by US military aid. Coptic expert Samuel Tadros ironically commented: "Perhaps I ought to join the president in his concern and call for restraint: I call upon the security forces to refrain from killing Christians, and upon Christians to refrain from dying."[24]

On Easter morning in 2012, a Protestant church in Kaduna, Nigeria, was targeted by a suicide car bombing that killed thirty-nine and wounded dozens, apparently the handiwork of Boko Haram, the Salafi network whose stated aim is to turn Africa's largest country into a sharia state. The Christmas before, Boko Haram had bombed St. Theresa's Catholic Church outside the capital Abuja killing forty-four worshipers, and also attacked various Christian churches in the towns of Jos, Kano, Gadaka, and Damaturu.

There was no official comment from the Obama administration about the monstrous example of anti-Christian persecution on the holy day of Easter. However, on April 8, 2012, that is, Easter, Secretary Clinton did manage to issue one press release. It announced that "today we celebrate the history, impact and culture of Romani people" (formerly called gypsies), and inveighed against Europe, demanding that it become "more inclusive."[25] But for the northern Nigerian Christians savagely attacked on one of their most important religious days, there was not a word of condolence.

Even worse, the day after the Nigeria church bombing, at a forum on US policy toward Nigeria held at Washington's Center for Strategic and International Studies, Clinton's assistant secretary of state for African affairs, Johnnie Carson—overlooking Boko Haram's self-proclaimed identity, pattern of behavior, statements, and very name, which means "Western education is a sin"—publicly denied that Boko Haram has religious motives. He went out of his way to stress: "Religion is not driving extremist violence in . . . northern Nigeria."[26] By June it had escalated with multiple church bombings every Sunday and with some Christians using indiscriminate violence against Muslims in retaliation.

Carson was articulating official US policy. Its theory is that Boko Haram is "exploiting religious differences" to "create chaos" to protest "poor government service delivery," poverty, and a variety of good-governance concerns. The United States Commission on International Religious Freedom found that Boko Haram's violence is indeed "religiously related."[27] Even Nigeria's Committee of Imams of the Federal Capital Territory has acknowledged that the church bombings are done in the name of Islam and condemned them as "deviant."[28]

Again, we are not asking for special privileges for Christians; the problem is that our political leaders often avoid any mention of Christians. Clearly, much more needs to be done by the United States and the rest of the West.

"IT WOULD HAVE BEEN CATASTROPHIC TO REMAIN IN A KIND OF SILENCE"

Some members of Congress are trying to make a difference. The stalwart US Congressional representatives Frank Wolf, Chris Smith, Trent Franks, and the late Donald Payne and Tom Lantos, have held hearings and press conferences on these issues.

In 2011, Representative Wolf introduced a bill (HR 440) to direct the president to appoint a Special Envoy to Promote Religious Freedom of Religious Minorities in the Near East and South Central Asia.[29] This measure could, like the Sudan envoy measure on which it is modeled, focus attention on religious persecution against Christians and other religious minorities where persecution is most widespread and intensifying. But, to make a difference, any envoy, or any congressional initiative, needs grassroots support.

While other Western governments have usually said little about the current plight of Middle Eastern Christians, on February 21, 2011, the EU council of foreign ministers "firmly condemned" recent violence and terrorist acts in "various countries" against Christians, as well as Muslim pilgrims and other religious groups. This statement was a result of lobbying by the Council of European Episcopal Conferences as well as the Orthodox, Protestant, and Anglican representatives of the Conference of European Churches. French Cardinal Jean-Pierre Ricard acknowledged the initial "reticence" of EU foreign ministers to speak up, and added: "It would have been catastrophic to remain in a kind of silence, of incapacity to speak."[30] He also hoped the sentiments expressed would "now be translated in concrete initiatives on the spot."

POLITICAL ACTION

Umar Mulinde grew up in a staunch Muslim home in the African nation of Uganda; his grandfather was an imam, and Umar was trained in Islamic thought from childhood. His Muslim beliefs went unchallenged until he went to college, where he faced other views.

One Sunday Umar visited a church for the first time. At the end of the service he walked to the front of the church and publicly converted from Islam to Christianity. As he walked out of the church, three of his Muslim friends saw that he had been inside. They later attacked him. "I knew that I would suffer beatings if I became a Christian, but I thought it would happen for awhile and then stop. I was wrong."

As time passed, Umar preached the Christian gospel, and before long had a church with a congregation of a thousand. On Christmas night 2011, as he walked out of his church, acid was thrown at him. It burned into the right side of his face, including his eye and part of his back. He recalls hearing his assailant declare "Allahu Akbar" three times as he slipped away into the crowd.

Mulinde's face is dramatically scarred and he has lost the sight in his right eye. Severe pain continues. Nonetheless, he plans to return to his church and his family in Uganda. "When I became a Christian, I was set free from legalism, fear, and hatred. My message today is one of Christ's love and forgiveness, and I will continue to preach it."[31]

One of the greatest challenges faced by those concerned about religious freedom is a sense of powerlessness. A paralyzing lassitude sometimes strikes when we see such a massive and deadly epidemic of intimidation, persecution, and violence as is faced by Christians around the world.

We, as citizens living in freedom, are not powerless. Sometimes within our given circumstances we are able to take steps on our own to help: as diplomats or members of the international business community, or as ordinary people by starting social media or Internet campaigns, by organizing mass letter writing and petitions to oppressive governments abroad, or by using music and art to raise awareness.

But one of the most effective means is to use our rights as citizens to influence the foreign policy of our own government. Even in extreme persecution, individuals can be rescued and helped by our country's actions and policies. We have told the story of Abdul Rahman, an Afghan who was put on trial for his life in 2006 after he converted to Christianity. The US State Department, after first saying it would wait for Afghanistan's judicial process to play out, firmly reminded the Karzai government of its international human rights obligations. After Rahman's case became an issue among Western Christians and other human rights advocates, his life was spared and he was spirited out of the country to safety.

These examples show that we can make a difference. But it often takes an influential government, applying both incentives and pressures—"carrots and sticks"—to move tyrants to change their ways.

There are many actions we can and must take, but many that yield the largest impact are undertaken through official foreign policies. One major example was stopping the forcible Islamization of Christians and animists in South Sudan. An independent South Sudan was born and religious freedom secured for millions of its residents, regardless of their religious beliefs. As we noted earlier, the US State Department stated it did not receive any reports of religious discrimination or abuse in South Sudan in the year after its independence.

But without a reinvigorated, grassroots base, our political leaders frequently fail to act. If we do not act, churches will not act, few NGOs will act, and our government will not act.

THE INTERNATIONAL RELIGIOUS FREEDOM ACT

Ordinary Americans can shape foreign policy. One example is the critically important International Religious Freedom Act (IRFA). This law has established a foreign policy focus on religious freedom, and an independent body to help those persecuted for their faith. Its history helps us to know ways to act.

Incensed by persecution habitually ignored by the American foreign policy establishment, a large, grassroots movement coalesced around what became the International Religious Freedom Act of 1998.[32] One crystallizing moment was a summit in January 1996 on worldwide religious persecution, held for American religious leaders. At this summit, which the Center for Religious Freedom organized, the National Association of Evangelicals released a Statement of Conscience, solemnly pledging "to do what is within our power to the end that the government of the United States will take appropriate action to combat the intolerable religious persecution now victimizing fellow believers and those of other faiths."[33]

This marked the beginning of a broad, faith-based mobilization that defeated even active opposition by foreign policy makers to secure the passage of the new law. The backbone of this movement was defined by Summit participants: one hundred key Christian leaders, later joined by Jewish, Hindu, Muslim, Buddhist, Baha'i, and other representatives of nearly every faith group.

REPORTING ON RELIGIOUS PERSECUTORS

IRFA mandates that the State Department report annually on the status of religious freedom in some two hundred foreign countries and territories, and then designate and sanction Countries of Particular Concern—places where religious persecution is "egregious, ongoing and systematic." These reports are more than a thousand pages long and accessible through the website www.state.gov/j/drl/rls/irf/. This is now the world's best repository of information on religious freedom.

While there is room for improvement, especially in reporting on increasing violations of the right to conscience in the West, these reports otherwise have been largely insulated from political considerations. For example, though it damaged the reputation of America's partner in Afghanistan when the Obama administration was struggling to maintain American public support for its war strategy, the 2011 US Department of State report on Afghanistan asserted that religious freedom was "deteriorating" under the Karzai government.

These respected nonsectarian resources help compensate for the failure of much of the mainstream media, which often overlooks the plight of Christians. David Aikman observed, "Western figures who think little of slighting evangelicals still carefully avoid offending Muslims. This complicates efforts to criticize Muslim persecution of Christians."[34] Others have secular blind spots and prefer to cover political prisoners, not religious prisoners, when they cover human rights abuses at all.[35]

IRFA'S CHILDREN

IRFA also established USCIRF, a commission appointed on a bipartisan basis by the president, the House of Representatives, and the Senate. It is an independent agency charged with recommending the world's worst religious persecutors for Country of Particular Concern status and suggesting nonbinding foreign policies to the government.[36]

USCIRF played a key role in recommending policies to end the North-South strife in Sudan, and prompted the State Department to designate as "egregious" persecutors China, Saudi Arabia, and Uzbekistan. It keeps the focus on egregious religious atrocities by our trading partners and strategic allies—Vietnam, Pakistan, Turkey, Iraq, and Egypt—when the State Department might rather not. Canada, the Netherlands, Germany, and the Philippines are now examining the USCIRF model.

In adopting IRFA, a broad interfaith coalition prevailed over a well-padded trade lobby and influential establishment figures such as then–Secretary of State Madeleine Albright (who has since gracefully recanted her opposition). But, since IRFA passed, while individuals and organizations do important and heroic work, the coalition behind it largely disbanded.

Because it lost public attention, IRFA is not fully effective. It has generated generally excellent reporting by the US Department of State and recommendations by USCIRF, but US policy typically fails to incorporate and act on these findings.

In democracies, political leaders respond when constituents care about the problem. We must remind elected officials of the importance of religious freedom. Fifteen years ago, a core group of activists and religious leaders worked with congressional leaders to light a prairie fire—a national, interfaith, grassroots mobilization to focus and institutionalize concern for religious freedom in US foreign policy. This fire needs rekindling.

As our endnotes show, you can now, as you could not twenty years ago, use the Internet easily to gather further information, offer financial help, and write to imprisoned or otherwise deprived Christians. This information can be sent to congressional representatives, senators, and the president, asking for specific action.

One priority should be appointing a Special Envoy to Promote Religious Freedom of Religious Minorities in the Near East and South Central Asia. An envoy could be a central point for foreign policy, supported by a steady flow of information. An envoy's pull will depend a great deal on public backing.

BEARING OTHERS' BURDENS

The world is changing quickly. The Arab Spring roils the Middle East. North Korea gets a new leader. South Sudan achieves independence. China is in long-term transition, and Burma is opening up. Cuba's Castro dictatorship and Saudi Arabia's monarchy are in their decrepitude. What comes next? Obviously, we don't know, but clearly much more needs to be done by the United States and the rest of the West, and especially by Christians who have the freedom to speak up.

In the face of our changing and increasingly dangerous world, we are called to help bear the burden of those who are carrying the cross in ways we can hardly imagine. The sobering words of Dietrich Bonhoeffer, a Christian pastor who died in a Nazis concentration camp for resisting Hitler's injustice, resonate today as perhaps never before. May they become a meditation for all who pray and watch on behalf of persecuted Christians around the world. May they inspire us to move forward with wisdom, courage, and strength in the midst of the persecution.

Christianity stands or falls with its revolutionary protest against violence, arbitrariness and pride of power and with its plea for the weak.

Christians are doing too little to make these points clear rather than too much. Christendom adjusts itself far too easily to the worship of power.

Christians should give more offense, shock the world far more, than they are doing now. Christians should take a stronger stand in favor of the weak rather than considering first the possible right of the strong.

—Pastor Dietrich Bonhoeffer,
sermon on 2 Corinthians 12:9

AFTERWORD

BY MOST REVEREND CHARLES J. CHAPUT, O.F.M. CAP., D.D., ARCHBISHOP OF PHILADELPHIA

"DEAR FRIENDS, DO NOT BE SURPRISED AT THE FIERY ORDEAL that has come on you to test you, as though something strange were happening to you. But rejoice inasmuch as you participate in the sufferings of Christ . . ." So wrote St. Peter to the early Christians. And so the story continues.

In today's deeply troubled world, we can no longer be surprised by the ongoing "fiery ordeal" encountered by the global Christian community. Tragically, it is neither strange nor unusual—in fact we are living in an age of intensifying anti-Christian persecution. And while Scripture asserts that persecution for righteousness's sake will always be with us, this hardly gives us who are not persecuted an alibi for complacency or resignation as we see Christians and other religious minorities facing atrocities we can hardly imagine.

The Bible gives us clear guidelines for helping the persecuted. It challenges us to pray for them as when the entire church gathered in prayer for the release of prisoners Peter and Paul. Again and again, in the story of the Good Shepherd, in the parable of the Good Samaritan, in Paul's encouragement to the church to use the opportunity "to do good to all people" and take special responsibility for "the family of believers," it calls us to loving action as a moral imperative. And, as we learn in the book of Acts, when Paul faced murder at the hands of an angry mob, he appealed for due process and a fair hearing before Caesar, asserting his civil and legal rights of Roman citizenship.

In reading the preceding pages, we cannot help but be shocked by the scores of distressing accounts from across the world. Every day, millions of women, men, and children face persecution, imprisonment, and even death simply because of their faith in Jesus Christ. They are forced to endure these abuses because one of their most fundamental human rights has been violated: the right of religious freedom.

A person's right to religious freedom under the protection of the law is a foundation stone of human dignity. No one, whether acting in the name of some political agenda or religious ideology, has the authority to interfere with that basic human right.

Religious freedom includes being able to worship as we choose. It's also the liberty to preach, teach, and practice our faith openly and without fear. And it involves even more than that. Religious freedom includes the right of religious believers, leaders, and communities to take part vigorously in a nation's public life.

Freedom of religion presumes two things.

First, "freedom of religion" presumes that we have free will as part of our basic human dignity. And because we can freely reason and choose, we will often disagree about the nature of God and the best path to knowing him. Some will choose to not believe in God at all—and they clearly have a right to their unbelief.

Second, "freedom of religion" presumes that questions about God, eternity, and the purpose of human life really do have vital importance for human happiness. And therefore we should have the freedom to pursue and live out the answers we find to these basic questions without government interference.

A few years ago I received a letter from a former Special Forces officer and graduate of West Point—a career army veteran—serving in Baghdad as a security adviser to Iraqi authorities.

A Catholic himself, he wrote to me about the harassment and violence Iraqi Christians face as part of their daily routine. He knew, as many Americans still don't, that large Christian Arab communities once thrived across the Middle East. Over the centuries, under pressure from repressive forms of Islam, Christian populations have slowly declined. But the past one hundred years have been especially brutal for Christians of the region.

In the letter, he wrote:

> I have come to know many of the surviving [Iraqi] Christians, both Eastern rite Catholic and Orthodox, who work here in [Baghdad's] International Zone. I had known as an academic item about the massacre of the [Christian] Armenians by the Ottoman Turks in 1915. What I had not known was that many of the areas currently occupied by Kurds—[southeast] Turkey, northern Iraq and northwest Iran—were originally . . . Christian. Not having enough manpower to kill all the Christians in their empire, the Ottomans "contracted out" the destruction of the Christians to their subject peoples. More than 750,000 were directly killed, died of disease and exposure, or starved to death. What's going on now [in Iraq] very much affects the remaining Christians here too.

Discrimination, deprivation of rights, and even bloodshed against Christians: all of these indignities have a long and troubling history in the Middle East that *predates* Western colonialism and American interventions by many years. The horrific attack and murders at Our Lady of Perpetual Help church (also translated as "Our Lady of Deliverance"), an Eastern rite Catholic community in Baghdad detailed in chapter 8 of this book, is a dramatic example in a long line of brutal acts designed to obliterate—either by killing or driving out—the ancient Iraqi Christian community. Observers quite rightly describe the continuing anti-Christian violence in Iraq as a form of "religious cleansing." In a recent letter to brother bishops, clergy, and lay Catholics across the United States, Mar Barnaba Yousif Habas—bishop of Our Lady of Deliverance Syriac Catholic Diocese covering the United States and Canada—pleaded for our solidarity and prayers. He warned that we are "witnessing an ongoing genocide and forced exodus of [Iraq's Christians] because they are Christians, and only because of their faith."

The so-called Arab Spring that began to unfold in 2011 has received a lot of positive media coverage. But very little of that coverage has mentioned that the turmoil in Muslim countries has also created a very dangerous situation for Christians and other religious minorities across North Africa and the Middle East. In Egypt, angry mobs have attacked Christian churches and monasteries, burning them to the ground and murdering the people inside. Christians have fled in large numbers from anti-Christian violence in Iraq and Syria. Meanwhile, in Saudi Arabia, it's illegal to own a Bible or wear a crucifix. In Pakistan, Christians face imprisonment, beatings, and even murder over accusations that they committed blasphemy against Islam by some word or deed that may not be supported by any evidence.

Pakistan has one of the world's strictest anti-blasphemy laws, which criminalizes defamation of Islam, and this results in extensive human-rights abuses. Allegations of blasphemy, which are often false and used to intimidate or settle personal scores, have resulted in the lengthy detention of Ahmadis, Christians, Hindus, and members of other religious minority communities, as well as Muslims whose views are deemed offensive by religious extremists. Criminal penalties for blasphemy include the death penalty or a sentence of up to life in prison. Who judges what constitutes blasphemy, a term that is open to arbitrary interpretation? Usually, it is Muslim extremists who rabble-rouse local mobs that threaten violence outside the jails and courthouses until a conviction is handed down. Fundamental freedoms of belief and expression are among the victims.

We also need to remember that religious freedom is under siege in many other cultures and countries. Remnants of communism still harass, imprison, torture, and kill Christians in China, Vietnam, Laos, Cuba, and perhaps most egregiously in North Korea. State authorities who cannot tolerate citizens who serve a higher, divine authority mistreat Christians in such places as Eritrea, Burma, and in vast portions of the former Soviet Union. Wherever Christians refuse to bow the knee to earthly rulers who claim what belongs to God, persecution abounds.

In his World Day of Peace message a few years ago, Pope Benedict XVI voiced his concern over the worldwide prevalence of "persecution, discrimination, terrible acts of violence and religious intolerance." We now face a global crisis in religious liberty. There is nothing remote or theoretical about this intolerance. It is bitterly real. It is being suffered by men, women, and children who belong to the family of Jesus Christ; for Christians in the West, they are *our* family, *our* church, *our* brothers and sisters. If we ignore them, we ignore our own baptism. As a Catholic bishop, I have a natural concern that Christian minorities in Africa and Asia bear the brunt of today's religious discrimination and violence. The Holy Father noted this same fact in his own remarks.

We should always remember that Christians are not the only victims. Data from the Pew Forum on Religion and Public Life are sobering. More than 70 percent of the world's people now live in nations where religious freedom is gravely restricted. As the authors of this book have documented, this ugly reality has only been getting worse. Principles that Americans find self-evident—the dignity of the human person, the sanctity of conscience, the separation of political and sacred authority, the distinction between secular and religious law, the idea of a civil society preexisting and distinct from the state—are not widely accepted elsewhere.

The modern world's system of international law is founded on the assumption of universal values shared by people of all cultures, ethnicities, and religions. In the sixteenth century, the Spanish Dominican priest Francisco de Vitoria envisioned something like the United Nations. An international rule of law is possible, he said, because there is a "natural law" inscribed in the heart of every person, a set of values that are universal, objective, and unchanging. The twentieth-century American theologian and priest John Courtney Murray argued in the same way. The natural law tradition presumes that men and women are religious by nature and that we are born with an innate desire for transcendence and truth.

These assumptions are at the core of the 1948 Universal Declaration of Human Rights. Many of the people who worked on this declaration, such as the great French philosopher Jacques Maritain, believed that this charter of international liberty also reflected the American experience.

Article 18 of the declaration famously says that "Everyone has the right to freedom of thought, conscience and religion; this right includes freedom to change his religion or belief; and freedom, either alone or in community with others and in public or private, to manifest his religion or belief in teaching, practice, worship and observance."

In this sense, then, the American model has already been applied. What we see today is a repudiation of that model by atheist regimes and secular ideologies, and also unfortunately by militant versions of some non-Christian religions. This global situation is made worse by the inaction of our own national leadership in promoting to the world one of America's greatest qualities: religious freedom.

This is regrettable for many reasons, not least because we urgently need an honest discussion on the relationship between Islam and the assumptions of the modern democratic state. In diplomacy and in interreligious dialogue we need to encourage an Islamic public theology that is both faithful to Muslim traditions and also open to liberal norms. A healthy distinction between the sacred and the secular, between religious law and civil law, is foundational to free societies. Christians, and especially Catholics, have learned the hard way that the marriage of church and state rarely works. For one thing, religion usually ends up the loser, an ornament or house chaplain for Caesar. For another, *all theocracies are utopian*—and every utopia ends up persecuting or murdering the dissenters who can't or won't pay allegiance to its claims of universal bliss.

This is a moment that determines who we really are as believers. We can't solve the problems of the world. But we *can* help those who are suffering for their faith and simply trying to live in peace with their neighbors in lands they've called home for centuries, long before the arrival of Islam.

Please pray for the Christian communities and other religious minorities being persecuted at this time in whichever country they may be.

We cannot change the direction of the world by ourselves or on our own. But that is not our job. Our calling is to let God *change us*, and then through us, God will change others and the world.

One central task for those of us living in the free countries is to remind our elected officials of the facts of religious persecution—including anti-Christian violence—around the world. And another, equally vital task is to *press* them to ensure that religious freedom abroad for all individuals becomes a real priority for the White House and our international diplomacy.

Please contact your senators and members of Congress. Urge them to ensure that the government of the United States is doing all it can to oppose religious persecution and advance religious freedom throughout the world. During the years I served as a commissioner on the US Commission on International Religious Freedom, I observed firsthand how such intervention can spare lives, result in prisoner releases, and rescue people from unspeakable oppression.

It was just such appeals that brought about an extraordinary foreign policy achievement for the Christians and animists of South Sudan: there, religious cleansing carried out over two decades by the fanatical Islamic Front regime in North Sudan, had resulted by 2005 in the killing of two million innocent people. In that year, American policy forged over the prior four years began to take effect and paved the way for South Sudan in 2011 to become an independent nation and free of Khartoum's rule. In 2012, the US State Department reported that, during its first year as an independent nation, the new government of the South "respected religious freedom in law and in practice." Moreover, there were "no reports of societal abuses of religious freedom or discrimination against individuals on the basis of their religious affiliation, belief, or practice, and prominent societal leaders took positive steps to promote religious freedom." In other words, galvanized by concerned citizens, American diplomatic action stopped religious genocide and opened the way for true religious freedom where everyone, of all religions, can now freely pray and practice his or her religion. The difference we can make by using our rights of citizenship is astonishing!

Ignorance of the world is a luxury we cannot afford. We must know our faith, know our world and its struggles—and then open our hearts, engage our minds, and lift our hands.

ACKNOWLEDGMENTS

PERSECUTED: THE GLOBAL ASSAULT ON CHRISTIANS IS A PROJECT of the Hudson Institute's Center for Religious Freedom. The Center is deeply grateful for the generosity of the Lynde and Harry Bradley Foundation, and of donors who wish to remain anonymous.

Our acknowledgments face an embarrassment of riches. Over the years we have worked on these issues, we have learned from many hundreds of people and organizations representing a broad array of churches and other religious or non-religious institutions and media, collectively reaching every country in the world. They are too many to name here. What we have done in partial acknowledgment of our debts is to refer to their information and insights in the many sources cited throughout the book and listed in the endnotes. We also cite a broad range of sources used in the wider society, but these organizations and individuals deserve our special tribute. We know them as reliable and responsible observers and reporters, who shine light upon the darkest corners of the world. Often their work puts them at direct risk, from the same hostile forces that threaten those on whom they report. We commend them to our readers who wish to continue following and learning more about the persecution of Christians worldwide.

We also wish to thank our excellent researchers Sarah Schlesinger, Bryan Neihart, Josh Turner, Andrew Marshall, Allison Kanner, and Marcie Gould, and to express our admiration for the expertise and wise counsel of our Hudson colleagues, Samuel Tadros, Kurt Werthmuller, and Hillel Fradkin.

Cameron Wybrow did excellent work on copyediting. Joel Miller and Janene MacIvor of Thomas Nelson were enthusiastic, patient, and encouraging.

Our special thanks to Eric Metaxas and Most Reverend Charles J. Chaput for kindly agreeing to write the Preface and Foreword.

We also thank Sarah Stern, chairman of the board of the Hudson Institute, and the directors, as well as Hudson president Ken Weinstein, chief operating officer John Walters, vice president for communications Grace Terzian, and director of program and staff planning Katherine Smyth.

Center advisory board chair James R. Woolsey deserves our deep gratitude for his stalwart support of the Center for Religious Freedom. For their belief in our work, we also express our appreciation to the other members of the advisory board: Zainab Al-Suwaij, Joseph Ghougassian, Mary Habeck, John Joyce, Rabiya Kadeer, Firuz Kazemzadeh, Richard Land, Theodore Roosevelt Malloch, Vo Van Ai, and George Weigel.

We wish to thank all the above for their work, assistance, and patience, and we emphasize that the above are not responsible for any errors in the book; nor should it be assumed that they agree with all its contents.

The Center for Religious Freedom is a privately funded research center of the Hudson Institute and promotes religious freedom as a component of US foreign policy. For further information contact: Hudson Institute's Center for Religious Freedom, 1015 15th St. NW, Suite 600, Washington DC 20005; http://crf.hudson.org.

NOTES

CHAPTER 1. THE CURRENT STATE OF AFFAIRS

1. Yeo-sang Yoon and Sun-young Han, *2009 White Paper on Religious Freedom in North Korea* (Seoul: Database Center for North Korean Human Rights, March 20, 2009), 145, http://www.uscirf.gov/images/2009%20report%20on%20religious%20freedom%20in%20north%20korea_final.pdf. Used with permission.
2. Yoon and Han, *2009 White Paper,* 142.
3. Saif Tawfiq, "Bus Bombings Show Plight of Christians in Iraq," *Reuters* (May 13, 2010), http://in.reuters.com/article/2010/05/13/idINIndia-48467920100513; "Bomb Attack Seriously Injures Christian Students," Compass Direct News (May 5, 2010), http://www.compassdirect.org/english/country/iraq/18691/.
4. Nina Shea, "Two Christians Freed; Two Peoples Held Captive," National Review Online (September 12, 2012), http://www.nationalreview.com/corner/316441/two-christians-freed-two-peoples-held-captive-nina-shea.
5. John Pontifex and John Newton, eds., *Persecuted and Forgotten? A Report on Christians Oppressed for their Faith, 2011 Edition* (Sutton, Surrey, UK: Aid to the Church in Need, 2011), 11, accessed July 23, 2012, http://www.holyseemission.org/pdf/Persecuted_&_Forgotten_2011.pdf.
6. Pew Forum on Religion and Public Life, *Global Christianity: A Report on the Size and Distribution of the World's Christian Population* (Washington, DC: Pew Research Center, 2011), http://www.pewforum.org/Christian/Global-Christianity-worlds-christian-population.aspx.
7. For all the bulleted points, see International Religious Freedom Act of 1998, H.R. 2431, 105th Cong. (1998), 5, http://www.state.gov/documents/organization/2297.pdf.
8. Ibid.
9. Meghan Clyne, "The Chinese Crackdown Continues," *Weekly Standard* (May 19, 2011), http://www.npr.org/2011/05/19/136456402/weekly-standard-the-chinese-crackdown-continues.
10. Paul Marshall, ed., *Religious Freedom in the World* (Lanham, MD: Rowman and Littlefield, 2007). For overviews of religious freedom and religious persecution in general, see the Global Restrictions on Religion reports

produced by the Pew Forum on Religion and Public Life (http://www.pewforum.org/), the annual reports on religious minorities produced by the First Freedom Center and the annual religious freedom reports produced by the Department of State and USCIRF.

11. Brian J. Grim, "Religious Persecution and Discrimination against Christians and Members of Other Religions" (Seminar presented to the European Parliament, Brussels, Belgium, October 5, 2010), http://www.eppgroup.eu/Press/pevel0/docs/101006grim-speech.pdf.
12. Pontifex and Newton, *Persecuted and Forgotten*; Terry Murphy, "New report reveals 75 percent of Religious Persecution Is Against Christians," United Kingdom/International (March 16, 2011), http://www.acnuk.org/news.php/205/ukinternational-new-report-reveals-75-percent-of-religious-persecution-is-against-christians.
13. There are several books on particular people or countries, but relatively few general overviews. See Ron Boyd-MacMillan, *Faith That Endures: The Essential Guide to the Persecuted Church* (Grand Rapids: Revell, 2006); Carl Moeller and David W. Hegg, *The Privilege of Persecution* (Chicago: Moody, 2011); Baroness Cox and Benedict Rogers, *The Very Stones Cry Out: The Persecuted Church: Pain, Passion and Praise* (London: Continuum, 2011). The annual *Operation World: The Definitive Prayer Guide to Every Nation* (Biblica Publishing) also contains much useful information. Paul Marshall and Nina Shea's *Silenced: How Apostasy and Blasphemy Codes Are Choking Freedom Worldwide* (New York: Oxford University Press, 2011) describes, among many other things, the treatment of converts to Christianity in the Muslim world and beyond. Eliza Grizwold's *The Tenth Parallel: Dispatches from the Fault Line Between Christianity and Islam* (New York: Farrar, Straus and Giroux, 2010) outlines conflict of Muslims and Christians from the Atlantic to the western Pacific. See also Lela Gilbert, *Baroness Cox: Eyewitness to a Broken World* (Grand Rapids: Monarch Books, 2007) and the International Institute for Religious Freedom's bi-yearly *International Journal for Religious Freedom*. Since many of the attacks on Christians and much of the antipathy toward Christians stems from bigoted understandings of conversion, see also Elmer John Theissen, *The Ethics of Evangelism: A Philosophical Defense of Proselytizing and Persuasion* (Downers Grove, IL: IVP Academic, 2011), which defends evangelism as ethical and its absence as unethical. Charles L. Tieszen's *Re-Examining Religious Persecution: Constructing a Theological Framework for Understanding Persecution* (Johannesburg: AcadSA Publishing, 2008) discusses many relevant theological issues.
14. "USCIRF Identifies World's Worst Religious Freedom Violators," United States Commission on International Religious Freedom (henceforth USCIRF), press release (March 20, 2012), http://www.uscirf.gov/news-room/press-releases/3707-uscirf-identifies-worlds-worst-religious-freedom-violators.html.

15. Joseph Mayton, "Christians Angry as Saudi Grand Mufti Calls for Churches to Be Destroyed," *Bikyamasr* (March 16, 2012), http://bikyamasr.com/62210/christians-angry-as-saudi-grand-mufti-calls-for-churches-to-be-destroyed/.
16. This historical section summarize parts of Philip Jenkins, *The Lost History of Christianity: The Thousand-Year Golden Age of the Church in the Middle East, Africa, and Asia—and How It Died* (New York: HarperOne, 2008); Paul Marshall, "God Looked East: The Disappearance of Christianity in Its Homeland," *Weekly Standard* (April 13, 2009), http://www.weeklystandard.com/Content/Protected/Articles/000/000/016/370hhcef.asp. See also Paul Marshall, "Elsewhere in Iraq," *Wall Street Journal* (August 22, 2003), http://online.wsj.com/article/SB106152420376841900.html; Thomas C. Oden, *How Africa Shaped the Christian Mind* (Downers Grove: InterVarsity, 2007).
17. Ibid.
18. Ibid.
19. Philip Jenkins, *The Next Christendom: The Coming of Global Christianity* (New York: Oxford University Press, 2002); Philip Jenkins, *The New Faces of Christianity: Believing the Bible in the Global South* (New York: Oxford University Press, 2006); Mark Noll, *The New Shape of World Christianity* (Downers Grove, IL: InterVarsity Press, 2009). Mark A. Noll and Carolyn Nystrom, in *Clouds of Witnesses: Christian Voices from Africa and Asia* (Downers Grove, IL: InterVarsity Press, 2011), provide a rich collection of pen portraits of recent leaders in the church outside the West.
20. Ibid.
21. George Holland Sabine and Thomas Landon Thorson, *History of Political Theory* (New York: Holt, Rinehart and Winston, 1961), 180. See also Henry Kissinger's statement, "Restraints on government derived from custom, not constitutions, and from the universal Catholic Church, which preserved its own autonomy, thereby laying the basis—quite unintentionally—for pluralism and democratic restrains on state power that evolved centuries later," in *Does America Need a Foreign Policy?* (New York: Simon and Schuster, 2001), 20–21. For background that suggests this was not "quite unintentional," see Brian Tierney, *Religion, Law and the Growth of Constitutional Thought, 1150–1650* (Cambridge: Cambridge University Press, 1982.
22. Paul Marshall, *God and the Constitution: Christianity and American Politics* (Lanham, MD: Rowman and Littlefield, 2002), 117.
23. Paul Marshall and Lela Gilbert, *Their Blood Cries Out*, Dallas: Word, 19979. See also Nina Shea, *In the Lion's Den* (Nashville: Broadman and Holman, 1997).
24. Benedict XVI, "Message of His Holiness Pope Benedict XVI for the Celebration of the World Day of Peace," the Vatican (January 1, 2011), accessed July 23, 2012, http://www.vatican.va/holy_father/benedict_xvi/messages/peace/documentshf_ben-xvimes_20101208_xliv-world-day-peace_en.html.

25. The following section is adapted, with permission, from Marshall, "God Looked East."

CHAPTER 2. CAESAR AND GOD: THE REMAINING COMMUNIST POWERS

1. "Gao Zhisheng in Jail After Disappearance," China Uncensored (March 22, 2012), http://www.chinauncensored.com/index.php ?option=com_content&view=article&id=470:gao-zhisheng-in-jail-after -disappearance&catid=48:most-censored&Itemid=108.
2. David Aikman, "The Worldwide Attack on Christians," *Commentary* (February 2012), http://www.commentarymagazine.com/article/ the-worldwide-attack-on-christians/.
3. " 'Disappeared' Human Rights Lawyer Gao Zhisheng Imprisoned in Remote Far Western China," ChinaAid (January 1, 2012), http://www.chinaaid.org/2012/01/flash-disappeared-human-rights -lawyer.html; "China: Gao Zhisheng ainsi que sa famille," Amnesty International (January 19, 2006), http://www.amnestyinternational .be/doc/actions-en-cours/les-actions-urgentes/article/chine-gao -zhisheng-ainsi-que-sa; "China: Lawyer Gao Zhisheng Given Three -Year Sentence," Christian Solidarity Worldwide (December 20, 2011), http://dynamic.csw.org.uk/article.asp?t=press&id=1287; Edward Wong, "Missing Chinese Lawyer Said to Be in Remote Prison," *New York Times* (January 1, 2012), http://www.nytimes.com/2012/01/02/world/asia /gao-zhisheng-missing-rights-lawyer-turns-up-in-remote-prison.html; Andrew Jacobs, "Family Visits Rights Lawyer Held in China," *New York Times* (March 28, 2012), http://www.nytimes.com/2012/03/29/world/asia /family-reports -prison-visit-with-long-missing-chinese-rights-lawyer.html.
4. "Forced Recantations of Faith Continue," Compass Direct News (January 18, 2010), http://www.compassdirect.org/english/country /vietnam/13976/; "Vietnamese Christian, Family, Forced into Hiding," Compass Direct News (April 1, 2010), http://www.compassdirect.org /english/country/vietnam/16932; USCIRF, *Annual Report of the United States Commission on International Religious Freedom 2011, Vietnam* (Washington, DC: USCIRF 2011), 205, http://uscirf.gov/images/ar2011 /vietnam2011.pdf.
5. "Testimony from Pastor Joo-Chan from North Korea," *Open Doors* (December 22, 2010), http://www.opendoorsusa.org/pray/prayer-updates/ 2010/december/Testimony-from-Pastor-Joo-Chan-from-North-Korea.
6. Promise Hsu, personal communication with Paul Marshall, August 9, 2010.
7. "Chinese Authorities Expel Shouwang Church Member from Beijing," ChinaAid (Thursday, June 30, 2011), http://chinaaiden.blogspot. com/2011/06/chinese-authorities-expel-shouwang.html. The description of events around Shouwang is based on "Beijing Shouwang Church

Announcement on January 1st Outdoor Worship Service—39 Week," ChinaAid (January 4, 2012), http://www.chinaaid.org/2012/01/beijing-shouwang-church-announcement-on_04.html.

8. Pray for Beijing Shouwang Church, Facebook profile, accessed July 12, 2012, http://www.facebook.com/note.php?note_id=332570033449084.
9. "Local Authorities Occupy, Demolish Government Three-Self Churches in Shandong, Jiangsu Provinces," ChinaAid (March 20, 2012), http://www.chinaaid.org/2012/03/local-authorities-occupy-demolish.html.
10. Ambassador James Sasser, meeting with Nina Shea and Peter Torry, president of Open Doors, at US Department of State, Washington, DC, January 1996.
11. Tim Gardam, "Christians in China: Is the Country in Spiritual Crisis?" *BBC News Magazine* (September 11, 2011), http://www.bbc.co.uk/news/magazine-14838749.
12. "Number of Christians in China and India," Lausanne Global Analysis (August 7, 2011), 4, http://conversation.lausanne.org/en/conversations/detail/11971#article_page_4.
13. "Sons of Heaven: Inside China's Fastest-Growing Non-Governmental Organisation," *Economist* (October 2, 2008), http://www.economist.com/node/12342509.
14. The Pew Forum on Religion and Public Life, *Global Christianity: A Report on the Size and Distribution of the World's Christian Population* (Washington, DC: Pew Research Center, 2011), http://www.pewforum.org/Christian/Global-Christianity-worlds-christian-population.aspx.
15. "Number of Christians in China and India," Lausanne Global Analysis, 4.
16. Paul Marshall and Lela Gilbert, *Their Blood Cries Out* (Dallas: Word, 1997).
17. Christopher Bodeen, "Shi Enhao, Underground Church Pastor, Sent to China Labor Camp," Huffington Post (July 26, 2011), http://www.huffingtonpost.com/2011/07/26/shi-enhao-underground-chu_n_909544.html; "Pastor Freed from Prison, Not Persecution," Mission Network News (February 7, 2012), http://www.mnnonline.org/article/16795; "Persecution Continues for Pastor Shi Enhao's Suqian House Church," ChinaAid (November 17, 2011), http://www.chinaaid.org/2011/11/persecution-continues-for-pastor-shi.html; Christopher Bodeen, "Top Chinese Church Leader Sentenced to Two Years," Associated Press (July 27, 2011), http://www.pewforum.org/Religion-News/Top-Chinese-church-leader-sentenced-to-2-years.aspx.
18. Meghan Clyne, "The Chinese Crackdown Continues," *Weekly Standard* (May 19, 2011), accessed July 23, 2012, http://www.npr.org/2011/05/19/136456402/weekly-standard-the-chinese-crackdown-continues; see also USCIRF, *Annual Report 2011*, 128–129.
19. USCIRF, *Annual Report 2011*, 129.
20. "Bishop Su Zhimin of Baoding, Hebei Is Still Detained by the Chinese

Government," the Cardinal Kung Foundation (November 6, 1997), http://www.cardinalkungfoundation.org/press/971106.htm; Nina Shea, *In the Lion's Den* (Nashville: Broadman and Holdman, 1997), 63.

21. USCIRF, *Annual Report 2011*, 129.
22. Wang Zhicheng, "Inner Mongolia: Campaign of Persecution Against Underground Church," AsiaNews.it (February 24, 2012), http://www.asianews.it/news-en/Inner-Mongolia:-campaign-of-persecution-against-underground-Church-24069.html.
23. Bernardo Cervellera, "Sheshan: Beijing's War and the Pope's 'Battle,' " AsiaNews.it (May 23, 2011), http://www.asianews.it/news-en/Sheshan:-Beijing's-war-and-the-Pope's-"battle"-21639.html.
24. Testimony of Nina Shea before the US House of Representatives, Committee on International Relations (Washington, DC: Hudson Institute: November 15, 2005), 4, http://www.hudson.org/files/publications/nina_shea_testimony.pdf.
25. Cheryl Wetzstein, "With 1-Child Policy, China 'Missing' Girls," *Washington Times* (January 27, 2010), http://www.washingtontimes.com/news/2010/jan/27with-1-child-policy-china-missing-girls/?page=all.
26. Rep. Chris Smith (NJ-04), "Statement at House Press Conference on Hu Visit to U.S." (Washington, DC: Congress of the United States House of Representatives, January 18, 2011), http://chrissmith.house.gov/UploadedFiles/Call_for_Chinese_President_Hu_to_Respect_Human_Rights.pdf.
27. "Update on Youqing Church," ChinaAid (September 30, 2010), http://www.chinaaid.org/2010/09/update-on-youqing-church.html.
28. USCIRF, *Annual Report 2011*, 130.
29. Stoyan Zaimov, "Underground Chinese Church Leader Freed After 10 Years," *Christian Post* (February 27, 2012), http://global.christianpost.com/news/underground-chinese-church-leader-freed-after-10-years-70394/.
30. "House Church in Hebei Repeatedly Targeted for Persecution; Members Detained, Sent to Labor Camp," ChinaAid (March 9, 2012), http://www.chinaaid.org/2012/03/house-church-in-hebei-repeatedly.html.
31. Stoyan Zaimov, "Li Ying's Release Credited to International Letter-Writing Campaign," *Christian Post* (February 27, 2012), http://global.christianpost.com/news/underground-chinese-church-leader-freed-after-10-years-70394/.
32. Magda Hornemann, "China: A Post-Communist Managerial State and Freedom of Religion or Belief," Forum 18 (March 20, 2012), http://www.forum18.org/Archive.php?article_id=1681.
33. USCIRF, *Annual Report 2011*, 125.
34. Ibid., 124.
35. "China Releasing Christian Mother; Other Believers Detained," ChinaAid (March 21, 2012), http://www.chinaaid.org/2012/03/china-releasing-christian-mother-other.html.

36. "Jailed Vietnam Priest in Hospital," Asia One News (November 17, 2009), accessed July 23, 2012, http://www.asiaone.com/News/Latest+News/Asia/Story/A1Story20091117-180453.html.
37. *Socialist Republic of Vietnam: Father Thadeus Nguyen Van Ly-Prisoner of Conscience.* (New York: Amnesty International, July 4, 2001), 6, http://www.amnesty.org/en/library/asset/ASA41/005/2001/en/633f6017-d933-11dd-ad8c-f3d4445c118e/asa410052001en.pdf; "Vietnam: USCIRF Condemns Seizing of Priest and Urges CPC Designation," USCIRF (July 27, 2011), http://www.uscirf.gov/news-room/press-releases/3643-vietnam-uscirf-condemns-seizing-of-priest-and-urges-cpc-designation.html; Testimony of Rev. Thadeus Nguyen Van Ly before the USCIRF (February 13, 2001), http://www.freedom-now.org/wp-content/uploads/2010/10/Testimony.swf; Senator Barbara Boxer, "Boxer Leads Bipartisan Group of Senators in Urging Vietnam to Refrain from Returning Father Ly to Prison," press release (March 11, 2011), http://boxer.senate.gov/en/press/releases/031111c.cfm; "Vietnam's Human Rights Defenders," Human Rights Watch (March 23, 2010), http://www.hrw.org/en/news/2010/03/24/testimony-sophie-richardson-tom-lantos-human-rights-commission; "Letter to His Relatives from Father Nguyen Van Ly in K1 Prison in Nam Ha," Reporters Without Borders (May 24, 2007), http://en.rsf.org/vietnam-letter-to-his-relatives-from-24-05-2007,22286.html; "Jailed Vietnam Priest in Hospital," Asia One News (November 17, 2009), http://www.asiaone.com/News/Latest+News/Asia/Story/A1Story20091117-180453.html.
38. Reg Reimer, *Vietnam's Christians: A Century of Growth in Adversity* (Pasadena: William Carey Library, 2011), 71.
39. "Authorities Raid, Threaten House Church," Compass Direct News (August 6, 2009), http://www.compassdirect.org/english/country/vietnam/4221.
40. J. B. An Dang, "Thai Ha Faithful in Procession to Ask for Return of Parish Land," AsiaNews.it (February 7, 2008), http://www.asianews.it/news-en/Th%C3%A1i-H%C3%A0-faithful-in-procession-to-ask-for-return-of-parish-land-11463.html; Nguyen Hung, "Priests, Lay People from Thai Ha Parish Who Asked to Speak to the Authorities Beaten and Arrested," AsiaNews.it (December 2, 2011), http://www.asianews.it/news-en/Priests,-lay-people-from-Thái-Hà-parish-who-asked-to-speak-to-the-authorities-beaten-and-arrested-23339.html; Nguyen Hung, Hanoi: "Attacks Continue Against Thai Ha Parish," AsiaNews.it (November 24, 2011), http://www.asianews.it/news-en/Hanoi:-attacks-continue-against-Thai-Ha-parish-23265.html.
41. Emily Nguyen, "Police in Hue Seizes Last Bit of Land Belonging to Loan Ly Parish," AsiaNews.it (October 21, 2009), http://www.asianews.it/index.php?l=en&art=16651&geo=5&size=A.
42. Lee Edwards, "Con Dau Persecution in Vietnam Continues," Global

Museum on Communism (July 1, 2010), http://www.globalmuseum oncommunism.org/content/con-dau-persecution-vietnam-continues.
43. J. B. An Dang, "A Con Dau Catholic Dies Shortly After Being Released by Police," AsiaNews.it (July 6, 2010), http://www.asianews.it/news-en/A -Con-Dau-Catholic-dies-shortly-after-being-released-by-police-18856 .html.
44. US Department of State, *July–December, 2010 International Religious Freedom Report*, Bureau of Democracy, Human Rights, and Labor (September 13, 2011), http://www.state.gov/j/drl/rls/irf/2010_5/168382 .htm.
45. Ibid.
46. Reg Reimer, *Vietnam's Christians*.
47. "Writer, Priest Handed Jail Sentences," Radio Free Asia (December 30, 2011), http://www.rfa.org/english/news/vietnam/sentences -12302011124923.html.
48. "Vietnamese Protestants Report Abuse, Despite Premier's Order," Radio Free Asia (May 25, 2005), http://www.radicalparty.org/en/content /vietnamese-protestants-report-abuse-despite-premiers-order.
49. "Montagnard Christians in Vietnam: A Case Study in Religious Repression" (New York: Human Rights Watch, March 30, 2011), 23, http:// www.hrw.org/node/97632.
50. Reg Reimer, *Vietnam's Christians*, 106.
51. US Department of State, "July–December, 2010 International Religious Freedom Report," (Washington, DC: Bureau of Democracy, Human Rights, and Labor, September 13, 2011), http://www.state.gov/j/drl/rls /irf/2010_5/168382.htm.
52. "Vietnam: Montagnards Harshly Persecuted," Human Rights Watch (March 30, 2011), http://www.hrw.org/en/news/2011/03/30 /vietnam-montagnards-harshly-persecuted.
53. Michael Benge, "Vietnam's War on Religion," *FrontPage Magazine* (September 16, 2009), http://archive.frontpagemag.com/readArticle .aspx?ARTID=36282.
54. USCIRF, *Annual Report 2011*, 198.
55. Montagnard Foundation, Inc., "Three Degar Were Forced to Renounce Their Faith," Unrepresented Nations and Peoples Organization (February 8, 2011), http://www.unpo.org/article/12247.
56. "Two Evangelists in Vietnam Sentenced to Prison," Compass Direct News (November 30, 2010), http://www.compassdirect.org/english/country /vietnam/29066.
57. "Christians Killed; Alarming Religious Freedom Abuses Continue," Voice of the Martyrs, Canada (May 5, 2011), http://www.persecution.net /la-2011-05-05.htm; "Release International Prayer Alert," Release International (May 24, 2011), http://www .releaseinternational.org/media/download_gallery/Prayer

%20Alert%20-%2024%20May%202011.pdf#xml=http://releaseinternational.org.master.com/texis/master/search/mysite.txt?q=laos&order=r&id=08894a70c42c88f5&cmd=xml; Emily Nguyen, "Vietnam Unleashes Wave of Repression Against Hmong Christians, at Least 49 Dead," AsiaNews.it (May 9, 2011), http://www.asianews.it/news-en/Vietnam-unleashes-wave-of-repression-against-Hmong-Christians,-at-least-49-dead-21507.html.

58. USCIRF, *Annual Report 2011*, 282.
59. "Hinboun District Police Authorities' Abuse of Power and Unlawful Arrest of Christians in Villages of Khammouan Province," Human Rights Watch for Lao Religious Freedom (HRWLRF) (January 5, 2011), http://www.hrwlrf.net/files/Download/AdvocacyNo1-2011.pdf.
60. "ASIA/LAOS—Church confiscated, Christians defined as 'enemies,'" Agenzia Fides (February 25, 2012), http://www.fides.org/aree/news/newsdet.php?idnews=31096&lan=eng.
61. *Cuba: Castro's War on Religion* (Washington, DC: Puebla Institute, May 1991).
62. USCIRF, *Annual Report 2011: Cuba*, 237, http://www.uscirf.gov/images/book%20with%20cover%20for%20web.pdf; "Cuba: Pastor's Wife Faces Court After Losing Baby in Attack," *Christian Today* (August 18, 2009), http://www.christiantoday.com/article/cuba.pastors.wife.faces.court.after.losing.baby.in.attack/24009.htm; US Department of State, *International Religious Freedom Report 2010: Cuba*, Bureau of Democracy, Human Rights, and Labor (November 17, 2010), http://www.state.gov/j/drl/rls/irf/2010/148748.htm. Note, the reports on the charges in this case diverge in the reports of USCIRF and the Department of State.
63. US Department of State, *International Religious Freedom Report 2010: Cuba*, Bureau of Democracy, Human Rights, and Labor (November 17, 2010), http://www.state.gov/j/drl/rls/irf/2010/148748.htm.
64. US Department of State, *International Religious Freedom Report 2010*: *Cuba* (see above); USCIRF, *Annual Report 2011: Cuba*, 237, http://www.uscirf.gov/images/book%20with%20cover%20for%20web.pdf; Charlie Boyd, "Disappointment After Cuban Pastor Loses Right to Appeal," *Christian Today* (February 1, 2010), http://www.christiantoday.com/article/disappointment.after.cuban.pastor.loses.right.to.appeal/25202.htm; "Cuban Government Backtracks on Verbal Assurances to Grant Pastor Exit Visa," Christian Solidarity Worldwide (January 19, 2012), http://dynamic.csw.org.uk/article.asp?t=press&id=1307&search=.
65. USCIRF, *Annual Report 2011: Cuba*, 237, 238.
66. "Religious Freedom in Cuba," (New Malden, Surrey, UK: Christian Solidarity Worldwide, 2010), 6, http://dynamic.csw.org.uk/article.asp?t=report&id=128&search=.
67. "Protestant Pastors Detained and Interrogated in Cuba," Christian Solidarity Worldwide (May 4, 2011), http://cswusa.com/Cubaihtml?id=629921#cuba050411.

68. US Department of State, *International Religious Freedom Report 2010: Cuba.*
69. "Religious Persecution in Cuba," Christian Solidarity Worldwide, http://www.csw.org.uk/cuba.htm; See also Human Rights Watch, "New Castro, Same Cuba: Political Prisoners in the Post-Fidel Era" (New York: Human Rights Watch, 2009), 28, http://www.hrw.org/sites/default/files/reports/cuba1109web_0.pdf.
70. US Department of State, *International Religious Freedom Report 2010: Cuba*; Shasta Darlington, "Family of Cuban Hunger Striker Headed to Miami," CNN (June 8, 2011), http://articles.cnn.com/2011-06-08/world/cuba.prisoner.family_1_orlando-zapata-tamayo-guillermo-farinas-hunger-strike?_s=PM:WORLD.
71. "Religious Persecution in Cuba," Christian Solidarity Worldwide, http://www.csw.org.uk/cuba.htm.
72. "Cuba Releases Jailed Dissident Oscar Elias Biscet," BBC News (March 11, 2011), http://www.bbc.co.uk/news/world-latin-america-12721318.
73. US Department of State, *International Religious Freedom Report 2010: Cuba.*
74. USCIRF, "A Prison Without Bars"; Yoon and Han, *2009 White Paper*, http://www.uscirf.gov/images/2009%20report%20on%20religious%20freedom%20in%20north%20korea_final.pdf.
75. USCIRF, "A Prison Without Bars," 15.
76. Ibid.
77. Ibid., 40.
78. "Christian Refugees Question Regime's Claims," Compass Direct News (April 23, 2009), http://www.compassdirect.org/english/country/northkorea/3166.
79. USCIRF, "A Prison Without Bars," 10.
80. Ibid., 12.
81. US Department of State, *International Religious Freedom Report 2010: Korea, Democratic People's Republic of*, Bureau of Democracy, Human Rights, and Labor (November 17, 2010), http://www.state.gov/j/drl/rls/irf/2010/148874.htm; Lord Alton and Baroness Cox, Chairman and Vice-Chairman of the U.K. All Party Parliamentary Group for North Korea, "Building Bridges Not Walls: The Case for Constructive, Critical Engagement with North Korea" (October 2010), http://www.scribd.com/doc/40523738/Building-Bridges-Not-Walls-Final-Report.
82. USCIRF, "A Prison Without Bars," 36.
83. Yoon and Han, *2009 White Paper*, 140.
84. USCIRF, "A Prison Without Bars," 10.
85. US Department of State, *International Religious Freedom Report 2010: Korea, Democratic People's Republic of*, Bureau of Democracy, Human Rights, and Labor (November 17, 2010), http://www.state.gov/j/drl/rls/irf/2010/148874.htm.

86. USCIRF, "A Prison Without Bars," 23.
87. "North Korean College Students Arrested with Christian Literature," Mission Network News (March 28, 2008), http://www.mnnonline.org/article/11055.
88. Yoon and Han, *2009 White Paper*, 140.
89. "U.S. Detainee Freed by N. Korea Arrives in Seoul," *Bangkok Post* (May 28, 2011), http://www.bangkokpost.com/news/asia/239378/us-detainee-freed-by-n-korea-arrives-in-seoul.
90. Kwang-Tae Kim, "Robert Park, U.S. Activist, Crosses Frozen River into North Korea," Huffington Post (December 26, 2009), http://www.huffingtonpost.com/2009/12/26/robert-park-us-activist-c_n_403847.html; Mark McDonald, "Activist Tells of Torture in North Korea Prison," *New York Times* (October 27, 2010), http://www.nytimes.com/2010/10/28/world/asia/28seoul.html?sq=robert%20park&st=cse&adxnnl=1&scp=4&adxnnlx=1311299213-WyWDTp/AK836wGcIiKmAKg; C. L. Lopez, "What Robert Park Learned in North Korea," *Christianity Today* (August 30, 2010), http://www.christianitytoday.com/ct/2010/augustweb-only/45-11.0.html.
91. Yoon and Han, *2009 White Paper*, 81.
92. USCIRF, "A Prison Without Walls," 23.
93. Ibid.
94. Ibid., 27.
95. Yoon and Han, *2009 White Paper*, 141–142.
96. US Department of State, *International Religious Freedom Report 2010: Korea, Democratic People's Republic of*, Bureau of Democracy, Human Rights, and Labor (November 17, 2010), http://www.state.gov/j/drl/rls/irf/2010/148874.htm.
97. Melanie Kirkpatrick, "China Delivers unto Evil, http://www.hudson.org/index.cfm?fuseaction=publication_details&id=8764; *Wall Street Journal* (Asia Edition, March 1, 2012), http://www.hudson.org/index.cfm?fuseaction=publication_details&id=8764#.
98. USCIRF, *Annual Report 2011*, 208, http://www.uscirf.gov/images/book%20with%20cover%20for%20web.pdf.
99. Lord Alton and Baroness Cox, chairman and vice-chairman of the U.K. All Party Parliamentary Group for North Korea, "Building Bridges Not Walls: The Case for Constructive, Critical Engagement with North Korea" (October 2010), http://www.scribd.com/doc/40523738/Building-Bridges-Not-Walls-Final-Report. 100. Yoon and Han, *2009 White Paper*, 142.

3. POST-COMMUNIST COUNTRIES: REGISTER, RESTRICT, AND RUIN

1. Felix Corley, "Belarus: Authorities Prepare Again to Expel New Life Church from Its Own Building," Forum 18 (August 24, 2009), http://www.forum18.org/Archive.php?article_id=1339; see also CSW Briefing, "Belarus: New Life Church Case" (April 2007); "New Life Church Newsletter" (October 2008), http://www.newlife.by/eng_news.php?skip=180.

2. "Another Massive Fine for Belarusian Church," Assist News Service (August 3, 2010), http://www.assistnews.net/Stories/2010/s10080016.htm.
3. US Department of State, *International Religious Freedom Report 2010: Russia*, Bureau of Democracy, Human Rights, and Labor, http://www.state.gov/j/drl/rls/irf/2010/148977.htm;
4. "As Russian Lutherans Come Under Suspicion for 'Terrorism,' Police Shows Ignorance About Religion," AsiaNews.it (March 15, 2010), http://www.asianews.it/news-en/As-Russian-Lutherans-come-under-suspicion-for-%E2%80%9Cterrorism%E2%80%9D,-police-shows-ignorance-about-religion-17885.html; see also, "Russia: Lutheran Extremists?" Forum 18 (March 23, 2010), http://www.forum18.org/Archivephp?article_id=1425.
5. "Murdered Human Rights Activists in Grozny, Chechnya Friends with Christians," Assist News Service (August 24, 2009), http://www.assistnews.net/Stories/2009/s09080162.htm.
6. *World Watch List,* Open Doors USA, accessed September 15, 2012, http://www.worldwatchlist.us/?utm_campaign=worldwatchlist&utm_source=odusa.
7. Library of Congress, Country Studies, Russia, "The Russian Orthodox Church," http://countrystudies.us/russia/38.htm.
8. Timothy Ware, *The Orthodox Church* (New York: Penguin, 1993), 145–146.
9. Wallace L. Daniel, *The Orthodox Church and Civil Society in Russia* (College Station, TX TAMU Press, 2006), 30.
10. JB's Reflections on Russia, "The Plot to Kill God—Unintended Consequences" (August 17, 2011), http://jb-russianreflections.blogspot.com/2011/08/plot-to-kill-god-unintended.html.
11. Daniel, *The Orthodox Church and Civil Society in Russia*, 69.
12. "CIA Agents in Mormon Disguise Are Probable to Work in Russia, a Renowned Sect Expert Believes," Interfax Religion News (August 21, 2008), http://www.interfax-religion.com/?act=news&div=5099.
13. Geraldine Fagan, "Russia: Notorious 'Anti-Cultists' on New 'Inquisition,'" Forum 18 (May 27, 2009), http://www.forum18.org/Archive.php?article_id=1300 ; see also "Orthodox Can Get Catholic and Lutheran churches—but Catholics and Lutherans Can't," Forum 18 (December 4, 2010), http://forum18.org/Archive.php?article_id=1521.
14. "One Complex of Measures Against Religious Communities," Forum 18 (June 29, 2011), http://forum18.org/Archive.php?article_id=1587.
15. "Russian Supreme Court Overturns Decision Closing Grace Church in Khabarovsk," *Russia Religion News*, http://www2.stetson.edu/~psteeves/relnews/1108a.html#04.
16. US Department of State, *International Religious Freedom Report 2010: Russia*, Bureau of Democracy, Human Rights, and Labor, http://www.state.gov/j/drl/rls/irf/2010/148977.htm.
17. "One Complex of Measures Against Religious Communities," Forum 18 (June 29, 2011), http://www.forum18.org/Archive.php?article_id=1587.

18. "Prosecutor Pursues Siberian Pentecostals," Russia Religion News, http://www2.stetson.edu/~psteeves/relnews/1105a.html#02.
19. "Authorities Try to Stop Children Attending Meetings for Worship," Forum 18 (December 8, 2011), http://www.forum18.org/Archive.php?article_id=1645.
20. "'Anti-terror' Raid on Old People's Home," Forum 18 (March 22, 2011), http://www.forum18.org/Archive.php?article_id=1554.
21. "Turkmenistan," USCIRF, *Annual Report 2011*, 172, http://www.uscirf.gov/images/book%20with%20cover%20for%20web.pdf..
22. "Worship Without State Registration 'Illegal'" Forum 18 (February 1, 2010), http://www.forum18.org/Archive.php?article_id=1401.
23. "Exit Bans, Haj Ban, Visa Denials Part of State Religious Isolation Policy," Forum 18 (February 2, 2010), http://www.forum18.org/Archive.php?article_id=1403; "Appeal Denied for Ilmurad Nurliev, Pentecostal Pastor Convicted by False Evidence," AsiaNews.it (November 16, 2010), http://www.asianews.it/news-en/Appeal-denied-for-Ilmurad-Nurliev,-Pentecostal-pastor-convicted-by-false-evidence-20010.html.
24. "Turkmenistan: Four Fines for Bibles, Prisoner Transferred," Forum 18 (March 27, 2012), http://www.forum18.org/Archive.php?article_id=1684.
25. "Appeal Denied for Ilmurad Nurliev," (see above).
26. "Turkmenistan," USCIRF, *Annual Report 2011* (see above), http://www.uscirf.gov/images/book%20with%20cover%20for%20web.pdf, 172.
27. "'Unpleasantness with the Law' for Worshipping?" Forum 18 (May 11, 2010), http://www.forum18.org/Archive.php?article_id=1443; US Department of State, *International Religious Freedom Report 2010: Azerbaijan*, Bureau of Democracy, Human Rights, and Labor, http://www.state.gov/j/drl/rls/irf/2010/148912.htm.
28. "'Without Registration, You Can't Pray,'" Forum 18 (December 22, 2011), http://www.forum18.org/Archive.php?article_id=1651.
29. US Department of State, *International Religious Freedom Report 2010: Azerbaijan*, http://www.state.gov/j/drl/rls/irf/2010/148912.htm.
30. "Jehovah's Witnesses Deported, Baptists Next," Forum 18 (September 11, 2009), http://www.forum18.org/Archive.php?article_id=1347.
31. Ibid.; "Biggest Expulsion in Eight Years," Forum 18 (January 9, 2007), http://wwrn.org/articles/23898/?&place=caucasus.
32. "'Infidel Santa' Killed in Tajikistan," RT News (January 2, 2012), http://rt.com/news/infidel-santa-killed-tajikistan-133/; "Man Dressed as 'Father Frost' Stabbed to Death in Tajikistan," *Guardian* (January 3, 2012), http://www.guardian.co.uk/world/2012/jan/03/man-father-frost-killed-tajikistan.
33. USCIRF, *Annual Report 2012*, 1, http://www.uscirf.gov/images/2012ARChapters/tajikistan%202012.pdf.
34. "Latest Religious Property Eviction, Religion Law Enters Force," Forum 18 (April 3, 2009), http://www.forum18.org/Archive.php?article_id=1279.
35. "Christians Criticize Tajik Bill Barring Youth from Churches, Mosques,"

Radio Free Europe/Radio Liberty (February 17, 2011), http://www.rferl.org/content/christians_criticize_tajik_bill_barring_youth_from_churches_mosques/2312867.html.

36. "Authorities 'Have the Right' to Raid Unregistered Worship," Forum 18 (March 30, 2011), http://www.forum18.org/Archive.php?article_id=1556.
37. See Lela Gilbert and Elizabeth Zelensky, *Windows to Heaven: Introducing Icons to Protestants and Catholics* (Grand Rapids: Brazos, 2005).
38. "Why Can't Derelict Church Be Relocated for Worship?" Forum 18 (February 14, 2011), http://www.forum18.org/Archive.php?article_id=1540.
39. Organization for Security and Cooperation in Europe, *Hate Crimes in the OSCE Region—Incidents and Responses, Annual Report for 2009* (Warsaw: November 2010), 33, http://www.osce.org/odihr/73636?download=true.
40. US Department of State, *International Religious Freedom Report 2010: Belarus*, http://www.state.gov/g/drl/rls/irf/2010/148914.htm.
41. "Belarus," USCIRF, *Annual Report 2011*, 228.
42. "'Appropriate Permission Is Needed,'" Forum 18 (July 30, 2010), http://www.forum18.org/Archive.php?article_id=1472.
43. "Authorities 'Have the Right' to Raid Unregistered Worship," Forum 18 (March 30, 2011), http://www.forum18.org/Archive.php?article_id=1556.
44. Geraldine Fagan, "New Controls on Foreign Religious Workers," Forum 18 (February 20, 2008), http://www.forum18.org/Archive.php?article_id=1090; "'We Are Reclaiming Our History as a Land of Religious Freedom,'" Forum 18 (May 22, 2008), http://www.forum18.org/Archive.php?article_id=1131; "Official Justifies Rejection of Religious Freedom Petition," Forum 18 (April 29, 2008), http://www.forum18.org/Archive.php?article_id=1121.
45. "Belarus," USCIRF, *Annual Report 2011*, 230.
46. Felix Corley, "'Forbidden Christ' and Right to Legally Challenge Warnings Forbidden," Forum 18 (November 11, 2010), http://www.forum18.org/Archive.php?article_id=1510.
47. "Criminal Records for Religious Activity," Forum 18 (April 1, 2010), http://www.forum18.org/Archive.php?article_id=1428; US Department of State, *International Religious Freedom Report 2010: Kazakhstan*, Bureau of Democracy, Human Rights, and Labor, http://www.state.gov/j/drl/rls/irf/2010/148793.htm
48. Svetlana Glushkova and Courtney Brooks, "Kazakhstan, Not Practicing What It Preaches, Puts Minority Religions Under Pressure," Radio Free Europe/Radio Liberty (February 17, 2011), http://www.rferl.org/content/kazakhstan_minority_religions_persecution/2307031.html.
49. "We Have Not Been Able to Pray and Worship Together," Forum 18 (January 18, 2012), http://www.forum18.org/Archive.php?article_id=1657.
50. "Christians Denied Burial Rights by Muslims in Kyrgyzstan," the Catholic-Christian Secular Forum (May 24, 2011), http://persecutedchurch.info/2011/05/24/christians-denied-burial-rights-by-muslims-in-kyrgyzstan/.

51. "Abai," personal interview with Lela Gilbert, February 26, 2012.
52. Stepan Danielyan, Vladimir Vardanyan, and Artur Avtandilyan, "Religious Tolerance in Armenia," the Collaboration for Democracy Centre (in conjunction with the OSCE Office in Yerevan), 23–24 (2009), http://www.osce.org/yerevan/74894.
53. US Department of State, *International Religious Freedom Report 2010: Armenia*, Bureau of Democracy, Human Rights, and Labor, http://www.state.gov/j/drl/rls/irf/2010/148908.htm.
54. Ibid.
55. Stepan Danielyan, Vladimir Vardanyan, and Artur Avtandilyan, "Religious Tolerance in Armenia," 31, http://www.osce.org/yerevan/74894. Spectacularly scenic Georgia bears a strong similarity to its neighbor Armenia. Both are built around ancient Christian religious traditions, and both churches extend deep roots into the countries' proud patriotic and nationalistic bedrock. The Georgian Orthodox Church, like the Armenian Orthodox Church, marks its beginning in the fourth century, perhaps earlier. Today's Georgian believers are deeply loyal to their church. Radio Free Europe reported in February 2011: "The authority of the Orthodox Church is perceived as unshakeable in Georgia. Opinion polls consistently show trust in the church at over 90 percent, a rating politicians can only dream of. The personal popularity of Patriarch Ilia II, who has led the church since 1977, is particularly high." See "Georgia's Showdown between Church and State," Radio Free Europe/Radio Liberty (February 20, 2011), http://www.rferl.org/content/commentary_georgia_churches/2314963.html. The few non-Orthodox Christian groups face restrictions on property rights and construction permits due to the reluctance of local authorities to issue building permits that could antagonize local Georgian Orthodox Church officials. See US Department of State, *International Religious Freedom Report 2010: Georgia*, Bureau of Democracy, Human Rights, and Labor, http://www.state.gov/j/drl/rls/irf/2010_5/168312.htm.
56. "Religious Freedom Survey," Forum 18 (December 17, 2009), http://www.forum18.org/Archive.php?article_id=1388.

CHAPTER 4. SOUTH ASIA'S CHRISTIAN OUTCASTES

1. "Orissa Christian Persecution Fact Finding Report," *South Asian Connection*, Evangelical Fellowship of India (September 10, 2008), http://www.southasianconnection.com/blogs/995/Orissa-Christian-Persecution-Fact-Finding-Report.html.
2. "Victim of Orissa, India Violence Rescued from Trafficking Ring," Compass Direct News (August 25, 2010), http://www.compassdirect.org/english/country/india/24732.
3. "Christians Concerned over Acquittals in Orissa, India Violence," Compass Direct News (September 30, 2011), http://www.compassdirect.org/english/country/india/9979.

4. “Annual Report: India,” (Washington, DC: USCIRF, May 2011), http://uscirf.gov/images/ar2011/india2011.pdf.
5. USCIRF, *Annual Report: India*, March 2012.
6. “Report Faults Indian Authorities in ’08 Anti-Christian Violence,” Zenit (December 21, 2011), http://www.zenit.org/article-34030?l=english; “Orissa: a Global Report on the 2008 anti-Christian Pogroms Is Released,” AsiaNews.it (December 6, 2011), http://www.asianews.it/news-en/Orissa:-a-global-report-on-the-2008-anti-Christian-pogroms-is-released-23373.html; “Kandhamal Violence Pre-planned, Say Officials,” *Cathnews-India* (November 22, 2011), http://www.cathnewsindiacom/2011/11/22/orissa-officials-testify-kandhamal-violence-pre-planned/.
7. “Kashmir Pastor Arrested for Baptising Seven Muslims,” AsiaNews.it (November 21, 2011), http://www.asianews.it/news-en/Kashmir-pastor-arrested-for-baptising-seven-Muslims-23237.html; Nirmala Carvalho, “Kashmir: Sharia Court Summons Fr Jim Borst on Proselytising Charges,” AsiaNews.it (December 9, 2011), http://www.asianews.it/news-en/Kashmir:-Sharia-court-summons-Fr-Jim-Borst-on-proselytising-charges-23395.html; “The High Court of Kashmir Blocks the Islamic Court and Saves Pastor Khanna,” Agenzia Fides (February 13, 2011), http://www.fides.org/aree/news/newsdet.php?idnews=30982&lan=eng.
8. For an overview of religious freedom in India, see Paul Marshall, ed., *The Rise of Hindu Extremism and the Repression of Christian and Muslim Minorities in India* (Washington: Freedom House, 2003).
9. These states include Orissa, Madhya Pradesh/Chhattisgarh, Arunachal Pradesh, Himachal Pradesh, Gujarat, and with some under consideration in Rajasthan (the Rajasthan law is awaiting consent by the president).
10. Justice M. N. Rao, *Freedom of Religion and Right to Conversion*, PL WEBJOUR 19 (2003), http://www.ebc-india.com/lawyer/articles/706.htm#Ref3#Ref3; USCIRF, *Annual Report: India*, (March 2012), http://www.uscirf.gov/images/Annual%20Report%20of%20USCIRF%202012(2).pdf.
11. American Center for Law and Justice, “Religious Freedom Acts: Anti-Conversion Laws in India,” (June 26, 2009), http://media.aclj.org/pdf/freedom_of_religion_acts.pdf; “Priest, Nun, Held for Forced Conversion,” *Pioneer* (India) (January 26, 1996).
12. “Life Term Adequate for Staines Murder Convicts: SC,” *Times of India* (January 21, 2011), http://articles.timesofindia.indiatimes.com/2011-01-21/india/28351453_1_dara-singh-graham-staines-minor-sons.
13. “Indian Pastor Shot in Bomb Attack on Church,” Compass Direct News (March 2009), http://www.compassdirect.org/english/country/india/2394.
14. US State Dept., Bureau of Democracy, Human Rights, and Labor, *International Religious Freedom Report: India* (November 17, 2010), http://www.state.gov/g/drl/rls/irf/2010/148792.htm.
15. “India Briefs: Recent Incidents of Persecution,” Compass Direct News

(December 30, 2011), http://www.compassdirect.org/english/country/india/article_1317439.html/.

16. "Karnataka Anti-Christian Attacks Intensify," the Catholic-Christian Secular Forum (December 29, 2011), http://persecutedchurch.info/2011/12/29hebron-assembly-church-and-pastors-house-ransaked-in-mangalore/.
17. "Hindu Nationalist Still Proud of Role in Killing Father of India," *New York Times* (March 2, 1998), http://www.nytimes.com/1998/03/02/world/hindu-still-proud-of-role-in-killing-the-father-of-india.html?pagewanted=all&src=pm.
18. *Our Nationhood Defined* (Nagpur: Bharat Publications, 1939), 37, quoted in Marzia Casolari, "Hindutva's Foreign Tie-up in the 1930s," *Economic and Political Weekly* (January 22, 2000), 224, http://www.epw.in/special-articles/hindutvas-foreign-tie-1930s.html.
19. For an overview of the RSS, see the articles in *Outlook* (April 27, 1998).
20. US State Dept., Bureau of Democracy, Human Rights, and Labor, *International Religious Freedom Report: India* (November 2007), http://www.state.gov/g/drl/rls/irf/2007/90228.htm.
21. "News Briefs: Recent Incidents of Persecution," Compass Direct News (March 6, 2007), http://www.compassdirect.org/english/country/india/2007/newsarticle_4793.html.
22. John Malhotra, "Believers 'Mercilessly' Beaten by Fanatics in Karnataka," *Christian Today* (December 10, 2010), http://in.christiantoday.com/articles/believers-mercilessly-beaten-by-fanatics-in-karnataka/5869.htm.
23. Lausanne Global Analysis, "Number of Christians in China and India," *The Lausanne Global Conversation* (August 7, 2011), http://conversation.lausanne.org/en/conversations/detail/11971#article, 4.
24. Anto Akkara, "Churches Angry That Indian Census Ignores 14 Million Christian Dalits," *Christianity Today* (February 1, 2001), http://www.christianitytoday.com/ct/2001/februaryweb-only/56.0c.html.
25. "Christian, Visiting Lepers Beaten, Jailed in India," Compass Direct News (June 20, 2011), http://www.compassdirect.org/english/country/india/article_113939.html.
26. John Malhotra, "Pentecostal Pastor Beaten and Arrested in India," *Christian Today* (September 29, 2010), http://www.christiantoday.com/article/pentecostal.pastor.beaten.and.arrested.in.india/26806.htm.
27. *Indian Express* (April 9, 2002).
28. USCIRF, *Annual Report: India* (March 2012), http://www.uscirf.gov/images/Annual%20Report%20of%20USCIRF%202012(2).pdf.
29. "Pastor's Father Beaten Unconscious in Attack in Rajasthan, India," Compass Direct News (July 5, 2011), http://www.compassdirect.org/english/country/india/article_114557.html.
30. Vishal Mangalwadi et al., *Burnt Alive: The Staines and the God They Loved* (Mumbai: GLS Publishing, 2000), 6.
31. "Claim in Killing of Christian Family in India," *New York Times* (February

5, 2002), http://www.nytimes.com/2002/02/05/world/claim-in-killing-of-christian-family-in-india.html?src=pm.

32. Ruben Banerjee and Ahmed Farzand, "Staines' Killing: Burning Shame," *India Today* (February 8, 1999), http://www.india-today.com/itoday/08021999/cover.html.
33. "Staines Was Not Inducing Tribals: CBI," *Hindu* (January 16, 2003).
34. Mangalwadi et al., *Burnt Alive*, 7, 9–10. Narayanan quotation from the front matter.
35. Celia W. Dugger, "47 Suspected Militants in India Charged in Missionary's Death," *New York Times* (January 25, 1999), http://www.nytimes.com/1999/01/25/world/47-suspected-militants-in-india-charged-in-missionary-s-death.html?src=pm.
36. "Burning Shame," *India Today* (see above).
37. "Key Witness Backtracks in Dara Singh Trial," Compass Direct News (April 21, 2001), http://www.compassdirect.org/english/country/india/2001/newsarticle_0680.html.
38. "Dara Singh's Mother Honoured," *Hindu* (December 21, 2002).
39. "Hindu Given Death for Killing Missionary," *New York Times* (September 23, 2003), http://www.nytimes.com/2003/09/23/world/hindu-given-death-for-killing-missionary.html?ref=grahamstaines; Nirmala Carvalho, "Murderer of Christian Missionary Graham Staines Asks for Early Release," AsiaNews.it (February 16, 2007), http://www.asianews.it/news-en/Murderer-of-Christian-missionary-Graham-Staines-asks-for-early-release-8510.html. On September 22, 2007, the Orissa High Court sentenced Singh to life for the murder of Catholic priest Arul Doss.
40. "Life Term Adequate for Staines Murder Convicts: SC," *Times of India* (January 21, 2011), http://articles.timesofindia.indiatimes.com/2011-01-21/india/28351453_1_dara-singh-graham-staines-minor-sons.
41. "Report in India Blames Attacks on Conversions to Christianity," Compass Direct News (February 8, 2011), http://www.compassdirect.org/english/country/india/32833/.
42. Mangalwadi et al., *Burnt Alive*. Narayanan quotation is from the front matter.
43. "Widow of Graham Staines: 'Do Not Give Up Hope, Pray for India,'" AsiaNews.it (January 20, 2009), http://www.asianews.it/news-en/Widow-of-Graham-Staines:-Do-not-give-up-hope,-pray-for-India-14257.html; "Missionary Widow Continues Leprosy Work," BBC News (January 27, 1999), http://news.bbc.co.uk/2/hi/asia-pacific/264326.stm.
44. International Christian Concern, "Nepalese Christians on hunger strike," reprinted in *Persecution and Prayer Alert* (April 14, 2011), http://www.persecution.net/np-2011-04-14.htm; "Dead Space: Christians Demand Burial Land in Crowded Kathmandu," *Christianity Today* (April 8, 2011), http://www.christianitytoday.com/ct/2011/aprilweb-only/deadspace.html.
45. "Nepal Christians Fight for Burial Rights: Nearly 200 Graves Face

Demolition," Compass Direct News (January 25, 2011), http://www.compassdirect.org/english/country/nepal/31797; see also "Hundreds of Hindu Sages Occupy Christian Tombs in Pashupatinath," AsiaNews.it (February 26, 2011), http://www.asianews.it/news-en/Hundreds-of-Hindu-sages-occupy-Christian-tombs-in-Pashupatinath-20886.html.

46. "Nepal Should Review Proposed Religious Restriction," World Evangelical Alliance Research Liberty Commission (March 24, 2011), http://worldea.org/news/3445; "Nepal: No Agreement on New Constitution as Peace Process Deadline Approaches," Christian Solidarity Worldwide (May 24, 2011), http://dynamic.csw.org.uk/article.asp?t=press&id=1175.
47. "Protecting Religious Freedom for a New Nepal," Christian Solidarity Worldwide, (briefing, August 2011), 4, http://dynamic.csw.org.uk/article.asp?t=report&id=141; "Prospects Dim for Religious Freedom in Nepal," *Christian Post* (March 30, 2011), http://www.christianpost.com/news/prospects-dim-for-religious-freedom-in-nepal-49636/.
48. "Protecting Religious Freedom for a New Nepal," 15, Christian Solidarity Worldwide, (see above).
49. Sudeshna Sarkar, "Nepal's Churches Live Under Threat, Discrimination," Compass Direct News (August 18, 2011), http://www.compassdirect.org/english/country/nepal/article_116602.html, and Human Rights Without Frontiers (August 22, 2011), http://www.hrwf.org/images/forbnews/2011/nepal%202011.pdf.
50. "Christians Protest to Demand Burial Grounds," Associated Press (March 3, 2011), http://www.washingtonpost.com/wp-dyn/content/article/2011/03/23/AR2011032304412.html, and Human Rights Without Frontiers (March 28, 2011), http://www.hrwf.org/images/forbnews/2011/nepal%202011.pdf.
51. "Update: Church Bombing Claims Third Victim," Voice of the Martyrs (June 3, 2009), http://www.persecution.net/np-2009-06-03.htm; see also Sudeshna Sarkar, "Christians in Nepal Attacked as Constitutional Deadline Nears: Bomb Goes Off in Front of Charity Office; Preachers Assaulted, Church Building Razed," Compass Direct News (November 25, 2011), http://www.compassdirect.org/english/country/nepal/article_123620.html; "Nepal: Bomb Outside Christian Charity Raises CSW's Concerns," Christian Solidarity Worldwide (December 13, 2011), http://dynamic.csw.org.uk/article.asp?t=news&id=1112.
52. Sudeshna Sarkar, "Christians Begin Legal Battle for Burial Ground," Compass Direct News (April 19, 2011), and Human Rights Without Frontiers (April 20, 2011), http://www.hrwf.org/images/forbnews/2011/nepal%20211.pdf; Sudeshna Sarkar, "Nepal's Churches Live Under Threat, Discrimination."
53. "Sri Lanka: Rev. Gnanaseelan Shot Dead—January 13, 2007," World Evangelical Alliance (January 2007), http://www.worldevangelicals.org/news/article.htm?id=865.
54. Paul Ciniraj, "16 Tamil Civilian Christians Killed by Bombing in Sri Lanka,"

Journal Chrétien (January 6, 2007), http://www.journalchretien.net/5358-16-Tamil-Civilian-Christians-Killed-by-Bombing-in-Sri-Lanka?lang=fr.

55. "Family Despairs as Reports Claim Recovered Body That of Mission Priest," Union of Catholic Asian News (June 11, 2007), http://www.ucanews.com/story-archive/?post_name=/2007/06/11/family-despairs-as-reports-claim-recovered-body-that-of-missing-priest&post_id=5889.
56. Anto Akkara, "Sri Lankan Priest, Companion Disappear amid Fighting," Catholic News Service (August 23, 2006), http://www.catholicnews.com/data/stories/cns/0604802.htm; "Family Despairs," Union of Catholic Asian News (June 11, 2007), http://www.ucanews.com/storyarchive/?post_name=/2007/06/11/family-despairs-as-reports-claim-recovered-body-that-of-missing-priest&post_id=5889; Danielle Vella, "Catholic Priest Disappears in Sri Lanka," AsiaNews.it (August 23, 2006), http://www.asianews.it/news-en/Catholic-priest-disappears-in-Sri-Lanka-7014.html.
57. "Family Despairs" (June 11, 2007), http://www.catholic.org/international/international_story.php?id=24349; Vella, "Catholic Priest Disappears in Sri Lanka" (see above).
58. "Family Despairs as Reports Claim Recovered Body That of Missing Priest" (see above).
59. "United Nations Human Rights Council, Universal Periodic Review: Sri Lanka," submission of the Becket Fund for Religious Liberty (February 8, 2008), http://www.lankaliberty.com/documents/Sri-Lanka-UPR-Jan-08.pdf.
60. "Ranjith Says Textbooks Defame the Church," Catholic News Asia (July 2, 2010), http://www.ucanews.com/story-archive/?post_name=/2010/07/02/ranjith-says-schoolbooks-defame-the-church&post_id=61193; "Proposal for an 'Anti-Conversion Law'; Christians Discriminated in Building Permits," Agenzia Fides (December 17, 2011), http://www.fides.org/aree/news/newsdet.php?idnews=30606&lan=eng-.
61. Benedict Rogers, "Buddhas's Fist," CatholicCulture.org (Morley Publishing Group, Inc., February 2005), http://www.catholicculture.org/culture/library/view.cfm?recnum=6395.
62. "Shooting Kills Pastor; Wife Critically Injured," Compass Direct News (February 21, 2008), http://www.compassdirect.org/english/country/srilanka/2008/newsarticle_5256.html.
63. W. Chandrapala, "Killing of Pastor: Motive Personal, Police Act Fast," *Sunday Times Online* (February 24, 2008), http://www.sundaytimes.lk/080224/News/news007.html.
64. "Sri Lanka: Funeral Held for Murdered Pastor," Christian Solidarity Worldwide (February 26, 2008), http://dynamic.csw.org.uk/article.asp?t=press&id=704.
65. "Sri Lanka: Dramatic Increase in Violence Against Christians," Christian Solidarity Worldwide (March 4, 2008), http://dynamic.csw.org.uk/article.asp?t=press&id=707; "GFA Bible College Comes Under Attack," Gospel

for Asia (March 13, 2008), http://www.gfa.org/news/articles/gfa-bible-college-comes-under-attack/; "Attacks on Bible School Continue," Compass Direct News (March 25, 2008), http://www.compassdirect.org/english/country/srilanka/2008/newsarticle_5307.html.

66. "Pastor Attacked in Sri Lanka," Christian Solidarity Worldwide (June 24, 2008), http://dynamic.csw.org.uk/article.asp?t=press&id=749.
67. "Pastor and Worker Attacked with Machete: Vineyard Community Church Pannala (Kurunegala District)," National Christian Evangelical Alliance of Sri Lanka, Church Attack Report March–April 2009, 25 Mar. 2009, http://www.nceasl.org/NCEASL/rlc/incident_report_2009.php; "Incident Reports: January–December 2009," Sri Lankan Christians (March 25, 2009), http://www.srilankanchristians.com/pages/posts/january---december-200931.php.
68. "Rash of Attacks on Christians Reported in Sri Lanka," Compass Direct News (August 17, 2009), http://www.compassdirect.org/english/country/srilanka/4665.
69. "Sri Lanka: Religious Freedom in the Post Conflict Situation," Christian Solidarity Worldwide (January 2010), http://dynamic.csw.org.uk/article.asp?t=report&id=123; "Rash of Attacks on Christians Reported in Sri Lanka," Compass Direct News (August 17, 2009), http://www.compassdirect.org/english/country/srilanka/4665.
70. Melani Manel Perera, "Buddhist Extremists Prevent Celebration of Mass near Colombo," AsiaNews.it (October 15, 2007), http://www.asianews.it/index.php?l=en&art=10556&theme=8&size=A.
71. Melani Manel Perera, "Catholic Church Attacked, Suspicions Fall on Buddhist Extremists," Asia News.it (December 9, 2009), http://www.asianews.it/news-en/Catholic-Church-attacked,-suspicions-fall-on-Buddhist-extremists-17072.html.
72. "Buddhist Extremists Brutally Attack Catholic Church in Sri Lanka," Catholic News Agency (December 11, 2009), http://www.catholicnewsagency.com/news/buddhist_extremists_brutally_attack_catholic_church_in_sri_lanka/.
73. Vishal Arora, "Official Recognition Eludes Christian Groups in Bhutan," Compass Direct News (February 1, 2011), accessed September 13, 2012, http://www.compassdirect.org/english/country/12469/32148.
74. Ibid.; see also Vishal Arora, "Buddhist Bhutan Proposes 'Anti-Conversion' Law," Compass Direct News (July 21, 2010), http://www.compassdirect.org/english/country/12469/23018.
75. "Official Recognition Eludes Christian Groups in Bhutan," Compass Direct News (February 2, 2011).
76. US Department of State, "Background Note: Bhutan" (February 2, 2010), http://www.state.gov./r/pa/ei/bgn/35839.htm; "Despite Democracy, Christians in Bhutan Remain Underground," Compass Direct News (January 25, 2010), http:/www.compassdirect.org

/English/country/12469/14394; "Christians in Bhutan Seek to Dispel Regime's Mistrust," Compass Direct News (September 9, 2011), http://www.compassdirect.org/english/country/12469/article_120136.html; Vishal Arora, "Legal Status Foreseen for Christianity in Buddhist Bhutan," Compass Direct News (November 4, 2010), http://www.compassdirect.org/english/country/12469/28077; Vishal Arora, "Official Recognition Eludes Christian Groups in Bhutan" (see above).

77. "Despite Democracy, Christians in Bhutan Remain Underground," Compass Direct News, http://www.compassdirect.org/English/country/12469/14394.
78. "Christians in Bhutan Seek to Dispel Regime's Mistrust," Compass Direct News, http://www.compassdirect.org/english/country/12469/article_120136.html; see also US Department of State, *International Religious Freedom Report 2010*, http://www.state.gov/j/drl/rls/irf/2010/148791.htm; Vishal Arora, "Official Recognition Eludes Christian Groups in Bhutan" (see above); "Despite Democracy, Christians in Bhutan Remain Underground" (see above).
79. "Christian in Bhutan Imprisoned for Showing Film on Christ," Compass Direct News (October 18, 2010), http://www.compassdirect.org/english/country/12469/27133.
80. Vishal Arora, "Christians in Bhutan Seek to Dispel Regime's Mistrust," (April 13, 2011), "Religious Conversion Worst Form of 'Intolerance,' Bhutan PM Says" (September 9, 2011), "Official Recognition Eludes Christian Groups in Bhutan" (January 2, 2011), Compass Direct News, http://www.hrwf.org/images/forbnews/2011/bhutan%202011.pdf.
81. Vishal Arora, "Legal Status Foreseen for Christianity in Buddhist Bhutan," Compass Direct News (November 4, 2010), http://www.compassdirect.org/english/country/12469/28077; "Despite Democracy, Christians in Bhutan Remain Underground" (see above); "WEA-RLC Report: Why Bhutan Wants Anti-Conversion Law?" World Evangelical Alliance, Religious Liberty Commission (December 13, 2010), http://www.worldevangelicals.org/commissions/rlc/rlc_article.htm?id=2489; Christians in Bhutan Seek to Dispel Regime's Mistrust" (see above); Vishal Arora, "Religious Conversion Worst form of 'Intolerance,' Bhutan PM Says," Compass Direct News (April 13, 2011), and Human Rights Without Frontiers (April 18, 2011), http://www.hrwf.org/images/forbnews/2011/bhutan%202011.pdf; Vishal Arora, "Official Recognition Eludes Christian Groups in Bhutan" (see above).
82. "Official Recognition Eludes Christian Groups in Bhutan," Compass Direct News, http://www.compassdirect.org/english/country/12469/32148.

CHAPTER 5. THE MUSLIM WORLD: A WEIGHT OF REPRESSION

1. US Department of State, *International Religious Freedom Report 2005: Jordan*, Bureau of Democracy, Human Rights, and Labor (November 8, 2005), http://www.state.gov/j/drl/rls/irf/2005/51602.htm; "Court Annuls

Christian Convert's Marriage," Compass Direct News (June 9, 2008), http://www.compassdirect.org/english/country/jordan/2008/newsarticle_5420.html.

2. In Kuwait, Christians are not abused, but apostasy and evangelism of Muslims is strictly forbidden. In February 2012, Kuwaiti parliamentarian Osama Al-Munawer, claiming that there were already too many churches in proportion to the size of the Christian community, announced that he was drafting legislation to ban the construction of churches and other houses of worship in the emirate. Joseph DeCaro, "Kuwaiti Legislators Call for Ban on Church Construction," Worthy News (February 22, 2012), http://www.christianpersecution.info/index.php?view=11285.
3. Julia Zappei, "Malaysia: Catholic Paper That Used Allah Can Print," Associated Press (January 8, 2009), http://wwrn.org/articles/29945/; "Malaysian Government Defeated by History: Christians Have Used the Word 'Allah' for Centuries," AsiaNews.it (February 25, 2009), http://www.asianews.it/index.php?l=en&art=14574; "Islamic Councils Against Catholic Magazine of Kuala Lumpur: Forbidden to Use the Word 'Allah,'" AsiaNews.it (November 25, 2008), http://www.asianews.it/index.php?l=en&art=13850; "Malaysia Restores 'Allah' Ban for Christians," Associated Press (March 2, 2009), http://www.foxnews.com/story/0,2933,503504,00.html; "Malaysia Court Suspends 'Allah' Ruling," Associated Free Press (January 6, 2010), http://www.google.com/hostednews/afp/article/ALeqM5jdjxJHhJSxwW0qXtF-tOv447Y4Sw.
4. James Hookway and Celine Fernandez, "Malaysia Says It Will Appeal 'Allah' Ruling," *Wall Street Journal* (January 4, 2010), http://online.wsj.com/article/SB126252276477713845.html; Rachel Harvey, "Malaysia Church Attacks Continue in Use of 'Allah' Row," BBC News (January 11, 2009), http://news.bbc.co.uk/2/hi/asia-pacific/8451630.stm; "Pig Head Find at Malaysia Mosques," BBC News (January 27, 2010), http://news.bbc.co.uk/2/hi/asia-pacific/8482267.stm; "Malaysia Won't Punish Muslims for Taking Communion," Associated Press (March 4, 2010), http://www.siasat.com/english/news/malaysia-wont-punish-muslims-taking-communion.
5. Allen V. Estabillo, "The (Religious) Minorities' Retort," *Southeast Asian Press Alliance* (May 12, 2010), http://www.seapabkk.org/seapa-fellowship/fellowship-2006-program/83-the-religious-minorities-retort.html.
6. Sahil Nagpal, "Body-Snatching divides religious in Malaysia," Top News (June 22, 2009), http://www.topnews.in/bodysnatching-divides-religions-malaysia-2180869.
7. Paul Marshall, "'Allah' by Any Other Name: The Government's Censorship Has Only Compounded Malaysia's Troubles," *Wall Street Journal*, Asia Edition (January 14, 2010), http://online.wsj.com/article/SB10001424052748704586504574655343534999778.html; see also Liz Gooch, "Malaysian Court Ends Ban on Book," *New York Times* (January 25, 2010), http://www.nytimes.com/2010/01/26/world/asia/26malaysia

.html?ref=world; "Govt Bans 37 Publications on Islam Containing Twisted Facts," BERNAMA News Agency (June 6, 2007), http://kpdnkk.bernama.com/news.php?id=265986&; Paul Marshall, Lela Gilbert, and Roberta Green, *Islam at the Crossroads: Understanding Its Beliefs, History and Conflicts* (Grand Rapids: Baker, 2002); Paul Wiseman, "In Malaysia, 'Islamic Civilization' Is Promoted," *USA Today* (November 3, 2004), http://www.usatoday.com/news/world/2004-11-03-malaysia-islam_x.htm.

8. "Seizure of 15,000 Bibles in Malaysia Stuns Christians," Compass Direct News (November 7, 2009), http://www.compassdirect.org/english/country/malaysia/11589/; Julia Zappei, "Malaysia Rejects Call to Release 10,000 Bibles," Associated Press (November 5, 2009), http://www.boston.com/news/world/asia/articles/2009/11/05/malaysia_rejects_call_to_release_10000_bibles/; Razak Ahmad, "Rising Christian Anger in Malaysia over Bible Seizures," Reuters (March 30, 2011), http://in.reuters.com/article/2011/03/30/idINIndia-55989920110330; "Malaysia Releases Malay-Language Bibles Impounded for Using 'Allah,'" Deutsche Presse-Agentur (March 15, 2011), http://www.monstersandcritics.com/news/asiapacific/news/article_1626201.php/Malaysia-releases-Malay-language-Bibles-impounded-for-using-Allah.
9. "Non-Muslims not to use 35 Islamic terms: Diktat," *Press Trust of India* (January 15, 2010), http://www.zeenews.com/news596153.html; see also Joseph Chinyong Liow, "No God But God: Malaysia's 'Allah' Controversy," *Foreign Affairs* (February 10, 2010), http://www.foreignaffairs.com/articles/65961/joseph-chinyong-liow/no-god-but-god.
10. Doug Bandow, "The Right Not to Be Muslim," *National Review Online* (June 8, 2007), http://article.nationalreview.com/?q=Y2IyZmU2NDljNmEwMjIxNGNmMzI4NzFjZmNiMTQ5YjI.
11. "Clause Doesn't Cover Muslims," *Star Online* (February 24, 2009), http://thestar.com.my/news/story.asp?file=/2009/2/24/parliament/3330271&sec=parliament/; Thio Li-Ann, "Apostasy and Religious Freedom: Constitutional Issues Arising from the Lina Joy Litigation," *Malayan Law Journal* 2, no. 1 (April 2006).
12. "M'sian Muslims Protest Ruling on Renunciation of Islam," *Straits Times* (May 16, 2008), http://www.asiaone.com/News/AsiaOne%2BNews/Malaysia/Story/A1Story20080516-65646.html. In 2008, the Islamic court of Penang ruled that Siti Fatimah Tan Abdullah had previously never really converted to Islam and so she was free to return to Buddhism, but the case has limited applicability. Sharanjit Singh, "Syariah High Court Declares Convert No Longer a Muslim," *New Straits Times* (May 8, 2008), http://www.malaysianbar.org.my/legal/general_news/landmark_decision_syariah_high_court_declares_convert_no_longer_a_muslim.html.
13. "Exposed to Other Faiths, Malaysian Muslims Are Ordered to Receive Counselling," *Freethinker* (October 10, 2011), http://freethinker.co.uk/2011/10/10/

exposed-to-other-faiths-malaysian-muslims-are-ordered-to-receive-counselling/; interviews by Paul Marshall, Kuala Lumpur, August 2011.

14. Salim Osman, "Time to Curb Malaysia's Racial Attack Dogs," *Straits Times Indonesia* (May 23, 2011), http://www.thejakartaglobe.com/opinion/time-to-curb-malaysias-racial-attack-dogs/442649.
15. Debra Chong, "Hasan Ali Says Gathering Proof of Christian Proselytism," *Malaysian Insider* (December 20, 2011), http://www.themalaysianinsider.com/malaysia/article/hasan-ali-says-gathering-proof-of-christian-proselytism.
16. "Murder in Anatolia. Christian missionaries and Turkish Ultranationalism," *European Stability Initiative* (January 12, 2011), http://www.esiweb.org/pdf/esi_document_id_124.pdf.
17. "Local Officials' Role Emerges in Malatya Murders," Compass Direct News (April 15, 2011), http://www.compassdirect.org/english/country/turkey/3019.
18. "Murder in Anatolia. Christian missionaries and Turkish Ultranationalism," *European Stability Initiative* (see above); "Local Officials' Role Emerges in Malatya Murders," Compass Direct News (April 15, 2011), http://www.compassdirect.org/english/country/turkey/3019; "Turkey: Malatya Murder Trial Continues on Fourth Anniversary of Deaths," Christian Solidarity Worldwide (April 18, 2011), http://dynamic.csw.org.uk/article.asp?t=press&id=1158.
19. Elif Shafak, "The Murder of Hrant Dink," *Wall Street Journal* (January 22, 2007), http://www.pen.org/viewmedia.php/prmMID/1141. "Prominent Turkish Journalist Hrant Dink Murdered in Istanbul," *USA Today* (January 19, 2007), http://www.usatoday.com/news/world/2007-01-19-TURK-JOURNALIST_x.htm.
20. Marshall and Shea, *Silenced*, 128.
21. Fethiye Çetin and Deniz Tuna, "Two Years On: Lawyers Summarise Dink Trial," *Bianet News* (January 19, 2009), http://www.bianet.org/english/minorities/112015-two-years-on-lawyers-summarise-dink-trial.
22. Ibid.; "Ergenekon Suspect to Give Testimony in Malatya Murder Case," *Today's Zaman* (January 17, 2009), http://www.todayszaman.com/tz-web/detaylar.do?load=detay&link=164331.
23. Consulate General of Greece in Istanbul, "The Ecumenical Patriarchate," http://www2.mfa.gr/www.mfa.gr/AuthoritiesAbroad/Europe/Turkey/GeneralConsulateKonstantinoupoli/en-US/Local+Greeks/The+Ecumenical+Patriarchate/.
24. Unpublished interview of Syriac Metropolitan Yusuf Cetin by Nina Shea, as part of the USCIRF delegation, March 2011, Istanbul, Turkey.
25. Orhan Kemal Cengiz, "Intolerance Record of the Week in Turkey," *Today's Zaman* (February 5, 2012), http://www.todayszaman.com/mobile_detailc.action?newsId=270473.
26. Elizabeth H. Prodromou and Nina Shea, "Religious Freedom for Turkey," The

Hill, Congress Blog, USCIRF (August 26, 2011), http://thehill.com/blogs/congress-blog/foreign-policy/178317-religious-freedom-for-turkey.

27. Association of Protestant Churches in Turkey, "Interview with Zekai Tanyar, the Chair of the Association of Protestant Churches in Turkey," *International Institute for Religious Freedom* (February 5, 2012), http://www.iirf.eu/index.php?id=178&tx_ttnews%5Btt_news%5D=1295&cHash=9fedc64120351ae637b358f45d21d7d9.
28. Mine Yildirim, "Turkey: Education Should Facilitate, Not Undermine, Freedom of Religion or Belief," Forum 18 (January 5, 2011), http://www.forum18.org/Archive.php?article_id=1526; "Intolerance and Discrimination Based on Religion or Belief," Human Rights Without Frontiers, newsletter (January 30, 2012).
29. "Persecution Complex: A Test of Whether Turkey Really Grasps the Concept of Religious Freedom," *Economist* (June 23, 2005), http://www.economist.com/node/4112336.
30. Mine Yildirim, "Turkey: The Diyanet—the Elephant in Turkey's Religious Freedom Room?" Forum 18 (May 4, 2011), http://www.forum18.org/Archive.php?article_id=1567.
31. Association of Protestant Churches in Turkey, "Interview with Zekai Tanyar, the Chair of the Association of Protestant Churches in Turkey," International Institute for Religious Freedom (February 5, 2012), http://www.iirf.eu/index.php?id=178&tx_ttnews%5Btt_news%5D=1295&cHash=9fedc64120351ae637b358f45d21d7d9.
32. USCIRF, *Annual Report 2011* (May 2011), http://www.uscirf.gov/images/book%20with%20cover%20for%20web.pdf, 322–323.
33. On other properties, see NAT da Polis, "Landmark Ruling in Turkey: Buyukada Orphanage Returned to the Orthodox Patriarchate," AsiaNews.it (November 9, 2010), http://www.asianews.it/news-en/Landmark-ruling-in-Turkey-Buyukada-orphanage-returned-to-the-Orthodox-Patriarchate-19938.html.
34. USCIRF, *Annual Report 2012*, 226, http://www.uscirf.gov/images/Annual%20Report%20of%20USCIRF%202012(2).pdf.
35. Ibid., 204.
36. "Turkey: Violation of Christian Graves; Bartholomew I: 'The Church Will Fight for Her Survival," *Oriente Cristiano* (November 3, 2010), http://orientecristiano.com/english-news/world-news-of-the-eastern-church/the-church-will-fight-for-her-survival.html.
37. USCIRF, *Annual Report 2012*, 204, http://www.uscirf.gov/images/Annual%20Report%20of%20USCIRF%202012(2).pdf.
38. Interview of Syriac Metropolitan Yusuf Cetin by Nina Shea, as part of the USCIRF delegation, March 2011, Istanbul, Turkey. Note also that there has been some limited success in the village of Kafro in Mardin Province, which has seen an influx of wealthy Syriacs returning from Europe. Again, eighty-seven families contributed to the restoration of two

Syriac churches in the Midyat village of Yemisli, which had been closed for services for thirty years; it reopened in 2010 with ceremonies attended by hundreds of Syriac émigrés from around the world and local Turkish officials. See "Syriac Churches in Turkey Hold First Ritual in 30 Years," *Hurriyet Daily News* (August 5, 2010), http://www.hurriyetdailynews.com/default.aspx?pageid=438&n=the-first-ritual-took-place-in-assyrian-churches-after-30-years-2010-08-05.

39. Marc Champion, "Turkey Allows Monastery Service," *Wall Street Journal* (August 16, 2010), http://online.wsj.com/article/SB10001424052748703382304575431400969083186.html.
40. Marshall and Shea, *Silenced*, 189.
41. Geries Othman, "Catholic Bishop Luigi Padovese Assassinated in Southern Turkey," *Catholic Online* (June 4, 2010), http://www.catholic.org/international/international_story.php?id=36811.
42. Annette Grossbongardt, "Fear Prevails After Priest's Murder," *Spiegel Online* (December 4, 2006), http://www.spiegel.de/international/spiegel/0,1518,411043,00.html.
43. "Catholic Priest Knifed in Turkey," BBC News (July 2, 2006), http://news.bbc.co.uk/2/hi/europe/5139408.stm.
44. "Turkey: Questions Emerge over Murder of Bishop Padovese," *Spero News* (June 8, 2010), http://www.speroforum.com/a/34418/Turkey-Questions-emerge-over-murder-of-Bishop-Padovese.
45. "Mgr Franceschini: Ultranationalist and Religious Fanatics Behind Bishop Padovese's Murder," AsiaNews (October 16, 2010), http://www.asianews.it/news-en/Mgr-Franceschini:-ultranationalist-and-religious-fanatics-behind-Bishop-Padovese%27s-murder-19743.html.
46. John Eibner, "Turkey's Christians Under Siege," *Family Security Matters* (May 20, 2011), http://www.familysecuritymatters.org/publications/id.9561/pub_detail.asp; "Mgr Franceschini: Ultranationalist and Religious Fanatics Behind Bishop Padovese's murder," AsiaNews.it (see above); "Priest in Southern Turkey Narrowly Avoids Sword-Wielding Suspects," *Hurriyet Daily News* (April 22, 2011), http://www.hurriyetdailynews.com/n.php?n=priest-avoided-being-killed-in-adana-at-easter-eve-2011-04-22.
47. Ziya Meral, *No Place to Call Home* (Surrey, UK: Christian Solidarity Worldwide, 2008), 53.
48. Syriac Universal Alliance, 2012 Turkey Report to the United Nations Headquarters in New York City, Human Rights Committee, December 30, 2011, 6–7, http://www2.ohchr.org/english/bodies/hr/docs/ngos/SyriacUniversalAlliance_Turkey_HRC104.pdf.
49. "Patriarch Murder Plot Merged with Ergenekon Case in Turkey," *Hurriyet Daily News* (May 5, 2011), http://www.hurriyetdailynews.com/default.aspx?pageid=438&n=rencber-case-merged-with-ergenekon-case-2011-05-05.

50. Murat-Yetkin, "Dink's Half-Solved Murder," *Hurriyet Daily News* (July 25, 2011), http://www.hurriyetdailynews.com/default.aspx?pageid=438&n=dink8217s-half-solved-murder-2011-07-25.
51. USCIRF, *Annual Report 2012*, 215, http://www.uscirf.gov/images/Annual%20Report%20of%20USCIRF%202012(2).pdf.
52. Henrik Ræder Clausen, *Cyprus: In the Shadow of the Half Moon* (2012), on file at the Hudson Institute's Center for Religious Freedom.
53. USCIRF, *Annual Report 2011* (May 2011), 331, http://www.uscirf.gov/images/book%20with%20cover%20for%20web.pdf.
54. Interviews by Nina Shea, as part of the USCIRF delegation to Cyprus, February 2011.
55. USCIRF, *Annual Report 2012*, 216, http://www.uscirf.gov/images/Annual%20Report%20of%20USCIRF%202012(2).pdf.
56. "Cyprus: USCIRF Concerned over Demolition of 200-Year-Old Church in Northern Cyprus," USCIRF (May 12, 2011), http://www.uscirf.gov/news-room/press-releases/3627-5122011-cyprus-uscirf-concerned-over-demolition-of-200-year-old-church-in-northern-cyprus-.html.
57. Interview of Fr. Zacharias by Nina Shea, as part of the USCIRF delegation to Cyprus, February 2011.
58. USCIRF, *Annual Report 2011* (May 2011), 332, http://www.uscirf.gov/images/book%20with%20cover%20for%20web.pdf.
59. US Department of State, *International Religious Freedom Report 2010: Morocco* (November 17, 2010), http://www.state.gov/j/drl/rls/irf/2010/148834.htm.
60. Ibid.
61. "Morocco Continues to Purge Nation of Foreign Christians," Compass Direct News (July 1, 2010), http://www.compassdirect.org/english/country/morocco/22151/.
62. Ibid. See also above: US Department of State, *International Religious Freedom Report 2010: Morocco.*
63. "Algeria Stalls Appeal of Converted Christian," Compass Direct News (December 16, 2011), http://www.christianpost.com/news/algeria-stalls-appeal-of-convicted-christian-65028/.
64. US Department of State, *International Religious Freedom Report 2010: Algeria* (November 17, 2010), http://www.state.gov/j/drl/rls/irf/2010/148812.htm.
65. "Six Christians Arrested in Eastern Algeria," International Christian Concern / Human Rights Without Frontiers International (November 4, 2011), http://www.hrwf.org/images/forbnews/2011/algeria%202011.pdf.
66. US Department of State, *International Religious Freedom Report 2010: Algeria* (November 17, 2010), http://www.state.gov/j/drl/rls/irf/2010/148812.htm.
67. US Department of State, *International Religious Freedom Report 2010: Jordan*, http:/www.state.gov/j/drl/rls/irf/2010/148826.htm; Marshall and Shea, *Silenced*, 122–123.

68. "Officials Deport More Christians, Deplore Compass Report: Church Council Condemnation of Article Came at Government's Urging," Compass Direct News (February 26, 2008), http://www.compassdirect.org/english/country/jordan/2008/newsarticle_5259.html.
69. "Christian Girls Kidnapped in Yemen Are Rescued," Compass Direct News (May 18, 2010), http://www.compassdirect.org/english/country/Yemen/19612.
70. US Department of State, *International Religious Freedom Report 2010: Yemen* (November 17, 2010), http://www.state.gov/j/drl/rls/irf/2010/148855.htm.
71. Personal interview by Lela Gilbert with Justus Reid Weiner (Resident Scholar at the Jerusalem Center for Public Affairs and a researcher specializing in persecution of Christians in the Palestinian territories), November 2011; Justus Reid Weiner, "Human Rights of Christians in a Palestinian Society," Jerusalem Center for Public Affairs (2004), 19, http://www.jcpa.org/text/Christian-Persecution-Weiner.pdf.
72. US Department of State, *2010 International Religious Freedom Report* (September 13, 2011), http://www.state.gov/j/drl/rls/irf/2010_5/168266.htm.
73. See Daniel Schwammenthal, "The Forgotten Palestinian Refugees," *Wall Street Journal* (December 28, 2009), http://online.wsj.com/article/SB10001424052748704304504574610022765965390.html; Maria MacKay, "Palestine's Christians Continue to Suffer Persecution," *Christian Today* (January 25, 2006), http://www.christiantoday.com/article/palestines.christians.continue.to.suffer.persecution/5106.htm.
74. US Department of State, *International Religious Freedom Report 2010: Israel and the Occupied Territories*, http://www.state.gov/j/drl/rls/irf/2010/148825.htm.
75. "Unknown Assailants Attack Christian School," Compass Direct News (June 4, 2008), http://www.compassdirect.org/english/country/palestinianterritories/2008/newsarticle_5416.html.
76. Liz Gooch, "For Malaysian Christians, an Anxious Holiday Season," *New York Times*, http://www.nytimes.com/2011/12/13/world/asia/for-malaysian-christians-an-anxious-holiday-season.html?pagewanted=all.
77. "Countries of Particular Concern," USCIRF, http://www.uscirf.gov/countries/countries-of-particular-concern.html.

CHAPTER 6. THE MUSLIM WORLD: POLICIES OF PERSECUTION

1. "Iran: Further information on Fear of Torture and Ill-Treatment /Possible Prisoners of Conscience," Amnesty International, http://www.iranrights.org/english/document-454-973.php; "Court Issues Verdict on 3 Farsi-Speaking Christians," Persecution.org (March 27, 2009), http://www.persecution.org/2009/03/27/court-issues-verdict-on-3-farsi-speaking-christians-in-shiraz/; "Iranian Christian Arrested Without Charges," Compass Direct News (June 9, 2008), http://archive.compassdirect.org/en

/display.php?page=news&idelement=5421&lang=en&length=short&backpage=archives&critere=&countryname=Iran&rowcur=0.

2. "Worker Escapes Death in Saudi," UCA News (October 11, 2011), http://www.ucanews.com/2011/10/11/worker-escapes-hanging-in-saudi/.
3. "Christian Couple Dies from Police Attack," Compass Direct News (August 6, 2008), http://www.compassdirect.org/english/country/iran/2008/newsarticle_5508.html.
4. "Iranian Christians Face Death Penalty in Iran," *BosNewsLife* (September 11, 2008), http://www.rferl.org/content/Two_Iranian_Christians_May_Face_Execution_For_Apostasy/1779217.html; "Iranian Church Leader Released—Son of Hanged Pastor Bailed on Charges of Anti-Govt Behavior," Release International (October 23, 2008), http://www.releaseinternational.org/pages/posts/iranian-church-leader-released--son-of-hanged-pastor-bailed-on-charges-of-anti-govt-activity451.php. For additional cases, see "Tortured Christian Flees," Compass Direct News (July 21, 2008), http://www.compassdirect.org/english/country/iran/2008/newsarticle_5478.html; "Christian Couple Dies from Police Attack," Compass Direct News, (see above); "Prosecutor Charges Two Christians with Apostasy," Iran Human Rights Voice (September 11, 2008), http://www.ihrv.org/inf/?p=884; "Matin Azad and Arash Basirat, Two Christians Charged with Heresy," Iran Human Rights Voice (October 4, 2008), http://www.ihrv.org/inf/?p=1060; "Court Finds Way to Acquit Christians Of 'Apostasy,' " Compass Direct News (October 30, 2008), http://www.compassdirect.org/english/country/iran/2008/newsarticle_5664.html; "Assyrian Iranian Minister Arrested in Urumieh by Security Agents," Farsi Christian News Network (October 1, 2008), http://www.fcnn.com/index.php?option=com_content&task=view&id=1760&Itemid=63.
5. "The Calvary of a Female Convert to Christianity," Human Rights Without Frontiers (June 9, 2009), in HRWF country report at http://www.hrwf.net/index.php?option=com_content&view=article&id=105:news-2008-catalogued-by-country&catid=38:freedom-of-religion-and-belief&Itemid=90.
6. "Rising Restrictions on Religion," the Pew Forum on Religion and Public Life (August 9, 2011), http://www.pewforum.org/Government/Rising-Restrictions-on-Religion(2).aspx.
7. "Pastor Flees Death Threats," Compass Direct News (January 30, 2009), http://www.compassdirect.org/english/country/saudiarabia/2009/newsarticle_5781.html.
8. "Living in Secret in Saudi Arabia: Interview with Scholar on Churches in the Middle East," Camille Eid interview on the television program *Where God Weeps* of the Catholic Radio and Television Network (CRTN) in cooperation with Aid to the Church in Need (April 4, 2011), http://www.zenit.org/article-32222?l=english; Zenit (April 4, 2011), http://www.ewtn.com/library/CHRIST/zsaudiar.htm.
9. Clifford May, "Destroy All Churches," *National Review Online* (March 22,

2012), http://www.nationalreview.com/articles/294112/destroy-all-churches-clifford-d-may.

10. Celestine Bohlen, "After 20 Years, a Mosque Opens in Catholicism's Back Yard," *New York Times* (June 22, 1995), http://www.nytimes.com/1995/06/22/world/after-20-years-a-mosque-opens-in-catholicism-s-back-yard.html?pagewanted=all&src=pm.
11. "Living in Secret in Saudi Arabia," Zenit (April 4, 2011), http://www.zenit.org/article-32222?l=english.
12. Galal Fakkar, "More Scholars Join Call for Stopping Supplications Against Non-Muslims," *Arab News* (January 11, 2011), http://www.arabnews.com/node/365140.
13. US Department of State, "Saudi Arabia," *International Religious Freedom Report 2009* (October 26, 2009), http://www.state.gov/j/drl/rls/irf/2009/127357.htm.
14. Nina Shea, "Ten Years On: Saudi Arabia's Textbooks Still Promote Religious Violence," *Hudson Institute Center for Religious Freedom* (September 11, 2011), 15, http://www.hudson.org/files/publications/SaudiTextbooks2011Final.pdf.
15. "Saudi Man Kills Daughter for Converting to Christianity," *Gulf News* (August 12, 2008), http://www.gulfnews.com/News/Gulf/saudi_arabia/10236558.html.
16. Shea, "Ten Years On," 16, http://www.hudson.org/files/publications/SaudiTextbooks2011Final.pdf.
17. NRO Symposium, "Bin Laden, No More," *National Review Online* (May 2, 2011), http://www.nationalreview.com/articles/266271/bin-laden-no-more-nro-symposium?pg=4.
18. Abdurrahman Wahid, "Right Islam vs. Wrong Islam," *Wall Street Journal* (December 30, 2005), http://www.libforall.org/news-WSJ-right-islam-vs.-wrong-islam.html.
19. Shea, "Ten Years On"; see the Center's four Saudi textbook studies at http://crf.hudson.org.
20. Meeting of Nina Shea with Saudi Education Minister Prince Faisal Al-Saud, in the office of the Education Ministry, Riyadh, Saudi Arabia, February 1, 2011.
21. US Department of State, "Saudi Arabia," *International Religious Freedom Report 2010* (November 17, 2010), http://www.state.gov/j/drl/rls/irf/2010/148843.htm.
22. "Living in Secret in Saudi Arabia," http://www.zenit.org/article-32222?l=english.
23. Jennifer Gold, "Persecution of Christians Increases in Saudi Arabia after New King Inaugurated," *Christianity Today* (August 25, 2005), http://www.christiantoday.com/article/persecution.of.christians.increases.in.saudi.arabia.after.new.king.inaugurated/3779.htm.
24. "Pastor Flees Death Threats," Compass Direct News (January 30, 2009),

http://www.compassdirect.org/english/country/saudiarabia/2009/newsarticle_5781.html.

25. "Eritrean Christian Facing Deportation from Saudi Arabia," Christian Solidarity Worldwide (July 20, 2011), http://dynamic.csw.org.uk/article.asp?t=press&id=1205&search=.
26. Nina Shea and Jonathan Racho, "Persecuted for Praying to God in Saudi Arabia," *National Review Online* (February 8, 2012), http://www.hudson.org/index.cfm?fuseaction=publication_details&id=8719.
27. US Department of State, "Saudi Arabia," *International Religious Freedom Report 2008*, http://www.state.gov/j/drl/rls/irf/2008/108492.htm.
28. "Pastor Flees Death Threats," Compass Direct News (January 30, 2009), http://www.compassdirect.org/english/country/saudiarabia/2009/newsarticle_5781.html.
29. "Saudi Arabia: Conditional Release for 12 Filipinos Accused of Proselytizing," AsiaNews.it (October 7, 2010), http://www.asianews.it/news-en/Saudi-Arabia:-conditional-release-for-12-Filipinos-accused-of-proselytizing-19655.html.
30. Rodolfo Estimo Jr., "12 Filipinos Arrested for Proselytizing Out on Bail," Arab News (October 6, 2010), http://www.arabnews.com/node/356966.
31. "Filipino Jailed in Saudi for 'Blasphemy,'" Catholic News Philippines (October 26, 2011), http://www.cathnewsphil.com/2011/10/26/filipino-jailed-in-saudi-for-blasphemy/.
32. "A Philippine Worker Has Been Arrested for Blasphemy; Bishops Appeal for His Release," Agenzia Fides (October 26, 2011), http://www.fides.org/aree/news/newsdet.php?idnews=30190&mode=print&lan=eng.
33. "Saudi Arabia Arrests Ethiopian Christians for 'Mixing with Opposite Sex,'" Persecution.org (December 21, 2011), http://www.persecution.org/2011/12/21/saudi-arabia-arrests-ethiopian-christians-for-mixing-with-opposite-sex/.
34. Ibid.
35. See video at http://www.youtube.com/watch?v=ZBd3DXBHa6M. Also see Nina Shea and Jonathan Racho, "Persecuted for Praying to God in Saudi Arabia."
36. "Saudi Arabia Deports 35 Ethiopian Christians for Practicing Their Faith," Persecution International Christian Concern (August 3, 2012), http://www.persecution.org/2012/08/03/saudi-arabia-deports-35-ethiopian-christians-for-practicing-their-faith/.
37. Shea and Racho, "Persecuted for Praying to God in Saudi Arabia."
38. "Saudi Arabia Authorities Release Christian Blogger," ReligionNewsBlog (April 20, 2009), http://www.religionnewsblog.com/23412/saudi-arabia-authorities-release-christian-blogger.
39. "Authorities Arrest Christian convert," Compass Direct News (January 28, 2009), http://www.compassdirect.org/english/country/saudiarabia/2009/newsarticle_5779.html. See also "KSA Arrests Blogger, Blocks His Site.

His Life at Risk as He Embraced Christianity," Arabic Network for Human Rights Information (January 14, 2008), http://anhri.net/en/reports/2009/pr0114.shtml; "Saudi Arabia: Authorities Release Christian Blogger," Compass Direct News (April 16, 2009), http://www.compassdirect.org/english/country/saudiarabia/2009/newsarticle_5881.html; Cairo Institute for Human Rights Studies, *Bastion of Impunity, Mirage of Reform: Human Rights in the Arab Region*, Annual Report 2009, 176, http://www.cihrs.org/wp-content/uploads/2012/01/2009-En.pdf
. Hamoud had been arrested twice before.

40. "Saudi Christian Convert Arrested and Jailed," AsiaNews.it (December 17, 2004), http://www.asianews.it/index.php?l=en&art=2134. Additional information provided in e-mail correspondence with a representative of International Christian Concern, April 1, 2008.
41. Center for Religious Freedom, *Saudi Publications on Hate Ideology Invade American Mosques* (Washington, DC: Freedom House, 2005), 12, 45, http://crf.hudson.org/files/publications/2005%20Saudi%20Report.pdf.
42. Ibid., 20.
43. "Saudi Teacher Jailed for Praising Jews," Newsmax.com (November 14, 2005), http://archive.newsmax.com/archives/ic/2005/11/14/95657.shtml.
44. "Jihad and the Saudi Petrodollar," BBC (November 15, 2007), http://news.bbc.co.uk/2/hi/middle_east/7093423.stm.
45. Neil MacFarquhar, "Saudi Reformers: Seeking Rights, Paying a Price," *New York Times* (June 9, 2005), http://www.nytimes.com/2005/06/09/international/middleeast/09saudi.html; Mahan Abedin, "Saudi Dissent More Than Just Jihadis," first published by Saudi Debate (June 15, 2006), http://www.e-prism.org/images/Saudi_dissent_more_than_just_ihadis_-_15-6-06.pdf; "Jihad and the Saudi Petrodollar," BBC (November 15, 2007), http://news.bbc.co.uk/2/hi/middle_east/7093423.stm.
46. Joseph Ghougassian, *The Knight and the Falcon: The Coming of Christianity in Qatar, a Muslim Nation*, (Escondido, CA: Lukas and Sons Publishers, 2008), 46. The following paragraphs summarize this work.
47. Ghougassian, *The Knight and the Falcon*, 30.
48. Ibid., 34–35.
49. An unofficial transcript of the court verdict is at http://www.foxnews.com/interactive/world/2011/10/01/iranian-court-ruling-on-christian-pastor/.
50. Ibid.
51. Paul Marshall, "Christian Pastor Faces Death Sentence in Iran," http://www.hudson.org/index.cfm?fuseaction=publication_details&id=8372. "Articles of Faith," *London Times* (September 29, 2011), http://www.hudson.org/index.cfm?fuseaction=publication_details&id=8372.
52. Kathryn Jean Lopez, "Pastor Faces Death in Iran for Apostasy; John Boehner Urges Iran to 'Abandon This Dark Path, Spare Yousef Nadarkhani's Life, and Grant Him a Full and Unconditional Release,'" September 28, 2011, http://www.nationalreview.com

/corner/278584/pastor-faces-death-iran-apostasy-john-boehner -urges-iran-abandon-dark-path-spare-youse.

53. "Foreign Secretary Calls on Iran to Overturn Iranian Church Leader's Death Sentence," Foreign and Commonwealth Office (September 28, 2011), http://www.fco.gov.uk/en/news/latest-news/?view=News&id =662412382.
54. "Iran News Falsely Reports Youcef Not Charged with Apostasy," *American Center for Law and Justice* (September 30, 2011), http://aclj.org/iran/iran-news-falsely-reports-youcef-not-charged-apostasy; Dan Merica, "Iranian Pastor Faces Death for Rape, not Apostasy—report," CNN (October 1, 2011), http ://articles.cnn.com/2011-09-30/middleeast/world_meast_iran-christian -pastor_1_violent-crimes-apostasy-execution?_s=PM:MIDDLEEAST; Nina Shea, "Iran Switches Charges Against Pastor for the Second Time," *National Review Online* (October 4, 2011), http://www.nationalreview.com /corner/279113/iran-switches-charges-against-pastor-second-time-nina-shea; "Iran: Nadarkhani Rejects 'Unconstitutional' Terms of Release," Christian Solidarity Worldwide (January 13, 2012), http://dynamic.csw.org.uk/article .asp?t=press&id=1305. Nina Shea, "Two Christians Freed; Two Peoples Held Captive," National Review Online (September 12, 2012), http://www .nationalreview.com/corner/316441/two-christians-freed-two-peoples-held -captive-nina-shea.
55. "Iran: Ten Iranian Christians Arrested at a Prayer Meeting," AsiaNews.it (February 10, 2012), http://www.asianews.it/news-en/Ten-Iranian -Christians-arrested-at-a-prayer-meeting-23936.html.
56. Iran Constitution, Article 167: "The judge is bound to endeavor to judge each case on the basis of the codified law. In case of the absence of any such law, he has to deliver his judgment on the basis of authoritative Islamic sources and authentic [fatawas]. He, on the pretext of the silence of or deficiency of law in the matter, or its brevity or contradictory nature, cannot refrain from admitting and examining cases and delivering his judgment," http://www.servat.unibe.ch/icl/ir00000_.html.
57. Paul Marshall, "Christian Pastor Faces Death Sentence in Iran," *London Times* (September 29, 2011), http://www.hudson.org/index.cfm ?fuseaction=publication_details&id=8372 by "Christian Arrested Without Charges," Compass Direct News (June 9, 2008), http://www.compassdirect .org/english/country/iran/2008/newsarticle_5421.html.
58. "Iran: Further information on Fear of Torture and Ill-Treatment /Possible Prisoners of Conscience," Amnesty International, http://www .iranrights.org/english/document-454-973.php; "Court issues verdict on 3 Farsi-Speaking Christians," *Farsi Christian News Network* (March 25, 2009), http://www.persecution.org/2009/03/27/court-issues-verdict -on-3-farsi-speaking-christians-in-shiraz/.
59. Damaris Kremida, "Iran Releases Two Christian Women from Evin Prison," Compass Direct News (November 18, 2009), http://www

.compassdirect.org/english/country/iran/11805/; "Authorities Tighten Grip on Christians as Unrest Roils," Compass Direct News (August 12, 2009), http://www.iranpresswatch.org/post/4679; "Iran Detains Christians Without Legal Counsel," Compass Direct News (January 28, 2010), http://www.compassdirect.org/english/country/iran/14572. For additional cases, see "Iranian Authorities Pressure Father of Convert," Compass Direct News (May 20, 2009), http://www.compassdirect.org/english/country/iran/3851; Roxana Saberi, "Iran Must Stop Persecuting Minority Religions," CNN (December 21, 2011), http://www.cnn.com/2011/12/21/opinion/saberi-iran-religion/index.html.

60. "Convert Couple Arrested, Tortured, Threatened," Compass Direct News (June 25, 2008), http://www.compassdirect.org/english/country/iran/2008/newsarticle_5448.html; "Safe at Last, by Grace of God, but They Still Need Your Prayers," *Open Doors* (July 7, 2009), available at http://www.undergroundnz.org/article/67/safe-at-last-by-grace-of-god-but-they-still-need-your-prayers.
61. Paul Marshall, "Iran Escalates Attacks on Christians," *National Review Online* (January 10, 2011), http://www.nationalreview.com/corner/256755/iran-escalates-attacks-christians-paul-marshall.
62. "Severe Intensification of Arrests and Imprisonment of Christians in Iran," Elam Ministries (January 25, 2011), http://www.elam.com/Editor/assets/briefing%20document%20changed%20date.pdf.
63. "Christians in Iran Sentenced for 'Crimes Against the Islamic Order,'" *CSW* (March 11, 2011), http://dynamic.csw.org.uk/article.asp?t=press&id=1126&search=.
64. Ibid.; "Iranian News Website Suspended After Reporting Burning of New Testaments," Christian Solidarity Worldwide (March 16, 2011), http://dynamic.csw.org.uk/article.asp?t=press&id=1135; Paul Marshall, "Iran Burns Bibles, Condemns Quran Burning," *National Review Online* (March 24, 2011), http://www.nationalreview.com/corner/263028/iran-burns-bibles-condemns-quran-burning-paul-marshall; "Iran: More Arrests of Christians and Bibles Confiscated," Christian Solidarity Worldwide (August 24, 2011), http://dynamic.csw.org.uk/article.asp?t=press&id=1219.
65. Paul Marshall, "Ahmadinejad Arrives in New York on a Wave of Religious Repression," *National Review Online* (September 19, 2011), http://www.nationalreview.com/corner/277589/ahmadinejad-arrives-new-york-wave-religious-repression-paul-marshall; "Iran: Detained Pastor Assaulted; Nadarkhani Verdict Extension Rumoured," Christian Solidarity Worldwide (December 16, 2011), http://dynamic.csw.org.uk/article.asp?t=press&id=1284.
66. Paul Marshall, "Iran Feels Pressure over Nadarkhani," *National Review Online* (October 2, 2011), http://www.nationalreview.com/corner/278929/iran-feels-pressure-over-nadarkhani-paul-marshall.

67. Testimony of Paul Marshall, "Religious Freedom and Persecution in Iran," Congressional Religious Freedom Caucus (IRF)(February 13, 2012), http://www.hudson.org/files/publications/MarshallReligiousFreedomTestimony021312.pdf, p. 5.
68. Paul Marshall, "Ahmadinejad Arrives in New York on a Wave of Religious Repression," Hudson Institute (September 19, 2011), http://www.hudson.org/index.cfm?fuseaction=publication_details&id=8333.
69. Ibid.; see also Marshall and Shea, *Silenced.*

CHAPTER 7. THE MUSLIM WORLD: SPREADING REPRESSION

1. Paul Marshall, "The Ongoing Attacks on Egypt's Coptic Christians," *National Review Online* (March 10, 2011), http://www.nationalreview.com/corner/261847/ongoing-attacks-egypts-coptic-christians-paul-marshall.
2. Mariam Faruqi, "A Question of Faith: A Report on the Status of Religious Minorities in Pakistan," *Jinnah Institute* (2011), 45–46, http://www.humanrights.asia/opinions/columns/pdf/AHRC-ETC-022-2011-01.pdf.
3. February 17, 2011, letter from prison is available from International Christian Concern, http://www.persecution.org/pdf/LetterandTranslation.pdf.
4. "Afghani Convert Musa Released; Another Christian Still in Prison," Compass Direct News (February 24, 2011), http://www.compassdirect.org/english/country/afghanistan/33433; "Afghan Prisoner Released from Prison and Safely Out of the Country," International Christian Concern (April 20, 2011), http://www.persecution.org/2011/04/20/afghan-christian-released-from-prison-and-safely-out-of-the-country/.
5. Representative Frank Wolf, "Trip Report: South Sudan Yida Refugee Camp" (February 2012), http://wolf.house.gov/uploads/Sudan%20Trip%20-%202012.pdf.
6. The Maldives is one of the most religiously repressive places in the world, on a par with Saudi Arabia. It claims to have a 100 percent Muslim population, and the government essentially bans any non-Muslim religious expression (and much Muslim expression, for that matter). The reason we have not included it separately is that there are few Christians and few incidents there. On September 29, 2010, a group of angry Muslim parents stormed a government school accusing Geethamma George, a Christian teacher from India, of drawing a cross in her class (she had in fact drawn a compass). She was removed from the island for her safety. "Muslims Force Expat Christian Teacher to Flee Maldives," Compass Direct News (October 5, 2010), http://www.compassdirect.org/english/country/23845/26545. In September 2011, Shijo Kokkattu, a Catholic teacher, also from India, was arrested after police found a Bible and a rosary in his house during a raid, and he was deported. "Maldives Arrests, Deports Indian Teacher for Owning Bible," Compass Direct News (October 21, 2011), http://www.compassdirect.org/english/country/23845/article_122214.html.

7. Testimony of Nina Shea, director, Hudson Institute's Center for Religious Freedom, before the Tom Lantos Human Rights Commission (TLHRC), "Under Threat: The Worsening Plight of Egypt's Coptic Christians," December 7, 2011, 3, http://www.hudson.org/files/publications/Shea-Egypt-testimony-12-7-11.pdf.
8. Mohamed Fadel Fahmy, "Prime Minister Says Egypt 'Scrambling' After at Least 23 Killed in Clashes," CNN (October 10, 2011), http://edition.cnn.com/2011/10/09/world/meast/egypt-protest-clashes/index.html?hpt=hp_t2; "Board's Report on the Event of Maspero," the National Council for Human Rights, http://www.nchregypt.org/ar/index.php?option=com_content&view=article&id=500:2011-11-02-19-51-28&catid=43:2010-03-09-13-00-53&Itemid=55 (Arabic version); Mai Elwakil, "State Media Coverage of Maspero Violence Raises Tempers," *Egypt Independent* (October 10, 2011), http://www.egyptindependent.com/node/503748; Maggie Michael, "24 Dead in Worst Cairo Riots Since Mubarak Ouster," Associated Press (October 9, 2011), http://news.yahoo.com/24-dead-worst-cairo-riots-since-mubarak-ouster-232452205.html.
9. Testimony of Nina Shea, director, Hudson Institute's Center for Religious Freedom, before the Tom Lantos Human Rights Commission (TLHRC), "Under Threat: The Worsening Plight of Egypt's Coptic Christians," December 7, 2011, 3, http://www.hudson.org/files/publications/Shea-Egypt-testimony-12-7-11.pdf.
10. Paul Marshall, "Attacks on Egypt's Copts Escalate," *National Review Online* (January 3, 2011), http://www.nationalreview.com/corner/256207/attacks-egypts-copts-escalate-paul-marshall.
11. Interview of Egyptian Coptic Orthodox and Protestant leaders by Nina Shea, February 2012, Washington, DC.
12. US Department of State, "International Religious Freedom Report 2010," Bureau of Democracy, Human Rights, and Labor (November 17, 2010), http://www.state.gov/j/drl/rls/irf/2010/148817.htm; The United States Commission on International Religious Freedom, *Annual Report 2011*, 55, http://www.uscirf.gov/images/book%20with%20cover%20for%20web.pdf; "Egyptian Panel Drops Maspero Massacre Case for 'Lack of Evidence," Assyrian International News Agency (April 28, 2012), http://www.aina.org/news/20120427193443.htm.
13. "Two Years of Sectarian Violence: What Happened? Where Do We Begin?—An Analytic Study of January 2008–January 2010," Egyptian Organization for Personal Rights (April 2010), http://eipr.org/sites/default/files/reports/pdf/Sectarian_Violence_inTwoYears_EN.pdf.
14. "USCIRF Identifies World's Worst Religious Freedom Violators: Egypt Cited for First Time," USCIRF (April 28, 2011), http://www.uscirf.gov/news-room/press-releases/3595-4282011-uscirf-identifies-worlds-worst-religious-freedom-violators-egypt-cited-for-first-time.html.
15. Jack Shenker, "Egypt's Coptic Christians Struggle Against Institutionalized Prejudice," *Guardian* (December 23, 2010), http://www.guardian.co.uk

/world/2010/dec/23/egypt-coptic-christians-prejudice; Mary Abdelmassih, "Egyptian Christians Clash with State Security Forces over Church Construction," Assyrian International News Agency (November 27, 2010), http://www.aina.org/news/20101126184013.htm.

16. "Bastion of Impunity, Mirage of Reform: Human Rights in the Arab Region Annual Report 2009," Cairo Institute for Human Rights Studies (December 8, 2009), 127, www.cihrs.org/wp-content/uploads/2012/01/2009-En.pdf.
17. Mustafa El-Menshawy, "One Step Forward, Two Steps Back," *Al-Ahram Weekly* (October 20–26, 2005), http://weekly.ahram.org.eg/2005/765/eg6.htm; Maamoun Youssef, "Stabbing of Nun Sparks Tension in Alexandria," *Independent Online* (October 20, 2005), http://www.iol.co.za/news/africa/stabbing-of-nun-sparks-tension-in-alexandria-1.256516#.T9Ib-9VSRLc; "Three Killed in Egypt Church Riot," BBC (October 22, 2005), http://news.bbc.co.uk/2/hi/middle_east/4366232.stm ;2009; Michael Slackman, "Egyptian Police Guard Coptic Church Attacked by Muslims," *New York Times* (October 23, 2005), http://www.nytimes.com/2005/10/23/international/africa/23egypt.html?_r=1.
18. Nina Shea, "Egypt's Copts Suffer More Attacks," *National Review Online* (March 5, 2011), http://www.nationalreview.com/corner/261405/egypt-s-copts-suffer-more-attacks-nina-shea; Wael Ali, "Rights Group Blames Security Forces for Imbaba Incident," *Egypt Independent* (September 5, 2011), http://www.egyptindependent.com/node/430326.
19. For example, see, Christopher Landau, "Egyptian Christian's Recognition Struggle," BBC (February 13, 2009), http://news.bbc.co.uk/2/hi/middle_east/7888193.stm; Article 98(f) specifies penalties of up to five years in prison and a fine of up to LE 1,000.
20. Paul Marshall, interview with Grand Sheik of Al-Azhar, Sheik Tantawi, August 1998. See also Paul Marshall, *Egypt's Endangered Christians* (Washington: Freedom House, 1999), and *Massacre at the Millennium* (Washington: Freedom House, 2001); "Egypt: Copts Appeal Religious Identity Ruling," Compass Direct News (June 25, 2007), http://www.compassdirect.org/english/country/egypt/2007/newsarticle_4921html.
21. "Egyptian Convert to Christianity Held Captive Since November 2009," Jubilee Campaign USA (July 14, 2010), http://www.persecution.org/2010/07/21/egyptian-convert-to-christianity-held-captive-since-november-2009/. In July 2007, Ali Gomaa, the grand mufti, made a controversial statement that apostasy only merited punishment in the afterlife. He later clarified that "apostates" could be punished on earth if they were "actively engaged in the subversion of society."
22. "Muslim Publics Divided on Hamas and Hezbollah: Most Embrace a Role for Islam in Politics," Pew Research Center (December 2, 2010), http://www.pewglobal.org/2010/12/02/muslims-around-the-world-divided-on-hamas-and-hezbollah/.

23. "Convert Locked into Mental Hospital," Compass Direct News (May 13, 2005), http://www.compassdirect.org/english/country/egypt/2005/newsarticle_3816.html; "Convert Released from Mental Hospital," Compass Direct News (June 21, 2005), http://www.compassdirect.org/english/country/egypt/2005/newsarticle_3860.html.
24. For background, see "Prohibited Identities," Human Rights Watch (November 12, 2007), http://www.hrw.org/reports/2007/11/11/prohibited-identities; for discriminatory laws concerning marriage, divorce, child custody, and inheritance, see Law no. 25 of 1920; Law no. 52 of 1929; Law no. 77 of 1943. Though it has not caused any hardship so far because no one has successfully converted from Islam, any convert loses his inheritance. This does not apply to converts to Islam.
25. "Egypt," in USCIRF *Annual Report 2008*, 224, http://www.uscirf.gov/images/AR2008/egyptar2008_full%20color.pdf.
26. "Egyptian Convert to Christianity Tortured, Raped in Egypt," Assyrian International News Agency (December 20, 2008), http://www.aina.org/news/20081219220247.htm; "Muslim Woman Who Converted to Christianity Arrested at Cairo Airport," Voice of the Copts (December 17, 2008), http://www.aina.org/news/20081216193035.htm.
27. "Egypt: Judge Tells of Desire to Kill Christian," Compass Direct News (January 27, 2009), http://www.compassdirect.org/english/country/egypt/1860.
28. "Prohibited Identities" says, "Conversion from Islam to Christianity is fraught with legal and social risks. . . . As a result, the number of persons born Muslim who have converted to Christianity is hard to gauge, but at a minimum it would appear to involve a score or more persons per year, and so cumulatively be in the hundreds if not thousands," Human Rights Watch. Anecdotal evidence from Egypt suggests the number may be much higher.
29. "Egypt Copt Jailed 45 Years After Father's Conversion," Associated Free Press (November 22, 2007), http://afp.google.com/article/ALeqM5gWAdeTNMOeMfyPaOwrYpODjNAQJA; "Father's Brief Conversion Traps Daughters in Islam," Compass Direct News (October 10, 2008), http://www.compassdirect.org/english/country/egypt/2008/newsrticle_5630.html; "Bahiya Detained," Watani International, http://www.arabwestreport.info/year-2008/week-19/62-bahiya-detained; "Christian in Muslim ID Case Wins Right to Appeal," Compass Direct News (December 2, 2008), http://www.compassdirect.org/english/country/egypt/2008/newsarticle_5708.html. HRW/EIPR reports that, as of November 2007, there were at least eighty-nine people struggling to have their religion officially recognized after their parents converted them against their will; see "Prohibited Identities."
30. "Muslim Sues for Right to Convert to Christianity," Compass Direct News (August 7, 2007), http://www.compassdirect.org/english/country

/egypt/newsarticle_4978.html; "Islamists Join Case Against Convert to Christianity," Compass Direct News (October 10, 2007), http://www.compassdirect.org/english/country/egypt/2007/newsarticle_5069html; "In Hiding, Convert Continues Fight for Rights," Compass Direct News (November 15, 2007), www.compassdirect.org/english/country/egypt/2007/newsarticle_5144html; "Egypt: Muslim Authorities Call for Beheading of Convert," *International Society for Human Rights* (August 30, 2007), http://www.ishr.org/index.php?id=697&tx_ttnews%5Btt_news%5D=762&tx_ttnews%5BbackPid%5D=296&cHash=c51802de6d; Pierre Loza, "Christian Convert Says He'll Stay the Course, Despite Threats," *Daily Star* (August 9, 2007), http://www.dailystaregypt.com/article.aspx?ArticleID=8706; "Egypt, Muslim Convert to Christianity Fears for Life," *Middle East Times* (August 14, 2007), http://www.metimes.com/print.php?StoryID=20070814-070417-8160r. Hegazy published a book of poems called *Sherine's Laugh*. In one poem, "Ashraf Pasha," he recalled the abuse he had suffered at the hands of Ashraf Ma'alouf, an SSI officer who reportedly tortured him for converting.

31. "Tempers Flare into Melee at Convert's Hearing," Compass Direct News (January 25, 2008), http://www.compassdirect.org/english/country/egypt/2008/newsarticle_5205.html/?view=Print; "Egypt: Court Rules Against Convert," Worthy Christian News (February 1, 2008), http://wwwworthynews.com/1585-egypt-court-rules-against-convert.
32. Paul Marshall, "Egypt's Identity Crisis," Hudson Institute, *Weekly Standard* (March 3, 2008), http://rs.hudson.org/index.cfm?fuseaction=publication_details&id=5463.
33. "Another Convert Tries to Change Religious Identification," Compass Direct News (August 7, 2008), http://www.compassdirect.org/english/country/egypt/2008/newsarticle_5510.html.
34. "Another Convert Tries to Change Religious Identification," Compass Direct News (August 7, 2008), http://www.compassdirect.org/english/country/egypt/2008/newsarticle_5510.html; Magdy Samaan, "Convert to Christianity Takes His Case to Court," *Daily News Egypt* (August 13, 2008), http://www.thedailynewsegypt.com/article.aspx?ArticleID=15722; "Egyptian Christian's Recognition Struggle," BBC (February 13, 2009), http://news.bbc.co.uk/2/hi/middle_east/7888193.stm; "Judge Ejects Lawyer for Christian from Court," Compass Direct News (January 13, 2009), http://www.compassdirect.org/english/country/egypt/ejection; "Ruling on Bid for Christian ID Expected Soon," Compass Direct News (February 10, 2009), http://www.compassdirect.org/english/country/egypt/2029.
35. "Egypt: Islamic Lawyers Urge Death Sentence for Egyptian Convert," Compass Direct News (February 27, 2009), http://www.compassdirect.org/english/country/egypt/2009/newsarticle_5826.html; "Egypt May Remove Religion from ID Cards," *Al Arabiya* (March 25, 2009), http://www.alarabiya.netarticles/2009/03/25/69227.html.

36. "Coptic Church Issues First Conversion Certificate," Compass Direct News (April 14, 2009), http://www.compassdirect.org/english/country/egypt/2009/newsarticle_5879.html; "Convert's Religious Rights Case Threatens Islamists," Compass Direct News (May 12, 2009), http://www.compassdirect.org/english/country/egypt/2009/newsarticle_5917.html.
37. "Court Denies Right to Convert to Second Christian," Compass Direct News (June 16, 2009), http://www.compassdirect.org/english/country/egypt/2009/newsarticle_5964.html.
38. "Muslim Egyptian Girl Who Converted to Christianity Subjected to Acid Attack," Assyrian International News Agency (April 17, 2010), http://www.aina.org/news/20100416201043.htm.
39. "The Disappearance, Forced Conversions, and Forced Marriages of Coptic Christian Women in Egypt," *Christian Solidarity International and Coptic Foundation for Human Rights* (November 2009), http://csi-int.org/pdfs/csi_coptic_report.pdf.
40. Press Release, "Congressional Members Urge State Department to Address Forced Marriage, Forced Conversion of Coptic Women and Girls in Egypt," *The Business Journals* (April 19, 2010), http://www.bizjournals.com/prnewswire/press_releases/2010/04/19/DC88930.
41. Press Release, "USCIRF Calls for Justice After Deadly Religious Violence in Egypt," USCIRF (May 10, 2011), http://www.uscirf.gov/news-room/press-releases/3626-5102011-uscirf-calls-for-justice-after-deadly-religious-violence-in-egypt.html; "Islamic Extremists Attack Churches in Cairo, Egypt," Compass Direct News (May 9, 2011), http://www.compassdirect.org/english/country/egypt/article_112197.html.
42. Kurt Werthmuller, "Copt's Murder a Test of Egypt's New Anti-Discrimination Law," *National Review Online* (October 31, 2011), http://www.hudson.org/index.cfm?fuseaction=publication_details&id=8452; Interviews by Hudson Institute Center for Religious Freedom, Mallawi, October 2011.
43. Rob Crilly and Aoun Sahi, "Christian Woman Sentenced to Death in Pakistan 'for Blasphemy,'" *Telegraph* (November 9, 2010), http://www.telegraph.co.uk/news/religion/8120142/Christian-woman-sentenced-to-death-in-Pakistan-for-blasphemy.html.
44. Bushra Khaliq, "Pakistan's Dark Journey," *International Viewpoint Online Magazine* (March 2011), http://internationalviewpoint.org/spip.php?article2005.
45. Rob Crilly and Aoun Sahi, "Christian Woman Sentenced to Death in Pakistan 'for Blasphemy,'" *Telegraph* (November 9, 2010), http://www.telegraph.co.uk/news/religion/8120142/Christian-woman-sentenced-to-death-in-Pakistan-for-blasphemy.html.
46. Jibran Khan, "Christmas in Prison for Asia Bibi, Sentenced to Death for Blasphemy," AsiaNews.it (December 20, 2011), http://www.asianews.it/news-en/Christmas-in-prison-for-Asia-Bibi,-sentenced-to-death-for-blasphemy-23485.html.

47. "Mr. Jinnah's Presidential Address to the Constituent Assembly of Pakistan, August 11, 1947," *Dawn, Independence Day Supplement* (August 14, 1999), http://www.pakistani.org/pakistan/legislation/constituent _address_11aug1947.html.
48. "Christian Students Discriminated at University Because They 'Do Not Learn the Koran,'" *Agenzia Fides* (February 15, 2012), http://www.fides. org/aree/news/newsdet.php?idnews=31015&lan=eng.
49. "Pakistan's Educational System Fuels Religious Discrimination," USCIRF (November 9, 2011), http://www.uscirf.gov/news-room/press-releases/3661 -pakistans-educational-system-fuels-religious-discrimination.html.
50. Azhar Hussain and Ahmad Salim with Arif Naveed, "Connecting the Dots: Education and Religious Discrimination in Pakistan: A Study of Public Schools and Madrassas," USCIRF (November 2011), 63, http://www.uscirf .gov/images/Pakistan-ConnectingTheDots-Email.pdf.
51. USCIRF *Annual Report 2011*, 110, http://www.uscirf.gov/images/book%20 with%20cover%20for%20web.pdf.
52. Jibran Khan, "Pakistani Christians 'Number One Target' After the Death of Bin Laden," AsiaNews.it (May 19, 2011), http://www.asianews.it/news-en /Pakistani-Christians-number-one-target-after-the-death-of-Bin-Laden -21603.html.
53. Jibran Khan, "Punjab: Armed Gang Attacks Protestant Clergyman Who Is Saved by Muslims," *AsiaNews.it* (May 31, 2011), http://www.asianews.it /news-en/Punjab:-armed-gang-attacks-Protestant-clergyman-who-is -saved-by-Muslims-21711.html.
54. "The Ideologies of South Asian Jihadi Groups," *Current Trends in Islamist Ideology*, vol. 1, March 21, 2005, 24, http://www.currenttrends.org/docLib /20060130_Current_Trends_vol_1.pdf.
55. David Forte, *Studies in Islamic Law* (San Francisco: Austin & Winfield, 1999). Also see, Marshall and Shea, *Silenced*, 85–86; Section 295-B of the Pakistani penal code, added in 1982 (incorporated through the implementation of Ordinance I) states, "Whoever wilfully defiles, damages or desecrates a copy of the Holy Qu'ran or of an extract there from, or uses it in any derogatory manner or for any unlawful purpose shall be punishable with imprisonment for life." And Section 295-C, added in 1986, declares: "Whoever by words, either spoken or written, or by visible representation, or by any imputation, innuendo, or insinuation, directly or indirectly, defiles the sacred name of the Holy Prophet Muhammad (peace be upon him) shall be punished with death, or imprisonment for life, and shall also be liable to fine." This can be found at "Religious Intolerance in Pakistan," Religious Tolerance, http://www.religioustolerance.org /rt_pakis.htm; Maarten G. Barends, "Sharia in Pakistan," pp. 65–85 of Paul Marshall, ed., *Radical Islam's Rules: the Worldwide Spread of Extreme Sharia* (Lanham, MD: Rowman and Littlefield, 2005). The stakes were raised even higher when in 1990 the Federal Sharia Court, where cases

involving Islamic issues are normally heard, ruled that, "The penalty for contempt of the Holy Prophet . . . is death and nothing else." While this is in principle binding, the government has not yet amended the law, which means that the provision for a life sentence still formally exists, and the government uses it as a concession to critics of the death penalty. See also Akbar S. Ahmed, "Pakistan's Blasphemy Law: Words Fail Me," *Washington Post* (May 19, 2002), http://www.wright-house.com/religions/islam/pakistan-blasphemy-law.html. Pakistan's Constitution guarantees freedom of religion and freedom of speech, but such freedoms are constitutionally "subject to any reasonable restrictions imposed by law in the interest of the glory of Islam."

56. Nina Shea, "Another Christian Martyred in Pakistan," *National Review Online* (December 4, 2011), http://www.nationalreview.com/corner/284856/another-christian-martyred-pakistan-nina-shea.
57. Marshall and Shea, *Silenced*, 87.
58. "Why the U.S. Must Oppose Blasphemy Laws—Not Just Their Abuse," *National Review Online* (August 21, 2012), http://www.nationalreview.com/corner/314600/why-us-must-oppose-blasphemy-laws-not-just-their-abuse-nina-shea. "Pakistan Must Repeal Its Blasphemy Laws," Farahnaz Ispahani and Nina Shea, Huffington Post (September 13, 2012), http://wwwhuffingtonpost.com/farahnaz-ispahani/pakistan-blasphemy-law_b_1882381.html.
59. Testimony of Nina Shea, director, Hudson Institute's Center for Religious Freedom before the Tom Lantos Human Rights Commission of the Committee on Foreign Affairs of the US House of Representatives, "Pakistan's Anti-Blasphemy Laws," October 8, 2009, 7, http://www.hudson.org/files/documents/SheaPakistan108.pdf.
60. "Illiterate Christian Acquitted of Blasphemy," Compass Direct News (June 16, 2003), http://www.compassdirect.org/english/country/pakistan/2003/newsarticle_2092.html.
61. Mariam Faruqi, "A Question of Faith: A Report on the Status of Religious Minorities in Pakistan," *Jinnah Institute* (2011), 40, http://www.humanrights.asia/opinions/columns/pdf/AHRC-ETC-022-2011-01.pdf.
62. "Pakistan's 'Blasphemy' Laws Pose Growing Threat," Compass Direct News (May 13, 2011), http://www.compassdirect.org/english/country/pakistan/article_112455.html.
63. "Punjab Governor Salman Taseer Assassinated in Islamabad," BBC (January 4, 2011), http://www.bbc.co.uk/news/world-south-asia-12111831; Nina Shea and Paul Marshall, "The Murder of a Muslim Moderate," *National Review Online* (January 4, 2011), http://www.nationalreview.com/corner/256307/murder-muslim-moderate-nina-shea.
64. Mosharraf Zaidi, "Taseer's Murder Another Sign of Dysfunctional Pakistani State," *Foreign Policy* (January 4, 2011), http://afpak.foreignpolicy.com/posts/2011/01/04/taseers_murder_another_sign_of_the_dysfunctional_pakistani_state.

65. Nina Shea, "Pakistan Hero Slain for Reform Efforts," *National Review Online* (March 2, 2011), http://crf.hudson.org/index.cfm?fuseaction =publication_details&id=7759.
66. Video: "Pakistani minister Shahbaz Bhatti predicted his own assassination—video," *Guardian* (March 2, 2011), http://www.guardian .co.uk/world/video/2011/mar/02/pakistani-minister-shahbaz-bhatti-video.
67. Nina Shea, "Pakistan Hero Slain for Reform Efforts," *National Review Online* (March 2, 2011), http://www.nationalreview.com/corner/261104 /pakistan-hero-slain-reform-efforts-nina-shea.
68. "Catholic Girl Killed in Faisalabad, a 'Martyr of the Faith,' " Agenzia Fides (December 2, 2011), http://www.fides.org/aree/news/newsdet.php?idnews =30488&mode=print&lan=eng.
69. Shafique Khokhar, "Faisalabad, 18-year-old Christian Woman Killed During an Attempted Rape," AsiaNews.it (December 2, 2011), http:// www.asianews.it/view4print.php?l=en&art=23336; Nina Shea, "Another Christian Martyred in Pakistan," *National Review Online* (December 4, 2011), http://www.nationalreview.com/corner/284856/another-christian -martyred-pakistan-nina-shea.
70. "Pakistan: A 12-year-old Christian Is Gang Raped for Eight Months, Forcibly Converted and Then 'Married' to Her Muslim Attacker," Asian Human Rights Commission (October 10, 2011), http://www.humanrights.asia/news/urgent -appeals/AHRC-UAC-199-2011; "12-year-old Christian Girl Abducted, Raped, and Then Told by Courts She Must Return to the Rapist Who Forced Her into Marriage!" British Pakistani Christian Association (October 12, 2011), http:// britishpakistanichristian.blogspot.com/2011/10/12-year-old-christian-girl -raped-for-8.html.
71. This is a summary of Mindy Belz, "Well-Founded Fear: Afghan Christians Face Growing Threats and Diminished Protection as US Pullout Nears," *World* (July 16, 2011), http://www.worldmag.com/articles/18301.
72. "Said Musa's Handwritten Letter," Barnabas Aid (November 16, 2010), http://www.barnabasfund.org/Said-Musas-handwritten-letter.html.
73. An excellent overview of Said Musa's case is given in Mindy Belz's, "Holding Fast," *World* (November 19, 2011), http://www.worldmag .com/articles/18822; see also Will Inboden, "Why Obama Needs to Intervene to Save a Persecuted Afghan Christian," *Foreign Policy* (February 18, 2011), http://shadow.foreignpolicy.com/posts/2011/02/18/why_obama _needs_to_intervene_to_save_a_persecuted_afghan_christian.
74. US Department of State, "July-December, 2010 International Religious Freedom Report," Bureau of Democracy, Human Rights, and Labor (September 13, 2011), http://www.state.gov/j/drl/rls/irf/2010_5/168240.htm.
75. Amir Shah, "Afghanistan Imposes Death Penalty for Conversion from Islam," Associated Press (January 8, 2001). In June 2001, this was amended so that foreigners caught proselytizing would be detained for three to ten days and then deported.

76. "Taliban Refuse Access to Jailed Christians," Compass Direct News (August 24, 2012), http://www.compassdirect.org/english/country/afghanistan/2001/newsarticle_0563.html.
77. Barry Bearak, "Afghans Shut Offices of 2 More Christian Relief Groups," *New York Times* (September 1, 2001), http://www.nytimes.com/2001/09/01/world/afghans-shut-offices-of-2-more-christian-relief-groups.html.
78. Pamela Constable, "We Are All Good Muslims," *Washington Post* (August 24, 2001), http://imgs.sfgate.com/cgi-bin/article.cgi?f=/c/a/2001/08/24/MN50203.DTL&hw=mohamed&sn=261&sc=036; Bearak, "Afghans Shut Offices of 2 More Christian Relief Groups," see above; "Taliban Refuse Access to Tailed Christians" Compass Direct News (August 29, 2001), http://www.compassdirect.org/english/country/afghanistan/2001/newsarticle_0563.html ; Amir Zia, "Foreign Aid Workers' Trial to Reopen Saturday in Kabul," Associated Press (September 27, 2001), http://www.boston.com/news/daily/27/aid_worker.htm; Molly Moore, "From Agony to Anxiety, Then Freedom," *Washington Post* (November 16, 2001), http://pqasb.pgarchiver.com/washingtonpost/access/90175118.html?FMT=ABS&FMST=ABS:FT&date=Nov+16%+2001&author=Molly+Moore&desc=From+Agony+To+Anxiety%2C+Then+Freedom%3B+Aid+Workers+Describe+Rescue+From+Taliban.
79. "Five Afghan Christians Martyred," Compass Direct News (September 9, 2004), http://www.compassdirect.org/english/country/afghanistan/2004/newsarticle_0208.html.
80. Fisnik Abrashi, "Taliban Threaten to Kill 18 Abducted South Korean Christians in Afghanistan," Associated Press (July 21, 2007), http://www.independent.co.uk/news/world/asia/taliban-threaten-to-kill-18-abducted-isouth-korean-christians-in-afghanistan-458079.html; Choe Sang-Hun, "Deal Is Set to Free Korean Hostages," *International Herald Tribune* (August 29, 2007).
81. Kathy Gannon, "6 Americans on Medical Team Killed in Afghanistan," Associated Press (August 7, 2010), http://www.washingtontimes.com/news/2010aug/7/6-americans-medical-team-killed-afghanistan/?page=all.
82. "Military Burns Unsolicited Bibles Sent to Afghanistan," *CNN* (May 22, 2009), http://edition.cnn.com/2009/WORLD/asiapcf/05/20/us.military.bibles.burned/index.html?eref=edition. See also "Probe Call in Afghan 'Convert' Row," Aljazeera.net (May 4, 2009), http://english.aljazeera.net/news/asia/2009/05/20095485025169646.html.
83. "11/04/2003: Afghanistan: Constitution Threatens to Institutionalize 'Taliban-lite,'" USCIRF press release (November 4, 2003), http://www.uscirf.gov/index.php?option=com_content&task=view&id=1473.
84. Paul Marshall, "Taliban Lite," *National Review Online* (November 7, 2003), http://old.nationalreview.com/comment/marshall200311070906.asp.
85. The Commission was referring to a draft of the constitution, but the relevant articles remained in the final version. See also Paul Marshall,

"Taliban Lite," *National Review Online* (November 7, 2003), http://old.nationalreview.com/comment/marshall200311070906.asp; "Afghanistan: Constitution Threatens to Institutionalize 'Taliban-lite,'" see above.

86. Alex Spillius, "Afghans to Carry on Stoning Criminals," *Telegraph* (January 25, 2002), http://www.telegraph.co.uk/news/worldnews/asia/afghanistan/1382687/Afghans-to-carry-on-stoning-criminals.html.
87. Nina Shea, "Sharia in Kabul?" *National Review Online* (October 28, 2002), http://www.hudson.org/index.cfm?fuseaction=publication_details&id=4607. See also Alex Spillius, "Afghans to Carry on Stoning Criminals," *Telegraph* (January 24, 2002), http://www.telegraph.co.uk/news/worldnews/asia/afghanistan/1382687/Afghans-to-carry-on-stoning-criminals.html; J. Alexander Their, "The Crescent and the Gavel," *New York Times* (March 26, 2006), http://www.nytimes.com/2006/03/26/opinion/26thier.html.
88. US Department of State, "July–December, 2010 International Religious Freedom Report," Bureau of Democracy, Human Rights, and Labor (September 13, 2011), http://www.state.gov/j/drl/rls/irf/2010_5/168240.htm.
89. Barbara G. Baker, "More Christians Arrested in wake of Afghan 'Apostasy' Case," Compass Direct News (March 23, 2006), http://www.crosswalk.com/1385441/; Abdul Waheed Wafa, "Preachers in Kabul Urge Execution of Convert to Christianity," *New York Times* (March 25, 2006), http://www.nytimes.com/2006/03/25/international/asia/25convert.html; "Hundreds Protest Report Afghan Convert to Be Freed," CNN (March 27, 2006); Daniel Williams, "Afghan Convert Arrives in Italy as Protests Mount in Homeland," *Washington Post* (March 30, 2006), http://wwrn.org/articles/20988/?&place=afghanistan.
90. Gebauer, Matthias, "A Community of Faith and Fear," *Spiegel Online* (March 30, 2006), http://www.spiegel.de/international/0,1518,408781,00.html.
91. Barbara G. Baker, "More Christians Arrested in Wake of Afghan 'Apostasy' Case," Compass Direct News (March 23, 2006), http://www.crosswalk.com/1385441/; Barbara Baker, "Whose Law in Afghanistan?" *Christianity Today* (May 1, 2006), http://www.christianitytoday.com/ct/2006/may/5.22.html. On other converts, see Santosh Digal, "Appeal for Afghan Christians, Sentenced to Death for Their Faith," AsiaNews.it (June 15, 2010), http://www.asianews.it/news-en/Appeal-for-Afghan-Christians,-sentenced-to-death-for-their-faith-18680.html#; Mindy Belz, "Kill the Christians: Lawmakers and Protesters in Afghanistan Are Calling for Just That," *World* (June 18, 2010), http://www.worldmag.com/webextra/16862; Emmanuel Duparcq, "Afghan Christians Live in Fear of Jail, Exile, or Worse," Associated Free Press (January 26, 2011), http://www.google.com/hostednews/afp/article/ALeqM5gGv-Whxe4Fa4tryEKRnNnE2g7eyA?docId=CNG.10d6ea3cf68994ed0615cc315002c75d.81.
92. Mindy Belz, "Well-Founded Fear: Afghan Christians Face Growing Threats and Diminished Protection as U.S. Pullout Nears," *World* (July

16, 2011), http://www.worldmag.com/articles/18301; Sam Jones, "Afghan Christians to Be Deported Despite Death Fears," *Guardian* (April 26, 2011), http://www.guardian.co.uk/uk/2011/apr/26/afghan-christians-deported-despite-death-fears.

93. Danna Harman, "Despite Opposition, Afghan Christians Worship in Secret," *Christian Science Monitor* (February 27, 2009), http://www.csmonitor.com/World/Asia-South-Central/2009/0227/p04s03-wosc.html.
94. "Priests Released Amid Wave of Abductions in Sudan," Compass Direct News (February 15, 2012), http://www.compassdirect.org/english/country/sudan/article_1402682.html.
95. "Muslim Relatives of Sudanese Christian Woman Pursue Her, Son," Compass Direct News (December 10, 2011), http://www.compassdirect.org/english/country/sudan/12443.
96. Thomas C. Oden, *How Africa Shaped the Christian Mind: Rediscovering the African Seedbed of Western Christianity* (Downers Grove, IL: InterVarsity Press, 2007); see also "One Hundred Years," the Catholic Archdiocese of Khartoum-Sudan, http://archdioceseofkhartoum.catholicweb.com/index.cfm/NewsItem?ID=130334&From=Home; Paul Bowers, "Nubian Christianity: The Neglected Heritage," *Africa Journal of Evangelical Theology*, iv.1 (1985), 3–23.
97. Soraya Sarhaddi Nelson, "Christians Flock to South Sudan, Fear Future in North," NPR (January 20, 2011), http://www.npr.org/2011/01/20/132930349/christians-flock-to-south-sudan-fear-future-in-north.
98. Marshall and Shea, *Silenced*, 144–145.
99. Josh Kron, "Sudan Leader to Accept Secession of South," *New York Times* (February 7, 2011), http://www.nytimes.com/2011/02/08/world/africa/08sudan.html.
100. Nina Shea, "I Take Back My Clooney Criticism," *National Review Online* (March 16, 2012), http://www.nationalreview.com/corner/293738/i-take-back-my-clooney-criticism-nina-shea.
101. "UNMIS Report on the Human Rights Situation During the Violence in Southern Kordofan Sudan," United Nations Mission in Sudan (UNMIS), (June 2011), 3, http://graphics8.nytimes.com/packages/pdf/world/20110823-UN-report-south-jordofan.pdf.
102. Eric Reeves, "Darfur . . . and now more genocide in Sudan?" *Christian Science Monitor* (August 4, 2011), http://www.sudanreeves.org/2011/08/04/darfur-and-now-more-genocide-in-sudan-the-christian-science-monitor-august-4-2011/.
103. Nina Shea, "Serial Genocide in Sudan," *National Review Online* (August 10, 2011), http://www.nationalreview.com/articles/274131/serial-genocide-sudan-nina-shea.
104. December 2011 letter of Bishop Macram Gassis, on file, Hudson Institute's Center for Religious Freedom. For the International Criminal Court's warrant for arrest of Ahmad Harun, see http://www.icc-cpi.int/iccdocs/doc/doc279813

.pdf; December 2011 letter of Bishop Macram Gassis, on file, Hudson Institute's Center for Religious Freedom.

105. CNN Wire Staff, "Bombs Hit Evangelical Bible School in Sudan, Group Says," CNN (February 2, 2012), http://articles.cnn.com/2012-02-02/africa/world_africa_sudan-bombing_1_south-sudan-bombs-sudanese-government?_s=PM:AFRICA.
106. Andrew Natsios, "Sudan's Oil Crisis Is Only Bashir's First Problem," *Foreign Affairs Online* (February 1, 2012), http://www.hudson.org/index.cfm?fuseaction=publication_details&id=8690.
107. U.S. Department of State, "International Religious Freedom Report for 2011, Executive Summary," http://www.state.gov/j/drl/rls/irf/religiousfreedom/index.htm#wrapper.
108. USCIRF, *Annual Report 2012*, 178–179, http://uscirf.gov/images/Annual%20Report%20of%20USCIRF%202012(2).pdf.
109. USCIRF, *Annual Report 2011*, 158–160, http://www.uscirf.gov/images/book%20with%20cover%20for%20web.pdf.
110. "North Sudan Church Still Too Fearful to Rebuild," *Christian Today* (August 27, 2011), http://www.christiantoday.com/article/north.sudan.church.still.too.fearful.to.rebuild/28506.htm.
111. "Afghani Convert Musa Released; Another Christian Still in Prison," Compass Direct News (February 24, 2011), http://www.compassdirect.org/english/country/afghanistan/33433.
112. "Clashes Erupt over Egypt Pig Cull," BBC (May 3, 2009), http://news.bbc.co.uk/2/hi/middle_east/8031490.stm.

CHAPTER 8: THE MUSLIM WORLD: WAR AND TERRORISM

1. Marshall and Shea, *Silenced*, 139.
2. "Indonesian 'Blasphemy' Law a Weapon for Radical Islam," Compass Direct News (May 12, 2010), http://www.compassdirect.org/english/country/indonesia/article_112397.html.
3. "Indonesia: A Prisoner of Truth," *Open Doors Youth* (August 24, 2009), http://undergroundnz.org/article/93/indonesia-a-prisoner-of-truth; see also "Village to Be Rebuilt Following Islamic Rampage," Compass Direct News (December 17, 2008), http://www.compassdirect.org/english/country/indonesia/2008/newsarticle_5737.html; "Indonesian Blasphemy Law a Weapon for Radical Islam," Compass Direct News (May 12, 2011), http://www.compassdirect.org/english/country/indonesia/article_112397.html.
4. "Death of Christian Leader in Iraq, Ominous Sign for Believers," *Mission Network News* (March 14, 2008), http://www.mnnonline.org/article/11006. See also, "Kidnapped Iraqi Archbishop Dead," BBC (March 13, 2008), http://news.bbc.co.uk/2/hi/middle_east/7294078.stm.
5. Nina Shea, "Iraq's Christians Still Under Siege." *National Review Online* (November 1, 2010), http://www.nationalreview.com/corner/251765/iraqs-christians-still-under-siege-nina-shea; Anthony Shadid, "Baghdad Church

Attacks Hit Iraq's Core," *New York Times* (November 1, 2010), http://www.nytimes.com/2010/11/02/world/middleeast/02iraq.html.

6. "Kidnapped Christian Doctor Freed in Critical Condition," Compass Direct News (September 22, 2009), http://www.compassdirect.org/english/country/iraq/9776.
7. "Escaping Mayhem and Murder," U.S. Conference of Catholic Bishops Migration and Refugee Services, Washington, DC (2007), 3, http://www.aina.org/reports/usccbiraq07.pdf.
8. Testimony of Commissioner Nina Shea, USCIRF, before the Tom Lantos Human Rights Commission, US House of Representatives, on Christian Minorities Under Attack: Iraq and Egypt, January 20, 2011, http://www.uscirf.gov/government-relations/congressional-testimony/3520-1212011-commissioner-nina-shea-testifies-on-recent-attacks-targeting-minorities-in-iraq-and-egypt.html.
9. "Church Bombings in Iraq Since 2004," Assyrian International News Agency (August 19, 2011), http://www.aina.org/news/20080107163014.htm.
10. "Iraq: International Religious Freedom Report," Bureau of Democracy, Human Rights, and Labor (November 17, 2010), http://www.state.gov/g/drl/rls/irf/2010/148821.htm; Steven Lee Myers, "Churches and Envoy Attacked in Iraq," *New York Times* (July 12, 2009), http://www.nytimes.com/2009/07/13/world/middleeast/13iraq.html?scp=1&sq=Rizko%20Aziz%20Nissan&st=cse; Jomana Karadsheh, "4 Killed, 32 Wounded as 6 Baghdad Churches Bombed," CNN (July 12, 2009), http://www.cnn.com/2009/WORLD/meast/07/12/iraq.violence/index.html?iref=allsearch.
11. John Leland and Omar Al-Jawoshy, "Christians Are Casualties of 10 Baghdad Attacks," *New York Times* (December 30, 2010), http://www.nytimes.com/2010/12/31/world/middleeast/31iraq.html; "Iraq church bombing wounds at least 20," CNN (August 2, 2011), http://articles.cnn.com/2011-08-02/world/iraq.church.attack_1_salvation-church-iraq-wounds?_s=PM:WORLD.
12. Interview of Canon Andrew White, the "Vicar of Baghdad," by Nina Shea, Washington, DC, June 2009.
13. UN Assistance Mission for Iraq, *UNAMI Human Rights Report* (January 1–June 30, 2008), 17, http://www.uniraq.org/documents/UNAMI_Human_Rights_Report_January_June_2008_EN.pdf.
14. Nina Shea, " 'Obliterating' Iraq's Christians," *Washington Post* (May 14, 2010), http://newsweek.washingtonpost.com/onfaith/guestvoices/2010/05/obliterating_iraqs_christians.html.
15. Ibid.
16. Ibid.
17. Nina Shea, "Their Last Christmas? Iraq's Endangered Non-Muslims," *National Review Online* (December 23, 2006), http://www.nationalreview.com/articles/219579/their-last-christmas/nina-shea.
18. http://www.aina.org/news/20050106124300.htm.

19. Nina Shea and James Rayis, "Christian Crisis: Chaldo Assyrians May Soon Leave Iraq en Masse," *National Review Online* (January 6, 2005), http://www.nationalreview.com/articles/213305/christian-crisis/nina-shea.
20. Pascale Warda, "Threats to Iraq's Communities of Antiquity" (Address at Public Hearing: 'Threats to Iraq's Communities of Antiquity,' Senate Russell Office Building, Washington, DC, July 25, 2007), USCIRF (July 25, 2007), http://uscirf.gov/component/content/article/160-iraq-press-releases/2171-threats-to-iraqs-communities-of-antiquity-testimony-by-pascale-warda.html.
21. "Iraq: Protect Christians from Violence," *Human Rights Watch* (February 23, 2010), http://www.hrw.org/en/news/2010/02/23/iraq-protect-christians-violence.
22. "Iraq: International Religious Freedom Report," Bureau of Democracy, Human Rights, and Labor (November 17, 2010), http://www.state.gov/g/drl/rls/irf/2010/148821.htm; "Kirkuk, a Christian Nurse Killed; Archbishop Sako: the Situation Is 'Worrying,'" Asia News.it (October 5, 2009), http://www.asianews.it/index.php?l=en&art=16496&size=A.
23. "Orthodox Christian Shot to Death in Mosul," Asia News.it (May 30, 2011), http://www.asianews.it/news-en/An-orthodox-Christian-is-shot-to-death-21701.html.
24. Steven Lee Myers, "Most Christians Are Fleeing Iraq in New Violence," *New York Times* (December 12, 2010), http://www.nytimes.com/2010/12/13/world/middleeast/13iraq.html?_r=1%20&%20pagewanted=all.
25. "Iraq Christian IDPs Find Refuge in Kurdish North," *Middle East Online* (December 28, 2010), http://www.middle-east-online.com/english/?id=43311.
26. John Leland, "Christians Exercise Caution for Christmas," *New York Times* (December 24, 2010), http://www.nytimes.com/2010/12/25/world/middleeast/25iraq.html?scp=5&sq=Baghdad%20Syriac%20Catholic&st=cse.
27. Ibid.
28. "Nigeria: Teacher on Trial After P-unishing Muslim Student," Compass Direct News (October 16, 2006), http://www.compassdirect.org/english/country/nigeria/2006/newsarticle_4594.html.
29. "Nigeria: Teacher Accused of Blasphemy Disappears," Compass Direct News (March 28, 2006), http://www.worthynews.com/894-teacher-accused-of-blasphemy-in-nigeria-disappears.
30. For background, see Paul Marshall, "The Next Hotbed of Islamic Radicalism," *Washington Post* (October 8, 2002), http://www.freedomhouse.org/article/next-hotbed-islamic-radicalism; on Islam and Christianity in sub-Saharan Africa, see the Pew Forum's survey, "Tolerance and Tension: Islam and Christianity in Sub-Saharan Africa," April 15, 2010, http://pewforum.org/docs/?DocID=515.
31. See Paul Marshall, *The Talibanization of Nigeria: Sharia Law and Religious Freedom* (Washington: Freedom House, 2002), and "Nigeria: Shari'a in

a Fragmented Country," in *Radical Islam's Rules: The Worldwide Spread of Extreme Shari'a Law*, ed. Paul Marshall (Lanham, MD: Rowman and Littlefield, 2005), 113–134.

32. Marshall and Shea, *Silenced*, 137.
33. "Nigeria Christian Killed over Blasphemy; Dozens Injured," BosNewsLife (February 13, 2008), http://www.bosnewslife.com/3435-3435-nigeria-christians-killed-in-riot-over-blasph; "Nigeria: Muslim Rioters Attack Christian in Kano," Compass Direct News (April 23, 2008), http://www.compassdirect.org/english/country/nigeria/2008/newsarticle_5344.html; "Nigeria: Mob Kills 50-year-old Man for 'Blasphemy,'" *Daily Trust News*, http://allafrica.com/stories/200808110940.html.
34. For background, see Edward Pentin, "Who Is Boko Haram and What Do They Want?" Zenit (February 9, 2012), http://www.zenit.org/article-34271?l=english.
35. Paul Marshall, "The Christmas Bombings in Nigeria," *National Review Online* (December 26, 2011), http://www.nationalreview.com/corner/286672/christmas-bombings-nigeria-paul-marshall.
36. "Boko Haram Resurrects, Declares Total Jihad," *Vanguard* (August 14, 2009), http://www.vanguardngr.com/2009/08/14/boko-haram-ressurects-declares-total-jihad. See also "Nigeria: Death Toll Climbs in Attack by Islamic Sect," Compass Direct News (August 7, 2009), http://www.compassdirect.org/english/country/nigeria/4505; Senan Murray and Adam Nossiter, "In Nigeria, an Insurgency Leaves a Heavy Toll," *New York Times* (August 3, 2009), http://www.nytimes.com/2009/08/04/world/africa/04nigeria.html; "Boko Haram Resurrects, Declares Total Jihad," see above.
37. Aminu Abubakar, "Nigerian Islamist Sect Threaten to Widen Attacks," *Agence France Presse* (March 29, 2010), http://www.google.com/hostednews/afp/article/ALeqM5j1FA1NJrS-ES89YWeX4f--kcQGmA.
38. "Violence in Yobe State, Nigeria Aimed Mainly at Christians," Compass Direct News (November 11, 2011), http://www.compassdirect.org/english/country/nigeria/article_123074.html.
39. Nina Shea, "Sunni Sect's Ruthless Violence Against Christians," *National Review Online* (December 26, 2011), http://www.nationalreview.com/corner/286674/sunni-sect-s-ruthless-violence-against-christians-nina-shea; Nina Shea, "Nigeria's Catholic Bishops Appeal for Help Against Religious Cleansing," *National Review Online* (January 4, 2012), http://www.nationalreview.com/corner/287118/nigeria-s-catholic-bishops-appeal-help-against-religious-cleansing-nina-shea.
40. "Nigeria: Dozens Dead in Church Bombings and Rioting," BBC (June 17, 2012), http://www.bbc.co.uk/news/world-africa-18475853.
41. Mike Oboh, "Islamist Insurgents Kill over 178 in Nigeria's Kano," Reuters (January 22, 2012), http://af.reuters.com/article/topNews/idAFJOE80L03L20120122; Laura Heaton, "Nigeria: Al-Qaeda-linked Group Gives

Christians 3-day Deadline," *Telegraph* (January 2, 2012), http://www.telegraph.co.uk/news/worldnews/africaandindianocean/nigeria/8988262/Nigeria-al-Qaeda-linked-group-gives-Christians-3-day-deadline.html.

42. "North Africa Qaeda Offers to Help Nigerian Muslims," Reuters (February 1, 2012), http://af.reuters.com/article/topNews/idAFJOE6100EE20100201. See also Christian Solidarity Worldwide (January 2012), "NIGERIA: Overview of Recent Violence"; Scott Stewart, "Nigeria's Boko Haram Militants Remain a Regional Threat," Stratfor (January 26, 2012), http://www.stratfor.com/weekly/nigerias-boko-haram-militants-remain-regional-threat?utm_source=freelist-f&utm_medium=email&utm_campaign=20120126&utm_term=sweekly&utm_content=readmore&elq=7d5a232d4567477d9382eece72aecd7e.
43. "Imam Abubakar Shekau," NNTV (January 12, 2012).
44. "Indonesian Christian Village Burnt to Ground by Neighbouring Muslims," Barnabas Aid (March 23, 2008), http://barnabasfund.org/US/News/Archives/Indonesian-Christian-village-burnt-to-ground-by-neighbouring-Muslims.html.
45. "Indonesia: Sunday School Teachers Sentenced to Three Years in Prison," Compass Direct News (September 1, 2005), http://www.compassdirect.org/english/country/indonesia/2005/newsarticle_3949.html.
46. "Indonesia: Court Rejects Legal Intervention for Jailed Teachers," Compass Direct News (January 24, 2006), http://www.compassdirect.org/english/country/indonesia/2006/newsarticle_4178.html.
47. Ibid. See also "Indonesia: Imprisoned Sunday School Teachers Released," Compass Direct News (June 8, 2007), http://www.compassdirect.org/english/country/indonesia/2007/newsarticle_4902.html.
48. Anita Rachman, "Indonesia: A Bad Year for Religious Rights," *Jakarta Globe* (December 26, 2011), http://setara-institute.org/en/content/indonesia-bad-year-religious-rights; "Anti-Christian Incidents Nearly Doubled in Indonesia in 2011," Compass Direct News (January 4, 2012), http://www.compassdirect.org/english/country/indonesia/article_1331441.html.
49. Hasyim Widhiarto, "Bekasi NU and PKS Back Sharia Law," *Jakarta Post* (June 29, 2010), http://www.thejakartapost.com/news/2010/06/29/bekasi-nu-and-pks-back-sharia-law.html.
50. Aubrey Belford, "For Indonesian Christians Gatherings Bring Tension," *New York Times* (July 31, 2010), http://www.nytimes.com/2010/07/30/world/asia/30iht-indo.html?partner=rssnyt&emc=rs; Ulma Haryanto, "Batak Church Cries Foul over 'Unfair' Treatment by Bekasi Administration," *Jakarta Globe* (July 27, 2010), http://www.thejakartaglobe.com/home/batak-church-cries-foul-over-unfair-treatment-by-bekasi-administration/387954; "Indonesian Church Leaders Wounded in Attack," Compass Direct News (September 15, 2010), http://www.compassdirect.org/english/country/indonesia/25551; "3 Jailed for

HKBP Church Attack," *Jakarta Post* (February 24, 2011), http://www.thejakartapost.com/news/2011/02/24/3-jailed-hkbp-church-attack.html.

51. The following examples of church closure and destruction in early 2010 are taken from the USCIRF *Annual Report: Indonesia* (May 11, 2011), http://uscirf.gov/images/ar2011/indonesia2011.pdf.
52. "Two Partially Constructed Church Buildings Burned," Compass Direct News (January 29, 2010), http://www.compassdirect.org/english/country/indonesia/14613/.
53. "Construction of Two Churches Stopped in Indonesia," Compass Direct News (March 25, 2010), http://www.compassdirect.org/english/country/indonesia/16748/.
54. "Theology Students in Indonesia Still Seek Facilities, Compensation," Compass Direct News (December 23, 2010), http://www.compassdirect.org/english/country/indonesia/30202/.
55. "Indonesia: Christian Lecturer Attacked in West Java," Compass Direct News (November 16, 2006), http://www.compassdirect.org/english/country/indonesia/2006/newsarticle_4629.html. On September 6, 2007, the Malang District Court sentenced forty-one members of the College Student Services Agency to five years in prison for creating a training video in which, allegedly, trainees placed Qur'ans on the ground. The following August, they were given reprieves as part of Indonesian Day celebrations. See "Indonesia," *International Religious Freedom Report 2009*, US Department of State, Bureau of Democracy, Human Rights, and Labor, http://www.state.gov/g/drl/rls/irf/2009/127271.htm.
56. Benting Reges, "East Java: 41 Christians Arrested for Blasphemy Against Islam," AsiaNews.it (May 2, 2007), http://www.asianews.it/index.php?l=en&art=9144; USCIRF *Annual Report: Indonesia* (May 2010), http://uscirf.gov/images/ar2010/indonesia2010.pdf.
57. Testriono, "New Research May Hold Key to Indonesia's Church-Building Controversy," *Common Ground News Service* (February 7, 2012), http://www.commongroundnews.org/article.php?id=30973&lan=en&sp=0; Elizabeth Kendal, "Indonesia: Saying 'NO' to Islamic Intolerance," Religious Liberty Monitoring (February 29, 2012), http://elizabethkendal.blogspot.com/2012/02/indonesia-saying-no-to-islamic.html.
58. "Bangladesh: Christian Convert's Life Threatened," Compass Direct News (October 16, 2008), http://www.compassdirect.org/english/country/bangladesh/2008/newsarticle_5634.html. For a similar case, see "Bangladesh: Muslims Drive Christian Grandparents from Home," Compass Direct News (January 14, 2009), http://www.compassdirect.org/english/country/bangladesh/expel.
59. US Department of State, *International Religious Freedom Report 2010, Bangladesh* (November 17, 2010) http://www.state.gov/j/drl/rls/irf/2010/148789.htm.
60. "Christians in Bangladesh Cleared of Charge of Offending Muslims,"

Compass Direct News (August 15, 2011), http://www.compassdirect.org/english/country/bangladesh/article_116225.html; Central Intelligence Agency, *The World Factbook: Bangladesh* (January 18, 2012), http:www.cia.gov/library/publications/the-world-factbook/geos/bg.html; US Department of State, *International Religious Freedom Report 2010, Bangladesh*, see above.

61. Abha Shankar, "US Islamists Take Issue with Bangladesh's Crackdown on Radicals," *IPT News* (September 29, 2010), http://www.investigativeproject.org/2207/us-islamists-take-issue-with-bangladeshs; US Department of State, *International Religious Freedom Report 2010, Bangladesh* (November 17, 2010), http://www.state.gov/j/drl/rls/irf/2010/148789.htm; Al-Alawi, Irfan, "Bangladesh Bans Arch-Jihadist's Writings," (New York: Hudson Institute, July 22, 2010), http://www.gatestoneinstitute.org/1430/bangladesh-bans-jihadist-writings.
62. US Department of State, *International Religious Freedom Report 2010, Bangladesh* (November 17, 2010), http://www.state.gov/j/drl/rls/irf/2010/148789.htm.
63. "Church Leaders Beaten at Police Station," Compass Direct News (August 29, 2011), http://www.compassdirect.org/english/country/bangladesh/article_116856.html.
64. For the large number and diversity of instances of religious persecution against Christians, see http://www.compassdirect.org/English/country/Bangladesh/.
65. "Christian Family Beaten, Cut—and Faces Charges," Compass Direct News (December 8, 2008), http://www.compassdirect.org/english/country/bangladesh/2008/newsarticle_5722.html.
66. "Italian Nun Killed in Somalia: Islamic Forces Suspected," Catholic World News (September 18, 2006), http://www.catholicculture.org/news/features/index.cfm?recnum=46538.
67. "Burial for Nun Killed in Somalia," BBC (September 21, 2006), http://news.bbc.co.uk/2/hi/5367972.stm; Elizabeth A. Kennedy, "Slain Nun Remembered as Devoted to Poor," Associated Press (September 21, 2006), http://www.4forums.com/political/religion-debates/8907-sister-leonella-sgorbati.html; "Anniversario del Martirio di Suor Leonella Sgorbati: la Sua Biografia," Fidei Donum (September 17, 2009), http://fideidonum.wordpress.com/2009/09/17/anniversario-del-martirio-di-suor-leonella-sgorbati-la-sua-biografia/.
68. "Somali Islamists Declare: 'We will slaughter Christians'—'Somalis are 100% Muslim and Will Always Remain So,'" *Militant Islam Monitor* (October 17, 2006), http://www.militantislammonitor.org/article/id/2474.
69. Simba Tian, "Somali Convert from Islam Whipped in Public," Compass Direct News (January 10, 2012), http://www.eurasiareview.com/10012012-somali-convert-from-islam-whipped-in-public/.
70. "Christian Aid Worker in Somalia Beheaded for Converting from Islam,"

Compass Direct News (October 27, 2008), http://www.compassdirect.org/english/country/somalia/2008/newsarticle_5661.html.

71. USCIRF *Annual Report: Somalia* (May 2011), 304, http://www.uscirf.gov/images/book%20with%20cover%20for%20web.pdf.
72. "From African Bush to Scotland Yard—the Murder Trail That Led to al-Qaida," *Guardian* (November 15, 2005), http://www.guardian.co.uk/world/2005/nov/15/rosiecowan.mainsection.
73. "Al-Shabab 'Join Ranks' with al-Qaeda," Al Jazeera (February 10, 2012), http://www.aljazeera.com/news/africa/2012/02/201221054649118317.html.
74. "Islamic Extremists Behead Another Convert in Somalia," Compass Direct News (February 8, 2012), http://www.compassdirect.org/english/country/somalia/article_1390864.html/.
75. "Islamic Extremists in Somalia Behead 17-year-old Christian," Compass Direct News (October 19, 2011), http://www.compassdirect.org/english/country/somalia/article_122124.html; "Somali Convert to Christianity Kidnapped, Beheaded," Compass Direct News (September 12, 2011), http://www.compassdirect.org/english/country/somalia/article_120184.html.
76. "November 3, 2001 Address of Osama Bin Laden," *Washington Post* (November 7, 2001); originally broadcast on Al Jazeera satellite television channel on November 3); Al Jazeera (January 4, 2004).

CHAPTER 9: CRUEL AND USUAL ABUSE

1. "Muslim Mob Severely Injured Three Christians, Ransacked Two Churches in Ethiopia," *Persecution News*, International Christian Concern (October 2, 2009), http://www.persecution.org/2009/10/02/muslim-mob-severely-injured-three-christians-ransacked-two-churches-in-ethiopia/.
2. "Third Christian This Year Dies in Military Prison," Compass Direct News (July 27, 2009), http://www.compassdirect.org/english/country/eritrea/2009/newsarticle_6034.html.
3. On recent persecution in the Maldives, Tanzania (Zanzibar), and the Philippines, see "Maldives Arrests, Deports Indian Teacher for Owning Bible," Compass Direct News (October 21, 2011), http://www.compassdirect.org/english/country/23845/article_122214.html; "Christians Live in Cloud of Fear in Zanzibar, Tanzania," Compass Direct News (September 5, 2011), http://www.compassdirect.org/english/country/tanzania/article_117316.html; "Christians Fear Failed Pact Increases Risk of Reprisals," Compass Direct News (October 7, 2011), http://www.compassdirect.org/english/country/philippines/2008/newsarticle_5628.html.
4. "Christians Forced from Village," Compass Direct News (September 16, 2011), http://www.compassdirect.org/english/country/mexico/article_120370.html.
5. Personal interview of Liz Kopp with Lela Gilbert, February 28, 2012.
6. The US Department of State, Bureau of Democracy, Human Rights, and Labor, "Israel," *International Religious Freedom Report 2010*, http://www.state.gov/j/drl/rls/irf/2010/148825.htm.

7. "More Shelling in Palu as Villagers Make Plans to Hold Christian Celebrations Elsewhere," *Karen Human Rights Group Update* (December 31, 2010), http://www.khrg.org/khrg2011/khrg11f1_update.html.
8. Caroline Cox, "Foreword," in Benedict Rogers, *Carrying the Cross* (Christian Solidarity Worldwide, 2006), 7, http://dynamic.csw.org.uk/article.asp?t=report&id=36.
9. Salai Bawi Lian, "Persecution of Chin Christians in Burma," speech at *International Conference on Persecuted Churches*, April 15–16, 2005, http://www.chro.ca/resources/religious-freedom/363-persecution-of-chin-christians-in-burma-international-conference-on-persecuted-churches.html.
10. "Burma," *Refugees International*, http://www.refintl.org/where-we-work/asia/burma.
11. Benedict Rogers, *Carrying the Cross* (Christian Solidarity Worldwide, 2007), 17–18, http://dynamic.csw.org.uk/article.asp?t=report&id=36.
12. U.S. Department of State, "Burma," *International Religious Freedom Report July–December 2010*, http://www.state.gov/g/drl/rls/irf/2010_5/168349.htm.
13. "Destruction of Cross in Chin (Burma) Condemned," Burma News International (August 25, 2010), http://bnionline.net/index.php/news/narinjara/9228-destruction-of-cross-in-chin-burma-condemned.html.
14. Rogers, *Carrying the Cross*, 39, http://dynamic.csw.org.uk/article.asp?t=report&id=36.
15. "Rangoon's Christians Banned from Worshipping," Mizzima (January 7, 2009), http://www.mizzima.com/news/inside-burma/1514-rangoons-christians-banned-from-worshiping.html.
16. Rogers, *Carrying the Cross*, 31, http://dynamic.csw.org.uk/article.asp?t=report&id=36.
17. Amy Alexander, "We Are Like Forgotten People," *Human Rights Watch* (January 28, 2009), http://www.hrw.org/node/79892/section/1.
18. "Global Christianity—A Report on the Size and Distribution of the World's Christians," *Pew Forum on Religion and Public Life* (December 19, 2011), http://www.pewforum.org/uploadedFiles/Topics/Religious_Affiliation/Christian/Christianity-fullreport-web.pdf; Rogers, *Carrying the Cross*, 12–14, http://dynamic.csw.org.uk/article.asp?t=report&id=36; Peter Pattisson, "Burma 'Orders Christians to Be Wiped Out,' " *Telegraph* (January 21, 2007), http://www.telegraph.co.uk/news/worldnews/1540121/Burma-orders-Christians-to-be-wiped-out.html; Amy Alexander, "We Are Like Forgotten People," *Human Rights Watch* (January 28, 2009), http://www.hrw.org/node/79892/section/1; USCIRF, *Annual Report: Burma* (May 2011), http://uscirf.gov/images/ar2011/burma2011.pdf. For further background, see Benedict Rogers, *A Land Without Evil: Stopping the Genocide of Burma's Karen People* (Grand Rapids: Kregel Publications, 2004).
19. "Karen Christians Among Victims in Attacks," Mission News Network (July 2, 2009), http://mnnonline.org/article/12914.

20. Tint Swe, "Burmese Leader in India Kneels Before the Buddha as Troops Shell Christian Village," AsiaNews.it (July 28, 2010), http://www.asianews.it/news-en/Burmese-leader-in-India-kneels-before-the-Buddha-as-troops-shell-Christian-village-19060.html.
21. "Tatmadaw Soldiers Shell Village, Attack Church and Civilian Property in Toungoo District," Karen Human Rights Group (November 25, 2011), http://www.khrg.org/khrg2011/khrg11b46.html.
22. Saw Yan Naing, "Ethnic Karen People Fight for Survival," the Media Project (August 17, 2011), http://www.themediaproject.org/article/karen-people-committed-survival?page=0,1.
23. Amy Alexander, "We Are Like Forgotten People," Human Rights Watch (January 28, 2009), 6, http://www.hrw.org/node/79892/section/1.
24. Rogers, *Carrying the Cross*, 22, http://dynamic.csw.org.uk/article.asp?t=report&id=36.
25. Human Rights Watch Interview with R. H. and M. T., Kuala Lumpur, April 12, 2008, 49, http://www.hrw.org/sites/default/files/reports/burma0109web_0.pdf.
26. Rogers, *Carrying the Cross*, 37.
27. Anonymous, "Violence in Kachin State: The Suffering and Unwavering Determination of the Kachin," Marist Fathers, *Social Justice Articles 2011*, http://www.maristfathers.org.au/Pages/6-SJ-articles-2011.htm#kachin.
28. "Burma: Kachin Christians Targeted," Release International (December 15, 2011), http://www.releaseinternational.org/pages/posts/burma-kachin-christians-targeted-919.php.
29. "Burma's Christian Civilians Attacked During Christmas," Compass Direct News (January 9, 2012), http://www.compassdirect.org/english/country/burma/article_1339709.html/; "DPA: Myanmar Army Accused of Ignoring President's Ceasefire Order," Refugees International (January 10, 2012), http://www.refugeesinternational.org/press-room/ri-in-the-news/dpa-myanmar-army-accused-ignoring-presidents-ceasefire-order; "Burma Gov't and Kachin Armed Group Hold Peace Talks in China," *Irrawady* (January 18, 2012), http://www2.irrawaddy.org/article.php?art_id=22877&Submit=Submit.
30. Edward Wong, "An Ethnic War Is Rekindled in Myanmar," *New York Times* (January 19, 2012), http://www.nytimes.com/2012/01/20/world/asia/ethnic-war-with-kachin-intensifies-in-myanmar-jeopardizing-united-states-ties.html?pagewanted=all.
31. Amy Jo Jones, "Karen Cyclone Victims Still Denied Aid in Burma," Christian Newswire (May 21, 2008), http://www.christiannewswire.com/news/993696682.html; "Myanmar Briefing: Human Rights Concerns a Month After Cyclone Nargis," Amnesty International (June 5, 2008), http://www.amnesty.org/en/library/asset/ASA16/013/2008/en/85931049-32e5-11dd-863f-e9cd398f74da/asa160132008eng.pdf.
32. "Christians Intentionally Neglected by Government," Mission Network

News (April 26, 2011), http://www.mnnonline.org/article/15644; "Church Collapse Kills 23; Still, Quake Victims Provide Relief Work," Mission Network News (April 8, 2011), http://www.mnnonline.org/article/15567.

33. "Burma Frees Dozens of Political Prisoners," BBC (October 12, 2011), http://www.bbc.co.uk/news/world-asia-pacific-15269259.
34. "Clinton Meets Burma (Myanmar) President Thein Sen, Aung San Suu Kyi," *Christian Science Monitor* (December 2, 2011), http://www.csmonitor.com/World/Asia-Pacific/2011/1202/Clinton-meets-Burma-Myanmar-President-Thein-Sein-Aung-San-Suu-Kyi; "Burma Frees High-Profile Dissidents in Amnesty," BBC (January 13, 2012), http://www.bbc.co.uk/news/world-asia-16540871.
35. Lally Weymouth, "Burma's President Gives His First Foreign Interview," *Washington Post* (January 19, 2012), http://www.washingtonpost.com/opinions/burma-president-thein-sein-country-is-on-right-track-to-democracy/2012/01/19/gIQANeM5BQ_story.html.
36. "The 45 Places to Go in 2012," *New York Times* (January 6, 2012), http://travel.nytimes.com/2012/01/08/travel/45-places-to-go-in-2012.html.
37. "Muslims Beat Evangelist to Death, Assault Pregnant Wife," Voice of the Martyrs (May 5, 2011), http://www.persecution.net/et-2011-05-05.htm. See also "Church Worker Killed by Muslims in Ethiopia," Barnabas Fund (May 4, 2011), http://barnabasfund.org/UK/News/Archives/Church-worker-killed-by-Muslims-in-Ethiopia.html.
38. "Spotlight on Ethiopia," *Global Christianity*, Pew Forum on Religion and Public Life (December 19, 2011), http://www.pewforum.org/Christian/Global-Christianity-ethiopia.aspx.
39. Pew Forum, *Global Restrictions on Religion Report* (2011), http://www.pewforum.org/Government/Global-Restrictions-on-Religion.aspx.
40. Simba Tian, "Christian Jailed in Ethiopia Accused of Desecrating Quran," Compass Direct News (October 7, 2010), http://www.compassdirect.org/english/country/ethiopia/26788/; "Alleged Qur'an Desecration Lands Ethiopian Christian Three Years in Prison," Persecution News, International Christian Concern (November 29, 2010), http://www.persecutionorg/2010/11/29/alleged-quran-desecration-lands-ethiopian-christian-three-years-in-prison/.
41. "Ethiopia Imprisons Christian Accused of Defacing Quran," Compass Direct News (November 29, 2010), http://www.compassdirect.org/english/country/ethiopia/15414/.
42. See page 270.
43. "Corpse of Ethiopian Christian Convert's Infant Dug up," Compass Direct News (May 27, 2009), http://www.compassdirect.org/english/country/ethiopia/4718.
44. Angel Rabasa, *Radical Islam in East Africa*, RAND—Project Air Force (Santa Monica: RAND, 2009); *Terrorism in the Horn of Africa*, US Institute of Peace (Special Report 113, January 2004).

45. "Ethiopia: Terrorism Verdict Quashes Free Speech," Human Rights Watch (January 19, 2010), http://www.hrw.org/news/2012/01/19/ethiopia-terrorism-verdict-quashes-free-speech.
46. "Radical Muslims Seek to Turn Ethiopia into an Islamist State," Voice of the Martyrs (November 10, 2011), http://www.persecution.net/et-2011-11-10.htm; see also "Ethiopian Government: Radical Wahhabi Muslims Seeking to Turn Ethiopia into an Islamic State," International Christian Concern (November 4, 2011), http://www.persecution.org/2011/11/04/ethiopian-government-radical-wahhabi-muslims-seeking-to-turn-ethiopia-into-an-islamic-state/.
47. Aaron Maasho, "Ethiopia's Religious Divides Flare Up in Violence," Reuters (March 24, 2011), http://af.reuters.com/article/topNews/idAFJOE72N0AH20110324?sp=true.
48. "Ethiopian Muslims Burn Down Christian Homes, Farms," Persecution News, International Christian Concern (September 29, 2010), http://www.persecution.org/2010/09/29/ethiopian-muslims-burn-down-christian-homes-farms/.
49. Diane Macedo, "Thousands of Christians Displaced in Ethiopia After Muslim Extremists Torch Churches, Homes," *Fox News* (March 24, 2011), http://www.foxnews.com/world/2011/03/24/thousands-christians-displaced-ethiopia-muslim-extremists-torch-churches-homes-2057387870/.
50. Ibid.; "Ethiopian Muslims Warn Christians to Convert, Leave City or Face Death," *Persecution News*, International Christian Concern (January 25, 2011), http://www.persecution.org/2011/01/25/ethiopian-muslims-warn-christians-to-convert-leave-city-or-face-death/.
51. "Ethiopian Gov't Says the Country Faces Threat Due to Intolerant Teachings of Wahhabism," *Persecution News*, International Christian Concern (October 10, 2011), http://www.persecution.org/?p=25890&upm_export=print.
52. "Eritrea: 3 More Christians Die Inside Military Prisons; Toll Now at 21," *Christian Post* (October 26, 2011), http://www.christianpost.com/news/eritrea-3-more-christians-die-inside-military-prisons-toll-now-at-21-59357/.
53. CIA, *The World Factbook* (February 25, 2012), https://www.cia.gov/library/publications/the-world-factbook/geos/er.html.
54. WikiLeaks, "How a U.S. Ambassador Understood Eritrean President Isaias Afewerki," (December 17, 2010), http://www.ethiomedia.com/augur/4272.html.
55. Ibid.
56. "US Embassy Cables: Djibouti in Talks to Defuse Eritrea Crisis," *Guardian* (December 8, 2010), http://www.guardian.co.uk/world/us-embassy-cables-documents/150529.
57. The US Department of State, Bureau of Democracy, Human Rights, and Labor, "Eritrea," *International Religious Freedom Report 2010*, http://www.state.gov/g/drl/rls/irf/2010_5/168406.htm.

58. "Eritrean Patriarch Under House Arrest as Government Repression Increases," *Christianity Today* (January 23, 2006), http://www.christiantoday.com/article/eritrean.patriarch.placed.under.house.arrest.as.government.repression.increases/5082.htm.
59. The US Department of State, "Eritrea," *International Religious Freedom Report 2010.*
60. USCIRF, *Eritrea 2011*, http://www.uscirf.gov/government-relations/other-advocacy-materials/3382-eritrea-advocacy-materials.html.
61. The US Department of State, "Eritrea," *International Religious Freedom Report 2010.*
62. "Wikileaks Exposes Torture of Eritrean Christians," International Christian Concern (February 3, 2011), http://www.persecution.org/crossingthebridge/2011/02/03/wikileaks-exposes-torture-of-eritrean-christians/.
63. "Eritrean Christians Tell of Torture," BBC (September 27, 2007), http://news.bbc.co.uk/2/hi/7015033.stm.
64. "Eritrea Cracks Down on Religion Even More as Woman Dies in Detention Center," Eritrea Human Rights Electronic Archive (February 2, 2010), http://www.ehrea.org/anothervictime.php.
65. "Asylum for Eritrean Gospel Singer," BBC (October 22, 2007), http://news.bbc.co.uk/2/hi/7056120.stm; "Update: Good News," Amnesty (November 3, 2006), http://www.amnesty.org.uk/actions_details.asp?ActionID=10.
66. The US Department of State, "Eritrea," *International Religious Freedom Report 2010.*
67. "Eritrean Christians Facing 'Unimaginable Suffering' in Egypt," *Christianity Today* (June 10, 2011), http://www.christiantoday.com/article/eritrean.christians.facing.unimaginable.suffering.in.egypt/28138.htm.
68. "Hostages, Torture, and Rape in the Desert: Findings from 284 Asylum Seekers about Atrocities in the Sinai," *Physicians for Human Rights Report* (February 23, 2011), http://www.phr.org.il/default.asp?PageID=100&ItemID=1044. Also see: Fox News (December 6, 2010), http://www.foxnews.com/world/2010/12/06/israel-fears-flood-migrants-threatens-state/.
69. "Eritrean Christians Facing 'Unimaginable Suffering' in Egypt," *Christianity Today* (June 10, 2011).
70. Caroline Cox, "Foreword," in Benedict Rogers, *Carrying the Cross*, 7.

CHAPTER 10: A CALL TO ACTION

1. "Saudi Arabian Officials Assault, Strip Search Christian Prisoners," *International Christian Concern* (January 24, 2012), http://www.persecution.org/2012/01/24/saudi-arabian-officials-assault-strip-search-christian-prisoners.
2. Marine Soreau, " 'Ecumenism of Martyrs' Presented as Path to Unity," Zenit (September 16, 2011), http://www.zenit.org/article-33454?l=english.

3. "Islamists in Somalia Behead Two Sons of Christian Leader," Compass Direct News (July 1, 2009), http://www.compassdirect.org/english/country/somalia/4482.
4. Elmer John Thiessen, *The Ethics of Evangelism: A Philosophical Defense of Proselytizing and Persuasion* (Downers Grove, IL: InterVarsity, 2011), eloquently defends evangelism as ethical and its absence as unethical.
5. "Christians and Lions," *Economist* (December 31, 2011), http://www.economist.com/node/21542195.
6. Letter provided to Nina Shea through the US Commission on International Religious Freedom (March 15, 2012); for fear of reprisal the author requested anonymity.
7. "Talk to Al Jazeera: Tauran: Christians Under Attack" (April 6, 2012), http://www.aljazeera.com/programmes/talktojazeera/2012/03/201231705416701698.html.
8. Joshua Muravchik, "The Fate of Middle Eastern Christians," Bush Center Blog (March 15, 2012), http://www.bushcenter.com/blog/2012/03/15/the-fate-of-middle-eastern-christians/.
9. Kurt Werthmuller, "State of Fear: Syria's Christians Face the Specter of Civil War and Sectarian Violence," Hudson Institute (February 3, 2012), http://www.hudson.org/index.cfm?fuseaction=publication_details&id=8708.
10. Kurt Werthmuller, "Failing Syria: Why the World Must Prepare Now for Assad's Fall and the Aftermath," http://crf.hudson.org/index.cfm?fuseaction=publication_details&id=8721; Huffington Post, (February 9, 2012), http://www.huffingtonpost.com/kurt-j-werthmuller/syria-violence-bashar-al-assad_b_1265069.html.
11. Paul Marshall, ed., *Religious Freedom in the World* (Lanham, MD: Rowman and Littlefield Publishers, 2008), 23.
12. Nina Shea, "The Middle East's Embattled Christians," http://www.hudson.org/index.cfm?fuseaction=publication_details&id=6667; *NationalReview Online* (December 23, 2009), http://www.nationalreview.com/articles/228851/middle-easts-embattled-christians/nina-shea.
13. Nina Shea, "'Obliterating' Iraq's Christians," http://www.hudson.org/index.cfm?fuseaction=publication_details&id=6999; *Washington Post Online* (May 14, 2010), http://onfaith.washingtonpost.com/onfaith/guestvoices/2010/05/obliterating_iraqs_christians.html.
14. Nina Shea, *In the Lion's Den* (Nashville: Broadman and Holman, 1997).
15. Faith J. H. McDonnell, "Become Aware and Take Action," Religious Liberty Program, Institute on Religion and Democracy, nd, http://www.theird.org/Page.aspx?pid=847&srcid=847.
16. Simon Roughneen, "Iraqi Christians: Round Trip to Death Street," *International Relations and Security Network (ISN)* (August 20 2008), http://www.isn.ethz.ch/isn/Current-Affairs/Security-Watch/Detail/?id=90264&lng=en.

17. Michael Youash, "Iraq's Minority Crisis and U.S. National Security: Protecting Minority Rights in Iraq," *American University Law Review*, vol. 24, issue 2, 347, http://digitalcommons.wcl.american.edu/cgi/viewcontent.cgi?article=1090&context=auilr.
18. John L. Allen Jr., "Ecumenism of the Martyrs," *National Catholic Reporter* (September 16, 2011), http://ncronline.org/blogs/all-things-catholic/ecumenism-martyrs-and-remembering-giancarlo-zizola.
19. Remarks by President George W. Bush to the American Jewish Committee (May 3, 2001), http://georgewbush-whitehouse.archives.gov/news/releases/2001/05/20010504.html.
20. Nina Shea, "The White House's Generic Response to an Act of Anti-Christian Terrorism," *National Review Online*, http://www.nationalreview.com/blogs/print/251901.
21. "Mosque Attack in Northern Israel," press statement, Victoria Nuland, Department Spokesperson, Office of the Spokesperson, Washington, DC (October 4, 2011), http://www.state.gov/r/pa/prs/ps/2011/10/175020.htm.
22. "Mosque Attack in the West Bank," press statement, Victoria Nuland, Department Spokesperson, Office of the Spokesperson, Washington, DC (January 11, 2012), http://www.state.gov/r/pa/prs/ps/2012/01/180460.htm.
23. "Obama 'Deeply Concerned' About Egypt Violence," CNN (October 10, 2011), http://www.cnn.com/2011/10/10/world/meast/egypt-protest-clashes/index.html?hpt=hp_t2.
24. Samuel Tadros, "Bloody Sunday in Cairo," *National Review Online* (October 12, 2011), http://www.nationalreview.com/blogs/print/279901.
25. "International Roma Day," press statement, Hillary Rodham Clinton, Secretary of State, Washington, DC (April 8, 2012), http://www.state.gov/secretary/rm/2012/04/187589.htm.
26. "Promise and Peril in Nigeria," presentation by Ambassador Johnnie Carson, assistant secretary of state for African Affairs, Center for Strategic and International Studies (April 9, 2012), http://csis.org/event/promise-and-peril-nigeria.
27. Leonard A. Leo and Rev. William Shaw, "In Nigeria: Getting Away with Murder," USCIRF Commissioners (January 25, 2012).
28. Nina Shea, "The Salafi War on Christians and U.S. Indifference," *National Review Online* (April 12, 2012), http://www.nationalreview.com/corner/295893/salafi-war-christians-and-us-indifference-nina-shea.
29. Frank Wolf, Bill Text 112th Congress (2011-2012) H.R.440.IH, http://thomas.loc.gov/cgi-bin/query/z?c112:H.R.440.IH.
30. "EU Condemns Anti-Christian Terrorist Acts," Zenit (February 22, 2011), http://www.zenit.org/article-31825?l=english.
31. Personal Interview with Lela Gilbert, March 2012.
32. For a history of IRFA and USCIRF, see Nina Shea, "The Origin and Legacy of the Movement to Fight Religious Persecution," *The Review of Faith and International Affairs*, vol. 6, no. 2, summer 2008, 25.

33. It was organized under the auspices of the Center for Religious Freedom, now with the Hudson Institute and at Freedom House. Hudson Institute's Michael Horowitz marshaled the participants, and Nina Shea invited the witnesses. See Nina Shea, *In the Lion's Den*, 95.
34. David Aikman, "The Worldwide Attack on Christians," *Commentary* (February 2012), http://www.commentarymagazine.com/article/the-worldwide-attack-on-christians/.
35. Paul Marshall, Lela Gilbert, and Roberta Ahmanson Green, *Blind Spot: When Journalists Don't Get Religion* (New York: Oxford University Press, 2008).
36. See www.uscirf.gov.

INDEX

ABOUT THE AUTHORS

Paul Marshall is a senior fellow at the Hudson Institute's Center for Religious Freedom, Washington, DC. He is the award-winning author of more than twenty books and has spoken on religious freedom, international relations, and radical Islam before Congress and the U.S. State Department and in many other nations.

Lela Gilbert is an award-winning author, who has written or cowritten more than sixty books. These include Saturday People, Sunday People: Israel through the Eyes of a Christian Sojourner, Blind Spot: When Journalists Don't Get Religion, and Baroness Cox: Eyewitness to a Broken World. She is a contributor to the Jerusalem Post, National Review Online, Weekly Standard Online, and other publications. She also is an adjunct fellow at Hudson Institute and resides in California and Jerusalem.

Nina Shea, an international human rights lawyer for thirty years, joined the Hudson Institute as a senior fellow in 2006. There she directs the Center for Religious Freedom, which she helped found in 1986. From 1999 to 2012, she served as a Commissioner on the US Commission on International Religious Freedom. Both Republican and Democratic administrations have appointed her a US delegate to the United Nations' main human rights body. She writes and speaks frequently on issues related to international religious freedom.